Cases in Financial Accounting

Cases in Financial Accounting

THOMAS R. DYCKMAN
ROBERT J. SWIERINGA
*Graduate School of Business
and Public Adminstration
Cornell University
Ithaca, New York*

Dame Publications, Inc.
P.O. Box 35556
Houston, Texas 77035

© DAME PUBLICATIONS, INC. 1981

All rights reserved. No part of this publication may be reproduced, stored in a retrieval system, or transmitted, in any form or by any means, electronic, mechanical, photocopying, recording, or otherwise, without the prior written permission of the publisher.

ISBN 0-931920-31-0
Library of Congress Catalog Card No. 81-67860

Printed in the United States of America

To Robert T. Sprouse

Preface

Cases in Financial Accounting provides a collection of relatively brief cases drawn from or based on actual corporate financial reports. The collection is designed for use as a supplement to a textbook in either a graduate or undergraduate intermediate accounting course or in a professional development program.

Objective The objective of this collection is to motivate and facilitate your learning of the concepts and terminology that are essential to an understanding of financial accounting and financial statements. By motivating you to use the concepts and terminology of financial accounting in realistic but often unfamiliar contexts, the cases are designed to enhance (1) your understanding of how accounting information is collected, adjusted or modified and presented to investors and others, (2) your understanding of and ability to critically evaluate published financial statements, and (3) your obtaining of a practical, working mastery of these concepts and terminology.

The cases assume a background in financial accounting that is equivalent to a one-quarter or one-semester introductory course. The cases focus on the accounting information presented in corporate financial statements. However, they assume and sometimes require a knowledge of the mechanics of double-entry bookkeeping, even though most cases are flexible in that these mechanics can be emphasized or de-emphasized as desired by your instructor.

Approach The dominant feature of the collection is the extensive use of financial statements actually prepared and published by publicly held corporations. Over the years, we have successfully used sets of corporate financial statements to demonstrate specific points in intermediate accounting courses at the Cornell Graduate School of Business and Public Administration and in various management development programs. We have found that use of these materials has simultaneously stimulated interest and enhanced learning.

The typical textbook approach to learning financial accounting emphasizes reading the information contained in the text and then working out the numerical solutions to exercises or problems. This approach provides a relatively comfortable learning environment. The text provides the necessary information and the exercises and problems are intended to provide you with feedback about how well you have learned this information.

Yet, several features of the textbook approach may encourage you to memorize this information instead of learning it. The exercises and problems tend to be closely tied to the information provided in the text. They use the same terminology as that used in the text and they rarely require you to obtain information from an outside source. They also tend to be very similar to examples provided in the text. If you have difficulty in working them you can usually find an example in the text to help you. In addition, they usually provide all the information required to work them and seldom include information that is not needed. As a result, you do not learn how to search for the information required to work problems or to resolve issues, you do not have to make assumptions or to consider alternative estimates that could be used and you do not have to choose which information to use and which information to ignore. Finally, they typically have unique correct solutions—you can determine whether you applied the information you obtained from the text correctly. However, in order to have unique solutions, the exercises and problems have to be simple and highly structured. The types of problems you can expect to deal with outside the classroom likely will be more complex, less structured and rarely will have unique solutions.

The typical case approach to learning financial accounting emphasizes analyzing situations described in a case and reaching conclusions about them. A case confronts you with a situation. In analyzing this situation you must decide what the issues are and make numerical calculations. You have to decide what information in the case you wish to rely on, to decide what additional information to search for and to consider alternative assumptions and estimates. In reaching conclusions you must identify and assess the strength of the arguments bearing on the issues. You must exercise judgment. Because individual judgments differ there is no unique correct solution to a case. In fact, the most important part of the learning process is the discussion of the case in which you and your colleagues will explain your positions, defend them, consider alternative positions and perhaps even modify your own position on the basis of the discussion. In this discussion you have the opportunity to become an active participant in a dynamic learning process, and this is the primary advantage of the case approach.

A major disadvantage of this approach is that you may become frustrated in this learning process, at least at first. Cases tend to be messy and disorderly. Different terms are sometimes used to describe the same thing. Conflicting information may be presented in the case and there may be no easy or simple way to "solve" the case. You can spend many hours on a case and still not exhaust the possibilities. You may come up with what you consider to be a reasonable position only to have it challenged in ways and for reasons you did not anticipate. You may find that the position that evolves in the discussion was one you did not consider or considered and rejected. You also may become unhappy about the fact that there is no correct position or solution for the case. It is likely that your initial frustrations will disappear as you become more accustomed to cases. In addition, it is important to realize that it may be easier for you to learn that realistic situations are not as simple as a text implies in an environment in which you have the resources of a text, other sources of information, an instructor and your colleagues readily available to help you.

The approach suggested by this collection of cases is a combination of the typical textbook and case approaches. A textbook will provide you with information about the concepts and terminology of financial accounting. We expect that you will familiarize yourself with this information and that your instructor will devote some time in class to this information. The cases in this collection will then be used to test your knowledge and understanding of these concepts and terminology in more realistic contexts. By not closely tying the cases to any one text, you will be encouraged to learn the information in the text and not to memorize it. The cases will also extend your knowledge and understanding of these concepts and terminology beyond the information presented in the text by encouraging you to seek information from various sources, to consider alternative assumptions and estimates, and to exercise judgment. To conserve your time and to focus your attention on the relevant issues, most cases are followed by a series of questions. You may find it useful to scan these questions before reading a case.

Courses in financial accounting enjoy a unique advantage over courses in other functional areas of business and even over management accounting courses. This advantage is ready access to published financial statements that illustrate financial accounting concepts and terminology in both immediate and practical ways. Even though most financial accounting texts provide some illustrations from published financial statements, this unique advantage has tended to be underexploited, in part because of a lack of materials reflecting a resourceful use of these statements. This collection of cases is designed to help you exploit this advantage by providing you with these materials in a useful form.

Organization

The cases are organized into nine sections. The cases in the first section focus on a general review of financial accounting, the use of balance sheets and income statements, and accounting for changes in accounting methods and extraordinary items. Many of these cases are designed to test your understanding of the relationships between balance sheet and income statement accounts.

The second and third sections focus on accounting for financial assets. Cases in the second section cover the use of present value concepts and methods to impute interest on receivables and payables and to account for leases. Cases in the third section concentrate on accounting for receivables and revenue recognition, including the use of the installment method.

The next three sections focus on inventories and operating assets, liabilities and stockholders' equity. Topics covered in the inventory cases include the use of FIFO, LIFO and replacement cost methods, the effects of these methods and changes in these methods on net income, and the liquidation of LIFO inventory quantities. The operating assets cases cover the acquisition, depreciation, exchange and disposition of these assets. The areas covered in the liabilities section include accounting for contingencies, deferred taxes and bonds. The cases in the stockholders' equity section focus on various preferred, common and treasury stock transactions and the calculation of earnings per share.

The last three sections focus on intercorporate investments, changes in financial position and price-level and fair value accounting. The intercorporate investments cases include accounting for marketable securities, unconsolidated subsidiaries, and business combinations. The cases in the financial position section concentrate on deriving the formal statement of these changes. Finally, the cases in the last section focus on accounting for general price-level changes and preparing and interpreting financial statements on the basis of replacement costs and fair values.

Acknowledgements We are indebted to Robert T. Sprouse of the Financial Accounting Standards Board for exposing us to the approach reflected in this collection of cases and we have dedicated this book to him. As a colleague of Thomas R. Dyckman at the University of California at Berkeley in 1961-1963 and of Robert J. Swieringa at Stanford University in 1968-1973, he stimulated our initial use of cases based on corporate financial statements to cover specific concepts and issues in our financial accounting courses. We are grateful to him for the many intellectually exciting class sessions which resulted from our use of this approach and which subsequently influenced our development of many of the cases included in this collection. Three of the cases included in this book were developed by Mr. Sprouse.

All of the cases included in this collection have been used in our intermediate accounting course at the Cornell Graduate School of Business and Public Administration. Some of the cases were motivated by articles and commentaries in various business periodicals, including *Barron's, Business Week, Forbes Magazine* and *The Wall Street Journal*. However, many of the cases resulted from our careful reading of publicly available annual reports and SEC Form 10-Ks from a wide variety of corporations. We are grateful to numerous students, colleagues and friends whose comments and suggestions resulted in many valuable improvements in the cases.

June 1981

Thomas R. Dyckman
Robert J. Swieringa

Contents

Section One   **Review of Financial Accounting**

1-1	Steak n Shake	3
1-2	J.M. Smucker Company	5
1-3	Wm. Wrigley, Jr. Company	7
1-4	Accounting for Various Events	12
1-5	Atlantic Richfield Company	14

Section Two   **Present Value and Leasing**

2-1	Colonial Commercial Corporation	19
2-2	Chart House Inc. (A)	21
2-3	Chart House Inc. (B)	23
2-4	American Technical Industries Inc.	25
2-5	Allied Chemical Corporation	26
2-6	Telefile Computer Corporation	28
2-7	Teleflex, Incorporated	30
2-8	Med General Inc.	33
2-9	Measurex Corporation	35
2-10	Computer Consoles, Inc.	41

Section Three   **Receivables and Revenue Recognition**

3-1	Career Academy, Inc.	47
3-2	General Development Corporation	55
3-3	Horizon Corporation	59
3-4	AMREP Corporation	67
3-5	Compugraphic Corporation	69
3-6	Allegheny Beverage Corporation	72
3-7	Great Southwest Corporation	76

xii Contents

Section Four — Inventories and Operating Assets

4-1	Koehring Company (A)	81
4-2	Allegheny Ludlum Industries, Inc. (A)	83
4-3	Chrysler Corporation	91
4-4	Lenox, Incorporated	97
4-5	E.I. Du Pont De Neumours & Company	99
4-6	Warner & Swasey Company	101
4-7	Corning Glass Works (A)	105
4-8	International Systems and Control Corporation	108
4-9	Georgia-Pacific Corporation (A)	111
4-10	W.R. Grace & Company (A)	113
4-11	Koppers Company, Inc.	117
4-12	Hoffman Electronics Corporation	119

Section Five — Liabilities

5-1	Owens-Illinois, Inc. (A)	123
5-2	Mohasco Corporation (A)	125
5-3	Koehring Company (B)	128
5-4	Bethlehem Steel Corporation (A)	132
5-5	Trans Union Corporation	136
5-6	Mohasco Industries, Inc. (B)	140
5-7	Associated Spring Corporation	149
5-8	American Savings and Loan Association	151
5-9	Louisville Gas and Electric Company	152
5-10	General Host Corporation	153
5-11	Allegheny Airlines	157
5-12	Fairchild Industries	159
5-13	Pan American World Airways	160
5-14	Mobil Corporation	162

Section Six — Stockholders' Equity

6-1	Bic Pen Corporation	165
6-2	Cannon Mills	167
6-3	American Consumer Industries, Inc.	169
6-4	Xonics, Inc.	170
6-5	Owens-Illinois, Inc. (B)	172
6-6	J.P. Stevens & Co., Inc.	174
6-7	Burlington Industries, Inc.	179
6-8	Crane Co. vs. American Standard, Inc., et al.	180
6-9	Gulf & Western Industries, Inc.	201
6-10	National Distillers	212
6-11	Bunker-Ramo Corporation	220
6-12	Computer Sciences Corporation	222
6-13	McDonnell Douglas Corporation	226
6-14	Georgia-Pacific Corporation (B)	228

Section Seven — Intercorporate Investments

7-1	W.R. Grace and Company (B)	235
7-2	Cooper Laboratories, Inc.	236
7-3	The Charter Company	238
7-4	Corning Glass Works (B)	240
7-5	Harte-Hanks Newspapers, Inc.	242
7-6	Time, Incorporated	247
7-7	Rockwell International	251
7-8	Giddings and Lewis Machine Tool Company	253
7-9	Borg-Warner Corporation	255
7-10	Crestek, Inc.	259
7-11	Emhart Corporation	261

Section Eight — Changes in Financial Position

8-1	Richard D. Brew and Company	269
8-2	Oxford Pendaflex Corporation	272
8-3	Evans Products Company	278
8-4	General DataComm Industries, Inc.	280
8-5	FlightSafety International	284
8-6	Gardner-Denver	286
8-7	Georgia-Pacific Corporation (C)	289
8-8	Allegheny Ludlum Industries, Inc. (B)	293

Section Nine — Price-Level and Fair Value Accounting

9-1	Westwood Manufacturing	297
9-2	Ayrshire Collieries Corporation	302
9-3	Crane Company	307
9-4	Indiana Telephone Corporation	309
9-5	Iowa Beef Processors	315
9-6	The Rouse Company	320
9-7	Bethlehem Steel Corporation (B)	329
9-8	Barber-Ellis of Canada, Limited (A)	333
9-9	Barber-Ellis Group (B)	335

Section One

Review of Financial Accounting

Case 1-1

Steak n Shake

The Consolidated Balance Sheets of Steak n Shake, Inc. and Subsidiaries for fiscal years ended September 30, 1974 and 1975 are shown.

Consolidated Balance Sheets

September 30	1975	1974
ASSETS		
Current Assets:		
Cash	$ 896,868	$ 824,454
Accounts receivable	75.389	50,916
Inventories	1,900,667	2,087,700
Properties to be sold and leased back	7,593,275	3,587,000
Prepaid expenses and other current assets	361,489	565,876
Total current assets	10,827,688	7,115,946
Property and equipment:		
Land	1,140,921	3,763,956
Building	2,226,549	3,632,483
Leasehold improvements	4,994,494	5,434,292
Equipment	11,624,859	8,241,127
	19,986,823	21,071,858
Less accumulated depreciation and amortization	8,173,097	6,882,937
Net property and equipment	11,813,726	14,188,921
Other assets, at cost less applicable amortization	220,800	285,348
	$22,862,214	$21,590,215
LIABILITIES AND STOCKHOLDERS' EQUITY		
Current Liabilities:		
Current portion of long-term debt	$ 70,208	$ 2,684,209
Accounts payable	1,965,327	1,662,858
Accrued expenses	2,191,741	1,894,959
Federal income taxes	633,343	764,916
Total current liabilities	4,860,619	7,006,942
Deferred federal income taxes	469,000	294,000
Long-term debt	3,648,750	2,412,208
Stockholders' equity:		
Common stock—par value $.50 per share: Authorized 3,000,000 shares; issued 2,514,876 shares	1,257,438	1,257,438
Additional paid-in capital	625,641	625,641
Retained earnings	12,000,766	9,993,986
Total stockholders' equity	13,883,845	11,877,065
	$22,862,214	$21,590,215

Required

1. The Consolidated Statement of Earnings for fiscal 1975 reported net earnings of $2,660,647. Compute the amount of cash dividends paid to stockholders during fiscal 1975.

2. During fiscal 1975 Steak n Shake sold and reclassified property and equipment costing $5,236,128 and having a net book value of $5,067,229. What was the cost of property and equipment acquired during fiscal 1975? What was the amount of depreciation and amortization of property and equipment charged to operations during fiscal 1975?

3. Steak n Shake follows the standard practice of including the current portion of long-term debt in current liabilities. Steak n Shake received $6,748,750 from the issuance of long-term debt in fiscal 1975. What was the total amount of long-term debt retired in fiscal 1975?

4. Steak n Shake's Consolidated Statement of Earnings for fiscal 1975 reported cost of goods sold of $14,516,848. Compute net purchases for fiscal 1975. Also compute approximate cash expenditures for merchandise in fiscal 1975.

5. The Consolidated Statement of Earnings for fiscal 1975 reported a provision for federal income taxes of $1,383,000. How much of this provision was currently payable? What was the total amount of payments made for federal income taxes in fiscal 1975?

Case 1-2

J.M. Smucker Company

The asset section of Smucker's Consolidated Balance Sheet for 1973 and 1974 is presented.

Consolidated Balance Sheets

Assets

	April 30, 1974	April 30, 1973
Current assets:		
Cash	$ 648,038	$ 1,198,321
Trade receivables, less allowances (1974–$104,840; 1973–$91,340)	5,131,219	3,812,656
Inventories:		
Finished products	6,800,345	5,989,866
Raw materials, containers and supplies	16,319,542	9,279,715
	23,119,887	15,269,581
Prepaid expenses	369,851	198,367
Total current assets	29,268,995	20,478,925
Other Assets	1,312,960	787,349
Property, Plant and Equipment		
Land and land improvements	1,443,780	1,326,162
Buildings and fixtures	10,304,252	8,299,978
Machinery and equipment	13,230,421	11,579,295
Construction in progress (estimated cost to complete $526,000)	430,985	864,137
	25,409,438	22,069,572
Allowances for depreciation (deduction)	(9,106,155)	(8,339,385)
Total Property, Plant and Equipment	16,303,283	13,730,187
Excess of Purchase Price Over Net Assets of Business Acquired	172,999	328,333
	$47,058,237	$35,324,794

6 Cases in Financial Accounting

Required

1. In 1974, Smucker included bad debt expense of $16,641 among its selling, distribution and administrative expenses in its 1974 Statement of Consolidated Income. What entry did Smucker make in 1974 to write off accounts it considered uncollectible?

2. During 1974 Smucker sold property, plant and equipment that cost $990,901 for its book value of $126,182. What entry did Smucker make in 1974 to record depreciation expense? (Assume that the sale took place on May 1, 1973.)

3. Smucker's 1974 Statement of Consolidated Income reveals that the cost of goods sold in 1974 was $69,984,721. What was the cost of goods manufactured in 1974?

4. Smucker's 1974 Statement of Consolidated Income reveals that the net sales in 1974 totaled $90,465,198. Assuming that all sales are on account, what was the total cash collections from customers in 1974?

Case 1-3

Wm. Wrigley Jr. Company

Shown are the Statement of Consolidated Earnings for the years ended December 31, 1974 and 1973, the Consolidated Balance Sheet for December 31, 1973, and the accounting policies and notes to the consolidated financial statements of Wm. Wrigley Jr. Company and wholly-owned associated companies.

Statement of Consolidated Earnings

Years ended December 31, 1974 and 1973

	1974	1973
Income:		
Net sales	$271,724,000	$231,868,000
Interest and dividends from investments	1,266,000	1,138,000
Miscellaneous other income—net	367,000	717,000
Total income	273,357,000	233,723,000
Costs and expenses:		
Materials, labor, and services consumed in making chewing gum and other products bought by customers	156,882,000	118,873,000
Selling, distribution, and general administrative expenses	81,780,000	76,163,000
Interest expense	674,000	791,000
Total costs and expenses	239,336,000	195,827,000
Earnings before income taxes	34,021,000	37,896,000
Income taxes:		
Federal	5,099,000	7,181,000
Foreign governments	9,515,000	9,329,000
States	1,251,000	1,538,000
Total income taxes	15,865,000	18,048,000
Net earnings for the year	$ 18,156,000	$ 19,848,000
Net earnings per outstanding share of capital stock	$ 4.61	$ 5.04

Depreciation has been included in the applicable classifications above, whereas in prior years depreciation was included as a separate line.

Statement of Consolidated Accumulated Earnings Retained for Use in the Business

Years ended December 31, 1974 and 1973

	1974	1973
Balance at the beginning of the year	$116,576,000	$109,130,000
Add:		
Net earnings for the year	18,156,000	19,848,000
Less—dividends declared ($3.00 per share in 1974 and $3.15 per share in 1973)	11,811,000	12,402,000
	6,345,000	7,446,000
Balance at the end of the year	$122,921,000	$116,576,000

Consolidated Balance Sheets

Assets	1973
Current assets:	
Cash	$ 8,599,000
Time deposits and certificates of deposit	7,556,000
Marketable securities, at cost (market value, 1974–$10,298,000; 1973–$10,655,000)	4,070,000
Accounts receivable	22,648,000
Inventories–	
Finished goods	7,136,000
Raw materials and supplies	38,480,000
Total inventories	45,616,000
Total current assets	88,489,000
Prepaid expenses and other assets	3,218,000
Property, plant and equipment, at cost:	
Land	6,436,000
Buildings and building equipment	63,917,000
Machinery and equipment	77,227,000
	147,580,000
Less accumulated depreciation	63,837,000
Total properties (net)	83,743,000
	$175,450,000

Liabilities and Stockholders' Equity	
Current liabilities:	
Notes payable to banks	$ 3,908,000
Accounts payable and accrued expenses	16,205,000
Dividends payable	1,575,000
Income taxes and other taxes payable	13,818,000
Total current liabilities	35,506,000
Accumulated deferred income taxes	3,670,000
Stockholders' equity:	
Capital stock, no par value– Authorized–8,000,000 shares Issued–4,000,000 shares	19,200,000
Accumulated earnings retained for use in the business	116,576,000
Accumulated earnings appropriated for guarantees under employment assurance contracts	2,000,000
	137,776,000
Less capital stock in treasury, at cost (63,032 shares)	1,502,000
Total stockholders' equity	136,274,000
	$175,450,000

Accounting Policies and Notes to Consolidated Financial Statements
December 31, 1974 and 1973

Consolidation and Foreign Exchange

The consolidated financial statements include the accounts of all wholly-owned associated companies after elimination of material intercompany amounts.

Assets and liabilities of international wholly-owned associated companies are translated at the rates prevailing at the balance sheet dates except for inventories and property, plant and equipment, which are translated at approximate rates prevailing on acquisition dates. Income and expenses are translated at weighted average rates for each year except for depreciation, which is translated at the same rates as applied to property, plant and equipment. All exchange adjustments are included in earnings. Net exchange gains aggregated $46,000 in 1974 ($870,000 in 1973).

Net assets at December 31, 1974 and 1973 and net earnings for the years then ended as reported for international wholly-owned associated companies included herein, stated in equivalent U.S. dollars, amounted to:

	1974	1973
Net current assets	$17,329,000	$15,413,000
All other assets—net	20,776,000	20,495,000
	$38,105,000	$35,908,000
Net earnings	$ 9,747,000	$10,301,000

Inventories

Inventories at December 31, 1974 and 1973 include $13,788,000 and $17,968,000, respectively, valued at cost on a last-in, first-out (LIFO) basis. If the average cost method of inventory accounting had been used, inventories would have been $16,945,000 and $9,497,000 higher than reported at December 31, 1974 and 1973, respectively. The other inventories are valued at the lower of cost (principally first-in, first-out basis) or market.

Property, Plant and Equipment

Expenditures for maintenance and repairs are charged to expense as incurred while major betterments and renewals are capitalized. When properties are sold or retired the cost and accumulated depreciation are removed from the accounts and the related gain or loss is included in earnings.

Depreciation is provided by the straight line method ($3,337,000 in 1974 and $3,058,000 in 1973) and accelerated methods ($5,508,000 in 1974 and $6,042,000 in 1973) over the estimated useful lives of the respective assets (buildings and building equipment—15 to 50 years; machinery and equipment—4 to 20 years).

Income Taxes

Deferred income taxes are provided for timing differences, principally depreciation, between financial and tax reporting. Investment tax credits, which are not significant in amount, are treated as a reduction of income taxes in the year the assets which gave rise to the credits are placed in service.

Federal income and foreign withholding taxes have not been provided on accumulated unremitted earnings (aggregating approximately $23,514,000 at December 31, 1974) of international wholly-owned associated companies which have been or are intended to be permanently reinvested in the operations of these companies. Foreign tax credits would be available to substantially reduce Federal income taxes resulting from distributions of such accumulated earnings.

Notes Payable to Banks

Interest rates for the Company's notes payable to banks ranged from 5¾% to 13½% (weighted average rate—12¼%) at December 31, 1974. The monthly average aggregate notes payable outstanding during 1974 was approximately $5,277,000 ($8,023,000 in 1973) with an approximate weighted average interest rate of 12% (8% in 1973). The maximum amount of aggregate notes payable outstanding at the end of any month during 1974 was $10,573,000 ($11,800,000 in 1973).

Unused lines of credit aggregated $14,978,000 at December 31, 1974. Of these lines of credit, one line is subject to a commitment fee of ¼ of 1% on $1,000,000, another to ½ of 1% on $1,000,000, with the balance not subject to such fees. Unused lines of credit are subject to periodic renewal and can be withdrawn upon the Company's request. At December 31, 1974, $16,500,000 of domestic credit lines and notes payable to banks are subject to 10-15% compensating balance arrangements.

Capital Stock

On March 14, 1973 the stockholders approved an increase in the authorized capital stock from 2,000,000 shares to 8,000,000 shares and a two-for-one stock split effective April 2, 1973. The share and per share data in the consolidated financial statements reflect the stock split.

Pensions

The Company and its major wholly-owned associated companies maintain group pension plans, principally insured, covering substantially all employees. Pension costs under these plans are funded as accrued and there are no significant unfunded vested benefits or, on a plan termination basis, past service liabilities at December 31, 1974. The cost of all plans charged to earnings was $2,273,000 in 1974 and $2,732,000 in 1973. The decrease in the 1974 cost is primarily due to a reduction in domestic funding requirements, which was partially offset by an $85,000 increase in the cost of foreign plans. The reduced funding in 1974 is the result of the consolidation of the various domestic plans into a single plan for funding purposes and revisions in actuarial cost methods and assumptions.

The board of directors has adopted certain amendments, effective January 1, 1975, to retirement plans for domestic employees to (a) consolidate the existing pension contracts, (b) make the plans non-contributory as to employees, (c) modify eligibility requirements, (d) permit eligible employees to be fully vested after ten years of service, (e) improve early retirement benefits for eligible employees who elect retirement dates prior to age 65, and (f) integrate a portion of the primary Social Security benefit. The amendments are subject to stockholder approval at the March 19, 1975 annual meeting.

The Company anticipates that the matters discussed in the two preceding paragraphs will not have a material effect on its results of operations in 1975 or future years and should stabilize the cost of the retirement program at a reduced percentage of payroll.

Litigation

In January of 1970 a group of mint growers, located in the States of Washington, Oregon, Idaho and Montana, filed a class action in the United States District Court, Western District of Washington, against a dealer in mint oils and the five largest United States purchasers of mint oils, including the Wm. Wrigley Jr. Company. One such purchaser has settled the claim against it and has been dismissed as a defendant; the other defendants are appealing the dismissal order. The mint growers' complaint alleges violations of certain Federal antitrust laws and seeks an injunction and treble damages which plaintiffs' counsel claims to be in the millions of dollars. The mint oil purchasers, including the Wrigley Company, have filed antitrust counterclaims against plaintiff mint growers charging them, among other things, with price-fixing. Company legal counsel are of the opinion that the claim against the Wrigley Company is without merit, that its counterclaim is meritorious and that the final outcome should not materially affect the Wrigley Company's consolidated financial statements, although any such lawsuit involves some risk and various costs to the Wrigley Company, including litigation expenses which must be incurred in defending it.

Section One | Review of Financial Accounting   11

Additional Information

1. Cash collections on Accounts Receivable during 1974 totaled $262,507,000.

2. Marketable Securities costing $1,416,000 were purchased during 1974.

3. Machinery costing $1,460,000 and fully depreciated was retired during 1974.

4. Wrigley borrowed (notes payable to banks) an additional $6,665,000 during 1974.

5. Dividends of $.40 per share were payable on December 31, 1974. (Round to the nearest thousand.)

6. Income taxes for 1974 totaled $15,865,000, including federal taxes of $5,099,000, foreign taxes of $9,515,000, and state taxes of $1,251,000. $1,834,000 of this total was deferred; cash payments for income taxes in 1974 amounted to $13,947,000.

7. Inventories on December 31, 1974 were as follows: Finished Goods, $9,428,000; Raw Materials and Supplies, $46,050,000. Also, prepaid expenses and other assets amounted to $3,828,000 on December 31, 1974.

8. During 1974, Wrigley purchased Land costing $15,000, Buildings and building equipment costing $921,000, and Machinery and equipment costing $8,384,000.

9. Accounts Payable and Accrued Expenses amounted to $20,357,000 on December 31, 1974.

10. Cash requirements resulted in drawing $2,871,000 of time deposits.

Required

Based on these statements and notes (and on the additional information provided), prepare:

1. Summary journal entries of the company's financial and operating transactions for 1974.

2. A consolidated balance sheet for December 31, 1974. (Assume all sales are on account.)

12 Cases in Financial Accounting

Case 1-4

Accounting for Various Events

For each of the following descriptions, identify the nature of the event described and indicate whether any debit or credit brought about by the event should be reported in the income statement or in the retained earnings statement under generally accepted accounting principles. Explain briefly the reasoning that led you to your choice.

Ashland Oil Company

During 1973, Ashland Oil, Inc. substantially resolved federal income tax issues for the years 1961 through 1967 relating primarily to income from crude oil transactions. The resulting income tax adjustment for these years and for similar issues for the years 1968 and 1969 resulted in a debit of $10,800,000.

McCrory Corporation

McCrory Corporation and its subsidiaries have several pension plans, one of which is contributory, covering certain of their employees. During the year ended January 31, 1974, the actuarial investment rate assumption used in computing pension cost was changed, resulting in a credit of $650,000.

National Distillers and Chemical Corporation

National Distillers and Chemical Corporation is engaged primarily in the production and marketing of petrochemicals, natural gas liquids, and sulfuric acid; alcoholic beverages and related products; brass mill products, tire valves, plumbing goods, forgings, graphic art supplies and related products; domestic wines and brandy; and textiles, primarily blankets.

In November 1975, the Company discontinued the manufacture and sale of double-knit apparel fabrics and wrote down the inventories, plant and equipment and other assets of the operation to estimated realizable value. Discontinuance of these operations resulted in a debit of $7,971,000.

Del E. Webb Corporation

During 1973, Del E. Webb Corporation filed a claim against the Government of Honduras for certain costs in excess of contract amounts required to be incurred in order to complete the construction of a highway in Honduras in prior years. The claim was included in accounts receivable from customers at December 31, 1973. The Government of Honduras initially indicated a desire to negotiate a mutually acceptable and timely settlement of the claim.

On November 12, 1974, representatives of Del E. Webb Corporation met with officials of the Government of Honduras to commence negotiating the amount of the claim. The Corporation was then informed that the Government of Honduras unconditionally rejected its claim and did not intend to negotiate a mutually acceptable settlement.

At December 31, 1974 the Honduras receivable amounted to $2,749,000 of claimed costs. The Corporation's earnings before taxes amounted to $9,292,000 in 1974.

How should this receivable be accounted for under generally accepted accounting principles?

Tastee Freez Industries, Inc.

The company made substantial sales of mobile units during the two years ended January 31, 1963, under contracts generally providing for payment over a five year period. The program was relatively new and insufficient time had elapsed to allow a good estimation to be made of uncollectibles. The firm's impressive reported net income for each of the two years was a result of overly optimistic appraisals of ultimate collectibility. On March 11, 1963, the common stock was listed on the American Stock Exchange. Later in 1963 the company went into receivership.

In general, how should a substantive change in the estimation of uncollectibles be accounted for in the company's financial statements? As it turned out, a subsequent epidemic of city ordinances forbidding vending from motor vehicles with the use of bells and other noise-makers was responsible for most of the losses. Under this condition, what treatment do you recommend? Does your answer depend on whether there was sufficient information available to accurately estimate the resulting uncollectibles at the time the revenues were recognized? Why or why not?

Case 1-5

Atlantic Richfield Company

The Consolidated Statement of Income and Retained Earnings of Atlantic Richfield Company for the years 1972 and 1971 is presented.

	1972	1971
Revenues:		
Sales and other operating revenues (including excise taxes)	$3,831,255,000	$3,658,437,000
Earnings of affiliated companies accounted for on the equity method	7,674,000	6,949,000
Interest and other revenues	60,504,000	57,591,000
	3,899,433,000	3,722,977,000
Expenses:		
Costs and operating expenses	2,325,076,000	2,130,604,000
Selling, delivery, general and administrative expenses	326,414,000	351,234,000
Taxes other than income taxes (note 10)	628,633,000	630,322,000
Depreciation, depletion, amortization and retirements	242,926,000	227,296,000
Interest	62,275,000	61,045,000
	3,585,324,000	3,400,501,000
Income before income taxes and extraordinary item	314,109,000	322,476,000
Provision for taxes on income (note 11)	121,593,000	111,943,000
Income Before Extraordinary Item	192,516,000	210,533,000
Extraordinary item (note 12)	3,045,000	(11,831,000)
Net Income	$ 195,561,000	$ 198,702,000
Earned Per Share (note 8)		
Income before extraordinary item	$3.40	$3.73
Extraordinary item	.06	(.21)
Net Income	$3.46	$3.52
Net Income Retained For Use In The Business:		
Balance January 1	$1,905,300,000	$1,837,749,000
Net income	195,561,000	198,702,000
Cash dividends:		
Preferred	(39,917,000)	(40,210,000)
Common (per share, 1972—$2.00; 1971—$2.00)	(91,937,000)	(90,941,000)
Balance December 31	$1,969,007,000	$1,905,300,000

The extraordinary charge of $3,045,000 was explained in footnote 12 as follows:

> The 1972 extraordinary credit of $3,045,000, after tax, reflects the gain from divestiture under a court decree of August 1970 of certain former Sinclair marketing, refining and related producing properties to Pasco, Inc. after offsetting extraordinary charges associated with a related program for restructuring and rebalancing facilities, relocating administrative activities, and the provision for writedown to realizable values reflecting planned modifications of agricultural chemical operations.
>
> The key elements of the restructuring and rebalancing program were dismantling and writeoff of portions of certain refineries, principally Philadelphia, reflecting the impact of the divestiture to Pasco, Inc. as well as the curtailment of certain marketing operations, withdrawal from marketing in certain Southern states extending as far west as Arizona. The consolidation and relocation of administrative activities included the transfer of corporate headquarters to Los Angeles, consolidation of the administrative centers in Chicago and Philadelphia into one unit located in Philadelphia, and the centralization of the responsibilities for the refining and marketing functions in Los Angeles.

The effect of these items was as follows:

	(thousands of dollars)		
	Credit (charge)	Income Taxes	Extraordinary Item
Divestiture under court decree	$89,391	$(24,100)	$65,291
Refining and marketing restructuring and rebalancing	(33,434)	7,800	(25,634)
Consolidation and relocation of offices (including $10,116 after tax for relocation of executive offices to Los Angeles)	(29,412)	7,000	(22,412)
Agricultural chemical assets— provision for writedown to realizable values	(18,500)	4,300	(14,200)
	$ 8,045	$ (5,000)	$ 3,045

Investment tax credits reflected in the above Income Taxes were $600,000.

The 1972 results of operations of the properties divested to Pasco, Inc. are included in the consolidated financial statements and operating statistics in the following amounts: crude oil production approximately 18,900 b/d; natural gas production approximately 48,400 b/d, while product sales amounted to approximately $14,700,000 (including excise taxes). The consolidated financial statements and operation statistics have not been restated to segregate these operations since this divestiture resulted in cash proceeds of approximately $156,900,000 and after considering interest on such funds the effect on earnings is not material.

The 1971 extraordinary charge of $11,831,000 (net of applicable income tax benefit of $5,300,000) reflects the Company's withdrawal from nuclear fuel operations.

Required

1. Which, if any, of the items in the Exhibit included in footnote 12 should be treated as extraordinary items for 1972? Why?

2. What is the impact of the treatment accorded these items by Atlantic Richfield on the net income reported for 1972?

3. Can you provide an explanation for the way Atlantic Richfield handled these items?

Section Two

Present Value and Leasing

Case 2-1

Colonial Commercial Corporation*

A standing complaint of innovators in any field is that they rarely win the recognition due them. Wall Street, we're happy to say, doesn't share this lamentable failure to reward creativity. Quite the contrary. A case in point is a little Curb number called Colonial Commercial Corporation. The company deserves credit for breaking new ground in two areas: its business and its accounting. On the first score, Colonial is a kind of glorified collection agency. There's nothing new, of course, in getting debtors to ante up. But Colonial has raised the fine old art of dunning to a different dimension. What it does essentially is seek out "distressed," to use the trade euphemism, portfolios of consumer accounts receivables, buy them at a sizable discount and then "liquidate" them — that is, collect.

Colonial's astuteness as both a connoisseur and collector in its specialized realm is evidenced by its rapid growth. Revenues climbed from a pittance in '65 to $5.32 million this year. Reported earnings, mostly nonexistent the first three years of this stretch, hit 63 cents a share last year vs. 44 cents in '69 and nine cents in '68. Moreover, the gains are accelerating rapidly: management expects earnings of $2.10 - $2.15 a share for '71. As noted, investors have responded warmly to the firm's success: the stock this year has soared from under 6 to a high of 36.

Colonial's contribution to creative accounting is perhaps best illustrated by its acquisition late last year of a small loan company in Chapter 11, Texas Consumer Finance. Colonial paid roughly $19 million for the firm: $900,000 for its equity and something like $18 million to satisfy the ill-fated outfit's creditors who held $32.7 million of its debt. By liquidating the Texas concern's loan portfolio, Colonial expects to realize $22.9 million, some $10 million this year and the rest in '72 and '73. That would suggest a gross profit of $3.9 million (arrived at by the sophisticated mathematical process of deducting the amount paid from the amount received).

However, Colonial's bookkeeping is not that — we almost said simple, but perhaps unimaginative is more apt. To begin with, the company uses the interesting concept of "present value" to cover the costs of its debt. Of the total purchase price, $5 million represented cash and the rest loans, including some $14 million in notes maturing at various times up to 15 years. However, the coupon on the bulk of those notes is 6% — or less than current market rates. Hence, Colonial has calculated what it might have made had it invested such funds at the higher current market return and subtracted the difference, some $4 million, from the original cost of $19 million. The result of this hypothetical exercise is to cut the "cost" of the acquisition to around $15 million and, coincidentally, boost the potential take to $7.6 million.

*Reproduced, with permission, from Alan Abelson's "Up and Down Wall Street" from the August 23, 1971 issue of *Barron's*.

Further, Colonial reckons that the other assets (besides the loan portfolio) of Texas Consumer Finance — primarily cash — were worth about $3 million. That sum, too, is sliced from the "cost" — which further reduces the amount paid to something like $12 million and, presto!, ups the potential gross to approximately $10.9 million.

What this lowering of costs via the magic of accounting means in terms of this year's earnings can be gauged with the help of a few figures. Colonial expects to collect $10 million of the $22.9 million from Texas Consumer's portfolio in '71. It will charge off $5.3 million as "cost"; other expenses include $500,000 for amortization of the discount of present value; $800,000 in interest on notes; and perhaps $400,000 or so to actually collect the money. This leaves roughly $3 million, or about $1.50 a share, largely tax free because of loss carry-forward, to report as earnings. Quite a chunk, in other words, of estimated net of $2.10-$2.15 a share.

By contrast, as we reckon it, had Colonial chosen to use the $19 million it actually paid for Texas Consumer as its cost base, it would show half as much in profits this year from the deal, or perhaps 70 cents a share, again largely tax free. That would put '71 earnings somewhere in the area of $1.40 a share. The difference is not exactly inconsequential for a company with a total market evaluation of $60 million, or 12 times stockholders' equity.

Far be it for us to question ingenuity in any sphere. Moreover, Colonial's brand of bookkeeping has the unqualified blessing of its auditors. Nonetheless, we can't help wonder what might happen one year if there isn't a juicy distressed portfolio to buy at a bargain. The company, of course, still will have to pay the interest on the money it borrowed in previous years to swing its deals. But, then, the strong card of innovators is that they can always come up with something new. Or, almost always.

Required Reconstruct the series of entries Colonial Commercial made to account for its acquisition of Texas Consumer Finance.

Case 2-2　　　　　　　　　　Chart House Inc. (A)

Chart House Inc. is the largest franchisee of Burger King restaurants, operating 262 such restaurants (24 of which are sub-franchised). The Company also operates 60 steak restaurants (five of which are franchised), including 21 Chart House restaurants, 36 Cork 'n Cleaver restaurants, and three Bodega restaurants, and one Chart House Seafood Inn.

Chart House Inc.'s Consolidated Statements of Income and Consolidated Statements of Shareholders' Investment for years ended December 31, 1974 and 1975 are presented. Note 4 to the Consolidated Financial Statements reveals that Chart House has a large number of noncancellable leases for restaurant land and buildings. Substantially all of these leases are noncapitalized financing leases. The present value of future minimum net rental payments as of December 31, 1974 was $39,379,000.

Consolidated Statements of Income
Dollars in thousands, except per share data

	Year Ended December 31, 1975	1974
Revenues	$138,084	$114,601
Costs and Expenses:		
Cost of Food and Supplies	$ 51,299	$ 46,048
Operating Expenses	56,711	45,116
Selling, General and Administrative Expenses	10,272	8,166
Depreciation and Amortization *(Note 1)*	4,564	3,790
Interest	1,854	1,797
Total Costs and Expenses	$124,700	$104,917
Income Before Provision for Income Taxes	$ 13,384	$ 9,684
Provision for Income Taxes *(Note 2)*:		
Currently Payable	$ 3,897	$ 2,840
Deferred to Future Periods	1,967	1,361
	$ 5,864	$ 4,201
Net Income	$ 7,520	$ 5,483
Net Income Per Share *(Note 7)*:		
Primary	$ 2.18	$ 1.59
Fully Diluted	$ 2.11	

Consolidated Statements of Shareholders' Investment
For the Years Ended December 31, 1975 and 1974
Dollars in thousands, except share amounts

	Common Stock		Treasury Stock		Total		Retained
	Shares	Amount	Shares	Amount	Shares	Amount	Earnings
Balance, December 31, 1973	3,533,596	$13,441	(78,522)	$ (1,041)	3,455,074	$12,400	$ 10,581
Net income for the year							5,483
Cash dividends declared ($.36 per share)							(1,146)
Balance, December 31, 1974	3,533,596	$13,441	(78,522)	$ (1,041)	3,455,074	$12,400	$ 14,918
Net income for the year							7,520
Income for short period (Note 1)							(62)
Exercise of stock options (Note 5)	400	4			400	4	
Cash dividends declared ($.54 per share)							(1,818)
Balance, December 31, 1975	3,533,996	$13,445	(78,522)	$ (1,041)	3,455,474	$12,404	$ 20,558

Required

1. Assume that Chart House decided to capitalize all previously noncapitalized leases on January 1, 1975.

    a.) What entry would have been made by Chart House to capitalize these leases on January 1, 1975?

    b.) How will the accounts included in the above entry affect Chart House's income statements and balance sheets over the life of these leases?

2. Assume that the average lease term (and average useful life of the assets involved) is 15 years and that the annual (minimum and average) rental payment in 1975 (and in each subsequent year) of $5,475,000 was made at the beginning of the year. Estimate the impact on Chart House's 1975 reported net income and primary earnings per share if it had capitalized all previously noncapitalized leases on January 1, 1975.

Case 2-3

Chart House Inc. (B)

Chart House Inc., the largest franchisee of Burger King restaurants, operated 278 such restaurants in Louisiana and the Gulf Coast Area, Northern Illinois, Indiana, Michigan, Virginia, Texas and California. In addition, the Company has sublicensed 54 such restaurants in Northern Illinois. The Company also operated 77 steakhouses in 25 states and four uniform limited-menu seafood restaurants in Louisiana as of December 31, 1977.

The Company is a lessee under a number of noncancellable lease agreements involving restaurant land and buildings and in accordance with the requirements of Statement of Financial Accounting Standards No. 13 (Accounting for Leases) has segregated minimum lease rentals into those portions relating to land and buildings, respectively. The buildings portion of the minimum rentals has been capitalized and the related asset and obligation recorded using the Company's incremental borrowing rate at the inception of the lease. The assets are amortized on a straight-line basis over the lease term and interest expense is accrued on the basis of the outstanding lease obligation. The portion of the minimum rentals relating to land is expensed as it accrues.

Excerpts from Chart House's December 31, 1977 and 1976 Consolidated Balance Sheets are presented. Additional information about capital leases is from Note (4) to Chart House's 1977 Annual Report.

Consolidated Balance Sheets

	As of December 31,	
Assets	**1977**	**1976**
Leased Property *(Notes 4 & 10)*:	*(In Thousands of Dollars)*	
Leased Property under Capital Leases, Less Accumulated Amortization of $6,848,000 in 1977 and $5,503,000 in 1976	$ 27,134	$ 26,368
Net Investment in Direct Financing Leases	2,919	1,377
Net Leased Property	$ 30,053	$ 27,745
Liabilities and Shareholders' Investment		
Current Liabilities:		
Current Portion of Long-Term Debt *(Note 3)*	$ 3,793	$ 3,247
Current Portion of Obligations under Capital Leases *(Note 4)*	1,033	924
Accounts Payable	5,819	5,657
Accrued Liabilities	7,594	6,263
Accrued Income Taxes	772	1,900
Dividends Payable	769	652
Total Current Liabilities	$ 19,780	$ 18,643
Long-Term Debt *(Note 3)*	$ 45,428	$ 31,858
Long-Term Obligations under Capital Leases *(Note 4)*	$ 31,606	$ 29,671
Deferred Credits:		
Income Taxes *(Note 2)*	$ 6,773	$ 3,935
Other	200	322
Total Deferred Credits	$ 6,973	$ 4,257

Capital Leases

The following is a reconciliation of the aggregate minimum payments under capital leases to the recorded liability at December 31, 1977:

Year Ended December 31:	(In Thousands of Dollars)
1978	$ 4,133
1979	4,139
1980	4,127
1981	4,040
1982	4,042
Later Years	48,488
Total Minimum Lease Payments	$ 68,969
Less: Amount Representing Interest	36,330
Total Obligations under Capital Leases	$ 32,639
Less: Current Portion	1,033
Long-Term Obligations under Capital Leases, with Interest Rates Ranging from 6½% to 13½% and a Weighted Average Interest Rate of 9.6%	$ 31,606

Total minimum lease payments have not been reduced by minimum sublease rentals of $4,067,000 due in the future under noncancelable subleases.

Amortization of leased property under capital leases was $1,707,000 and $1,575,000 and interest expense on the outstanding obligations under such leases was $2,922,000 and $2,775,000 in 1977 and 1976, respectively.

Required

1. Assume that there were no dispositions or sales of leased property under capital leases in 1977. Also assume that leased property under capital leases that was one-fifth depreciated or amortized was transferred to Chart House's property and equipment accounts to correct a classification error. What entries did Chart House make in 1977 to account for its capital leases?

2. Assume that the minimum lease payments for 1978 will be made on December 31, 1978. What entry will Chart House make on this date to record this payment under existing noncancellable lease agreements?

Case 2-4

American Technical Industries, Inc.

American Technical Industries Inc. is a leading manufacturer of artificial Christmas trees. The Company makes or imports and markets such related items as ornaments, garlands, wreaths, and artificial shrubs. The Company also turns out machinery, parts and assemblies for government and industry, including manufacturers of computers, electric typewriters, copiers and other electronic products. The Company operates on a March 31 fiscal year.

The following note was included in the notes to American Tech's Consolidated Financial Statements for the years ended March 31, 1977:

Subsequent Events

In December 1976, the Company acquired land and a building in Aurora, Illinois, for approximately $790,000. In April 1977, the Company sold such property to the City of Aurora for the same amount. The funds received by the Company represent proceeds from the issuance by the City of Aurora of an Industrial Development Revenue Bond in the principal amount of $790,000 maturing April 1, 1992 with interest on the rate of 7.875% per annum.

Simultaneous with the sale the Company entered into a lease agreement with the City of Aurora for rental by the Company of the above mentioned land and building for a period of fifteen years commencing April 1, 1977. Under the terms of the lease agreement the Company is required to make semi-annual rental payments on April 1 and October 1 of $45,300 to a Trustee appointed by the City. The payments are to be applied to interest on the Bond and repayment of the $790,000 principal upon maturity. At the end of the lease term the property reverts to the Company for a nominal amount. Such lease will be accounted for by the Company as a capital lease for financial reporting purposes...

Required

1. If the Industrial Development Revenue Bond is issued by the City of Aurora, why should a liability appear on American Tech's Balance Sheet?

2. Why would American Tech choose to acquire the use of this property in this indirect manner?

3. Assuming that the land and building represented 25% and 75%, respectively, of the total consideration, what entries did American Tech make in fiscal 1978 to account for the transactions relating to the property and lease?

Case 2-5

Allied Chemical Corporation

Allied Chemical Corporation's December 31, 1972 Consolidated Balance Sheet included the following items:

Consolidated Balance Sheets

	1972	1971
Current liabilities		
Accounts payable and accrued liabilities	$ 184,490,000	$ 162,446,000
Notes and loans payable	3,624,000	23,144,000
Taxes payable	22,410,000	16,520,000
Total current liabilities	210,524,000	202,110,000
Long-term debt	383,856,000	399,354,000
Capitalized lease obligations	55,140,000	56,183,000
Deferred income	19,086,000	19,412,000
Deferred income taxes	71,092,000	61,812,000
Accrued pension obligations	84,900,000	94,150,000
Total liabilities	$ 824,598,000	$ 833,021,000

Capitalized Lease Obligations

The Notes to Allied Chemical's 1972 Financial Statements included the following note:

> Capitalized lease obligations relate principally to plants and facilities financed by industrial development revenue bonds, the principal and interest on which will be covered by rental payments made by the Company. Under certain conditions, as provided in the lease agreements, the Company has the option to purchase these plants and facilities for amounts which will be sufficient to redeem and retire all outstanding bonds. These transactions and certain others are being treated for accounting and tax purposes as though the facilities were constructed and owned by the Company. Annual lease payment requirements approximate $4,500,000 from 1973 through 1993. The principal amounts of lease payments due within one year are $2,037,000 and $1,892,000 at December 31, 1972 and 1971, respectively, and are included in notes and loans payable.

Required

1. Assume that Allied Chemical Corporation signed its lease obligations financed by industrial development revenue bonds on December 31, 1971:

   a.) What entry did Allied Chemical Corporation make on December 31 to record these obligations?

   b.) How will the accounts included in the above entry affect Allied Chemical Corporation's income statements and balance sheets over the life of these leases?

2. Assume that Allied Chemical Corporation's annual lease payment on the Capitalized Lease Obligations was $4,500,000 in 1972:

   a.) What entry did Allied Chemical Corporation make in 1972 to record this payment?

   b.) What was the approximate effective rate of interest used by Allied Chemical Corporation to capitalize these lease obligations?

Case 2-6

Telefile Computer Corporation

Telefile Computer Corporation is in the computer accessories business. Its specialty is the design and sale of data storage systems — disks, magnetic tape transports, and computer memories. It also offers data-communication processors and a range of peripherals such as printers and card reading equipment.

Telefile's Consolidated Balance Sheets for September 30, 1975 and 1974 are presented. Only the asset sections are provided. Noncancellable long-term lease contracts which are in substance equivalent to installment sales are accounted for as sales at the discounted present value of rentals to be collected during the primary term of the lease. The related cost of the leased equipment is charged to cost of sales

Consolidated Balance Sheets

ASSETS (Note 6):	1975	1974
CURRENT:		
Cash	$ 174,139	$ 143,110
Trust certificate of deposit		186,000
Accounts and notes receivable, trade, less allowance for doubtful accounts of $1,500 in 1975 and 1974 (Note 2)	1,004,551	787,646
Lease receivables, due within one year, net of deferred finance income of $15,154 in 1975 and $6,635 in 1974 (Note 2)	58,225	20,560
Inventories (Note 3)	749,558	298,034
Other	31,964	42,864
Total current assets	2,018,437	1,478,214
Revenue-earning equipment, at cost, less allowance for depreciation of $254,453 in 1975 and $64,953 in 1974 (Note 4)	608,731	395,667
Property and equipment, at cost, less accumulated depreciation of $6,833 in 1975 and $41,948 in 1974 (Note 5)	96,205	59,117
Accounts and notes receivable (Note 2):		
Time sales, due after one year	833,634	13,760
Lease receivables, due after one year, net of deferred finance income of $16,124 in 1975 and $7,182 in 1974	132,752	60,806
Shareholders	1	1
Organization costs, net of accumulated amortization of $10,484 in 1975 and $8,276 in 1974	562	2,770
Deferred finance charges and other assets	11,432	38,686
	$3,701,754	$2,049,021

Required

1. What is the present value of Telefile's lease receivables at September 30, 1975?

2. On October 1, 1975, the U.S. Government acquired one of Telefile's telecommunications systems under a lease arrangement. The U.S. Government could have acquired the system for a cash sales price of $164,400, but they preferred to acquire it under a 10-year lease arrangement. The lease is noncancellable and requires cash payments of $21,000 at the beginning of each of the 10 years. Maintenance and service are contracted for separately under either sales or lease arrangements. The cost to Telefile of developing, manufacturing and installing this system was $157,000.

   a.) Prepare the journal entries that Telefile used to account for this lease in fiscal 1976 assuming this lease was a captial lease.

   b.) Prepare the journal entries that Telefile used to account for this lease in fiscal 1976 assuming this lease was an operating lease.

   c.) Prepare the journal entries that Telefile used to account for this lease in fiscal 1976 assuming that the installment method was used.

Case 2-7　　　　　　　　　　Teleflex, Incorporated

Teleflex, Incorporated manufactures and services precision control equipment; develops, manufactures and applies corrosion resistant coatings; and manufactures a line of extruded fluoroplastic products used in the aircraft and nuclear power industries. The company also designs and manufactures commercial controls, control systems, instruments, and other products having application in the automotive, marine and other industries. Teleflex's 1978 and 1977 Consolidated Balance Sheets are presented.

Teleflex, Incorporated	December 31, 1978	December 25, 1977*
Assets		
Current assets		
Cash and cash equivalents	$ 2,695,300	$ 1,127,300
Accounts receivable, less allowance for doubtful accounts, 1978—$393,800; 1977—$360,600	9,413,600	9,041,800
Inventories		
Raw material and manufactured parts	8,239,100	7,919,800
Work-in-process and finished goods	4,539,900	3,882,400
Prepaid expenses	341,900	148,000
Total current assets	25,229,800	22,119,300
Plant assets, at cost, less accumulated depreciation and amortization	10,193,300	9,813,700
Equity investment and patents, net of amortization	1,190,100	860,000
	$36,613,200	$32,793,000
Liabilities and shareholders' investment		
Current liabilities		
Current portion of borrowings and capital lease obligations	$ 1,030,300	$ 542,200
Accounts payable and accrued expenses	6,058,000	5,044,700
Estimated income taxes payable	813,800	841,900
Total current liabilities	7,902,100	6,428,800
Long-term borrowings	10,604,300	11,036,800
Obligations under capital leases	1,658,300	1,716,400
Deferred income taxes	877,000	714,000
	21,041,700	19,896,000
Shareholders' investment		
Preference shares, par value $1		
Authorized—500,000 shares		
Outstanding—none	—	—
Common shares, no par value		
Authorized—3,000,000 shares		
Outstanding—1978—1,398,810 shares; 1977—1,346,146 shares	5,421,000	5,010,700
Retained earnings	10,150,500	7,886,300
Total shareholders' investment	15,571,500	12,897,000
	$36,613,200	$32,793,000

The accompanying notes are an integral part of the consolidated financial statements.
*Restated (see Notes 3 and 5).

Note 3 which describes the company's lease arrangements is presented below. The company's effective income tax rate for 1978 was 48%. The expected income tax rate for 1979 also is expected to be 48%.

Note 3 — Lease arrangements

Capital leases:

In 1978, the company adopted the retroactive provisions of Statement of Financial Accounting Standards No. 13, Accounting for Leases. Accordingly, all financial data for years prior to 1978 presented in the consolidated financial statements and ten year summary have been restated.

As a result of the retroactive capitalization of these leases, consolidated net income has been reduced in 1978 and 1977 by $19,000 or $.01 per share, and $21,900 or $.01 per share, respectively. The cumulative effect of this accounting change for years prior to 1977 has been reflected as a decrease of $138,400 in retained earnings at the beginning of year 1977 in the accompanying financial statements.

The following analysis reflects the leased property which is included in plant assets (see Note 2):

	1978	1977
Land and buildings	$ 1,997,200	$ 1,997,200
Accumulated amortization	(653,700)	(560,500)
Net capitalized leases	$ 1,343,500	$ 1,436,700

Future minimum lease payments under capital leases together with the present value of the net minimum lease payments as of December 31, 1978 are:

1979	$ 228,800
1980	228,800
1981	228,800
1982	228,800
1983	228,800
After 1983	2,130,400
Net minimum lease payments	3,274,400
Amount representing interest	(1,558,000)
Present value of net minimum lease payments (including $58,100 currently due)	$1,716,400

Operating leases:

Future minimum rental payments under operating leases that have initial or remaining noncancellable lease terms in excess of one year at December 31, 1978 are:

1979	$295,000
1980	202,000
1981	126,000
After 1981	61,000
Total	$684,000

The total rental expense for all operating leases for the years ended 1978 and 1977 was $336,000 and $304,000, respectively.

Required

1. Assume Teleflex made a lease payment of $228,800 in 1978. Estimate the principal amount of capital lease obligations included in the "current portion of borrowings and capital lease obligations" line item at December 25, 1977.

2. Assume that no new capital leases will be added in 1979 and that depreciation and amortization are provided on the straight-line method for financial reporting purposes.

    a. What entries will Teleflex make in 1979 to account for its capital leases? (Amounts can be derived from the information given.)

    b. Estimate the effect of lease capitalization on consolidated net income in 1979.

Case 2-8

Med General Inc.

Med General Inc. manufactures and markets a wide range of medical and surgical equipment and supplies for the health care industry. Products include (1) transcutaneous electrical nerve stimulators (TENS) used to control acute and chronic pain, (2) muscle stimulators and biofeedback equipment used in rehabilitation programs, and (3) surgical products, especially fiberoptic lights, vesselcare aids and TENS systems used to control pain in postoperative surgical cases. The company was founded in 1969 and went public in 1972. The company's products are marketed by 400 dealers in the United States and 40 dealers in 75 countries overseas.

Med General's 1978 annual report included the following note:

Note 12: Commitments and Contingencies —
Capital Lease

During 1978, the company's wholly-owned subsidiary, Med General Laboratories, LTD. leased manufacturing space in Shannon, Ireland for 25 years at approximately $43,125 per year. The lease agreement provides an option for the subsidiary to purchase the property within the first three years of the lease agreement at a cost of approximately $412,000. If such option is exercised, the subsidiary will receive a grant from the government of Ireland of 35% of the purchase price. The lease agreement has been accounted for as a capital lease and the property has been capitalized at a cost reflecting interest rates appropriate at the inception of the lease.

Future minimum lease payments under the capital lease, by years, together with the present value of minimum lease payments as of December 31, 1978 are:

Year Ending December 31:	
1979	$ 43,125
1980	43,125
1981	43,125
1982	43,125
1983	43,125
Later years	862,500
Total net minimum lease payments	1,078,125
Less amount representing interest	737,125
Present value of net minimum lease payments	341,000
Less current amount	(40,450)
	$ 300,550

Med General's 1979 annual report included the following schedule of "minimum lease payments under the capital-lease, by years, together with the present value of minimum lease payments as of December 31, 1979:"

Year Ending December 31:	
1980	$ 43,125
1981	43,125
1982	43,125
1983	43,125
Later years	862,500
Total net minimum lease payments	$1,035,000
Less amount representing interest	696,155
Present value of net minimum lease payments	$ 338,845
Less current amount	(2,593)
	$ 336,252

The lease for the manufacturing space in Shannon, Ireland provides for monthly payments of $3,593 per month. Assuming that payments are made at the end of each month, the implicit interest rate reflected in the lease contract is 12%, compounded monthly. Selected present value of an ordinary annuity of one factors are given below:

Monthly Periods	Present Value Factors
300	94.9466
288	94.3056
276	93.5834
12	11.2551

Required

1. Assume that the lease for the manufacturing space in Shannon, Ireland was signed on December 31, 1978. What was the effect on net income in 1979 of Med General's accounting for this lease as a capital lease instead of as an operating lease?

2. How did Med General calculate the current portion of the capitalized leased obligation at December 31, 1978? How does this calculation compare with the one used for the current portion of this obligation at December 31, 1979?

3. Assume that in 1980, Med General was considering the possibility of leasing a warehouse which was built in November 1973 with an estimated life of 40 years. The specifics of the proposed lease were as follows:

Date:	December 1, 1980
Term:	25 years
Ownership:	Ownership retained by lessor
Purchase option:	None
Executory costs:	To be billed separately
Cancellation clause:	Noncancellable
Monthly payment:	$15,000 (due at the beginning of each month)

Assume that Med General's incremental borrowing rate was 12%. Through appraisal reports, the fair value of the land and building have been estimated at $367,485 and $1,070,955, respectively.

How should this lease be accounted for under generally accepted accounting principles? Why?

Case 2-9 Measurex Corporation

Selected excerpts from Measurex Corporation's 1972 and 1971 Consolidated Statements of Income, Balance Sheet, and Notes to Consolidated Financial Statements are presented.

Consolidated Statements of Income

Operating Revenues	1972	1971
Sales	$15,201,000	$8,041,000
Rental and service income	1,135,000	572,000
	16,336,000	8,613,000
Cost of sales, rentals and services	7,058,000	3,073,000
Gross profit	9,278,000	5,540,000
Selling, general and administrative expenses	6,414,000	3,458,000
	2,864,000	2,082,000
Interest income	607,000	275,000
Interest expense	(584,000)	(383,000)
	23,000	(108,000)
Income before taxes on income and extraordinary credit	2,887,000	1,974,000
Taxes on income	1,160,000	940,000
Income before extraordinary credit	1,727,000	1,034,000
Extraordinary credit—reduction of provision for federal income taxes through utilization of net operating loss carry-forward	—	545,000
Net income	$ 1,727,000	$1,579,000
Net income per common and common equivalent share:		
Income before extraordinary credit	$ .71	$ .52
Extraordinary credit	—	.27
Net income	$ .71	$ .79

Consolidated Balance Sheets

Assets	1972	1971
Current assets:		
Cash	$ 1,871,000	$ 1,150,000
Current portion of lease contracts receivable	2,619.000	893,000
Accounts receivable	1,457,000	2,063,000
Inventories	4,991,000	2,735,000
Prepaid expenses	26,000	131,000
Total current assets	10,964,000	6,972,000
Lease contracts receivable less current portion and valuation provision	17,222,000	5,989,000
Systems leased to others under short-term leases (including installation costs), at cost less accumulated depreciation and amortization of $261,000 (1972) and $174,000 (1971)	1,066,000	1,691,000
Residual value of systems leased to others under long-term leases	691,000	691,000
Fixed assets, at cost less allowance for depreciation	2,631,000	1,466,000
Investment in new product development less accumulated amortization of $814,000 (1972) and $451,000 (1971)	1,491,000	962,000
Other	592,000	525,000
	$34,657,000	$18,296,000

Liabilities

	1972	1971
Current liabilities:		
Long-term debt due within one year	$ 210,000	$ 147,000
Trade accounts payable	955,000	693,000
Accrued expenses:		
Payroll and payroll related items	989,000	466,000
Initial and continuing services	421,000	212,000
Other	218,000	195,000
Deferred taxes on income	150,000	40,000
Total current liabilities	2,943,000	1,753,000
Long-term debt less amount due within one year	10,386,000	9,033,000
Deferred taxes on income	1,229,000	355,000
	14,558,000	11,141,000

Contingent liabilities

Shareholders' Equity

Preferred stock, $1 par value:
Authorized: 1,000,000 shares; issued and outstanding: none

	1972	1971
Common stock, without par value: Authorized: 5,000,000 shares; issued and outstanding: 2,597,284 shares (1972) and 1,927,406 (1971)	68,000	34,000
Additional paid-in capital	17,865,000	6,682,000
Retained earnings	2,166,000	439,000
	20,099,000	7,155,000
	$34,657,000	$18,296,000

Notes to Consolidated Financial Statements

1. Summary of Significant Accounting Policies

Basis of Consolidation:
The accompanying consolidated financial statements include the accounts of the Company and its subsidiaries all of which are wholly owned excepting directors' qualifying shares. All significant intercompany items have been eliminated.

Lease Accounting:
Measurex offers its customers both short-term and long-term leases. Generally, short-term leases have terms from 12 to 42 months and long-term leases have terms from 66 to 102 months.

Substantially all the amounts shown as "Sales" are represented by long-term leases accounted for on the financing method. Such method recognizes as revenue at the time of shipment of a system an amount equal to the lesser of (a) the discounted amount of future committed lease payments discounted at a rate which the Company believes approximates the customer's borrowing rate or (b) the cash purchase price of the system. The excess of the aggregate committed lease payments over the discounted amount of such payments is recognized as interest income on the sum-of-the-digits method over the term of the lease.

In years prior to 1972 it was the Company's practice to record residual value on financing leases; had this practice been continued in 1972 net income would have been increased by approximately $336,000, or $.15 per share. (In fiscal year 1972 the American Institute of Certified Public Accountants published an Accounting Interpretation recommending that in accounting for financing leases residual value not be recorded; the Company has conformed to this recommendation.)

Short-term leases are accounted for on the operating method whereby the aggregate rentals are reported as revenue on a straight-line basis over the term of the leases. Under the operating method the statement of income reflects, as expenses, depreciation of the leased property and amortization of the installation costs.

Since its inception it has been the Company's practice to grant its customers an initial period, generally six months following installation, in which to evaluate the system. During the initial period the customer may return the system and require the refund of all rentals theretofore paid. Although no systems have been returned through November 30, 1972, provisions have been made which management believes to be sufficient to provide for losses which may result from returns.

See Note 2.

Inventory Valuation:
Purchased parts and components are stated at the lower of average cost or market. Finished sub-assemblies and systems and work in process are stated at the lower of standard cost (which approximates actual cost) or market.

See Note 3.

Properties:
The Company provides for depreciation and amortization by charges to expense which are sufficient to write off the costs of the assets over their estimated useful lives, on a straight-line basis.

The basis for computing depreciation and amortization is as follows:

Class of Property	Estimated Useful Lives
Systems leased to others under short-term leases	9 Years
Installation costs on systems leased to others under short-term leases	4 Years
Buildings	25-40 Years
Machinery and equipment	2-10 Years

Investment in New Product Development:
The Company is capitalizing new product development costs which are identifiable to significant new systems or products having a potential commercial value; those costs not meeting these criteria are charged to selling, general and administrative expense currently. The capitalized costs are being amortized to expense over the anticipated useful life of the system or product, or three years from the beginning of routine production, whichever is shorter. Costs applicable to projects abandoned are written off in the year of abandonment.

See Note 5.

Taxes on Income:
Deferred taxes are provided on all significant differences between taxable income and pre-tax income as shown in the accompanying consolidated statements of income except taxes are not provided on the income of the Company's Domestic International Sales Corporation subsidiary inasmuch as management believes that the payment of taxes on such income can be deferred indefinitely by investing and distributing such income as the DISC regulations allow.

Investment tax credit on fixed assets is recognized on the flow-through method. Generally, it is the Company's policy to allow the end-user of the leased Measurex system to claim the related investment tax credit; unclaimed investment tax credit is recognized by the Company either as additional sales or as financing income over the term of the lease.

Deferred taxes arise principally as a result of the following differences between taxable income and pre-tax income as shown in the accompanying consolidated statements of income:

(a) new product development costs which have been deferred in the accompanying financial statements are expensed for tax purposes,

(b) long-term leases, which are reported under the financing method for financial statement purposes, are reported under either the installment method or the operating method for tax purposes, and

(c) losses upon non-collection and system return are deducted for tax purposes as the losses are incurred.

See Note 8.

Net Income per Common and Common Equivalent Share:
Net income per common and common equivalent share has been computed based upon the average number of common shares outstanding during the year assuming the exercise of employee stock options and stock warrants to the extent that such options and warrants were dilutive. In this computation, the proceeds from the assumed exercise of the options and warrants are assumed to have been used to purchase shares of common stock at the average market price for the period such options and warrants were outstanding. The number of shares used in the computation was 2,429,000 in 1972 and 1,994,000 in 1971.

2. Lease Contracts Receivable

Lease contracts receivable are summarized below:

	1972	1971
Aggregate lease payments to be received under long-term leases accounted for under the financing method	$25,939,000	$9,079,000
Less unearned financing income	4,449,000	1,774,000
	21,490,000	7,305,000
Less amount due within one year	2,619,000	893,000
	18,871,000	6,412,000
Less reserve for non-collection and system returns	1,649,000	423,000
	$17,222,000	$5,989,000

For a more complete description of lease transactions, see Note 1—"Lease Accounting."

The aggregate amount of principal payments due in years subsequent to 1972 are set forth below:

1973	$ 2,619,000
1974	3,048,000
1975	3,201,000
1976	3,343,000
1977	3,277,000
Thereafter	6,002,000
	$21,490,000

With respect to certain leases which have been or will be accounted for under the financing method, the Company has arranged financing with Manufacturers Hanover Trust Company ("Manufacturers") in amounts not to exceed $7,456,000 through November 30, 1973. Pursuant to such arrangement, the Company sells to Manufacturers such lease contracts receivable and related equipment on a full recourse basis and participates with Manufacturers in revenues received from the customers pursuant to purchase or lease renewal options. The effective interst rate of this arrangement varies between 8¾% and 10%. As of November 30, 1972 the Company had received $3,456,000 from Manufacturers pursuant to this agreement and was contingently liable to Manufacturers for approximately $2,990,000 of such amount.

3. Inventories

Inventories are as follows:

	1972	1971
Purchased parts and components	$3,077,000	$1,232,000
Finished sub-assemblies and systems	1,064,000	1,085,000
Work in process	850,000	418,000
	$4,991,000	$2,735,000

See Note 1—"Inventory Valuation."

4. Fixed Assets

Details of fixed assets less allowance for depreciation are set forth below:

	1972	1971
Buildings (under construction in 1971)	$1,127,000	$ 350,000
Machinery and equipment	1,025,000	537,000
Leasehold improvements	—	9,000
	2,152,000	896,000
Less allowance for depreciation (see Note 1—"Properties")	293,000	164,000
	1,859,000	732,000
Land	772,000	734,000
	$2,631,000	$1,466,000

5. New Product Development

Total new product development expenditures:

	1972	1971
Capitalized (before amortization)	$ 915,000	$ 631,000
Charged to operating expenses currently	953,000	634,000
	$1,868,000	$1,265,000
Amortization of capitalized costs	$ 363,000	$ 273,000

See Note 1—"Investment in New Product Development."

6. Long-Term Debt

Details of long-term debt are presented below:

	1972	1971
Credit agreement with banks	$ 8,935,000	$7,110,000
4% mortgage payable in annual installments of $83,000	249,000	332,000
8¾% mortgage payable in monthly installments from 1973 to 1998	1,050,000	380,000
Capitalized lease obligations on equipment used by Measurex (8¾% interest rate)	362,000	158,000
2% above prime subordinated note	—	1,200,000
	10,596,000	9,180,000
Less amount due within one year	210,000	147,000
	$10,386,000	$9,033,000

The credit agreement with Bank of America and Manufacturers Hanover Trust Company allows the Company to borrow up to $20,000,000 through November 30, 1973. The funds borrowed as of November 30, 1973 are repayable in 66 monthly installments beginning in December 1973. The monthly installments are determined by a formula related to the Company's rental receipts, but in no case will the installments be less than 1/66th of the November 30, 1973 borrowed funds.

Borrowings under the credit agreement bear interest at ½% above the prime interest rate to November 30, 1973 and thereafter at 1% above prime. In addition, the Company is required to maintain compensating balances with the bank equal to the greater of 20% of the borrowed funds or $1,000,000; such compensating balance requirements at November 30, 1972 raise the Company's cost of borrowed funds under this agreement to approximately 7½% per annum.

The credit agreement prohibits payment of cash dividends and requires the Company to keep working capital and indebtedness within specified levels. As collateral for the credit agreement, the banks may require the Company to assign its rights to future rentals on certain systems leased to end users. As of January 23, 1973, the banks had not requested any collateral.

As of January 23, 1973, borrowings under the credit agreement have increased to $11,565,000.

The aggregate amount of principal payments of long-term debt required to be paid for each of the five years following fiscal year 1972 is set forth below:

1973	$ 210,000
1974	1,817,000
1975	1,802,000
1976	1,693,000
1977	1,661,000
Thereafter	3,413,000
	$10,596,000

Subsequent to November 30, 1972, the Company arranged for a $7 million Eurocurrency borrowing.

7. Profit-Sharing Plans

The Company presently has an employee cash profit-sharing plan whereby up to 10% of the consolidated pre-tax income may be contributed to the plan. The plan is subject to annual renewal and has been renewed for 1973. The Company's contributions under the plan are set forth below:

	Percent of Pre-Tax Income	Amount
Year ended November 30, 1972	7.9%	$248,000
Year ended November 30, 1971	8.2%	178,000

The Company also has an annually renewable bonus plan whereby the Company's president is paid 1% of pre-tax (and pre-profit-sharing) income.

8. Taxes on Income

The components of taxes on income are as follows:

	1972	1971
Provision for federal income taxes which would be required in the absence of the availability of the net operating loss carry-forward		$545,000
Deferred taxes	$1,283,000	475,000
Investment tax credit (recognized under the flow-through method)	(123,000)	(80,000)
	$1,160,000	$940,000

As of November 30, 1972 the Company had a net operating loss carry-forward for federal income tax purposes of approximately $9,000,000 of which amount approximately $500,000 will expire in 1973, $700,000 in 1974, $1,500,000 in 1975, $400,000 in 1976 and $5,900,000 in 1977, if not theretofore used to reduce taxable income. If the net operating loss carry-forward is utilized, it will not affect financial statement income in the year of utilization but will reduce federal income taxes otherwise payable.

In 1972 the Company formed a Domestic International Sales Corporation ("DISC"). Through the proper utilization of a DISC, federal income taxes on transactions with foreign customers may be indefinitely deferred. The 1972 statement of income includes $430,000 of DISC-related income for which no federal income tax provision has been made inasmuch as management believes they will be able to defer the payment of such tax indefinitely.

See Note 1—"Taxes on Income."

9. Qualified Stock Option Plans

Under the Company's qualified stock option plans, 405,000 shares of common stock have been reserved for granting of options to officers and key employees of which 150,000 shares are subject to shareholder approval. Options may be granted at prices not less than 100% of the fair market value of the stock at the date of grant and become exercisable either ⅓ each year commencing two years from the date of grant or ¼ each year commencing one year from the date of grant. Options expire if not exercised within five years from the date of grant. Information concerning options granted under the plans is set forth below:

	Shares Available for Grant	Options Outstanding Shares	Price per Share	Total
Balance, December 1, 1971	30,802	179,124	$.33-$15	$1,670,000
Additional shares reserved for grant	150,000			
Options granted	(58,750)	58,750	$17-$32	1,424,000
Options terminated	9,852	(9,852)	$10-$32	(147,000)
Options exercised		(65,878)	$.33-$15	(331,000)
Balance, November 30, 1972	131,904	162,144	$.33-$32	$2,616,000
Options exercisable at November 30, 1972		30,286	$.33-$15	$ 280,000

10. Warrants

At November 30, 1972, the Company has the following warrants to purchase common stock outstanding:

Shares	Price per Share	Expiration Date
12,000	$15.00	December 29, 1975
18,000	$13.33	May 30, 1977

Auditors' Report

To the Board of Directors
Measurex Corporation

We have examined the consolidated balance sheet of Measurex Corporation and Subsidiary Companies as of November 30, 1972, and the related consolidated statements of income, shareholders' equity and changes in financial position for the year then ended. Our examination was made in accordance with generally accepted auditing standards and accordingly included such tests of the accounting records and such other auditing procedures as we considered necessary in the circumstances. We previously examined and reported upon the consolidated financial statements of Measurex Corporation and Subsidiary Companies for the year ended November 30, 1971.

In our opinion, the above-mentioned financial statements present fairly the consolidated financial position of Measurex Corporation and Subsidiary Companies at November 30, 1972 and 1971, and the consolidated results of their operations and changes in financial position for the years then ended, in conformity with generally accepted accounting principles applied on a consistent basis, except for the change, with which we concur, in accounting for residual value on finance leases as described in Note 1 of Notes to Consolidated Financial Statements.

Lybrand, Ross Bros. & Montgomery

Lybrand, Ross Bros. & Montgomery
Palo Alto, California

January 23, 1973

Required

1. Describe the method Measurex uses to account for its long-term leases.

2. Do you consider Measurex's use of this method to be appropriate? Why or why not?

3. What is Measurex's estimate of the present value of its lease contracts receivable at November 30, 1972?

4. Assume that all of the long-term lease contracts signed by Measurex in 1972 were signed on November 30, 1972 (the Corporation's fiscal year-end) and that these contracts provide for seven annual rentals of $2,621,000 to be received on December 1 of each year. In addition, assume that the present value of these rentals (using a 7% discount rate) is $15,201,000 at November 30, 1972 and that the equipment leased under these contracts cost Measurex $6,090,000 to manufacture.

   a.) What is the total profit Measurex will recognize over the term of the lease contracts signed on November 30, 1972?

   b.) How much of this total profit will be recognized in income in 1972 using Measurex's present methods of accounting for these leases?

   c.) How much of this total profit will be recognized in income in subsequent years?

   d.) How much of this total profit would be recognized in income in 1972 if Measurex used the alternative method of accounting for these leases?

   e.) How much of this total profit would be recognized in income in each of the seven years if Measurex used the alternative method for accounting for these leases?

Section Two | Present Value and Leasing 41

Case 2-... Computer Consoles, Inc.

...esigns, develops, manufactures and markets
...nagement systems which more efficiently auto-
... and retrieval of information. The Company is
...er, New York, and its customers are primarily
...ted in the United States and abroad.
...nc. offers its equipment (systems) for sale or lease to
...lease is recorded by the Company using the present
...eam as of the date the installation is accepted by the
...sales-type lease contracts are sold to Computer Consoles
...n (CCLC), a wholly-owned subsidiary of Computer
...an amount equal to the discounted (present) value of the

...tement of Income and December 31, 1977 Balance Sheet of
...ented. CCLC commenced operations in May 1977. Assume that
...s on equipment lease contracts includes only sales-type leases.

Statement of Income

**THE PERIOD FROM THE INCEPTION OF OPERATIONS
(May 4, 1977) TO DECEMBER 31, 1977**

REVENUES (Note 1):	
Lease income earned	$ 792,014
Residual income	559,535
	$1,351,549
EXPENSES:	
Interest (Note 5)	$ 641,577
Loan commitment fees (Notes 2 and 3)	46,572
General and administrative	139,342
	$ 827,491
Income before provision for income taxes	$ 524,058
PROVISION FOR FEDERAL AND STATE INCOME TAXES (Note 1)	262,027
NET INCOME	$ 262,031
NET INCOME APPLICABLE TO:	
Common shareholder	$ 246,031
Preferred shareholder	16,000
	$ 262,031

Consolidated Balance Sheets

COMPUTER CONSOLES LEASING CORPORATION
BALANCE SHEET
DECEMBER 31, 1977

ASSETS

Cash	$ 110,975
Restricted cash (Note 3)	1,632,599
Receivables on equipment lease contracts, less unearned income of $3,562,546 (Notes 1, 4 and 5) (Schedule XII)	12,748,720
Notes receivable from affiliate (Note 2)	775,406
Organization expenses, net of accumulated amortization of $24,853 (Note 1)	161,544
Other assets	86,367
	$15,515,611

LIABILITIES AND STOCKHOLDERS' INVESTMENT

LIABILITIES:

Accounts payable and accrued expenses	$ 208,229
Rental income collected in advance	334,139
Payable to affiliates	2,102,689
Deferred Federal income taxes (Note 1)	210,027
Senior loans payable to a bank (Note 5)	12,038,496
Total liabilities	$14,893,580

STOCKHOLDERS' INVESTMENT (Notes 1, 2 and 5):

Preferred stock, 8% cumulative, $100 par value - Authorized and outstanding, 3,000 shares	$ 300,000
Common stock, $.10 par value - Authorized and outstanding, 60,000 shares	6,000
Capital in excess of par value	54,000
	$ 360,000
Retained earnings - Beginning of period	$
Net income for the period	262,031
	$ 262,031
Total stockholders' investment	$ 622,031
	$15,515,611

Required

1. In 1977, CCLC collected $3,806,347 on its lease receivables. How much did CCLC pay to Computer Consoles, Inc. for the purchase of sales-type lease contracts in 1977? (The collections include interest and principal.)

2. The equipment (systems) subject to Computer Consoles, Inc.'s sales-type leases in 1977 was designed and manufactured for a cost of $8,984,940. What entries did Computer Consoles, Inc. make in 1977 to record the sale of the sales-type lease contracts to CCLC?

3. Assume that the sales-type lease contracts Computer Consoles, Inc. sold to CCLC were in reality operating leases. Consistent with Financial Accounting Standards Board Statement No. 13, what entry would have been made by Computer Consoles, Inc. in 1977 to record the sale of the lease contracts to CCLC?

4. Assume that instead of selling its sales-type lease contracts to CCLC, Computer Consoles, Inc. retained these contracts and received the cash collections on these contracts in 1977. If Computer Consoles, Inc. had used the installment method to account for these accounts, what entries would have been made by Computer Consoles, Inc. in 1977?

5. Assume that the minimum aggregate lease payments reflected in the balance of the receivables on equipment lease contracts at December 31, 1977 are payable in six equal annual installments to be received on January 1 of each year. What entries will CCLC make in 1978 to account for its receivables on equipment lease contracts?

Section Three

Receivables and Revenue Recognition

Case 3-1   Career Academy, Inc.

Excerpts from the 1969 Consolidated Financial Statements of Career Academy, Inc. are provided.

Accounting Methods Change

On January 30, 1970, Career Academy announced a retroactive charge in the accounting methods used to determine income from the sale of Directorships. The following is a comprehensive explanation of this change and its effect on past and future income.

Reasons for the Change

Late in 1969 and early in 1970 a number of publications, including the Wall Street Journal and the Journal of Accountancy, carried articles that discussed the accounting methods used by firms deriving a significant portion of their income from the sale of franchises. These articles suggested that the liberal attitude toward recognizing all income at the time of sale should possibly be replaced by more conservative methods. We reaffirmed, with the concurrence of our auditors, the validity of our accounting methods and that our system avoided the problem areas being pointed out in the articles.

Nevertheless, a high degree of speculation and uncertainty arose during the third and fourth weeks in January 1970 within the financial community as to whether we would change our methods and how our income might be affected by a change. This speculation involved a number of different earnings projections, based on various accounting methods. The result was a seriously confused and uncertain condition that demanded clarification on our part.

Since we felt our existing accounting methods, and certain alternative methods were equally acceptable, we decided to adopt a more conservative method in order to end the uncertainty and speculation. Our auditors, Arthur Andersen & Co., concurred with our decision.

Accordingly, the new accounting method was retroactively instituted for 1969 and prior years.

The Effects of the Change

Since this change in accounting methods was a retroactive one, it not only affects the present and future years, but also all prior years. The major effect of the change involves the deferral of Directorship revenue. You will find this change reflected in our December 31, 1969, balance sheet under the heading "Unearned Directorship Revenue." The indicated net deferral as of that date is $8,258,982, of which $1,049,329 is estimated to be realized within one year.

It should also be pointed out that there is a reserve of $2,070,000 for possible losses on installment Notes Receivable from Directorships.

In 1969, the change in accounting methods resulted in a reduction of net income from 85¢ per share to 43¢ per share. In addition, the Notes to Financial Statements in this report contain references to and further explanations of the new accounting method.

The Substance of the Change

Our former accounting method provided that all income from a sale of a Directorship was recognized at the time a contract was signed. Under the new method, we will recognize income from the sale of Directorships on the basis of several performance criteria—the principal one being the number of students enrolled by the Directorship organization each year.

An amount equal to approximately 15% of the sale price is recorded as income over a period of one to two years. The remaining revenues will be recognized over an estimated 5 to 7 year period on the basis of the number of students enrolled by the Directorship organization each year.

Certain costs, directly associated with the establishment of Directorship organizations will be amortized against income on the same basis.

Section Three | Receivables and Revenue Recognition 49

	1969	1968 (Note 1)
Consolidated Statement of Income		
REVENUES (Notes 2 and 3):		
Income from students	$16,541,501	$12,613,757
Income from directorships	1,907,300	789,516
	$18,448,801	$13,403,273
COSTS AND EXPENSES:		
Instruction	$ 2,816,990	$ 2,445,820
Selling, general and administrative	10,762,006	8,033,536
Provision for doubtful accounts and student contract terminations	696,781	602,000
	$14,275,777	$11,081,356
Operating Income	$ 4,173,024	$ 2,321,917
OTHER INCOME (EXPENSE):		
Interest expense	$ (270,206)	$ (189,490)
Other income, net	301,228	211,075
	$ 31,022	$ 21,585
Income before provision for income taxes	$ 4,204,046	$ 2,343,502
FEDERAL AND STATE INCOME TAXES: (Note 4)		
Current	$ 300,000	$ 260,000
Deferred	1,928,000	982,000
	$ 2,228,000	$ 1,242,000
Net income	$ 1,976,046	$ 1,101,502
EARNINGS PER COMMON AND COMMON EQUIVALENT SHARE (Note 9)	$.43	$.25

	1969	1968 (Note 1)
Consolidated Statements of Paid-in Surplus and Retained Earnings		
PAID-IN SURPLUS		
Balance, beginning of year	$2,034,541	$ 661,912
Add—		
Excess of proceeds from exercise of options and warrants over par value of common stock issued (Note 7)	24,445	25,139
Excess of conversion price of 5 1/8% debentures converted over par value of common stock issued, less related unamortized bond discount	1,281,915	1,043,540
Excess of fair market value over par value of common stock issued in connection with employment agreements	—	303,950
Balance, end of year	$3,340,901	$2,034,541
RETAINED EARNINGS		
Balance, beginning of year	$1,888,690	$2,399,112
Retroactive effect of the change in accounting for income from sale of directorships (Note 3)	—	1,389,574
Balance, as restated	$1,888,690	$1,009,538
Add—Net income for the year	1,976,046	1,101,502
	$3,864,736	$2,111,040
Deduct—		
Transfer to common stock in connection with 2-for-1 stock split of August 20, 1968, effected in the form of a 100% stock dividend	—	222,350
Balance, end of year (Note 5)	$3,864,736	$1,888,690

Consolidated Balance Sheets

Career Academy, Inc. and Subsidiaries Consolidated Balance Sheets

Assets	1969	1968 (Note 1)
CURRENT ASSETS:		
Cash and certificates of deposit	$ 1,026,514	$ 799,738
Notes and accounts receivable -		
Tuition and fees (Note 2)	$15,749,039	$10,967,548
Amounts due from divisional and regional directors for advertising and supplies	3,966,626	1,661,110
Installment notes -		
Directors	1,300,000	901,496
Students	196,062	-
	$21,211,727	$13,530,154
Less - Allowance for doubtful accounts and student contract terminations	(4,363,500)	(2,077,000)
	$16,848,227	$11,453,154
Prepaid expenses and commissions	2,385,043	1,971,030
Total current assets	$20,259,784	$14,223,922
INSTALLMENT NOTES RECEIVABLE, less current amounts:		
Directors, less reserves of $2,070,000 in 1969 and $1,570,000 in 1968 (Note 3)	$ 9,111,299	$ 5,405,527
Students	1,708,059	-
	$10,819,358	$ 5,405,527
FIXED ASSETS AND LEASEHOLD IMPROVEMENTS, at cost, less accumulated depreciation of $883,677 in 1969 and $569,802 in 1968 (Notes 5 and 11)	$ 3,504,286	$ 2,718,033
OTHER ASSETS:		
Deferred charges, less amortization	$ 418,781	$ 308,556
Unamortized bond discount	194,423	160,334
Cost in excess of net assets of acquired companies	806,132	568,811
Other	513,757	487,948
	$ 1,933,093	$ 1,525,649
	$36,516,521	$23,873,131

Section Three | Receivables and Revenue Recognition 51

Liabilities	1969	1968 (Note 1)
CURRENT LIABILITIES:		
Current maturities of long-term debt	$ 46,139	$ 70,109
Note payable to bank	500,000	–
Accounts payable	517,706	641,846
Accrued expenses—		
Salaries and commissions	2,002,113	1,722,795
Future cost of instruction (Note 2)	471,200	409,316
Other	114,705	79,181
Income taxes payable	286,195	–
Deferred income taxes (Note 4)	3,501,408	1,607,408
	$ 7,439,466	$ 4,530,655
Unearned tuitions and fees (Note 2)	6,456,560	5,816,517
Unearned directorship revenues	1,049,329	774,443
Total current liabilities and unearned revenues	$14,945,355	$11,121,615
UNEARNED DIRECTORSHIP REVENUES, less related costs and amounts estimated to be realized in one year (Note 3)	$ 7,209,653	$ 5,286,223
LONG-TERM DEBT, less current maturities (Note 5)	$ 6,694,507	$ 3,091,602
STOCKHOLDERS' INVESTMENT:		
Preferred stock, 500,000 shares authorized (Note 10)	$ –	$ –
Common stock, $.10 par value, authorized 10,000,000 shares, issued and outstanding 4,613,685 shares in 1969 and 4,504,603 shares in 1968 (Notes 5, 7 and 10)	461,369	450,460
Paid-in surplus	3,340,901	2,034,541
Retained earnings (Note 5)	3,864,736	1,888,690
	$ 7,667,006	$ 4,373,691
	$36,516,521	$23,873,131

Notes to Financial Statements

(1) Basis of Consolidation

The consolidated financial statements include the accounts of the Company's subsidiaries. All material intercompany transactions and account balances have been eliminated in consolidation.

In October, 1969, the Company acquired all of the outstanding stock of Humboldt Institute, Inc. in exchange for 30,888 shares of Career Academy, Inc. common stock and merged Humboldt into a wholly-owned subsidiary of Career. This acquisition was accounted for as a pooling of interest, and accordingly, the financial statements for 1969 and 1968 include the accounts of Humboldt Institute, Inc. for those years. Revenue from Humboldt student enrollments was $940,255 in 1969 and $692,284 in 1968. Net income had no effect on earnings per common and common equivalent share.

In October, 1969, the Company also acquired certain assets of Airline Personnel Training by Humboldt, Inc. (Airline) for $250,000. This transaction has been accounted for as a purchase, and accordingly, the results of operations of Airline have been included in the consolidated statement of income since date of acquisition. Gross revenues for the period were $31,000.

The Company's investment in Airline exceeded the underlying book value of the assets acquired by $237,321, and this amount has been included in cost in excess of net assets of acquired companies in the accompanying balance sheet.

(2) Accounting for Student Revenues and Income

The full amount of tuitions and fees for student home study enrollment contracts is recorded as income at the time the contract is signed since the majority of the costs are incurred and all course materials are provided at this time. Estimated additional costs, consisting primarily of the estimated costs to grade lessons submitted and commissions, are accrued and charged currently against income.

Resident student income is recorded during the period in which the student attends the school.

(3) Accounting for Directorship Revenue and Income

Enrollments for the Company's courses are sold through independent marketing organizations. Rights to sell enrollments are sold by the Company to divisional and regional directors based upon the population of the area purchased.

In 1969, the Company retroactively changed its method of accounting for income from the sale of directorships. Sales of directorships are now recorded as "Unearned Directorship Revenues" with a corresponding charge to "Directorship Notes Receivable." Unearned directorship revenue is reduced and income recognized in amounts equal to approximately 15% of the sales price of a directorship. This income is recorded over a period of one to two years and is in relation to costs charged against income as the directorship organization is established.

The remaining unearned directorship revenue will be recognized on a student enrollment basis, estimated to be over a period of five to seven years. The Company had previously recorded the entire sales price to a director in the period in which the contract was signed.

The costs directly associated with the establishment of the directorship organizations for the Company's present courses have been deferred. These costs will be amortized against income over seven years or in proportion to the recognition of unearned directorship revenue based upon student enrollments, whichever is sooner. The deferred costs, and the provision for possible losses in collection, have been deducted from unearned directorship revenue in the accompanying balance sheet.

The effect of this change was to reduce net income by $1,967,506 in 1969 and $1,614,092 in 1968 or $.42 and $.35 per common and common equivalent share respectively. Retained earnings as of December 31, 1967, have been reduced by $1,389,574 from amounts previously reported.

(4) Deferred Income Taxes

The provision for income taxes has been computed on the income as reflected in the accompanying consolidated statement of income which has been determined on the accrual basis. For income tax purposes the Company determines taxable income on the cash basis. Accordingly, taxes provided in the accompanying statement of income which are not currently payable have been classified as deferred income taxes.

(5) Long-Term Debt

Long-term debt at December 31, 1969, consists of the following:

	Current	Long-Term
5⅛% convertible subordinated debentures due September 1, 1987	$ -	$1,496,000
5½% convertible subordinated notes, due May 1, 1989	-	5,000,000
6% mortgage note, due in 1985	7,000	165,604
5.56% mortgage note, due in 1972	14,000	21,103
Various installment notes, payable over three years	25,139	11,800
	$46,139	$6,694,507

The 5⅛% subordinated debentures are convertible at any time into common stock at $15.50 per share. As of December 31, 1969, 96,623 shares of unissued common stock are reserved for issuance upon conversion under this option. The debentures can be called for redemption upon 30 days notice at redemption prices ranging from 104.442% of the principal amount in 1970 to 100% of the principal amount starting in 1982.

On May 1, 1969, the Company entered into a Note Purchase Agreement for the sale, in four semiannual installments, of $10,000,000 of 5½% convertible subordinated notes due May 1, 1989. As of December 31, 1969, $5,000,000 of these notes were sold and the remaining notes will be sold in May and November, 1970. The notes are convertible at any time into common stock at $43.74 per share. As of December 31, 1969, 228,624 shares of unissued common stock are reserved for issuance upon conversion under this option. Beginning May 1, 1971, the notes can be called for redemption upon 30 days notice at prices ranging from 105.5% of the principal amount in 1971 to 100% starting in 1988. In addition, in order for the notes to be called for redemption during the three consecutive twelve month periods commencing May 1, 1971, the market value of the Company's common stock must be equal to or exceed 130%, 135% and 145%, respectively, of the conversion price for 30 days prior to notice of redemption. The

Agreement also provides for annual sinking fund payments of $1,000,000 per year from 1979 through 1988.

Under the terms of the 5⅛% convertible subordinated debenture agreement and the 5½% convertible subordinated Note Purchase Agreement, retained earnings existing at June 30, 1967, of $2,090,379 is restricted as to the payment of cash dividends and purchase of company stock.

(6) Lease Commitments

The Company leases offices and instructional space at various locations. At December 31, 1969, the Company's obligation for annual rents under such leases amounted to approximately $684,000. These leases will expire at various dates through 1986.

(7) Employees' Stock Option Plan

Under the Company's Qualified Stock Option Plan adopted in 1964, as amended, 300,000 shares of common stock were reserved for option to employees. Options are granted at the fair market value of the shares at the date of grant and expire five years from that date. They may be exercised only while the optionee is employed by the Company and generally not before five years from the date of employment or four years and six months from the date of grant, whichever is later, unless the option committee reduces such periods. The shares of common stock purchased through the exercise of an option may not be

Required

1. Discuss the alternatives that Career Academy, Inc. could have used to account for revenue from the sale of Directorships and evaluate each by applying generally accepted accounting principles to this situation.

2. What is the nature of the "Unearned Directorship Revenues" account? What attributes cause this account to be classified among the liabilities? Do you consider any alternative method of disclosure to be acceptable or preferable?

3. The Consolidated Statement of Retained Earnings reflects the retroactive effect of the change in accounting for income from sale of Directorships. Describe how this amount was determined and how it will affect Career Academy, Inc.'s future income statements and balance sheets.

Case 3-2

General Development Corporation

The 1971 and 1970 Consolidated Balance Sheets and Statements of Income and Retained Earnings of General Development Corporation are presented. Notes 1 and 2 to the Consolidated Financial Statements describe General Development's revenue recognition policy.

Consolidated Balance Sheets

	1971	1970
Assets		
Cash (Note 5)	$ 6,619,000	$ 5,106,000
Contracts receivable on homesite sales (estimated receipts in 1972, $41,000,000) (Note 1)	280,723,000	235,829,000
Less, allowance for loss on contract cancellations (Note 2)	39,800,000	36,500,000
	240,923,000	199,329,000
Mortgages and other receivables	6,886,000	4,333,000
Land and improvements, at cost (Note 4)	38,895,000	48,062,000
Houses, completed or under construction, at cost	4,474,000	3,898,000

	1971	1970		
Property, plant and equipment, at cost (Notes 3 and 4)	$54,197,000	$49,242,000		
Less, allowance for depreciation (Note 3)	13,138,000	10,980,000		
	$41,059,000	$38,262,000	41,059,000	38,262,000

	1971	1970
Other assets and deferred charges	3,304,000	1,727,000
	$342,160,000	$300,717,000
Liabilities		
Accounts payable	$ 3,862,000	$ 3,941,000
Accrued liabilities	14,364,000	12,580,000
Customers' deposits	4,030,000	2,240,000
Estimated homesite improvement costs (Notes 1 and 2)	40,600,000	42,700,000
Deferred federal income taxes (Note 1)	94,675,000	76,250,000
Mortgages payable (Note 4)	15,468,000	18,793,000
Notes payable (Note 5)	33,450,000	29,498,000
	206,449,000	186,002,000
Commitments and contingencies (Notes 1, 10 and 11)		
Stockholders' Equity		
Common stock, $1 par value; authorized 15,000,000 shares, issued and outstanding 9,879,590 and 9,641,594, respectively (Notes 5, 6, 7 and 8)	9,880,000	9,642,000
Capital contributed in excess of par value (Note 7)	45,948,000	39,885,000
Retained earnings, as annexed (Note 5)	79,883,000	65,188,000
	135,711,000	114,715,000
	$342,160,000	$300,717,000

Consolidated Statements of Income and Retained Earnings

	1971	1970
Sales		
Homesites	$116,191,000	$ 98,360,000
Houses	17,358,000	16,038,000
Other	7,423,000	6,071,000
	140,972,000	120,469,000
Cost of sales	48,094,000	40,612,000
Gross profit	92,878,000	79,857,000
Interest income on contracts receivable	14,802,000	11,911,000
	107,680,000	91,768,000
Commissions, advertising and other selling expenses	35,436,000	30,885,000
Provision for loss on cancellation of contracts receivable	17,953,000	15,245,000
General and administrative expenses	12,929,000	10,152,000
Other expenses, net, principally interest	2,406,000	2,462,000
	68,724,000	58,744,000
Income before provision for deferred federal income taxes	38,956,000	33,024,000
Provision for deferred federal income taxes	18,425,000	15,875,000
Net income	20,531,000	17,149,000
Retained earnings, beginning of year	65,188,000	51,318,000
Less, 2% stock dividend (Note 7)	(5,836,000)	(3,279,000)
Retained earnings, end of year (Note 5)	$ 79,883,000	$ 65,188,000
Net income per share and equivalent share (Note 9)	$2.03	$1.70*

*Adjusted for 2% stock dividend declared in May, 1971.

1. The Company records the full sales price of a homesite sold under an installment contract at the time the purchaser makes his first standard monthly installment payment or when the down payment approximates 5% or more of the selling price. Substantially all of the 1971 contracts require payments over an average period of ten years. Interest on the contract balance is recorded as income as monthly payments on the sales contracts are received.

Expenses related to a homesite sale are charged against income at the time of sale. Such expenses comprise average cost of unimproved land by development area, capitalized mortgage interest and real estate taxes, estimated closing costs, sales commissions and estimated cost of required improvements, such as roads and canals.

Sales of homesites are generally made in advance of the completion of land improvements and the cost of such development work to be completed in the future is recorded as an estimated liability. Under the terms of the Company's installment sales contracts, the required improvements must be completed by approximately the scheduled date of the customer's final installment payment. The unexpended cost to complete areas from which homesites have been sold is presently estimated by management to be $85,000,000. The Company presently plans annual expenditures for such improvement of approximately $13,500,000 in 1972, and decreasing annual amounts thereafter until 1980. Provision for $40,600,000 of such amount applicable to homesites sold to December 31, 1971 is shown on the balance sheet as estimated homesite improvement cost. The Company has also agreed to provide water service in certain areas in which homesites have been sold. The cost of the required utility facilities will be capitalized as construction progresses.

Sales of houses and all related costs

and expenses are recorded at the time of the closings.

Other sales and related costs and expenses are recorded at the time the income is earned by the Company.

Advertising, selling and administrative expenses are charged against income as incurred.

Payment of substantial amounts of federal income taxes provided on financial statement income has been deferred since income from homesite sales is reported for tax purposes principally on an installment basis as collections on the homesite contracts are received.

2. The Company provides for losses on future cancellations of contracts receivable on homesite sales by charges to income sufficient to maintain an allowance considered adequate on the basis of loss and collection experience. Cancellation of a sales contract in the year of sale results in the elimination of the sale and related accrued expenses from income of that year.

Cancellation of a sales contract in a year subsequent to the year of sale results in a reduction of the allowance for loss on contract cancellations by the excess of the remaining unpaid balance of the contract over the cost of the unimproved land, capitalized mortgage interest and real estate taxes, estimated closing costs, unpaid sales commissions and estimated cost of required improvements. The Company's policy generally is to cancel sales contracts on which no payment has been received for approximately six months.

At December 31, 1971, approximately 91% of the total number of installment contracts outstanding were current or prepaid. Contracts are classified as current only if all payments due up to the end of the preceding month have been received.

An industry accounting guide titled "Accounting for Retail Land Sales" was issued by the American Institute of Certified Public Accountants in early 1973. This guide specified the conditions under which accrual or installment methods were to be used. Payments under either method were to be treated as deposits and not recognized as sales until they were at least equal to ten percent of the contract price, the cancellation period had expired, and promised performance had become predictable.

Under the new rules, the accrual method was required on a project-by-project basis if **all** of the following conditions had been met:

1. The properties clearly were to be useful for residential or recreational purposes when the payment period was completed.

2. The company's financial capabilities assured its ability to fund or bond the planned improvements.

3. The project's planned improvements must have progressed beyond preliminary stages and there was evidence that the work was to be completed according to plan.

4. The receivable could not be subordinated to new loans on the property, except for construction purposes and collection experience on such contracts had to be the same as those not subordinated.

5. Collection experience of the project had to indicate that collectibility of receivable balances was reasonably predictable and that ninety percent of the contracts in force six months after sales were recorded would be collected in full.

All other contracts were to be accounted for by the installment method under which revenue was to be recognized as payments were received and related selling costs could be deferred.

The new accrual method required deferment of a portion of the contract price to cover cost and profit applicable to future development work and discounted contracts receivable to yield an interest rate equal to the retail installment credit rate. The new standards applied to financial statements for the period ending December 31, 1972 and called for restatement of the results for the three latest fiscal years.

Required

1. At what point did General Development recognize revenue from the sale of homesites in 1971? What alternative points could General Development have used to recognize revenue from these sales?

2. Assume that on January 1, 1972 General Development sold a homesite costing $3,450 for $15,000 to be received in six equal annual payments of $3,050 beginning on December 31, 1972. The payments include principal and interest. Also assume that the retail installment credit interest rate was ten percent on January 1, 1972 and that General Development incurred related selling costs of $4,500.

   a.) How much profit and interest income from this sale would have been recognized by General Development in 1972 if it had used the accrual method?

   b.) How much profit and interest income from this sale would have been recognized by General Development in 1972 if it had used the installment method?

   c.) How much profit and interest income from this sale would have been recognized by General Development in 1972 if it had used the cost recovery method?

Case 3-3   Horizon Corporation

The following letter to shareholders was included with Horizon Corporation's report for the nine months ended February 28, 1973:

Dear Shareholder:

The Company, in accordance with the provisions of the Accounting Guide for Retail Land Sales issued by the American Institute of Certified Public Accountants in February, 1973, has conformed its interim financial statements to the requirements of the Guide and restated its financial statements of prior years for purposes of comparability.

The guidelines provide for two different methods described as the "Accrual" and "Installment" Methods. The Installment Method is generally more conservative in that a smaller portion of profits on current period sales is reflected in current period income.

The Company has determined that a delay of approximately six months from dates contracts are entered into would enable it to meet all of the requirements for the recording of its land sales under the accrual method since at that time the contracts would meet the collectibility test required for this method. Nevertheless, the Company does not believe at this time that the users of its financial statements are best served by the presentation of current financial statements which reflect sales entered into at an earlier period. For this, and other reasons which management feels are in the best interests of the Company, the installment method of accounting has been adopted.

In assessing the performance of the Company, it is most important that the reader of the financial statements have a clear understanding of the impact thereon through use of the installment method.

The economics which determine the degree of profitability from the Company's operations, i.e., sales, collectibility of receivables, control of costs and expenses, etc., are in no way affected by the accounting method which serves as a foundation for the preparation of periodic financial statements.

The accounting methods utilized serve to control the timing of income recognition in such periodic statements. Thus, the ultimate income recognition from a project for which a total operating cycle has been completed should be the same under any accounting method. However, income recognition for any interim period within the total cycle will be influenced by the accounting method employed.

The use of the installment method by the Company effectively results in the spreading of income recognition from land sales over the terms of the related contracts, as receivable payments are received. The unrecognized portion of the gross profit from recorded land sales (deferred profit) is reflected in the Company's balance sheet as a deduction from gross contracts receivable.

Reported results of operations under the installment method do not require a charge against income to provide a reserve for anticipated losses on cancelled contracts since income recognition is based upon cash collections. Accordingly, losses on cancelled contracts will apply to the deferred profit which has not as yet been recognized in income. As a result, a portion of the deferred profit on recorded sales will not reach the income recognition stage.

Accountingwise, the installment method, as applied to retail land sales operations, consists of two stages which can be characterized as being similar to "holding patterns." These stages - "Deposit" and "Profit Deferral" ultimately result in "Profit Recognition." A discussion of each follows:

Deposit

Until such time as the sale contracts entered into qualify for recording in the books of account as sales, pursuant to criteria established in the Accounting Guide, all payments received from purchasers (down payments, receivable principal and interest) are recorded as customer deposits payable and reflected in the balance sheet as a liability to purchasers. Among the requirements which are prerequisite to the recording of sales is one which requires that payments received from the purchaser (including interest) equal or exceed 10 percent of the contract sales price.

Consistent with a basic accounting principle which requires a proper matching of revenues and costs, all applicable direct costs associated with sales in the deposit stage (including direct selling costs) are deferred and not charged against income until the sales are recorded. Interest received on contracts receivable is similarly deferred and not credited to income. Unrecoverable deferred costs must be charged against income when contracts are cancelled while in the deposit stage; forfeited payments received would be credited to income upon cancellation.

When all requirements for the recording of sales are met at the time contracts are initially processed, the deposit stage for such land sales would be eliminated.

Profit Deferral

When contracts in the deposit stage qualify for recording, the contract prices (principal) are reflected as sales in the income statement. All applicable direct costs are simultaneously charged against income. Receivables arising from recorded contracts are reflected in the balance sheet, net of principal payments received while the contracts were in the deposit stage.

Deferred profit applicable to recorded sales is computed and deducted (1) from sales in the income statement and (2) from receivables in the balance sheet. The formula for computation of the deferred profit is designed to effectively spread selling expenses related to recorded sales as charges against income ratably over the terms of the related receivables.

Profit Recognition

Interest on contracts which have been recorded as sales is credited to income upon receipt. Interest received, and deferred, while contracts were in the deposit stage is credited to income at the time such contracts are recorded as sales.

Each dollar of receivable principal collected represents in part a recovery of costs relating to land sold, including deferred selling expenses, and in part a realization of profit. The portion of receivable principal collections during each period attributable to profit realization are credited to income, with a comparable reduction in the deferred profit account reflected in the balance sheet.

If all recorded receivables were collected in full and no revisions to cost of sales were required (certain costs to be incurred in the future are estimated at time of recording the sale), the total deferred profit would be credit to income over the terms of the related receivables. However, a portion of recorded receivables will be uncollectible, through contract cancellations, and subsequent revisions to estimated costs, upward or downward, will probably be required.

Cost revisions will be accounted for as an adjustment of the deferred profit. If upward cost revisions are in excess of the applicable deferred profit, a charge against income of the period in which the excess becomes known will occur.

Uncollected receivable balances applicable to cancelled contracts will result in certain costs being recovered (land which may be resold and costs which will not be incurred — future improvement costs and recoverable salesmen's commissions) and the loss of the related deferred profit. An excess of the uncollected receivable balances over recovered costs and lost deferred profit will represent unrecovered deferred selling expenses which must be charged against income at time of cancellation.

****

The results of operations for the third fiscal quarter of the current year were, as expected, down from the year-earlier period. For the current third quarter, net income was $1,796,000, equal to 40¢ per share; for the nine months, net income was $5,549,000, or $1.24 per share.

Deferred profit at February 28, 1973, was $110,276,000 compared to $96,790,000 a year earlier. As noted, these profits have not been reflected in net income and will contribute to net income in future periods as our receivables are collected.

In addition, sales contracts carried in deposit status at February 28, 1973 amounted to $2,618,000 as compared to $4,960,000 at February 29, 1972. These sales contracts, less cancellations, will be recorded in future periods and the profits thereon will also be deferred and recognized in income as payments thereon are received. The low level of "deposit status" accounts (approximately 3% of the annualized recorded sales) results from the continued high level of down payments received at the time of sale (average 13.5%).

The restatement of prior periods had the effect of lowering the earnings reported under previous accounting methods, which reductions have been deferred to later periods. The cumulative effect of the restatement resulted in a reduction of $41,009,000 in retained earnings as previously reported at May 31, 1972.

We remarked in our earlier six-month report that unfavorable levels of land sales, operating expenses and housing margins accounted for the decline in earnings in the second quarter.

During the third quarter, modest improvements in land sales, operating expenses and housing margins were achieved as compared to the second quarter of the current fiscal year, and progress continues to be made on other fronts, including strong overall site development activity at existing projects. Perhaps the most significant event in the quarter was the completion of first registrations of property in the Company's new community near Houston, where sales will begin in the fourth quarter of this year. This project will become a major contributor to sales and earnings during Fiscal 1974.

Again, it is important to recognize that the new accounting procedures in no way affect the Company's operations, and that Horizon remains one of the most profitable companies in the land development and building industry, with a return on shareholders' equity of 18% for the nine months ending February 28, 1973.

While we see no sharp increases in earnings over current rates in the final quarter, we are optimistic that our seasoned organizations and exciting new products will result in improved results beginning in 1974.

Respectfully submitted,

Joseph Timan,
Chairman of the Board and Chief Executive Officer

Sidney Nelson,
President and Chief Operating Officer

Consolidated Statements of Income

HORIZON CORPORATION and SUBSIDIARIES

Consolidated Statements of Income
(Unaudited)
(000 omitted)

	Nine Months Ended February 28		Three Months Ended February 28	
	1973	1972*	1973	1972*
Revenues				
Sales of land	$63,288	$74,078	$18,985	$26,069
Sales of houses	17,503	14,559	5,353	6,258
Interest income	8,657	6,720	2,964	2,413
Profit deferred on current land sales	(32,980)	(44,110)	(9,732)	(15,606)
Deferred profit recognized	17,246	16,784	5,618	5,660
Miscellaneous, net	312	182	62	45
	74,026	68,213	23,250	24,839
Costs and Expenses				
Cost of sales - land and houses	20,967	18,803	6,327	7,515
Expenses	42,135	34,951	13,380	12,509
	63,102	53,754	19,707	20,024
Income before provision for income taxes	10,924	14,459	3,543	4,815
Provision for income taxes (principally deferred)	5,375	7,128	1,747	2,374
Net income	$ 5,549	$ 7,331	$ 1,796	$ 2,441
Earnings per share	$1.24	$1.65	$ .40	$ .55

*Restated to conform with the AICPA Industry Accounting Guide for Retail Land Sales.

HORIZON CORPORATION and SUBSIDIARIES

Consolidated Statements of Income for the Three Years Ended

May 31, 1972*

(Unaudited)
(000 omitted)

	Year Ended May 31		
	1972	1971	1970
Revenues			
Sales of land	$102,267	$84,289	$57,103
Sales of houses	19,933	12,627	7,398
Interest income	9,335	6,546	4,055
Profit deferred on current land sales	(60,424)	(49,803)	(35,182)
Deferred profit recognized	22,945	16,611	10,953
Miscellaneous, net	288	193	265
	94,344	70,463	44,592
Costs and expenses			
Cost of sales - land and houses	26,889	17,759	11,461
Expenses	48,154	38,495	25,437
	75,043	56,254	36,898
Income before provision for income taxes	19,301	14,209	7,694
Provision for income taxes (principally deferred)	9,436	6,785	4,125
Net income	$ 9,865	$ 7,424	$ 3,569
Earnings per share	$2.23	$1.68	$ .80

*Restated to conform with the AICPA Industry Accounting Guide for Retail Land Sales.

Consolidated Balance Sheets

HORIZON CORPORATION and SUBSIDIARIES

Condensed Consolidated Balance Sheet

February 28, 1973

(Unaudited)

Assets		
Cash		$ 3,683,000
Receivables (principally contracts receivable from land sales)	$193,122,000	
Less - Allowance for travel credits	(5,912,000)	
Accumulated deferred profit	(110,276,000)	
	(116,188,000)	76,934,000
Inventory of land and houses		76,060,000
Other assets - net		12,458,000
		$169,135,000
Liabilities		
Notes and loans payable		$ 31,319,000
Long term debt		47,953,000
Other liabilities		16,240,000
		95,512,000
Federal and state income taxes, principally deferred		29,486,000
Stockholders' Equity		
Common stock (4,468,531 shares outstanding)	$ 45,000	
Capital in excess of par value	15,687,000	
Retained earnings	28,603,000	
	44,335,000	
Less - Treasury stock (27,983 shares)	(198,000)	44,137,000
		$169,135,000

Required

1. Do you agree that "the economics which determine the degree of profitability from the Company's operations, i.e., sales, collectibility of receivables, control of costs and expenses, etc., are in no way affected by the accounting method which serves as a foundation for the preparation of periodic financial statements?" Why or why not?

2. Describe the sequence of entries Horizon will make in applying the installment method.

3. Describe the "profit deferred on current land sales" and "deferred profit recognized" items in the Consolidated Statements of Income for the three years ended May 31, 1972.

4. How much gross profit did Horizon recognize in income from the sales of land and houses in each of the three years ended May 31, 1972?

5. How much additional gross profit would Horizon have reported in each of the three years ended May 31, 1972 if it had used the sales or accrual method?

Case 3-4

Amrep Corporation

AMREP Corporation is the developer of three new communities — Rio Rancho Estates, Silver Springs Shores and Eldorado at Santa Fe. This involves the sale of lots (primarily homesites) and the construction and sale of single family homes, condominium apartments, and commercial buildings. AMREP also engages in the national and international distribution of magazines and paperback books.

AMREP's Consolidated Balance Sheets (asset section only) as of April 30, 1974 and 1975 are presented:

AMREP Corporation and Subsidiaries

Consolidated Balance Sheets

	1975	1974
ASSETS		
Cash (includes certificates of deposit—1975—$1,921,119; 1974—$1,952,617)	$ 5,227,057	$ 3,878,366
Marketable securities—At cost which approximates market	3,957,164	3,845,632
Contracts receivable on homesite sales, net of unrealized profit (1975— 1974—$51,000,860)		52,380,267
Mortgages and other receivables	7,351,968	11,246,948
Inventory of land and homes for sale—At cost—		
Land and improvements	17,241,139	27,535,488
Homes	3,346,075	5,482,588
Condominium apartments	6,748,977	9,644,107
Construction and other inventories—At cost	501,515	575,928
Land held for bulk sale	4,584,723	—
Property, plant and equipment—At cost— Net of allowance for depletion and depreciation	18,770,584	19,291,774
Deferred marketing expenses	2,702,542	7,107,369
Other assets	3,008,781	4,539,111
Excess of cost of investments over net assets acquired	5,205,440	5,216,440
	$	$150,744,018

AMREP's Notes to the Financial Statements included this excerpt:

A Summary of Significant Accounting Policies

HOMESITE SALES

The Company sells homesites in communities principally under installment contracts which require payments over an average period of seven years.

Homesite contracts are recorded as sales at the time customers' total payments (principal and interest) amount to at least 10% of the contract price and any refund period has expired. Until a contract qualifies for recording, customer total payments are recorded as deposits. Marketing costs applicable to deposit sales are deferred and charged to income as homesite contracts are recorded as sales.

Income from recorded homesite sales is recognized on the installment basis of accounting. On this basis, the full sales price of a homesite is included in revenues at the time the sale qualifies for recording. Related costs and expenses, consisting of land and improvement costs and marketing expenses, are recorded at the time the sale is recorded. The excess of homesite sales and revenues over related costs and expenses is deferred and recognized in income as customers' payments are received, using average profit rates for each community.

Interest on recorded installment contracts is included in income when it is received.

Upon cancellation of a homesite sale, the excess of the unpaid contract balance over related costs of land and improvements and deferred profit is charged to income. The Company's general policy is to cancel contracts on which no payment has been received for approximately four months.

Required

1. Provide general journal entries for the following events:

   a.) Homesites costing $3,681,148 were recorded as sales for $27,631,493 under installment contracts. Cash downpayments (in addition to customer deposits of $2,737,425) amounted to $3,400,862.

   b.) AMREP collected $35,394,918 (including interest of $7,190,021) on homesite sales contracts during fiscal 1975. These collections included $16,871,474 on installment receivables arising from sales completed in years prior to fiscal 1975 (and having an average gross profit percentage of 80 percent) and the remainder on fiscal 1975 installment sales recorded in requirement (a) above.

   c.) Installment receivables arising from sales of homesites prior to fiscal 1975 and having unpaid balances of $5,714,305 and an average gross profit percentage of 83 percent were cancelled in fiscal 1975. The unrecovered cost of the homesites represented by these receivables was transferred to the land and improvements inventory account.

2. Answer each of the following questions:

   a.) What was the gross contracts receivable on homesite sales account balance at April 30, 1975?

   b.) What is the unrealized profit account balance at April 30, 1975?

   c.) How much gross profit from sales of homesites in fiscal 1975 was included in AMREP's Consolidated Statement of Income for fiscal 1975?

Case 3-5

Compugraphic Corporation

The Balance Sheet (asset section only), Statement of Income and (selected) Notes to Financial Statements from the 1974 annual report of Compugraphic Corporation are presented.

Consolidated Balance Sheets

September 28, 1974 and September 29, 1973

ASSETS	1974	1973
CURRENT ASSETS:		
Cash	$ 1,834,017	$ 1,005,223
Receivables, less reserve of $439,000 in 1974 and $295,000 in 1973 (Notes 1, and 4)	12,930,231	9,427,254
Inventories, at lower of cost (first-in, first-out) or market	15,532,140	10,808,737
Federal and State taxes recoverable	235,574	630,429
Prepaid expenses and advances	532,586	484,118
Total current assets	31,064,548	22,355,761
INVESTMENT IN UNCONSOLIDATED SUBSIDIARY (Note 7)	4,572,504	2,118,090
PROPERTY AND EQUIPMENT, AT COST (Note 1):		
Font masters and letter characters	5,522,090	3,966,352
Less depreciation	(1,659,297)	(915,582)
	3,862,793	3,050,770
Other property and equipment:		
Machinery and equipment	4,210,758	2,443,268
Leasehold improvements	1,067,267	886,874
Furniture and fixtures	453,029	320,740
Total other property and equipment	5,731,054	3,650,882
Less depreciation and amortization	(1,633,083)	(1,025,563)
	4,097,971	2,625,319
Net property and equipment	7,960,764	5,676,089
OTHER ASSETS	191,626	227,730
	$43,789,442	$30,377,670

Statements of Income

For the years ended September 28, 1974, and September 29, 1973

	1974	1973
NET SALES (Note 1)	$61,412,981	$47,084,024
COST OF SALES	33,293,195	26,547,531
Gross Profit	28,119,786	20,536,493
EXPENSES:		
Installation, service, and warranty	5,418,034	4,602,797
Engineering, research and development	2,407,916	1,819,120
Employee profit sharing (Note 2)	1,032,600	705,000
Selling, general and administrative	10,832,501	7,617,515
Interest	1,402,063	881,771
Total Expenses	21,093,114	15,626,203
INCOME BEFORE FEDERAL AND STATE INCOME TAXES AND EARNINGS OF UNCONSOLIDATED SUBSIDIARY	7,026,672	4,910,290
PROVISION FOR INCOME TAXES (Note 6)	2,468,000	1,544,095
INCOME BEFORE EARNINGS OF UNCONSOLIDATED SUBSIDIARY	4,558,672	3,366,195
EARNINGS OF UNCONSOLIDATED SUBSIDIARY (Note 7)	245,692	118,090
NET INCOME	$ 4,804,364	$ 3,484,285
NET INCOME PER COMMON SHARE (Note 8)	$ 2.62	$ 1.91

NOTES TO FINANCIAL STATEMENTS

1. REPORTING AND ACCOUNTING POLICIES

PRINCIPLES OF CONSOLIDATION

The accompanying financial statements include the accounts of the Company and its wholly-owned subsidiary, Compugraphic International Corporation. All material intercompany balances and transactions have been eliminated in consolidation. As explained in Note 7, Graphic Credit Corporation, the Company's wholly-owned finance subsidiary organized in 1973, has not been consolidated and is reflected on the equity method in the accompanying financial statements.

REVENUE ACCOUNTING

The Company manufactures phototypesetting equipment for sale or lease. Under the principal lease program, the Company offers customers five-year non-cancellable lease contracts which in turn are sold to the Company's wholly-owned finance subsidiary. Under other lease programs, the lease contracts are sold to an independent third party for a discounted amount. The net proceeds to the Company under these lease programs equal or exceed the normal selling price of the equipment and together with regular sales are recognized as sales revenue when the equipment is shipped to a customer in accordance with the provisions of Accounting Principles Board Opinion No. 27. Reserves are provided at that time for the estimated installation and warranty costs as well as contingencies related to defaults by customers under the third party leases.

7. UNCONSOLIDATED FINANCE SUBSIDIARY

The Company's investment in Graphic Credit Corporation, its wholly-owned finance subsidiary, is stated at cost plus equity in undistributed earnings. This subsidiary purchases at a discount lease contracts receivable under the Company's five-year lease program. The discount rate used is higher than the finance subsidiary's cost of borrowing at the time of purchase.

The following is a summary of the finance subsidiary's balance sheet at September 28, 1974 and September 29, 1973 and income statement for the year ended September 28, 1974 and for the period from March 8, 1973 (date of incorporation) to September 29, 1973.

Balance Sheet	1974	1973
Assets:		
Receivables on equipment leases net of reserve for losses	$23,104,201	$8,609,435
Less deferred finance income	(5,007,906)	(2,040,479)
Cash and other assets	1,195,350	61,054
	$19,291,645	$6,630,010
Liabilities and Stockholders' Investment:		
Current notes payable	$5,700,000	$4,000,000
Long term note payable	8,000,000	—
Other liabilities	1,019,141	511,920
Stockholders' investment	4,572,504	2,118,090
	$19,291,645	$6,630,010

Statement of Income	1974	1973
Finance income	$2,168,016	$573,676
Interest expense	1,107,670	75,944
Provision for bad debts	434,076	196,812
Other expenses	79,579	40,630
Provision for income taxes	300,999	142,200
Net income	$245,692	$118,090

Required

1. Compugraphic Corporation: 76% of Compugraphic's total sales are domestic sales and about 34% of these domestic sales are affected by means of 5 year non-cancellable lease contracts that are sold to the Company's wholly-owned finance subsidiary. Assume that the Company's 1974 gross profit percentage applies to all of its domestic sales and that all of the domestic sales for 1974 were completed on October 1, 1973 (the beginning of the 1974 fiscal year):

    a.) How much gross profit was included in the Company's 1974 Statement of Income from domestic sales affected by lease contracts sold to the finance subsidiary?

    b.) Assume that all of the domestic sales for 1974 are receivable in annual installments beginning on October 1, 1973. In 1974, the Company received $15,000,000 on account from its 1974 domestic sales. How much gross profit would have been included in the Company's 1974 Statement of Income from 1974 domestic sales if the Company had used the installment method (pro rata) to account for these sales?

2. Compugraphic Corporation: Assume that all of Compugraphic's 1974 sales were on account, and that cash collections from customers totaled $57,648,000 in 1974. How much bad debt expense was included in the Company's 1974 Statement of Income?

3. Graphic Credit Corporation: Assume that all of Graphic Credit Corporation's receivables on equipment leases on September 28, 1974 were purchased from Compugraphic on that date and that the present value method is used to account for these receivables. Also assume that the reserve for losses on September 28, 1974 was zero and that these receivables are payable in 5 equal annual installments beginning on October 1, 1974.

    a.) What is the present value of these receivables on equipment leases on September 28, 1974?

    b.) What is the approximate interest rate used to discount these receivables?

    c.) What entries would be made on September 28 and October 1, 1975?

Case 3-6

Allegheny Beverage Corporation (ABC)*

ABC and its subsidiaries are engaged principally in the production and distribution of soft drinks and the sale of vending machines. The soft drinks, primarily carbonated beverages, are sold mainly in Pennsylvania, Maryland, Virginia and West Virginia. The vending machines and a proprietary line of carbonated beverages are sold under the trade name of Valu Vend throughout the United States and Puerto Rico. The Company also operates a brewery in Baltimore, and a bottling equipment reconditioning business in Athens, Georgia.

Allegheny Beverage reported net income of $3,275,501 in its 1971 Annual Report, released in early May 1972. They also reported earnings from operations of $1.05 per share on net sales of $72,770,506. Included in its report was a letter to the firm's stockholders describing a change in the firm's auditors. The following paragraphs from the Chairman of the Board's letter are relevant to that change.

> Prior to the time its audit begins, the Company receives a letter from the certified public accounting firm stating what information will be needed, how long they estimate the audit to take, and what fee will be charged for the audit. For the 1971 audit, Alexander Grant estimated a fee not to be in excess of the staggering amount of $150,000, and a completion date of February 23, 1972. Our internal accounting staff had been working closely with Alexander Grant throughout the year, and had determined to adopt the accrual method of accounting which is the method used in our industry. This is the basis on which our six months earnings, our nine months earnings, and our preliminary year-end earnings were reported. On March 2, one week after the audit was scheduled to have been completed, we were informed by the Baltimore office of Grant that their position had been reversed by their Chicago office, and that we must defer earnings from our Valu Vend subsidiary. During a long discussion, we were requested to provide supporting information from similar companies. This was done and our accounting method was substantiated. Also, at that same meeting, we were told that if we chose to terminate Grant because of their change of position, certification would be given for all divisions except Valu Vend.
>
> After much additional research and many meetings, on March 18, 1972, the Baltimore Grant office once again was prepared to return to the accrual method of accounting with substantially the same figures we had reported preliminarily. A meeting was held at the Grant main offices in Chicago on March 21, and we were informed that they would not accept our accrual accounting and proposed a hybrid approach which was unacceptable to us. We had no choice but to recommend to our Board that Grant be terminated.

---

*This case was prepared from publicly available sources. The situation was suggested by a case written by Donald F. Bryant under the supervision of Professor David F. Hawkins and Lecturer Mary Wehle.

We agreed to pay the remaining fees for the audit to date, which should have been approximately $30,000 and Grant agreed to cooperate with a new auditor in the changeover, make available their work papers for review, and to certify the divisions other than Valu Vend as promised by the Baltimore office. Two days later, we were told that if we didn't pay them $77,000 ($100,000 had been paid to date) that we would not be able to have access to their work papers, and were furthermore told that there would be no certification whatsoever. We had no choice but to submit to this pressure in order to finish the audit.

Valu Vend, a wholly-owned subsidiary of Allegheny Beverage, was described more fully along with its revenue recognition procedures in footnote 2 to Allegheny's financial statements.

Valu Vend, Inc. (a wholly-owned subsidiary) was formed in December 1970 to sell vending machines and the products to be vended through such machines. Valu Vend has adopted the policy of recognizing revenue from the sale of vending machines and related costs and expenses at the time a machine is sold. The machines are sold under conditional sales contracts with payments due over a four-year period. If income on these sales had been deferred until collected, primary earnings per share for 1971 would have been $.62.

Installment notes receivable under conditional sales contracts aggregated $19,150,000 after allowance for doubtful accounts of $505,000 at December 31, 1971. Finance charges to customers included in such receivables aggregated $3,875,000 at December 31, 1971 and are reflected as a deferred item. Such charges will be taken into earnings as installment payments are received.

The firm's 10K reveals the following concerning Valu Vend's operations.

The Company commenced its Valu Vend program in 1971 shortly after incorporation of Valu Vend, Inc., as a subsidiary in December 1970. During 1971 Valu Vend's business consisted of two complementary programs: (1) the sale of beverage vending machines to distributor appointees and to others, and (2) the sale of Valu Vend carbonated beverages distributed through such vending machines. The Valu Vend programs are national in scope.

Valu Vend sells its machines under conditional sales contracts. Under these contracts, a purchaser is required to make a $50 down payment and to pay the balance in equal monthly installments over a 48-month period after purchase. Under moratorium plans, the first of such monthly payments may begin 120 days or 210 days after the date of purchase, but all payments are completed within 48 months after purchase.

The new auditors, Benjamin Botwinick & Co., included the following paragraph in their opinion.

As described in Note 2, the Valu Vend, Inc. subsidiary in its inception year reported income from vending machine sales on the accrual method. This method of reporting is consistent with that generally accepted by the vending machine industry. Notes receivable from such sales will be collected over a four-year period from the date of sale. Because of the limited history of Valu Vend, Inc., the collectibility of the notes and the adequacy of the allowance for doubtful accounts thereon will be re-evaluated in future periods.

Allegheny Beverage also had unamortized startup costs incurred during the initial production period of a new bottling plant during 1971 of $3,409,000.

The Board Chairman summarized the Company's operations as follows:

> Earnings from operations totaled $1.05 per share. We had two extraordinary items causing a reduction in total earnings of 13¢ per share. Approximately 5¢ was due to the sale of all remaining airplanes in our leasing company which has now discontinued operations. The remaining 8¢ was due to a guarantee issued three years ago, which after much litigation, the company was called upon to meet. This call actually occurred in 1972 but a reserve was established for the expense in 1971. We are pleased with our net of 92¢ per share which is approximately a 300% increase in earnings over 1970.

Comments on the Installment Method

The installment method of recognizing income is a conservative procedure. Rather than recognizing the contract price as revenue and deducting related expenses at the time of sale, a gross profit margin is calculated on the sale. This gross profit margin, the contract price less identifiable expenses is converted to a percentage and applied to each installment received as a means of recognizing income.

For example, suppose a retail land sales company sells land costing $30,000 for $60,000 with the sales price to be received in three equal annual payments of $20,000. The gross margin is $60,000 - $30,000 = $30,000 and the gross margin percentage is 50 percent. This percentage is applied to the yearly installment of $20,000 resulting in $10,000 of income per year. Period expenses not traceable to specific sales would be deducted from the $10,000 (plus any other income) in determining net income.

An alternative method would show the total revenue from the contract less all expenses and less the gross profit deferred.

The installment method is allowed under certain circumstances for tax purposes, but its use in financial reporting is severely restricted by APB 10 paragraph 12 which states "Profit is deemed to be realized when a sale in the ordinary course of business is affected, unless the circumstances are such that collection of the sale price is not reasonably assured... Accordingly it concludes that, in the absence of the circumstances referred to above, the installment method of recognizing revenue is not acceptable." In a footnote, the Board goes on to say, "the Board recognizes that there are exceptional cases where receivables are collectible over an extended period of time and, because of the terms of the transactions or other conditions, there is no reasonable basis for estimating the degree of collectibility. When such circumstances exist, and as long as they exist, either the installment method or the cost recovery method of accounting may be used. (Under the cost recovery method, equal amounts of revenue and expense are recognized as collections are made until all costs have been recovered, postponing any recognition of profit until that time.)"

Required

1. Are you satisfied with the Company's statement of a 300 percent increase in net-per-share?

2. How should the Valu Vend activities be accounted for by Allegheny?

3. What would you have done if you were Alexander Grant in this Case? What obligations do you have, if any, to the new auditor and to the firm's shareholders?

Case 3-7

Great Southwest Corporation*

A. Bryant Ranch

In 1968 Great Southwest Corporation sold the Bryant Ranch for $31,000,000 to a limited partnership formed to purchase the land. Great Southwest reported the transaction as a sale and recorded a profit in that year of $8,558,176 and deferred $827,833 as a reported profit in 1969. The purchaser made a cash payment of $6,000,000 of which $600,000 was assigned to principal and $5,400,000 to prepaid interest. A note for $30,400,000 at a 7% annual rate was given for the balance, and under the terms of the note no principal payments were to be paid for the first 15 years after the transaction through 1983. There was no personal liability on the note and as required by California law, the only recourse was against the land. During this 15-year period, interest in the flat amount of $1,000,000 per year was to be paid. After 1984, principal payment plus accrued as well as current interest payments were to be made over a five-year period to amortize the note. Among other aspects of the terms of the transaction, Great Southwest was obligated under certain conditions to make certain improvements and also pay certain other costs.

Required

1. What entry did Great Southwest make in 1968 to record the sale of Bryant Ranch?

2. Evaluate Great Southwest's accounting for this sale. In particular, how does this transaction relate to criteria for revenue recognition?

B. Six Flags Over Texas

In June 1969, Great Southwest Corporation sold an amusement park in Texas known as Six Flags Over Texas for $40,000,000. A commission of 5% on the purchase price was paid to a real estate firm by Great Southwest in connection with the sale. The purchaser, a limited partnership, made a cash payment of $5,432,670 of which $1,500,000 was assigned to principal and $3,932,670 to prepaid interest by Great Southwest. The purchaser also gave a 7% mortgage note for $38,301,585. This note was to be paid off in equal installments over the next 35 years.

The note was secured by the amusement park properties. In addition, the agreement allowed GSC continuing exclusive management of the park and Great Southwest retained certain risk of loss and opportunity for gain factors. (Moreover, Great Southwest could not be removed as general partner prior to 1997 except under certain limited circumstances.)

As part of the transaction, Great Southwest agreed to refrain from competi-

---

*This case was prepared from publicly available sources. The situation was suggested by a case written by Professor John K. Shank.

tion with Six Flags Over Texas for a period of 10 years. The new owners considered this aspect of the deal to be critical in their purchase decision.

Great Southwest carried the park properties on the books at an original cost of $14.2 million with accumulated depreciation of $4.8 million.

Required

1. How should Great Southwest record this transaction?

   a.) When it took place (prior to APB Opinion No. 21)?

   b.) After APB Opinion No. 21, assuming the value of the consideration received was $40 million?

2. Provide the entries for Great Southwest for June 1970 for cases (a) and (b) of question 1. Assume a June fiscal year for convenience.

3. Why do you believe this transaction was attractive to the buyer?

Section Four

Inventories and Operating Assets

Case 4-1 Koehring Company (A)

Koehring Company's 1973 Consolidated Balance Sheet (asset section only) and 1973 Consolidated Statement of Earnings are presented below. Note that Koehring Company uses the LIFO method of inventory accounting.

Consolidated Balance Sheets

assets	1973	1972
	(Dollars in Thousands)	
CURRENT ASSETS:		
Cash	$ 19,636	$ 16,437
Receivables	58,114	56,532
Inventories — At current cost (approximates first-in, first-out method)	137,614	120,295
Less — Allowance to reduce domestic inventories to cost on the last-in, first-out method	(31,261)	(28,052)
	106,353	92,243
Prepaid expenses	1,780	1,263
Total current assets	185,883	166,475
INVESTMENTS AND OTHER ASSETS:		
Investments in and advances to unconsolidated and 50% owned companies	17,477	14,292
Other investments — at cost	2,020	2,478
Miscellaneous assets	4,027	4,374
	23,524	21,144
PROPERTY, PLANT AND EQUIPMENT:		
Land	3,087	3,345
Buildings and improvements	34,013	33,265
Machinery and equipment	63,851	60,331
Construction in progress	9,117	3,148
	110,068	100,089
Less — Accumulated depreciation	55,925	53,796
	54,143	46,293
EXCESS COST OF ACQUIRED COMPANIES OVER RELATED EQUITY	9,941	9,941
	$273,491	$243,853

Consolidated Statement of Earnings

	1973	1972
	(Dollars in Thousands)	
REVENUES:		
Net shipments	$367,829	$291,204
Royalties and service fees	3,161	2,329
	370,990	293,533
COSTS AND EXPENSES:		
Cost of products sold	285,043	224,648
Selling, administrative and general expenses	59,140	52,281
Interest and other financing expenses, less interest earned ($5,267,000 and $4,780,000, respectively)	12,424	8,187
	356,607	285,116
Earnings before income taxes and extraordinary items	14,383	8,417
PROVISION FOR INCOME TAXES:		
Current	3,922	2,035
Deferred	2,410	1,667
	6,332	3,702
	8,051	4,715
EQUITY IN NET EARNINGS OF UNCONSOLIDATED AND 50% OWNED COMPANIES	2,372	1,746
Earnings before extraordinary items	10,423	6,461
EXTRAORDINARY ITEMS		(1,268)
Net earnings	$ 10,423	$ 5,193

Required

1. The cost of goods sold for 1973 would have been what amount if Koehring had used the FIFO method of accounting for these inventories?

2. Assuming a 48% federal income tax rate, earnings retained in the business would have been increased by what amount if Koehring had used the FIFO method of accounting for these inventories instead of adopting LIFO in 1957?

3. What would have been the effect on net working capital at December 31, 1973 if Koehring had used the FIFO method of accounting for these inventories?

4. Assuming a 48% federal income tax rate, additional federal income taxes of approximately what amount would have been paid or accrued from 1957 to 1973, inclusive if Koehring had used the FIFO method of accounting for these inventories?

Case 4-2

Allegheny Ludlum Industries, Inc. (A)*

Allegheny Ludlum is a major steel producer engaged in the manufacture and sale of specialty steels and alloys (mainly stainless steel and nickel base alloys), consumer products, and other products including cemented tungsten carbide, industrial products and magnetic and electronic materials. The Company entered the consumer products field in 1967 by acquiring True Temper Corporation and expanded its position in 1969 by acquiring Jacobsen Manufacturing.

Allegheny Ludlum used the LIFO method of accounting for inventories in 1969 having switched to it in 1950. At the time the Company originally switched to LIFO raw material prices had been rising and the IRS had recently approved LIFO as an acceptable method of inventory valuation. Most of the other major steel producers also switched to LIFO about this time and were still using this method in 1969.

Allegheny's financial summary of their 1969 annual report contained the following paragraphs:

Effects of LIFO Accounting

For a number of years, the Corporation has used the Last-in First-Out (LIFO) method of accounting for its steel inventories. In periods of extended inflation, coupled with uncertain supplies of raw materials from foreign sources, and rapid increases and fluctuations in prices of raw materials such as nickel and chrome-nickel scrap, earnings can be affected unrealistically for any given year.

Because of these factors, Allegheny Ludlum will apply to the Internal Revenue Service for permission to discontinue using the LIFO Method of accounting for valuing those inventories for which this method has been used. If such application is granted, the LIFO reserve at December 31, 1969 of $12,300,000 would be eliminated which would require a provision for income taxes of approximately $6,150,000. The Corporation will also seek permission to pay the increased taxes over a ten-year period. If Allegheny Ludlum had not used the LIFO method of accounting during 1969, net earnings for the year would have been increased by approximately $1,500,000.

On March 4, 1970 the *Wall Street Journal* reported that Allegheny Ludlum was seeking approval from the IRS to discontinue using LIFO. The Company believed the change was necessary "because of the effect of continued inflationary increases in [the] cost of raw materials." The change would increase Allegheny Ludlum's net income substantially. The increase would be due to a gain on the extinguishing of LIFO reserves set up in previous years. The Company indicated the gain would be treated as an extraordinary item.

*This case was prepared from publicly available sources. The situation was suggested by a case written by Professor John K. Shank.

Furthermore, Allegheny was petitioning the IRS to spread the increased tax payment over a ten-year period.

On April 15 the *Wall Street Journal* reported that opposition to the planned change had surfaced from United Corporation, a closed-end investment company which controlled 5.8 percent of the voting stock in Allegheny Ludlum. A spokesman for Allegheny Ludlum indicated that the decision to alter inventory reporting was "a management decision approved by the board." As such it did not require stockholder approval and was not scheduled in the agenda for the April 24 stockholder meeting. On the other hand, William M. Hickey, president of United, argued that dropping LIFO would cost Allegheny six million in increased Federal income taxes.

On April 17, the *Wall Street Journal* reported that Allegheny Ludlum had scheduled a special shareholders' meeting to discuss the issue. The debate at this meeting was heated. Mr. Richard Smith, counsel of United, labeled the change "an unnecessary dissipation of corporate cash" and called on the directors to disapprove the change. This move was soundly defeated. However, Allegheny agreed to submit the proposal to a vote at a special shareholders meeting if the IRS approved the request.

Selected portions of Allegheny's financial reports are presented.

Statement of Consolidated Earnings and Earned Surplus
Year ended December 31, 1969 with comparative figures for 1968 (Note 1)

	1969	1968
Sales and revenues:		
Sales	$536,467,782	$487,886,449
Interest, dividends, royalties and other—net	2,142,791	2,800,520
	538,610,573	490,686,969
Costs:		
Employee costs (Note 10):		
Wages and salaries	167,186,276	150,426,045
Social security taxes	7,798,203	6,927,109
Pensions and other (Note 9)	25,997,519	23,254,394
	200,981,998	180,607,548
Materials, services and other costs (Note 10)	269,078,614	245,225,136
Depreciation and amortization (Note 5)	13,513,230	12,857,955
Interest and amortization of debenture expense	6,194,703	4,083,720
State, local and miscellaneous taxes	6,308,901	5,561,142
Federal taxes on income, including $6,226,000 deferred taxes (1968—$2,948,000) (Notes 5 and 9)	20,183,000	19,474,400
Total costs and income taxes	516,260,446	467,809,901
Net earnings	22,350,127	22,877,068
Balance in earned surplus at beginning (1968 adjusted by $8,538,454 representing earned surplus of pooled subsidiaries) (Note 1)	154,450,304	147,615,312
	176,800,431	170,492,380
Deduct—Dividends declared:		
On $3.00 Convertible Preferred Stock—$3.00 per share	4,998,505	3,938,031
On $2.70 Cumulative Preferred Stock (Note 6)	120,536	108,546
On Common Stock—$2.40 per share	11,363,923	11,228,563
By pooled subsidiaries to former shareowners	431,347	766,936
	16,914,311	16,042,076
Balance in earned surplus at end (Note 6)	$159,886,120	$154,450,304
Earnings per common share (Note 10):		
Primary	$3.44	$3.58
Fully diluted	$3.27	$3.35

See accompanying notes to financial statements.

Consolidated Balance Sheets

	1969	1968
ASSETS		
Current Assets		
Cash	$ 10,981,416	$ 9,912,103
Marketable securities—at cost (approximately market) and accrued interest	409,416	409,416
Notes and accounts receivable—trade, less estimated allowances of $910,333 (1968—$960,109)	66,187,027	51,519,456
Miscellaneous accounts receivable	1,805,991	1,817,497
Inventories (Note 2):		
Raw material	20,898,597	22,258,978
Semi-finished	82,953,011	70,734,562
Finished	33,165,618	32,993,793
Supplies	3,203,763	3,022,748
	140,220,989	129,010,081
Prepaid expenses (Note 9)	9,836,111	4,749,156
Total current assets	229,440,950	197,417,709
Investments (Note 3)	8,182,559	8,169,702
Fixed Assets—at Cost:		
Land	4,142,978	4,027,115
Buildings, machinery and equipment	408,076,470	377,692,025
	412,219,448	381,719,140
Less Accumulated depreciation and amortization	210,929,712	199,414,778
	201,289,736	182,304,362
Unamortized Expenses	702,024	750,035
Excess of Cost of Investments in Subsidiaries over Equities in Net Assets at Date of Acquisition	1,311,896	156,295
	$440,927,165	$388,798,103

See accompanying notes to financial statements.

	1969	1968
LIABILITIES		
Current Liabilities:		
Notes payable and current portion of long-term debt	$ 17,743,772	$ 13,496,480
Accounts payable—trade	24,372,904	18,499,118
Accrued liabilities:		
Payrolls, royalties and other expenses (Note 9)	14,638,259	10,515,441
Vacation allowances	8,530,942	7,929,589
Taxes, other than Federal taxes on income	5,321,336	3,619,974
	28,490,537	22,065,004
Dividends payable—preferred	1,510,429	1,170,021
Provision for Federal income taxes (Note 9)	4,445,309	903,645
Total current liabilities	76,562,951	56,134,268
Long-Term Debt (Note 4)	99,408,277	78,168,947
Reserves (Note 9)	10,322,963	11,261,297
Deferred Federal Income Taxes (Note 5)	5,241,535	—
Capital Stock and Surplus:		
Capital stock (Notes 1, 6 and 7):		
$3.00 Convertible Preferred Stock—$1.00 par value—authorized 2,200,000 shares; outstanding 2,013,905 shares (1968—2,012,468)	2,013,905	2,012,468
Cumulative Preferred Stock, issuable in series—no par value—authorized 1,000,000 shares—none outstanding	—	—
Shares; outstanding 4,748,978 shares (1968—4,731,641)	4,748,978	4,731,641
Surplus:		
Capital surplus (Note 8)	82,973,354	82,270,096
Earned surplus (Note 6)	159,886,120	154,450,304
	249,622,357	243,464,509
Less Cost of 4,500 common shares in treasury	230,918	230,918
	249,391,439	243,233,591
	$440,927,165	$388,798,103

Notes to Financial Statements

December 31, 1969

(1) Principles of consolidation:

The consolidated financial statements include the accounts of the Corporation and all wholly owned domestic and Canadian subsidiaries. In both the current and prior year are the accounts (on a calendar year basis) of companies (Jacobsen Manufacturing Company, National Material Corporation and Good Steel Service, Inc.) acquired in 1969 in transactions, recorded as poolings of interests, involving the issue or delivery of 610,210 shares of $3.00 Convertible Preferred Stock and 60,900 shares (including 38,500 held in treasury) of Common Stock.

(2) Inventories:

Inventories are stated at cost, which is not in excess of market. Cost was determined under the "last-in, first-out" method as to steel inventories. Other inventories are stated at standard (which approximates actual) or average cost. The amount applied to reflect inventories under the "last-in, first-out" method was increased by $3,085,325 during 1969 to $12,302,942 at year end.

(3) Included herein are:

Investments in unconsolidated affiliated companies, at cost, less reserves of $1,400,000	$6,464,679
Miscellaneous investments, at cost	1,717,880
	$8,182,559

The Corporation's equity in unconsolidated affiliated companies exceeded the carrying values by approximately $15,719,000 at December 31, 1969 and the Corporation's share of the net earnings for the year then ended amounted to approximately $526,000. During the year dividends $68,200 were received from these companies.

(4) Long-term debt:

Accounts due beyond one year:
Notes payable

3% Notes due January 1, 1972	$ 3,400,000
3.75% Notes due September 15, 1977	4,200,000
4⅝% Notes due May 1, 1990	25,000,000
5¼% Notes due May 1, 1979	1,700,000
6% Note due September 1, 1976	600,000
Prime rate notes and other obligations due January 15, 1971 and September 16, 1972	787,500
Bank Notes due November 15, 1971	39,000,000
Other notes	297,352
	74,984,852
4% Convertible Subordinated Debentures due October 1, 1981	5,703,200
4¾% Sinking Fund Debentures due June 1, 1986	11,375,000
3.6% to 6% Rental obligations due to 1989	7,345,225
	$99,408,277

Annual prepayments are required: on the 3% Notes, $100,000; on the 3.75% Notes, $600,000; on the 4⅝% Notes, $1,250,000 beginning in 1971; on the 5¼% Note, $200,000; on the 6% Note, $100,000; on the Prime rate notes and other obligations, $562,500; on the other notes, $60,400; on the 4% Convertible Subordinated Debentures, $810,000; on the 4¾% Sinking Fund Debentures, $725,000; and on the Rental obligations, approximately $385,000.

The Bank Notes represent borrowings under a bank credit agreement whereby the Corporation may borrow up to $45,000,000 during the period ending November 15, 1971, such borrowings bearing interest at the prime rate. On November 15, 1971, the Corporation may convert the then outstanding borrowings and the remaining unborrowed portion under the credit agreement into a term borrowing bearing interest at the rate of ¼ of 1% interest in excess of the prime rate and repayable quarterly over a five-year period.

The 4% Convertible Subordinated Debentures are convertible into shares of Common Stock. At December 31, 1969, the conversion price, which is subject to adjustment, was $52.00 per share and 109,677 shares of Common Stock were reserved for conversion.

The various Notes and the Indentures under which the Debentures were issued contain provisions restricting the payment of dividends on Common Stock (otherwise than in capital stock). However, no portion of the consolidated earned surplus was thereby restricted at December 31, 1969. The Notes and Indentures also contain various other restrictions relating to additional indebtedness, mortgages and liens and the purchase or redemption of capital stock or subordinated indebtedness.

The Rental obligations consist of indebtedness under certain lease-purchase agreements; the leased properties have been treated as assets and related lease obligations have been treated as the long-term indebtedness.

(5) Depreciation and deferred Federal income taxes:

The Corporation and its subsidiaries provide depreciation for financial reporting purposes based on straight-line rates whereas accelerated rates are utilized primarily for tax purposes. Deferred Federal income taxes applicable to the excess of depreciation used for tax purposes over that provided for financial reporting purposes amounted to $3,563,000 in 1969.

• • • • • • • • • • • • • • •

(11) Subsequent event:

On March 3, 1970, the Corporation announced its intention to apply to the Internal Revenue Service for permission to discontinue the "last-in, first-out" (LIFO) method of accounting as to steel inventories commencing with the year 1970. The amount of the LIFO reserve at December 31, 1969 was $12,302,942 and the elimination thereof would require a provision for income taxes of approximately $6,150,000. The Corporation will ask permission to pay the additional income taxes over a ten-year period.

Accountant's Report Peat, Marwick, Mitchell & Co.
Certified Public Accountants
Henry W. Oliver Building
Pittsburgh, PA 15222

The Shareowners and the Board of Directors Allegheny Ludlum Steel Corporation:

We have examined the consolidated balance sheet of Allegheny Ludlum Steel Corporation and subsidiaries as of December 31, 1969 and the related statement of earnings and earned surplus for the year then ended. Our examination was made in accordance with generally accepted auditing standards, and accordingly included such tests of the accounting records and such other auditing procedures as we considered necessary in the circumstances.

In our opinion, the accompanying consolidated balance sheet and statement of consolidated earnings and earned surplus present fairly the financial position of Allegheny Ludlum Steel Corporation and subsidiaries at December 31, 1969 and the results of their operations for the year then ended, in conformity with generally accepted accounting principles applied on a basis consistent with that of the preceding year.

Peat, Marwick, Mitchell & Co.
January 27, 1970 (except for Note 11
as to which the date is March 3, 1970)

Required

1. What reasons caused Alleheny Ludlum to switch to LIFO in 1950 and why do they wish to switch off LIFO in 1969? Was their action justified in 1950? Explain.

2. Do you sympathize with the United Corporation's objections, as a stockholder in Allegheny Ludlum?

3. How would the change affect the 1970 reports?

4. Is this item appropriately handled as an extraordinary item under current official pronouncements?

Case 4-3 Chrysler Corporation*

Chrysler Corporation is the third largest producer of cars and trucks in the United States. It also manufactures vehicles for the armed services. Despite its size, the firm has been dominated by its major competitors, Ford and General Motors. This has caused Chrysler's competitive position to deteriorate sharply in bad times.

The industry generally and Chrysler in particular, was experiencing substantive problems in 1970. Inflationary pressures were strong and labor unrest was on the rise in the automobile industry. General Motors had, for example, recently emerged from a strike which had idled production for over 10 weeks.

Chrysler's sales and net earnings had dropped precipitously during the fourth quarter of 1970, a period when new models are released and normally a strong sales period. The Company's stock reflected these pressures, falling as low as $16 from a high of $72 in 1968, as well as drops in overseas sales and Chrysler's poor competitive situation with respect to smaller cars then gaining in popularity with consumers.

Under these pressures Chrysler found it necessary to take a number of actions to improve its financial situation. These included tightening cost control, organizational changes designed to increase efficiency, a review and cutback of large capital expenditures and a vigorous marketing effort related to its existing products.

It was at this time that the firm also reviewed its accounting policies. Chrysler, as well as Ford and General Motors, used essentially conservative accounting procedures. All three companies expensed research and development costs in the year in which they arose. All three used accelerated depreciation methods for most if not all of their fixed assets. They deferred any investment tax credits. Finally, current pension costs were funded although all three companies had a substantive potential liability for past service costs.

One of two main differences in the accounting practices followed by the three firms related to inventories.† Ford and General Motors were essentially on a FIFO system. Chrysler, on the other hand, used basically a LIFO system. In 1970, however, Chrysler elected to convert to a FIFO system and to retroactively restate their 1969 operational data to be comparable. In making this change, Chrysler, in a letter to its shareholders, noted, "The other three U.S. automobile manufacturers have consistently used the FIFO method. Therefore, the reported loss for 1970 and the restated profit for 1969 are on a comparable basis as to inventory valuation with the other three companies."

The impact of the accounting change could only be discerned by a careful examination of the Company's financial reports and the accompanying footnotes. The financial reports for Chrysler in 1970 and the two major footnotes of relevance are included.

*This case was prepared from publicly available sources. The situation was suggested by a case written by Professor John K. Shank.

†The other major difference related to Goodwill. Only General Motors amortized Goodwill.

Consolidated Balance Sheets

ASSETS December 31	1970	1969*
Current Assets:		
Cash	$ 95,807,393	$ 78,768,440
Marketable securities—at cost and accrued interest	60,607,134	230,562,926
Accounts receivable (less allowance for doubtful accounts: 1970—$15,700,000; 1969—$13,400,000)	438,852,496	477,880,423
Refundable United States taxes on income	80,000,000	—
Inventories (See Inventories—Accounting Change note)	1,390,681,228	1,335,198,128
Prepaid insurance, taxes and other expenses	83,299,833	80,087,753
Income taxes allocable to the following year	17,415,554	27,186,281
TOTAL CURRENT ASSETS	2,166,663,638	2,229,683,951
Investments and Other Assets:		
Investments in and advances to associated companies outside the United States	24,907,266	15,496,619
Investments in and advances to unconsolidated subsidiaries	675,212,687	577,052,868
Income taxes allocable—noncurrent	22,301,845	32,465,250
Other noncurrent assets	44,971,952	55,814,937
TOTAL INVESTMENTS AND OTHER ASSETS	767,393,750	680,829,674
Property, Plant and Equipment:		
Land, buildings, machinery and equipment	2,949,256,417	2,825,623,645
Less accumulated depreciation	1,593,482,362	1,451,750,556
	1,355,774,055	1,373,873,089
Unamortized special tools	447,449,636	379,153,112
NET PROPERTY, PLANT AND EQUIPMENT	1,803,223,691	1,753,026,201
Cost of Investments in Consolidated Subsidiaries in Excess of Equity	78,491,382	78,184,245
TOTAL ASSETS	$4,815,772,461	$4,741,724,071

*Restated to reflect the change made in 1970 in accounting for inventories.

See notes to financial statements.

LIABILITIES AND SHAREHOLDERS' INVESTMENT December 31	1970	1969*
Current liabilities:		
Accounts payable and accrued interest.	$1,095,984,194	$1,116,607,970
Short-term debt	374,186,273	477,442,371
Payments due within one year on long-term debt	34,572,552	39,825,038
Taxes on income	43,136,332	9,969,436
TOTAL CURRENT LIABILITIES	1,547,879,351	1,643,844,815
Other Liabilities:		
Deferred incentive compensation	2,726,641	7,493,823
Other employee benefit plans	63,462,301	55,575,476
Deferred investment tax credit	21,774,580	25,598,022
Unrealized profits on sales to unconsolidated subsidiaries	49,280,076	47,336,034
Other noncurrent liabilities	68,733,595	89,870,533
TOTAL OTHER LIABILITIES	205,977,193	225,873,888
Long-Term Debt:		
Notes and debentures payable	671,053,172	466,951,466
Convertible sinking fund debentures	119,999,000	119,999,000
TOTAL LONG-TERM DEBT	791,052,172	588,950,466
International Operations Reserve	35,500,000	35,500,000
Minority Interest in Net Assets of Consolidated Subsidiaries	79,742,516	95,149,271
Shareholders' Investment:		
Represented by Common Stock—par value $6.25 a share: Authorized 80,000,000 shares; issued and outstanding 49,498,979 shares at December 31, 1970 and 47,942,136 shares at December 31, 1969	309,368,619	299,638,350
Additional paid-in capital	484,020,938	455,739,253
Net earnings retained for use in business	1,362,231,672	1,399,028,028
TOTAL SHAREHOLDERS' INVESTMENT	2,155,621,229	2,154,405,631
TOTAL LIABILITIES AND SHAREHOLDERS' INVESTMENT	$4,815,772,461	$4,741,724,071

*Restated to reflect the change made in 1970 in accounting for inventories.

CONSOLIDATED STATEMENT OF NET EARNINGS

Year ended December 31	1970	1969*
Net sales	$6,999,675,655	$7,052,184,678
Equity in net earnings [loss] of unconsolidated subsidiaries	(6,210,013)	(6,286,309)
Other income and deductions	(19,962,022)	23,261,424
	6,973,503,620	7,069,159,793
Cost of product sold, other than items below	6,103,250,974	5,966,732,377
Depreciation of plant and equipment	176,758,139	170,305,745
Amortization of special tools	172,568,348	167,194,002
Selling and administrative expenses	386,041,866	431,706,851
Pension and retirement plans	121,406,136	114,577,630
Interest and long-term debt	46,998,713	31,702,530
Taxes on income (credit)	(21,400,000)	91,700,000
	6,985,624,176	6,973,919,135
NET EARNINGS [LOSS] INCLUDING MINORITY INTEREST	(12,120,556)	95,240,058
Minority interest in net loss of consolidated subsidiaries	4,517,536	3,730,564
NET EARNINGS [LOSS]	$ (7,603,020)	$ 98,971,222
Average number of shares of Common Stock outstanding during the year	48,693,200	47,390,561
Net earnings [loss] a share	$(0.16)	$2.09

*Restated to reflect the change made in 1970 in accounting for inventories and to conform to 1970 classifications. The 1969 net earnings and net earnings a share, as previously reported, were $88.8 million and $1.87 respectively. See Inventories—Accounting Change note.

CONSOLIDATED STATEMENT OF ADDITIONAL PAID-IN CAPITAL

Year ended December 31	1970	1969*
Balance at beginning of year	$ 455,739,253	$ 421,184,933
excess of market price over par value of newly issued shares of Common Stock sold to the thrift-stock ownership programs (1,556,843 in 1970; 927,276 in 1969)	28,281,685	33,796,320
Excess of option price over par value of shares of Common Stock issued under the stock option plans (none in 1970; 25,172 in 1969)	—	758,000
Balance at end of year	$ 484,020,938	$ 455,739,253

CONSOLIDATED STATEMENT OF NET EARNINGS RETAINED FOR USE IN THE BUSINESS

Year ended December 31	1970	1969*
Balance at beginning of year	$1,399,028,028	$1,351,453,762
Adjustments (for the years 1957 through 1968)		43,309,750
As restated		1,394,763,512
Net loss	(7,603,020)	
Net earnings as restated		98,971,222
	1,391,425,008	1,493,734,734
Cash dividends paid ($0.60 a share in 1970 and $2.00 a share in 1969)	29,193,336	94,706,706
Balance at end of year	$1,362,231,672	$1,399,028,028

*Restated to reflect the change made in 1970 in accounting for inventories.

Selected Notes to Financial Statements

Inventories — Accounting Change

Inventories are stated at the lower of cost or market. For the period January 1, 1957 through December 31, 1969 the last-in first-out (LIFO) method of inventory valuation had been used for approximately 60% of the consolidated inventory. The cost of the remaining 40% of inventories was determined using the first-in, first-in (FIFO) or average cost methods. Effective January 1, 1970 the FIFO method of inventory valuation has been adopted for inventories previously valued using the LIFO method. This results in a more uniform valuation method throughout the Corporation and its consolidated subsidiaries and makes the financial statements with respect to inventory valuation comparable with those of the other United States automobile manufacturers. As a result of adopting FIFO in 1970, the net loss reported is less than it would have been on a LIFO basis by approximately $20.0 million, or $0.40 a share. Inventory amounts at December 31, 1969 and 1970 are stated higher by approximately $110.0 million and $150.0 million, respectively, than they would have been had the LIFO method been continued.

The Corporation has retroactively adjusted financial statements of prior years for this change. Accordingly, the 1969 financial statements have been restated resulting in an increase in Net Earnings of $10.2 million, and Net Earnings Retained for Use in the Business at December 31, 1969 and 1968 have been increased by $53.5 million and $43.3 million, respectively.

For United States income tax purposes the adjustment to inventory amounts will be taken into taxable income ratably over 20 years commencing January 1, 1971.

Taxes on Income

Taxes on income as shown in the consolidated statement of net earnings include the following:

	1970	1969
Currently payable:		
United States taxes [credit]	$[81,800,000]	$50,000,000
Other Countries	44,300,000	36,300,000
Deferred Taxes	16,100,000	[6,000,000]
As previously reported		80,300,000
Adjustment in deferred taxes for change in inventory valuation		11,400,000
Total taxes on income [credit]	$[21,400,000]	$91,700,000

The change in inventory valuation resulted in a reduction in income taxes allocable to to the following year of approximately $56.0 million at December 31, 1969.

Reductions in taxes resulting from the investment credit provisions of the Internal Revenue Code are being taken into income over the estimated lives of the related assets. The amounts of such credits which were reflected in net earnings were $6,300,000 in 1970 and $5,400,000 in 1969.

Required

1. What entry is needed on January 1, 1970 to bring the accounts into line recognizing the shift to FIFO? What was the balance in the account "income taxes allocable to the following year under LIFO in 1969?"

2. How much will the change cost Chrysler: In 1970? In future years?

3. What reasons does Chrysler give for wishing to make the change? Do you accept their reasons? Would you as a stockholder be pleased with Chrysler's decision?

4. Has Chrysler given adequate disclosure? Is the change treated appropriately under the requirements of APB 20? Need it be?

5. Determine the change in the cost of sales resulting from the restatement for 1969.

6. Can you explain the $80,000,000 for refundable U.S. taxes on income for 1970?

Case 4-4 Lenox, Incorporated

Lenox, Incorporated is a manufacturer of china products, crystal and glassware, silver-plated holloware, engagement and wedding rings, fashion jewelry, class rings, emblematic jewelry and awards, candles, soaps and waxes. The asset section of Lenox's December 31, 1974 and 1975 Consolidated Balance Sheet is presented.

Consolidated Balance Sheets

ASSETS		
CURRENT ASSETS	**1975**	**1974**
Cash	$ 3,747,000	$ 3,774,000
Short-term investments at cost, which approximates market	2,579,000	927,000
Receivables, less reserves — 1975, $1,069,000; 1974, $762,000	25,871,000	25,501,000
Inventories		33,354,000
TOTAL CURRENT ASSETS		63,556,000
OTHER ASSETS		
Prepayments and deferred items	1,355,000	1,512,000
Sundry investments	2,231,000	1,660,000
	3,586,000	3,172,000
PROPERTY, PLANT AND EQUIPMENT, at cost		
Land and land improvements	1,600,000	1,600,000
Buildings and leasehold improvements	15,242,000	14,925,000
Machinery and equipment	19,222,000	23,351,000
	36,064,000	39,876,000
Less: Accumulated depreciation and amortization	16,755,000	18,721,000
	19,309,000	21,155,000
TOTAL ASSETS		$87,883,000

Assume that in 1975 Lenox decided to adopt the last-in, first-out (LIFO) method of valuating inventories. It previously had used the lower of cost (on a first-in, first-out method) or market to value these inventories. Also assume that Lenox's effective income tax rate for 1975 was 48%, that its December 31, 1974 inventory reflected 10,000 units at $3.34 per unit, that its December 31, 1975 inventory included 8,755 units and that its 1975 purchases were as follows:

Period	Units	Price Per Unit	Total
1st Quarter	2,500	3.450	$ 8,625
2nd Quarter	3,092	3.550	10,975
3rd Quarter	5,580	3.600	20,088
4th Quarter	9,015	3.670	33,086
Total	20,187		$72,774

Required

1. Prepare the appropriate note to Lenox's 1975 financial statements describing the change from FIFO to LIFO and its effect on the balance sheet and income statement.

2. On January 10, 1976, an independent auditor determined that 2,000 units of inventory (costing $3.67 per unit) had been excluded from inventory. These units were in transit and had been shipped f.o.b. shipping point by the vendor. The purchase was recorded on December 15, 1975 upon receipt of the invoice. What adjusting entries should the auditor suggest be made on January 10, 1976?

Case 4-5 E.I. Du Pont Neumours & Company

The Consolidated Balance Sheet (asset section only) and the Consolidated Income Statement of E.I. Du Pont De Nemours & Company are presented. In 1973, the Company adopted the last-in, first-out (LIFO) method of accounting for certain material components of inventory which comprised some 5% of the dollar value of consolidated inventories at December 31, 1973. In 1974, LIFO accounting was extended to the material, labor, and overhead components of substantially all domestic inventories, which comprised about 62% of the dollar value of consolidated inventories at December 31, 1974. If inventory values were shown at current cost (determined by the average cost method) rather than at LIFO values, inventories would have been $382,700,000 and $14,100,000 higher than reported at December 31, 1974 and December 31, 1973, respectively.

Consolidated Balance Sheet

(Dollars in millions)

	December 31 1974	December 31 1973
Assets		
Current Assets		
Cash and Marketable Securities	$ 128.0	$ 365.4
Accounts and Notes Receivable	1,011.4	923.3
Inventories	1,420.3	924.9
Prepaid Expenses	71.0	31.3
Total Current Assets	2,630.7	2,244.9
Plants and Properties	7,668.5	6,785.9
Less: Accumulated Depreciation and Obsolescence	4,540.6	4,162.1
	3,127.9	2,623.8
Other Assets		
Investment in Nonconsolidated Affiliates—at Equity in Net Assets	88.6	62.4
Goodwill, Patents, and Trademarks	53.3	54.1
Other Assets & Investments	79.3	67.3
Total Other Assets	221.7	183.8
Total	$5,980.3	$5,052.5

Consolidated Income Statement

(Dollars in millions, except per share)

Sales	$6,910.1	$5,964.0
Other Income	67.1	72.0
Total	6,977.2	6,036.0
Cost of Goods Sold and Other Operating Charges	5,051.9	3,878.6
Selling, General, and Administrative Expenses	675.1	595.4
Depreciation and Obsolescence	506.4	450.3
Interest on Borrowings	62.0	34.7
Total	6,295.4	4,959.0
Earnings Before Income Taxes and Minority Interests	681.8	1,077.0
Provision for Income Taxes	267.0	480.5
Earnings Before Minority Interests	414.8	596.5
Minority Interests in Earnings of Consolidated Subsidiaries	11.3	10.9
Net Income	403.5	585.6
Dividends on Preferred Stock	10.0	10.0
Amount Earned On Common Stock	$ 393.5	$ 575.6
Earnings Per Share of Common Stock	$ 8.20	$ 12.04

Required

1. Calculate the effect of Du Pont's use of LIFO (rather than current [average] cost) on net income and earnings per share for the year ended December 31, 1974. (Assume that minority interests in earnings of consolidated subsidiaries are unaffected by the Company's use of LIFO.)

2. Assume that Du Pont's 1973 inventory represents a basic layer of 1 billion units and that the difference between the 1973 and 1974 LIFO inventories represent an additional LIFO layer of .5 billion units. Also assume that in the first quarter of 1975 Du Pont purchased 1 billion units for $1.263 billion and sold 1.4 billion units for $2.8 billion. (Note that all dollar amounts in Du Pont's financial statements are stated in millions.) By what amount will Du Pont's gross profit for the first quarter of 1975 be higher or lower under LIFO than under the (weighted) average cost method?

Case 4-6

Warner & Swasey Company

Warner & Swasey is a leading builder of industrial machinery and equipment, including machine tools, construction equipment and textile machinery. Warner & Swasey's net income in 1976 increased substantially, climbing to $10.2 million or $2.90 per common share, a 70% increase over 1975 earnings before cumulative effect adjustment. J. T. Bailey, the Company's Chief Executive Officer, stated in his letter to shareholders that heavy stress was placed on getting the Company's inventory situation in hand. Management reviewed and refined inventories at divisions throughout the company, and succeeded in reducing the overall inventory level by more than $15 million.

Note B to the 1976 financial statements, Consolidated Balance Sheets (asset sections only), Consolidated Statements of Income for 1976 and 1975, and excerpts from Warner & Swasey's Note W to SEC Form 10-K are presented.

Notes to Financial Statements

NOTE B—Inventories

Inventories are priced at the lower of approximate cost (primarily using the last-in, first-out method) or market. If all inventories had been priced using the first-in, first-out method, inventories would have increased approximately $17,684,000 and $14,924,000 at December 31, 1976 and 1975, respectively. During 1976, inventory quantities were reduced resulting in a liquidation of LIFO layers carried at lower costs prevailing in prior years as compared with the cost of 1976 purchases. The effect of this liquidation increased net income by approximately $1,200,000 or $.34 per share.

Since inventory records are maintained by product line, a separation of amounts into major classes is practicable only through physical inventories. Inventories were determined at various dates during the latter part of the year. Had the amounts been determined as of a specific date, it is estimated that the percentage composition by major classes would have been as follows:

	1976	1975
Finished parts and products	36%	30%
Work in process	32	36
Raw materials and purchased parts	32	34
	100%	100%

Effective January 1, 1975, the Company changed its method of costing domestic inventories, pursuant to internal Revenue Service regulations, for both financial and tax reporting purposes to include in inventory certain indirect production costs which were previously accounted for as period costs. The Company believes that the newly adopted method of inventory costing will provide a better matching of revenues and expenses and is, therefore, preferable to the method previously used. The effect of the change in 1975 was to increase inventory by $1,300,000, and net income by $1,027,000 ($.30 a share). Of the total cumulative effect $764,000 is not taxable and the remainder is taxable over a ten-year period commencing with 1975.

Consolidated Balance Sheets

	December 31 1976	1975
	(In Thousands of Dollars)	
ASSETS		
Current Assets		
Cash	$ 5,053	$ 6,496
Receivable from finance subsidiary — Note C	1,299	1,938
Trade accounts receivable	40,257	40,603
Inventories — Note B	72,558	88,286
Prepaid expenses	3,491	4,271
Total Current Assets	122,658	141,594
Investments and Other Assets		
Equity in net assets of finance subsidiary — Note C	13,835	13,100
Investments at approximate equity	1,377	1,311
Other investments and sundry assets	6,016	4,845
Excess of cost over purchased net assets	2,494	2,494
	23,722	21,750
Property, Plant and Equipment		
Land	4,449	4,571
Buildings	36,986	38,769
Machinery and equipment and other facilities	85,476	83,895
	126,911	127,235
Less allowances for depreciation	63,397	59,430
	63,514	67,805
	$209,894	$231,149

Consolidated Statements of Income

	Year Ended December 31 1976	1975
	(In Thousands of Dollars Except Per Share Amounts)	
Net sales	$251,185	$251,888
Other income — net	1,967	1,091
	253,152	252,979
Deductions from income:		
Cost of products sold	164,962	175,518
Selling, engineering, administrative and general expenses	67,591	62,437
Interest expense	4,625	6,947
	237,178	244,902
Income Before Income Taxes and Cumulative Effect of a Change in Accounting Principle	15,974	8,077
Income taxes — Note H	6,850	3,050
	9,124	5,027
Net income of finance subsidiary	1,090	996
Income Before Cumulative Effect of a Change in Accounting Principle	10,214	6,023
Cumulative effect on prior years of changing inventory costing method — Note B	—0—	1,027
Net Income	$ 10,214	$ 7,050
Earnings per share of Common Stock — Note A:		
Income before cumulative effect of a change in accounting principle	$2.90	$1.72
Cumulative effect on prior years of changing inventory costing method	—0—	.30
Net income	$2.90	$2.02

The following tables represent the financial data and the replacement cost values in compliance with Section 210.3-17 of Regulation S-X.

Balance Sheet Items

	(In Thousands of Dollars)			
	Replacement		Historical	
	Cost	Accum. Depr.	Cost	Accum. Depr.

At December 31, 1976:

Inventories	$ 93,300		$ 72,558	
Property, Plant & Equipment (Land and construction in progress excluded)				
Buildings	$ 87,000	$ 34,000	$ 36,227	$ 13,149
Machinery and Equipment and Other Facilities	197,000	121,000	82,934	48,187
Totals	$284,000	$155,000	$119,161	$ 61,336

Income Statement Items

	(In Thousands of Dollars)			
	Replacement		Historical	
	Cost	Accum. Depr.	Cost	Accum. Depr.

For the Year Ended December 31, 1976:

Cost of Sales including $11,750 replacement cost depreciation and $7,130 historical cost depreciation	$174,000		$164,962	
Other Depreciation Expense	$ 1,050		$ 685	

Required

1. Calculate Warner & Swasey's net income for 1976 assuming that the Company had not liquidated LIFO layers.

2. Some accountants have advocated using an adjustment to cost of goods sold for the excess cost of replacing liquidated LIFO inventories. Assume that Warner & Swasey decided to maintain December 31, 1975 inventory levels by replacing any liquidated inventories at December 31, 1976 in January 1977. Assume that any difference between LIFO and expected purchase cost at December 31, 1976 will also exist in January 1977. Warner & Swasey's effective tax rate was 43 percent in 1976.

    a.) What entry would Warner & Swasey have made in December 1976 to adjust the 1976 Consolidated Statement of Income if the procedure referred to above had been used?

    b.) What entry would Warner & Swasey have made in January 1977 to record the replacement of liquidated inventories if the procedure referred to above had been used?

3. Calculate Warner & Swasey's net income for 1976 assuming the Company had consistently used FIFO to account for its inventories.

4. Using the replacement cost information included in Warner & Swasey's SEC Form 10-K, estimate the amount of holding gains included in the Company's 1976 net income.

Case 4-7

Corning Glass Works (A)

Corning Glass Works is an international producer of glass and glass-ceramics products, and related products involving corollary technologies, for use in the home, science and industry. It traces its origins to a glass business established in 1851.

Corning's 1976 and 1975 Consolidated Statements of Income and Retained Earnings are presented along with its Consolidated Balance Sheets.

Consolidated Statements of Income and Retained Earnings
Years Ending January 2, 1977, and December 28, 1975

(In thousands, except per share amounts)	1976	1975
Net sales	$1,025,905	$938,959
Cost of sales	701,647	708,455
	324,258	230,504
Selling, general and administrative expenses	166,773	151,819
Research and development expenses	48,857	42,285
	215,630	194,104
Income from Operations	108,628	36,400
Royalty, interest and dividend income	18,038	11,317
Interest expense	(19,704)	(21,802)
Other income (deductions), net	3,745	(5,211)
Taxes on income	(51,874)	(7,723)
Income before minority interest and equity earnings	58,833	12,981
Minority interest in (earnings) loss of subsidiaries	(595)	2,617
Equity in earnings of associated companies	25,475	15,539
Net Income (per share, $4.74/1976; $1.76/1975)	83,713	31,137
Retained Earnings at beginning of year	446,081	439,649
Dividends		
Preferred stock—$3.50 per share	(11)	(14)
Common stock—per share, $1.50/1976; $1.40/1975	(26,481)	(24,691)
Retained Earnings at end of year	$503,302	$446,081

Consolidated Balance Sheets

January 2, 1977, and December 28, 1975 (In thousands, except shares)

	1976	1975
Assets		
Current Assets		
Cash	$ 20,425	$ 19,723
Short-term investments, at cost which approximates market value	165,216	91,876
Receivables, net of doubtful accounts and allowances—$6,724/1976; $6,691/1975	135,696	142,833
Inventories	154,647	142,471
Prepaid expenses including deferred taxes on income	38,802	17,454
Total current assets	514,786	414,357
Investments		
Associated companies, at equity	142,715	121,027
Other, at cost	3,488	3,490
	146,203	124,517
Plant and Equipment, at cost		
Land	14,820	14,957
Buildings	166,116	166,633
Equipment	580,027	571,697
Accumulated depreciation	(414,518)	(394,403)
	346,445	358,884
Goodwill	9,631	12,974
Other Assets	10,212	10,715
	$1,027,277	$921,447
Liabilities and Stockholders' Equity		
Current Liabilities		
Loans payable	$ 27,775	$ 35,998
Accounts payable	41,020	30,118
Taxes on income payable	54,451	19,643
Wages and employe benefits	44,845	44,463
Other accrued liabilities	42,199	40,841
Advance payments on long-term contracts, net	8,256	—
Total current liabilities	218,546	171,063
Provisions for Furnace Repairs and Other Expenses	24,551	24,713
Loans Payable Beyond One Year	167,173	172,686
Deferred Investment Credits and Deferred Taxes on Income	15,936	10,580
Minority Interest in Subsidiary Companies	562	91
Preferred Stock	309	331
Common Stockholders' Equity		
Common stock, including excess over par value—Par value $5 per share; authorized—25,000,000 shares	96,898	95,902
Retained earnings employed in the business	503,302	446,081
Total common stockholders' equity	600,200	541,983
	$1,027,277	$921,447

Corning uses the LIFO method of determining cost for substantially all inventories. The following note was included in Corning's Notes to its 1976 and 1975 Consolidated Financial Statements (current cost is the same as FIFO cost):

5. Inventories. Inventories used in the determination of cost of sales were:

Dollars in thousands	January 2, 1977	December 28, 1975	December 29, 1974
Finished goods	$ 80,446	$ 77,558	$ 81,199
Work in process	51,462	39,486	63,938
Raw materials and accessories	38,856	39,203	42,776
Supplies and packing materials	16,844	21,092	23,245
Total inventories valued at current cost	187,608	177,339	211,158
Reduction to LIFO valuation	(32,961)	(34,868)	(16,710)
Balance sheet valuation	$154,647	$142,471	$194,448

Required

1. What was Corning's gross margin in 1976 using the LIFO method?

2. What was Corning's gross margin in 1976 using the FIFO method?

3. Why did the gross margins differ in 1976 under the LIFO and FIFO methods?

4. Corning's 1976 Form 10-K disclosed that the replacement cost of goods sold would have exceeded the LIFO cost of goods sold by about $2,012,000 and that the replacement cost of inventories at January 2, 1977 would have exceeded the FIFO cost of these inventories by $14,251,000. Assume that purchases in 1976 were equal to the replacement cost of purchases. What was the replacement cost of inventories at December 28, 1975?

Case 4-8

International Systems and Controls Corp.

International Systems & Controls Corporation is engaged in engineering, manufacturing, trading and financial operations worldwide. ISC has activities in over 60 countries.

The Company's principal markets are in the development of energy, forestry and agricultural resources; and in grain, food, pulp, chemical and petrochemical processing.

The Consolidated Statement of Income and the Asset portion of the Consolidated Balance Sheet are shown. Also included are selected portions from the Financial Review and the Notes relating to revenues.

Consolidated Balance Sheets

Assets — June 30, 1976 and 1975

	1976	1975
Current assets:		
Cash	$ 39,621,000	$ 26,207,000
Certificates of deposit	437,000	5,757,000
Marketable securities at cost (which approximates market)	4,541,000	—
Accounts and notes receivable, less allowance for doubtful items—$646,000 (1975—$904,000)	64,191,000	56,165,000
Unbilled receivables	32,506,000	27,703,000
Inventories	14,085,000	12,663,000
Prepaid expenses and deposits	1,894,000	2,287,000
Plant facilities and assets held for sale	—	1,288,000
Total current assets	157,275,000	132,070,000
Investments and other assets:		
Accounts and notes receivable, less current portion	7,962,000	3,018,000
Investments in unconsolidated subsidiaries and 50%-owned companies	9,163,000	9,703,000
Excess of cost over equity in net assets of consolidated subsidiaries	8,900,000	7,689,000
Costs applicable to future operations	2,845,000	2,433,000
Plant facilities and assets held for sale	988,000	2,299,000
Other investments, at cost	2,265,000	3,115,000
Other assets	5,879,000	4,580,000
	38,002,000	32,837,000
Property, plant and equipment, at cost ($2,198,000 fully depreciated at June 30, 1976):		
Land	825,000	858,000
Buildings	6,919,000	6,363,000
Machinery and equipment	12,252,000	10,131,000
	19,996,000	17,352,000
Less accumulated depreciation	8,351,000	7,130,000
	11,645,000	10,222,000
	$206,922,000	$175,129,000

As discussed below, revenues for 1976 include the net proceeds from the sale of two-thirds of the Company's 15% interest in Kalingas, a joint venture it developed under an arrangement with the government in Iran to establish a facility for the manufacture of liquified natural gas (LNG) for sales in international markets.

Revenues

Also, 1976 revenues include the net proceeds, in the amount of $1,108,000, from sales of assets no longer utilized by the Company.

Income

Finally, the 1976 period includes approximately $4,671,000 after taxes from the sale of a portion of the Company's interest in Kalingas, and approximately $712,000 after taxes on the sale of certain assets, as described above.

Consolidated Statement of Income

Years ended June 30, 1976 and 1975

	1976	1975
Revenues	$339,203,000	$320,317,000
Costs and expenses:		
Cost of sales and services	272,702,000	260,392,000
Selling, engineering and administrative expenses	45,464,000	40,534,000
Depreciation	1,306,000	1,256,000
Interest expense	2,291,000	4,477,000
	321,763,000	306,659,000
Income before provision for income taxes, minority interest and discontinued operations	17,440,000	13,658,000
Provision for income taxes:		
Current	3,439,000	2,323,000
Deferred	5,423,000	4,655,000
	8,862,000	6,978,000
Minority interest	163,000	45,000
Income from continuing operations	8,415,000	6,635,000
Loss from discontinued operations	—	376,000
Net income	$ 8,415,000	$ 6,259,000
Weighted average number of common shares and common equivalent shares outstanding	1,583,136	1,583,136
Earnings per common share and common equivalent share after dividends on preferred stocks:		
Income from continuing operations after dividends on preferred stocks	$4.40*	$3.34*
Loss from discontinued operations	—	(.24)
Net income	$4.40*	$3.10*

*After deductions equal to $.92 and $.86 in 1976 and 1975 respectively, per common share and common equivalent share to account for dividends paid and charged on preferred stocks of $1,453,000 in 1976 and $1,355,000 in 1975.

Required

1. Explain the essence of the following accounts as best you can.

   a.) Costs applicable to future operations.

   b.) Excess of cost over equity in net assets of consolidated subsidiaries. (Is this account appropriately located?)

   c.) Unbilled Receivables.

   d.) Plant facilities and assets held for sale.

   e.) Other assets.

2. What does the parenthetical note just below "Property, plant and equipment" mean?

3. Discuss the Company's treatment of the sale of two-thirds of their 15% interest in Kalingas, and the proceeds from the sale of other assets. Do you believe the accounting treatment accorded these items is consistent with good theory?

Case 4-9

Georgia-Pacific Corporation (A)

Georgia-Pacific Corporation is a leading manufacturer and distributor of a wide range of forest products. The asset section of Georgia-Pacific's Consolidated Balance Sheet for 1973 and an excerpt from Note 5 to Georgia-Pacific's 1973 Consolidated Financial Statements are presented.

Consolidated Balance Sheets

December 31

(Amounts in thousands)	1973	1972
		(Note 1)
Assets		
Current assets:		
Cash	$ 36,640	$ 34,380
Marketable securities, at cost which approximates market	22,200	22,160
Receivables (less reserves of $5,350 in 1973 and $2,840 in 1972)	200,900	183,230
Inventories, at the lower of cost or market (Note 3)	321,490	258,390
Prepaid expenses	8,220	7,470
Total current assets	$ 589,450	$ 505,630
Timber and timberlands, at cost less depletion (Note 4)	$ 325,880	$ 244,870
Property, plant and equipment (Note 5):		
Land, buildings, machinery and equipment, at cost	$1,593,230	$1,382,550
Less—Reserves for depreciation (Note 7)	538,610	460,670
	$1,054,620	$ 921,880
Noncurrent receivables and other assets	$ 32,070	$ 27,670
	$2,002,020	$1,700,050

5. Depreciation and Capitalization Policies:

Provisions for depreciation of buildings, machinery and equipment have been computed using straight-line composite rates based upon the estimated service lives of the various units of property. The effective straight-line composite rates for the principal classes of property and equipment are as follows:

Land improvements	5 to 7%
Buildings	2 to 5%
Machinery and equipment	5 to 20%

Maintenance and repairs and replacements of minor units of property are charged to expense as incurred. Replacements of major units of property are capitalized and the replaced properties retired No gain or loss is recognized on normal property dispositions; property cost is credited to the asset accounts and charged to the depreciation reserve accounts and any proceeds are credited to the depreciation reserve accounts. When there are abnormal dispositions of property, the cost and related depreciation reserves are removed from the accounts and any gain or loss is reflected in income.

Required Assume (1) that Georgia-Pacific's disposition of property in 1973, was not abnormal, (2) that its purchase of property (at cost) in 1973 totaled $244,970, and (3) that the depreciation expense for property was $99,560. What entries did Georgia-Pacific make in 1973 to record its disposition of property (Land Improvements, Buildings, Machinery and Equipment)?

Case 4-10

W.R. Grace & Company (A)

W. R. Grace & Co. is an international chemical company with interests in natural resources and consumer products and services. Grace's specialty chemical business involves the processing of raw and intermediate chemical-based materials into products used in a wide variety of industrial applications and in packaging and plastics. In addition, Grace is a major factor in the domestic agricultural chemical industry, producing nitrogenous and phosphate fertilizers. Grace has a significant investment in natural resources, especially within the United States, with reserves of petroleum, natural gas and low-sulfur coal. Consumer products constitute the third area of Grace's business activities. W. R. Grace's Consolidated Statement of Income and Balance Sheet for 1977 are included along with selected notes. (Amounts are stated in thousands, except per share amounts.)

On January 1, 1975, W.R. Grace purchased equipment costing $107,962,000. This equipment had a useful life of 5 years with no estimated salvage value. On July 1, 1977, W.R. Grace sold this equipment for its book value as of that date. This sale constituted the only disposition of properties and equipment in 1977. W.R. Grace uses the straight-line method to depreciate equipment and records depreciation expense only at the date for which financial statements are produced except in the case of conversions.

Consolidated Statement of Income

Years Ended December 31,	1977	1976
Sales and operating revenues	$3,976,233	$3,628,406
Dividends, interest and other income	16,261	19,320
	3,992,494	3,647,726
Cost of goods sold and operating expenses	2,733,678	2,522,201
Selling, general and administrative expenses	734,938	666,584
Depreciation, depletion and lease amortization	132,042	115,397
Interest expense	75,230	68,248
Research and development expenses	32,007	28,280
Net foreign exchange (gains) losses	5,822	(5,816)
Net (gains) losses on disposal of business	17,158	(810)
	3,730,875	3,394,084
Income before taxes	261,619	253,642
Income taxes	121,144	120,992
Net income	$ 140,475	$ 132,650
Earnings per share	$ 3.71	$ 3.51
Earnings per share assuming full dilution	$ 3.44	$ 3.25

Consolidated Balance Sheet

Assets December 31,	1977	1976
CURRENT ASSETS		
Cash, including time deposits of $67,862 (1976—$58,900)	$ 89,861	$ 78,629
Marketable securities	90,109	155,035
Notes and accounts receivable, less allowances of $24,584 (1976—$17,439)	546,385	500,817
Inventories	608,014	585,090
Prepaid expenses	40,227	30,755
Total Current Assets	1,374,596	1,350,326
Long term receivables and other assets	158,536	151,114
Investments in and advances to partnerships and less than majority owned companies	120,637	136,856
Properties and equipment, net	1,216,950	1,127,878
Goodwill, less amortization of $16,230 (1976—$13,822)	70,244	74,461
	$2,940,963	$2,840,635

Liabilities		
CURRENT LIABILITIES		
Loans payable	$ 146,811	$ 170,020
Accounts payable	329,202	316,503
Income taxes	119,248	106,231
Other current liabilities	157,967	121,117
Total Current Liabilities	753,228	713,871
Deferred revenue from sales of future natural resource production	17,779	29,373
Long term debt	754,401	773,839
Foreign social law obligations and other noncurrent liabilities	54,052	52,619
Deferred income taxes	117,934	100,961
Equity of minority shareholders in unconsolidated subsidiaries	16,426	15,683
	1,713,820	1,686,346
SHAREHOLDERS' EQUITY	1,227,143	1,154,289
	$2,940,963	$2,840,635

Section Four | Inventories and Operating Assets 115

Notes to Financial Statements

Note 3— Investments in and Advances to Partnerships and Less Than Majority Owned Companies

The Company has 50% interests in partnerships for developing certain coal properties and manufacturing phosphoric acid and ammonia. In addition, the Company has investments in less than majority owned companies, principally a 49% interest in an ammonia manufacturing company in Trinidad and a 50% interest in a pulp and paper manufacturing company in Colombia. A summary of the financial position of these partnerships and less than majority owned companies is set forth below:

	1977	1976
Total assets	$ 417,229	$ 334,831
Total liabilities	337,138	143,506
Net assets	$ 80,091	$ 191,325
Company's equity and advances	$ 91,319	$ 121,743
Investments in and advances to other partnerships and less than majority owned companies	29,318	15,113
	$ 120,637	$ 136,856

At December 31, 1977, the Company had guaranteed certain obligations totaling $80,750 incurred by two of the partnerships. No loss is anticipated under these guarantees.

The Company's equity in the results of operations of partnerships and less than majority owned companies was not significant in either year. Dividends received from less than majority owned companies amounted to $2,982 (1976—$2,280).

Note 4— Properties and Equipment

Properties and equipment include:

	1977	1976
Land	$ 82,719	$ 81,372
Natural resource properties	326,855	275,247
Buildings	438,955	396,163
Machinery, equipment and other	1,125,848	1,053,566
Projects under construction	56,335	57,231
	2,030,712	1,863,579
Accumulated depreciation, depletion and lease amortization	(813,762)	(735,701)
	$1,216,950	$1,127,878

In 1977, the Company adopted the provisions of Statement of Financial Accounting Standards No. 13 which changed standards of financial accounting and reporting for leasing arrangements. This change was adopted retroactively and had no significant effect on net income.

Future minimum lease payments and the related present value of capital lease payments are:

	Capital Leases	Operating Leases
1978	$ 15,963	$ 30,412
1979	15,185	25,593
1980	14,444	21,938
1981	13,414	19,026
1982	12,823	17,737
Later years	117,205	255,008
Total minimum lease payments	189,034	$ 369,714
Interest	(91,674)	
Present value of net minimum lease payments	$ 97,360	

The Company's total rental expense for operating leases was $44,819 (1976—$42,405), including $2,468 (1976—$1,778) of contingent rentals. Sublease rentals were not significant in either year.

Required

1. What entries did W. R. Grace make on July 1, 1977 to record the disposition of the equipment? Assume depreciation is recognized for the actual period over which the equipment is used.

2. How much did W. R. Grace expend on new properties and equipment in 1977?

3. What entry did W. R. Grace make on December 31, 1977 to record depreciation depletion and lease amortization expense for the year 1977?

Case 4-11 Koppers Company, Inc.

Koppers Company, Inc. is a diversified manufacturing corporation with specialized engineering and construction capabilities. The company has 284 operating locations and makes more than 100 types of products.

The fixed asset sections of Koppers' 1979 and 1978 Consolidated Balance Sheets are presented.

Consolidated Balance Sheet

ASSETS

December 31, 1979	1978	Koppers Company, Inc. and Subsidiaries		Explanations
($ Thousands)				
24,446	20,570			
5,400	9,309	Funds held by trustee for capital expenditures		
		Fixed assets, at cost:	9	**9.** The original amount paid for Company-owned buildings, machinery and equipment.
87,581	73,428	Buildings		
745,924	626,548	Machinery and equipment		
833,505	699,976			**10.** Accumulation of the portion of the original amount paid for fixed assets that has been allocated to operating costs since the assets were purchased.
373,461	327,591	Less accumulated depreciation	10	
460,044	372,385			
18,241	16,645	Assets under capital leases, net of accumulated amortization of $12,336 in 1979 and $12,852 in 1978 (Note 5)		
51,888	43,767	Depletable properties, less accumulated depletion of $15,865 in 1979 and $12,997 in 1978	11	**11.** Cost of properties having exhaustible resources, such as timber and stone, reduced for resources used in the past.
25,598	24,855	Land		
555,771	457,652			
19,839	18,107	Other assets		
$1,138,119	$1,034,207		12	**12.** The total net cost assigned to everything Koppers owns.

Kopper's Statement of Accounting Policies included the following description of the company's accounting for fixed assets:

Fixed Assets
Buildings, machinery and equipment are depreciated on the straight-line method over their useful lives. All ordinary maintenance and repair expenses are charged to operations. Extraordinary repairs, which materially extend the life of property, are generally charged to accumulated depreciation. Timber and mineral properties are depleted on the basis of units produced.
    When land, standing timber or property units are sold, the difference between selling price and cost, after recognition of accumulated depreciation and depletion, is reflected as Other income.

During 1979, major repairs of $1,720,000 were charged to accumulated depreciation. Also, assume that there were only two exchanges or dispositions of buildings, machinery and equipment in 1979:

a. In July 1979, Koppers exchanged machinery which cost $10,244,000 to acquire in Januuary 1973 for similar machinery having a fair value of $15,845,000 and paid $11,275,600 cash boot.

b. In December 1979, Koppers exchanged machinery which cost $5,040,000 when it was purchased in January 1976 for similar machinery having a fair value of $4,635,000 and received $1,545,000 cash boot.

All machinery is assumed to have a ten year useful life.

Required

1. What is the primary justification for charging major repairs to accumulated depreciation?

2. What entries did Koppers make in 1979 to account for buildings, machinery and equipment based on the information given.

Case 4-12

Hoffman Electronics Corporation

Hoffman Electronics Corporation produces airborne navigation systems, military and civilian communications systems and multi-media education systems and equipment that are marketed both domestically and internationally. The Company also distributes video tape recording systems and designs and installs individual, master and community television antennas and closed circuit television systems as well as markets solderless terminals and connectors.

The asset and shareholders' equity sections of Hoffman's Consolidated Balance Sheets at December 31, 1972 and 1973 are presented.

Consolidated Balance Sheets

ASSETS	1973	1972
CURRENT ASSETS:		
Cash (Note 3)	$ 804,594	$ 799,673
Accounts receivable, less allowance for doubtful accounts (1973–$89,574; 1974–$112,284)	8,870,209	6,285,507
Income taxes refundable (Note 4)	492,357	–
Inventories, at the lower of cost (first in, first out) or market	4,842,137	4,136,614
Government contract inventories, less progress payments (1973–$11,287,074; 1972–$7,035,450) (Note 1)	5,686,584	6,288,695
Prepaid expenses (Note 4)	1,242,239	965,768
Total current assets	21,938,120	18,476,257
PROPERTY, PLANT AND EQUIPMENT, at cost (Note 1):		
Land	563,938	563,938
Buildings and improvements	4,878,576	4,500,268
Machinery and equipment	11,528,771	9,935,633
	16,971,285	14,999,839
Less–Accumulated depreciation and amortization	7,078,271	5,543,527
	9,893,014	9,456,312
OTHER ASSETS, at cost (Note 1):		
Patent and license agreement (less accumulated amortization of $383,223 in 1973 and $230,717 in 1972) and other	882,377	1,037,537
Deferred product development costs (less accumulated amortization of $1,127,586 in 1973 and $562,174 in 1972)	1,012,859	499,552
	1,895,236	1,537,109
	$33,726,370	$29,469,678
SHAREHOLDERS' EQUITY (Note 6):		
Preferred stock, without par value– Authorized–600,000 shares Outstanding–none		
Common stock, par value $.50 per share– Authorized–3,000,000 shares Outstanding–1,796,755 shares at December 31, 1973 and 1972 (including 73,576 shares held in treasury at December 31, 1973 and 41,576 at December 31, 1972)	898,377	898,377
Additional paid-in capital	4,182,293	4,182,293
Retained earnings	12,805,659	12,675,235
	17,886,329	17,755,905
	$33,726,370	$29,469,678

Prior to 1974, Hoffman's policy was to capitalize research and development costs applicable to specific product lines to the extent that they were recoverable from firm orders. Product development costs applicable to audio-visual learning techniques were capitalized and amortized as units were sold; all other research and development costs were charged to expense as incurred.

In 1974, Hoffman changed its policy, as recommended by the FASB Statement No. 2, to charge all research and development costs to expense as incurred. This change in accounting method was treated as a prior period adjustment, and the December 31, 1973 balance of retained earnings was restated for the effect, net of income taxes (48 percent), of applying retroactively the new method of accounting.

Required

1. What criteria usually must be met for an event to be treated as a prior period adjustment?

2. What entry did Hoffman make to restate the December 31, 1973 balance sheet to reflect this change in accounting? Assume that the development costs have been expensed for income tax purposes.

Section Five

Liabilities

Case 5-1

Owens-Illinois, Inc. (A)

Owens-Illinois, Inc. is one of the world's leading and most diversified manufacturers of packaging products. Owens-Illinois, Inc.'s 1976 Annual Report included the following paragraph in the Statement of Significant Accounting Policies:

Glass Melting Furnaces. In domestic units the estimated cost of the next periodic rebuild of a glass melting furnace is accrued during the furnace's current operating life and carried in the reserve for rebuilding furnaces. No tax deduction is allowed for this provision. When the furnace is rebuilt, the actual cost is charged against the reserve and is deducted as an expense for tax purposes. Foreign subsidiaries generally follow the practice of depreciating the actual cost of a rebuild over the estimated life of that rebuild.

The actual cost of rebuilding glass melting furnaces in 1976 was $9,599,648. The Company's actual tax rate was 36.3% in 1976 and 35.9% in 1975. The liability section of the Company's 1976 and 1975 Consolidated Balance Sheets is presented. (Amounts are stated in thousands.)

	1976	1975
Liabilities and Shareholders' Equity		
Current liabilities:		
Short-term loans	$ 20,042	$ 20,041
Accounts payable	141,148	136,502
Salaries and wages	67,691	60,247
U.S. and foreign income taxes	48,615	28,043
Other accrued liabilities	79,768	65,891
Long-term debt due within one year	33,941	13,878
Total current liabilities	391,205	324,602
Long-term debt	551,793	571,856
Reserves and other credits:		
Reserve for rebuilding furnaces	53,749	45,647
Deferred taxes	94,500	76,523
Obligations under foreign pension plans	46,261	36,633
Other liabilities and reserves	11,712	9,254
	206,222	168,057
Minority shareholders' interests	38,477	35,379
Shareholders' equity:		
Preferred shares	13,413	14,198
Preference shares (liquidation preference, 1976-$65,706; 1975-$66,394)	13,141	13,279
Common shares	44,187	43,455
Capital in excess of stated value	143,473	71,548
Retained earnings	793,320	705,493
	1,007,534	847,973
	$2,195,231	$1,947,367

Required

1. What entries did Owens-Illinois make in 1976 to account for the costs of rebuilding glass melting furnaces?

2. Assume that Owens-Illinois, Inc.'s income before taxes and glass melting furnace rebuilding costs was $191,739,000 in 1976 for both accounting and tax purposes. What entry did Owens-Illinois make in 1976 to record the provision for income taxes and income taxes payable?

Case 5-2   Mohasco Corporation (A)

Mohasco Corporation operates in four industries: carpets, furniture, distribution and furniture rental. Mohasco's 1979 and 1978 Consolidated Statements of Income and Consolidated Balance Sheets (asset sections only) are presented.

Consolidated Statements of Earnings   Mohasco, Inc.

Years ended December 31, 1979 and 1978

	1979	1978
	(In thousands)	
Net sales and other revenues	$747,100	712,517
Cost of sales	584,167	556,333
Selling, administrative and general expenses	132,903	122,579
	717,070	678,912
Operating income	30,030	33,605
Interest on indebtedness	16,634	13,127
	13,396	20,478
Other income (expenses), net (note 3)	(1,716)	704
Earnings before income taxes and minority interest in subsidiary company	11,680	21,182
Provision for income taxes (note 4)	3,930	9,592
Earnings before minority interest in subsidiary company	7,750	11,590
Minority interest in subsidiary company	21	110
Net earnings	$ 7,729	11,480
Net earnings per share of common stock (note 1)	$ 1.16	1.73

See accompanying notes to consolidated financial statements.

Consolidated Balance Sheets — Mohasco, Inc.

December 31, 1979 and 1978

	1979	1978
Assets	(In thousands)	
Current assets:		
Cash	$ 12,046	14,261
Accounts and notes receivable:		
Trade	111,583	104,227
Other	6,026	3,356
	117,609	107,583
Less allowance for doubtful accounts	6,392	5,030
	111,217	102,553
Inventories (note 1)	124,716	128,424
Prepaid expenses (note 4)	14,662	10,427
Total current assets	262,641	255,665
Excess of cost over underlying net assets of companies acquired, less accumulated amortization	4,509	4,648
Other assets	3,692	4,654
Rental furniture, at cost, less accumulated depreciation of $7,520,000 in 1979 and $6,816,000 in 1978	19,766	16,058
Property, plant and equipment, at cost:		
Land	6,496	6,264
Buildings	66,975	64,376
Buildings capitalized under long-term leases	22,159	19,983
Machinery and equipment	146,184	132,691
Leasehold improvements	11,087	10,831
Construction in progress	5,914	4,448
	258,815	238,593
Less accumulated depreciation and amortization	125,556	115,506
	133,259	123,087
	$423,867	404,112

Mohasco's summary of significant accounting policies included the following note:

Income Taxes

The Company provides deferred income taxes when timing differences occur in reporting income and expenses for financial statement purposes and income tax purposes.

The Company follows the policy of including the full amount of the investment tax credit in earnings in the year in which the credit is allowable for Federal income tax purposes.

Required Assume that the following information is available about differences between Mohasco's accounting and tax income:

1. Tax depreciation exceeded book depreciation by $1,422,000 in 1979.

2. The Company uses the write-off method of accounting for bad debt expense in the tax return.

3. Pension expenses in the income statement exceeded those included in the tax return by $631,000.

4. The income statement included $155,000 of tax exempt income.

5. The income statement included a provision of $2,000,000 [in other income (expenses)] in 1979 for estimated losses on sales of equipment, relocation costs and other expenses related to the closing of the carpet manufacturing plant in Merced, California. None of these estimated losses were included in the tax return.

The Company's effective tax rate was about 49% before consideration of investment tax credits of $1,785,000 which were included in earnings in 1979.

Reconstruct the entry Mohasco made in 1979 to record the provision for income taxes.

Case 5-3   Koehring Company (B)

Koehring Company is a manufacturer of specialized machinery for the construction and natural-resource industries—cranes and excavators, compaction equipment, water-well drills, light construction equipment, farm equipment, and hydraulic components and systems. The business is international in scope, with foreign sales accounting for 41 percent of 1978 shipments. Koehring operates 21 plants in six countries and markets its products worldwide, mainly through a network of independent dealers and distributors.

Koehring's 1978 and 1977 Consolidated Statements of Earnings and Consolidated Balance Sheets are presented.

Koehring Company and Consolidated Subsidiaries
Consolidated Statement of Earnings
For the Years Ended November 30, 1978 and 1977

	1978	1977
	(Dollars in Thousands)	
Net Shipments	$416,721	$361,607
Costs, Expenses, and Other Income:		
Cost of products sold	312,752	265,893
Selling, administrative, and general expenses	72,720	66,173
Interest and other financing expenses (income) —		
Interest expense	6,626	6,700
Financing charges from Koehring Finance Corporation	7,421	5,622
Earnings of Koehring Finance Corporation before income taxes	(4,201)	(2,997)
Interest income	(1,424)	(1,182)
Royalties and service fees	(2,978)	(2,101)
	390,916	338,108
Earnings before income taxes and equity in net earnings of 50%-owned companies	25,805	23,499
Provision for Income Taxes	12,887	13,232
	12,918	10,267
Equity in Net Earnings (Loss) of 50%-Owned Companies	(1,125)	261
Net Earnings	$ 11,793	$ 10,528
Earnings Per Common Share:		
Primary	$ 3.45	$ 3.03
Fully diluted	$ 3.27	$ 2.91

Koehring Company and Consolidated Subsidiaries
Consolidated Statement of Earnings Retained in the Business
For the Years Ended November 30, 1978 and 1977

	1978	1977
	(Dollars in Thousands)	
Balance at Beginning of Year	$75,922	$69,242
Net earnings for the year	11,793	10,528
Deduct — Cash dividends declared:		
On convertible preferred stock:		
Series G, 5%, $1.50 a share	25	25
Series H, 5½%, $2.75 a share	1,074	1,146
Series I, 5%, $2.50 a share	336	336
On common stock — $.90 a share in 1978 and $.80 a share in 1977	2,657	2,341
	4,092	3,848
Balance at End of Year	$83,623	$75,922

The accompanying "Notes" are an integral part of these statements.

Koehring Company and Consolidated Subsidiaries
Consolidated Balance Sheet
November 30, 1978 and 1977

Assets	1978	1977
	(Dollars in Thousands)	
Current Assets:		
Cash and commercial paper	$ 25,800	$ 23,916
Receivables	57,739	56,560
Inventories	117,160	96,834
Prepaid expenses	2,309	2,499
Total current assets	203,008	179,809
Investments and Other Assets:		
Investments in and advances to unconsolidated and 50%-owned companies	27,759	26,352
Other assets	8,618	6,497
	36,377	32,849
Property, Plant, and Equipment, at Cost:		
Land	4,106	3,356
Buildings and improvements	45,538	42,407
Machinery and equipment	67,815	62,303
Construction in progress	5,528	2,546
	122,987	110,612
Less — Accumulated depreciation	52,290	51,130
	70,697	59,482
Excess Cost of Acquired Companies Over Related Equity	5,163	6,023
	$315,245	$278,163

Liabilities and Shareholders' Investment	1978	1977
	\multicolumn{2}{c}{(Dollars in Thousands)}	
Current Liabilities:		
Payable to banks, international	$ 2,292	$ 651
Dividends payable	357	376
Trade accounts payable	25,368	16,647
Accrued liabilities	30,872	33,643
Income taxes —		
Current	24,525	6,479
Deferred	9,534	5,549
Payments due within one year on long-term debt	6,160	5,416
Total current liabilities	99,108	68,761
Long-Term Debt	69,521	64,003
Other Liabilities and Deferred Credits:		
Retirement and pension plans	7,867	5,176
Deferred income taxes	10,109	19,685
Other noncurrent liabilities	4,684	3,500
	22,660	28,361
Shareholders' Investment:		
Convertible preferred stock	28,269	28,269
Common stock	6,229	6,229
Additional paid-in capital	9,848	9,976
Earnings retained in the business	83,623	75,922
	127,969	120,396
Less — Cost of treasury stock	4,013	3,358
Total shareholders' investment	123,956	117,038
	$315,245	$278,163

The accompanying "Notes" are an integral part of this balance sheet.

Koehring Company's provision for future income taxes has been made to recognize the deduction of certain costs and the recognition of certain revenues for financial statement purposes in amounts different from those for income tax purposes. Note 8 to the financial statements is presented below. The balance of the deferred income taxes account at November 30, 1978 was increased by $3,487,000 as the result of Koehring's acquisition and consolidation of two French corporations in 1978. (Dollars in thousands except per share amounts.)

8. Income Taxes

The provision for income taxes, including the provision for income taxes of Koehring Finance Corporation accounted for on the equity basis, consists of the following:

	1978	1977
Currently payable:		
United States	$16,314	$ 3,243
Foreign	4,081	1,906
State and local	1,570	331
	$21,965	$ 5,480
Deferred:		
United States	$ (8,416)	$ 7,216
Foreign	(662)	536
	$(9,078)	$ 7,752
Total provision for income taxes	$12,887	$13,232

Deferred tax expense results from timing differences in the recognition of revenue and expense for tax and financial statement purposes. The primary source of these differences relates to deferred income, including installment sales of $(8,958) in 1978 and $6,839 in 1977.

Total tax expense of $12,887 in 1978 and $13,232 in 1977 results in effective tax rates of 49.9% and 56.3%, respectively. Differences between the statutory U.S. Federal income tax rate of 48% and the company's actual effective tax rate are summarized as follows:

	1978	1977
Statutory federal income tax rate	48.0%	48.0%
Taxes on foreign earnings provided at greater than U.S. rate, net	—	2.5
State and local income taxes, net of federal benefit	1.6	1.9
Foreign subsidiary losses (earnings) without tax benefit (expense)	(0.4)	2.0
Investment tax credit on assets purchased	(2.1)	(2.1)
Effects of translation	(0.5)	1.9
Amortization of goodwill	3.5	0.7
Other, net	(0.2)	1.4
Actual effective tax rate	49.9%	56.3%

Deferred income taxes are not required on the foreign subsidiaries' undistributed earnings which are considered to be permanently invested. It is estimated that no additional U.S. income taxes will be paid on such undistributed earnings should they be remitted.

Required

1. Reconstruct the entry Koehring made in 1978 to record the provision for income taxes.

2. Calculate the total amount of income tax payments made by Koehring in 1978.

3. Assume that the information provided in Note 8 about installment sales and the following data represent all of the differences between Koehring's accounting and tax income:

    a. Tax depreciation exceeded book depreciation by an undisclosed amount.

    b. Product liability losses in the income statement exceeded those included in the tax return by $1,540,000.

    c. The income statement included $1,895,000 of permanently invested and undistributed earnings of foreign subsidiaries that are not subject to tax and $1,864,000 of amortized goodwill.

    Using a 50% tax rate and applying the net-change method, calculate the amount by which tax depreciation exceeded book depreciation. (Hint: Reconstruct the calculations of the totals for the current and deferred income tax amounts.)

Case 5-4

Bethlehem Steel Corporation (A)

Bethlehem Steel Corporation is an integrated steel producer engaged primarily in the manufacture and sale of steel and steel products. It is the second largest producer in the United States. It is also engaged in marine construction, including the building and repairing of ships and the building of mobile offshore oil drilling platforms, and in the manufacture of plastic products.

Bethlehem's 1977 and 1976 Consolidated Statements of Income and Income Invested in the Business and its 1977 and 1976 Consolidated Balance Sheets are presented.

Consolidated Statement of Income and Income Invested in the Business

	1977	1976
	(dollars in millions)	
Revenues:		
Net sales	$5,370.0	$5,248.0
Interest, dividends and other income	40.2	56.7
	$5,410.2	$5,304.7
Costs and Expenses:		
Cost of sales (Note C)	$4,863.2	$4,485.9
Depreciation	300.1	275.6
Selling, administrative and general expense	284.6	271.5
Interest and other debt charges	82.5	77.7
	$5,530.4	$5,110.7
Income (Loss) before Non-recurring Items and Provision (Credit) for Taxes on Income	$ (120.2)	$ 194.0
Non-recurring Items:		
Estimated costs of closedown of certain steelmaking and related facilities (Note B)	$ 750.0	—
Flood expense	41.0	—
	$ 791.0	—
Income (Loss) before Provision (Credit) for Taxes on Income	$ (911.2)	$ 194.0
Provision (Credit) for Taxes on Income (Note L)	$ (463.0)	$ 26.0
Net Income (Loss) $(10.27) and $3.85 per share	$ (448.2)	$ 168.0
Income Invested in the Business, January 1	2,185.9	2,105.3
	$1,737.7	$2,273.3
Deduct: Dividends ($1.50 and $2.00 per share)	65.5	87.4
Income Invested in the Business, December 31	$1,672.2	$2,185.9

Consolidated Balance Sheets

	1977	1976
ASSETS	(dollars in millions)	
Current Assets:		
Cash	$ 55.4	$ 45.6
Marketable securities, at cost (approximating market)	183.4	355.6
Receivables, less allowances of $6,300,000 and $6,100,000	496.7	421.5
Refund of income taxes paid in prior year (Note L)	134.0	38.4
Inventories (Note C)	626.2	834.1
Total Current Assets	$1,495.7	$1,695.2
Investments in Associated Companies Accounted for by Equity Method (Note E)	125.0	116.9
Investments in Other Associated Enterprises	96.7	97.4
Long-term Receivables	36.1	24.8
Property, Plant and Equipment, Less Accumulated Depreciation (Note D)	2,988.3	2,963.4
Deferred Income Taxes (Note L)	80.4	—
Miscellaneous Assets (Note F)	76.7	79.8
Total	$4,898.9	$4,977.5
LIABILITIES AND STOCKHOLDERS' EQUITY		
Current Liabilities:		
Accounts payable	$ 313.9	$ 274.8
Accrued employment costs	286.6	241.5
Accrued taxes	129.5	165.9
Debt due within one year	3.3	12.9
Current portion of estimated future liability for costs attributable to the closedown of certain steelmaking and related facilities (Note B)	115.1	—
Other current liabilities	130.1	127.3
Total Current Liabilities	$ 978.5	$ 822.4
Liabilities Payable after One Year	150.8	140.8
Deferred Income Taxes (Note L)	—	298.6
Estimated Future Liability For Costs Attributable to the Closedown of Certain Steelmaking and Related Facilities (Note B)	435.9	—
Long-term Debt (Note G)	1,154.8	1,023.1
Total Liabilities	$2,720.0	$2,284.9
Commitments (Note H)		
Stockholders' Equity (Note I)		
Common stock—$8 par value—Authorized 80,000,000; issued and outstanding 45,987,118 shares	$ 576.0	$ 576.0
Income invested in the business	1,672.2	2,185.9
	$2,248.2	$2,761.9
Less: 2,322,031 and 2,321,540 shares of Common Stock held in treasury, at cost	69.3	69.3
Total Stockholders' Equity	$2,178.9	$2,692.6
Total	$4,898.9	$4,977.5

During 1977, Bethlehem announced the closing or curtailment of a number of operations and the attendant work force reductions. The biggest cutbacks began in August 1977, at which time Bethlehem announced that the annual steelmaking capacity of the Lackawanna plant would be permanently reduced from 4.8 to 2.8 million tons and that the Johnstown plant's annual steelmaking capacity would be permanently reduced by 0.6 million tons to 1.2 million tons. Note B to the 1977 Consolidated Financial Statements stated:

B. Closedown of Certain Steelmaking and Related Facilities

On August 18, 1977, the Corporation announced a plan to close down certain steelmaking and related facilities, to reduce capital expenditures and to reduce hourly and salaried work forces. The decision to close down these facilities resulted in a pre-tax charge against income of $750 million. This amount may be summarized as follows (in millions):

Employment related closedown costs	$483
Write-off of facilities, net of estimated salvage	167
Other costs associated with reduction of capacity	100
	$750

The employment related closedown costs include an estimate of the present value of unfunded costs of pensions and of the costs of other benefits accruing to terminated and laid-off employees including, among other things, continued life and other insurance benefits and supplemental unemployment benefits. The write-off of facilities represents the net book value of abandoned plant and equipment adjusted for estimated proceeds of sales or realizable scrap value and losses incurred as a result of the termination of certain in-progress capital projects. Other costs associated with the reduction of capacity include the writedown to scrap value of inventory quantities considered unusable, anticipated operating losses to the date of closedown of certain facilities and estimated losses under certain contracts and agreements whose terms are no longer favorable to Bethlehem following the reduction of capacity.

In the opinion of management, based on available information, the $750 million charge is a reasonable estimate of the costs and expenses associated with the plan to close down these facilities. However, there are uncertainties in estimating amounts payable in future years, and, therefore, it is possible that future adjustments will be made to this charge. The extent to which such adjustments will increase or decrease the charge cannot be determined at this time.

Required

1. What entries did Bethlehem make in 1977 to account for the costs attributable to the closedown of certain steelmaking and related facilities?

2. Bethlehem's provision (credit) for taxes on income reflects the tax effects of reporting income, expense and tax credits at different times for financial accounting purposes and for income tax purposes. The deferred income taxes account was affected by the following three items in 1977:

a.) Depreciation for tax purposes was $345.6 million in 1977.

b.) $96.5 million of investment tax credit carryforwards and foreign tax credits were debited to deferred income taxes in 1977.

c.) Certain expenses associated with the reduction in capacity were not deductible for tax purposes in 1977.

Assume that Bethlehem's average (and marginal) combined Federal and state income tax rate was .508 in 1977. Bethlehem deducted what amount of expenses associated with the reduction in capacity for tax purposes in 1977? (Hint: Analyze the deferred taxes account!)

Case 5-5

Trans Union Corporation*

Trans Union is a holding company engaging primarily in full service leasing of railway tank cars, which are either built by them or to their specification by other firms. The firm also manufactures waste treatment equipment and systems, charters ocean vessels and engages in some real estate development.

During the early 1970's the management of Trans Union was concerned with the way they were required under GAAP to deal with deferred taxes.

For Trans Union, the deferred tax account rose primarily because depreciation on tank cars could be taken on an accelerated basis for tax purposes while the straight-line method was used for financial reporting. Management believed the recognition of an increased tax expense for the total effect of the difference in taxable income due to accelerated depreciation was inappropriate and so informed its stockholders in the president's letter accompanying the 1972 report. Some portions of this letter appear below with selected portions of Trans Union's financial statements.

> On page 10 we have set out the gross revenues for 1972 and have then deducted the related expenses. All of the expenses which we have deducted on this page have already been paid or will be paid in early 1973. The one exception to this statement is deferred taxes, which we have deducted in the amount of approximately $13.4 million. Unlike the other expenses, this $13.4 million will not be paid for an average of approximately 18 years! During this 18-year period we are not required to pay any interest on this amount, but we are still required to deduct it today just as though it had already been paid.
>
> It is common knowledge that a dollar due in 18 years is not worth a dollar today. Who would pay one dollar today for just the right to receive one dollar 18 years from now? The same principle applies to expenses. An obligation to pay $13.4 million in 1990 does not require us to set aside $13.4 million today. If we were to set aside only half that amount today and were to earn 4% interest on it, it would total $13.4 million in 1990.
>
> In other words, when a liability is due at some time in the future, simple logic says we should discount the amount to determine what the real liability is today. If that were done in our case, we would deduct substantially less than $13.4 million in determining our 1972 income, and our earnings per share would be materially higher.
>
> Our statement that we will pay the deferred taxes 18 years from now is quite conservative. There are well known authorities who argue cogently that the $13.4 million will really never be paid unless the Company were to liquidate its tank car fleet and go out of business, and very likely not even then. These authorities include one of the very top auditing firms and the head of one of the most prestigious graduate schools of business in the country.
>
> We have been forced to account for our deferred taxes by ignoring the 18 year delay in payment, because the Accounting Principles Board (APB) has so ruled. It is interesting to note that at one time the APB created a subcommittee of its own members to study the problem of deferred taxes. In 1966 that committee expressed a preference for

---

*This case was prepared from publicly available sources. The situation was suggested by a case written by Guillermo J. Fernandez under the supervision of Professor John K. Shank.

discounting, but the APB overruled them. The APB prohibited discounting until a further research study could be made, but they have actually done nothing on the subject in the six years since that time.

It is also pertinent to point out that the handling of deferred taxes required by the APB is directly contrary to the handling they require for pension liabilities. If an employee works for us in 1972 and thereby acquires the right to receive a pension of $1,000 in the year 1990, the APB will not permit us to deduct $1,000 in 1972 but will permit a deduction of only the discounted amount of such future payment. This is directly opposite to the treatment they require for deferred taxes, and the reason for this inconsistency has never been explained by the APB.

Signed,

J. W. VanGorkom,
President

The main question raised by management concerns the accounting for deferred taxes. The issue is covered by APB Opinion 11. The opinion considers three possible alternatives. Excerpts from selected paragraphs of APB 11 follow: Paragraph 18. "Interperiod tax allocation under the **deferred method** is a procedure whereby the tax effects of current timing differences are deferred currently and allocated to income tax expense of future periods when the timing differences reverse." Paragraph 19. "Interperiod tax allocation under the **liability method** is a procedure whereby the income taxes expected to be paid on pretax accounting are accrued currently. ...The differences between income tax expense and income taxes payable in the periods in which the timing differences originate are either liabilities for taxes payable in the future or assets for prepaid taxes." Paragraph 20. "Interperiod tax allocation under the **net of tax method** is a procedure whereby the tax effects (determined by either the deferred or liability methods) of timing differences are recognized in the valuation of assets and liabilities and the related revenues and expenses. The tax effects are applied to reduce specific assets or liabilities on the basis that tax deductibility or taxability are factors in their valuation."

In later paragraphs the Board also considers and rejects the position that "income tax expense of a period equals income taxes payable for that period."

TRANS UNION CORPORATION AND SUBSIDIARIES
Consolidated Statement of Income
For the Years Ended December 31, 1968-1972
(Dollars in Thousands)

	1972	1971	1970	1969	1968
Revenues:					
Net Sales	$135,387	$110,324	$109,053	$109,532	$ 92,564
Services	153,931	145,936	134,404	120,832	115,924
Net Income from Finance Lease Business	1,223	570	132	—	—
Net Income from 50% Owned Companies	1,202	1,483	787	688	(287)
Interest Income	1,642	1,992	1,427	850	467
Royalties and Other	1,573	1,586	877	695	737
Amortization of Investment Tax Credit	462	432	388	302	211
	$295,420	$262,322	$247,068	$232,899	$209,616
Costs and Expenses:					
Cost of sales	$102,123	$ 83,433	$ 80,676	$ 83,132	$ 71,175
Cost of services	81,492	79,282	68,422	61,954	61,318
Selling, General and Administrative Services	46,747	40,965	40,997	37,492	28,777
Interest Expense	19,693	18,026	17,372	15,067	10,868
Minority Interest in Ecodyne Corporation	335	—	—	—	—
	$250,390	$221,706	$207,467	$197,645	$172,138
Net Income Before Income Taxes	$ 45,030	$ 40,616	$ 39,601	$ 35,254	$ 37,478
Provision for Income Taxes:					
Current	$ 4,750	$ 2,418	$ 2,315	$ 2,737	$ 6,086
Deferred	13,440	13,980	13,440	10,850	9,920
Investment Tax Credit (Deferred)	890	1,172	1,995	1,973	1,834
	$ 19,080	$ 17,570	$ 17,750	$ 15,560	$ 17,840
Net Income Before Extraordinary Items	$ 25,950	$ 23,046	$ 21,851	$ 19,694	$ 19,638
Extraordinary Items, Net of Income Taxes	—	6,060	1,890	1,625	—
Net Income (Including Extraordinary Items)	$ 25,950	$ 29,106	$ 23,741	$ 21,319	$ 19,638
Per Share of Common Stock—					
Net Income Before Extraordinary Items	$2.61	$2.32	$2.20	$1.98	$1.97
Extraordinary Items	—	.61	.19	.16	—
Net Income (Including Extraordinary Items)	2.61	2.93	2.39	2.14	1.97

Required

1. Assuming discounting of deferred taxes is appropriate, estimate as best you can the impact of discounting on Trans Union's 1972 financial statements. Trans Union showed Deferred Federal Income Taxes of $132.5 million on December 31, 1972.

2. Describe how the different treatments discussed by in APB Opinion 11 paragraphs 18-20 would affect the accounts of Trans Union in general terms.

3. How do you believe the accounting for deferred taxes should be done?

Case 5-6

Mohasco Industries, Inc. (B)*

The Comparative Consolidated Balance Sheet for December 31, 1967 and 1966 published in the 1967 Annual Report of Mohasco Industries, Inc. included two related accounts:

(1) **Among the assets:** "Non-current mortgage note receivable, secured by properties in Amsterdam," $5,754,229 at December 31, 1967 and $6,325,676 at December 31, 1966.

(2) **Among "other non-current liabilities":** "Long-term rentals on Amsterdam properties," $3,106,548 at December 31, 1967 and $3,494,881 at December 31, 1966.

Note 3 accompanying the financial statements in the 1967 Annual Report reads as follows:

Mortgage Note Secured by Properties in Amsterdam:
The mortgage note receivable and interest thereon are due in equal quarterly installments of $219,282 to October 1, 1976, which sums are to be applied first to interest and the balance to principal. The properties securing the mortgage note are leased by Mohasco Industries, Inc.; the liability for rentals due over the term of the lease, net of estimated future tax effect, was provided in a prior year.

These accounts originated in 1958 when, in accordance with its policy of minimizing its investment in plant buildings and land, Mohasco sold its plant buildings situated in Amsterdam, New York. The buildings comprised approximately 2,200,000 square feet of floor space. Simultaneously, it arranged to continue its carpet manufacturing operations in those buildings under an 18-year lease.

None of the machinery and equipment in the plant was included in the sale. The Amsterdam property was sold for $10,500,000 of which $2,500,000 was in cash and the balance a Note Receivable secured by a First Mortgage. The lease called for rental payments net of related tax deductions, of $388,455 **in 1958** and $388,333 in subsequent years.

---

*This case was prepared by Professor Robert T. Sprouse of the Graduate School of Business, Stanford University, as a basis for class discussion.
The case is based on information contained in the Annual Reports of Mohasco Industries, Inc. 1958-1968 inclusive and in the Mohasco Industries, Inc. case appearing in Leonard E. Morrissey, *Contemporary Accounting Problems* (Englewood Cliffs, N.J.: Prentice-Hall, Inc. 1963) pp. 383-390.

The gain on sale was reported as a "special credit" in Mohasco's 1958 income statement and a liability for the lease obligation was established by a "special charge" in the 1958 income statement. The lease rental payment made during 1958 was charged against the liability.

Note 4 to the 1958 financial statements described the transaction as follows:

Sale and lease of Amsterdam properties:
In December 1958 certain land and buildings in Amsterdam, New York ... were sold for cash of $2,500,000 and a 5 percent purchase money mortgage receivable of $8,000,000 and thereupon these properties were leased to Mohasco Industries, Inc. The gain on this sale, $8,450,923 net of applicable state taxes and expenses (no federal income taxes payable because of tax loss carryforward) is included as a special item in the statement of income. The mortgage receivable and interest thereon are due in equal quarterly installments of $130,084 from April 1, 1959 to October 1, 1966 and $219,282 thereafter to October 1, 1976 which sums are to be applied first to interest and the balance to principal.

The liability for rentals due over the term of the lease, net of the estimated future tax effect, has been provided by a special charge in the statement of income.

Mohasco Industries, Inc. was the name adopted in 1955 when Alexander Smith, Inc. merged with Mohawk Carpet Mills, Inc. Mohasco's major business is the manufacture and sale of wool and synthetic rugs and carpets.

At December 31, 1955, the date of the merger, Mohasco acquired Alexander Smith's accumulated tax loss carryover of $33,275,000. Of this amount, $10,490,000 remained to be used in 1959 and 1960. Without benefit of such carryover, 1958 net income before special charges would have been subject to federal income taxes of approximately $2,990,000 and the gain on sale of Amsterdam properties subject to taxes of about $1,975,000. Net income reported in 1956 and 1957, not subject to federal income taxes, was $3,653,638 and $3,266,078, respectively.

In Mohasco's December 31, 1958 Balance Sheet, the mortgage note receivable is reported partly current and partly non-current. Mohasco's Income Statement for the Year ended December 31, 1958 is shown.

Condensed Balance Sheet as of December 31, 1958

ASSETS
Current Assets:

Cash	$ 4,453,630
Accounts and notes receivable, less allowance for discounts and doubtful accounts	
Trade	12,364,622
Other	759,448
Inventories of raw materials, work in process, finished goods and supplies	28,373,141
Prepared expenses and defined charges	624,241
	$46,575,082
Mortgage and other notes receivable, non-current:	
Secured by properties in Amsterdam (note 4)	$ 7,877,389
Other	3,060,797
Total Mortgage and other notes receivable non-current	$10,938,186
Investments and advances	$ 914,946
Operating property, plant and equipment (note 4)	$57,292,408
Less accumulated depreciation and amortization	24,632,574
Operating property, plant and equipment-net	$32,659,834
	$91,088,048

LIABILITIES
Current liabilities:

Long-term debt due within one year	$ 1,832,695
Accounts payable	3,969,619
Accrued expenses	3,299,221
Total current liabilities	$ 9,101,535
Long-term debt	$14,583,929
Other non-current liabilities:	
Long-term rentals on Amsterdam properties (note 4)	$ 6,601,545
Estimated liability under pension plans	1,408,980
Other liabilities and deferred credits	251,397
Total other non-current liabilities	$ 8,261,922
Shareowners' equity:	
Capital stock:	
Cumulative preferred, par value $100:	
3½ per cent series	$ 3,794,800
4.20 per cent series	4,004,000
Common, par value $5	15,334,625
Capital surplus	3,629,518
Earned surplus	32,377,719
Total shareowners' equity	$59,140,662
	$91,088,048

Income Statement For Year Ended December 31, 1958

Net sales	$89,698,979
Cost of sales	69,693,763
Gross profit on sales	$20,005,216
Selling, general and administrative expenses	13,880,938
Operating income	$ 6,124,278
Interest on borrowings	1,069,443
	$ 5,054,835
Other income — net:	
Interest and royalties	$ 1,024,181
Gain on disposal of property, plant and equipment	1,164
Other	71,660
	$ 1,097,005
Net income before special items	$ 6,151,840
Special credit-gain on sale of Amsterdam properties (Note 4)	8,450,923
	$14,602,763
Special charge — provision for long-term rentals on Amsterdam properties (Note 4)	6,990,000
Net income after special items	$ 7,612,763

Comparative Consolidated Balance Sheet

December 31, 1967 and 1966

Assets

	1967	1966
Current assets:		
Cash	$ 3,976,531	$ 4,637,527
Accounts and notes receivable, less allowance for discounts and doubtful accounts:		
Trade	25,022,554	23,178,203
Other	2,029,632	2,115,082
Inventories of raw materials, work in process, finished goods and supplies (note 2)	52,898,680	54,770,385
Prepaid expenses and deferred charges	2,999,301	2,572,710
Total current assets	86,926,698	87,273,907
Non-current mortgage note receivable, secured by properties in Amsterdam (note 3)	5,754,229	6,325,676
Investments, at cost, and other assets:		
Foreign affiliate	1,197,438	796,714
Other investments	261,478	316,478
Other assets	445,665	459,007
Total investments and other assets	1,904,581	1,572,199
Property, plant and equipment:		
Machinery and equipment	69,982,601	70,269,941
Buildings, including capitalized leases $11,759,299 ($11,434,299 in 1966)	36,096,938	35,019,958
Leasehold improvements	6,625,008	6,140,040
	112,704,547	111,429,939
Less accumulated depreciation and amortization	51,129,588	47,667,511
	61,574,959	63,762,428
Land	1,262,088	1,272,701
Construction in progress	1,329,855	1,165,199
	64,166,902	66,200,328
	$158,752,410	$161,372,110

Liabilities

Current liabilities:	1967	1966
Notes payable—short term	$ 6,952,555	$ 8,893,845
Current maturities of long-term debt (note 4)	2,746,539	1,859,289
Accounts payable	11,146,802	10,558,699
Accrued expenses	6,872,531	6,008,707
Federal and State income taxes (note 6)	2,013,533	1,254,790
Total current liabilities	29,731,960	28,575,330
Long-term debt, less current maturities:		
Twenty-year promissory note (note 4)	28,350,000	30,000,000
Other notes (note 4)	2,000,000	1,280,000
Capitalized lease obligations	8,870,476	9,346,180
Total long-term debt	39,220,476	40,626,180
Other non-current liabilities:		
Long-term rentals on Amsterdam properties (note 3)	3,106,548	3,494,881
Estimated liability under pension plans	606.396	639,281
Deferred Federal income taxes	2,883,210	2,857,070
Other liabilities	833,017	2,054,806
Total other non-current liabilities	7,429,171	9,046,038
Shareowners' equity:		
Capital stock:		
Cumulative preferred, par value $100 per share (note 5):		
3½% series, 26,058 shares (27,338 in 1966) authorized and issued, less 1,900 shares (2,640 in 1966) in treasury	2,415,800	2,469,800
4.20% series, 30,510 shares (31,605 in 1966) authorized and issued, less 4,465 shares (3,490 in 1966) in treasury	2,604,500	2,811,500
Common, par value $5 per share; authorized 5,000,000 shares; issued 3,818,605 shares (3,791,105 in 1966) (note 7)	19,093,025	18,955,525
Capital surplus	10,058,972	9,903,244
Retained earnings (note 4)	49,750,367	50,026,128
	83,922,664	84,166,197
Less common stock in treasury, at cost—100,000 shares (70,800 in 1966)	1,551,861	1,041,635
Total shareowners' equity	82,370,803	83,124,562
	$158,752,410	$161,372,110

A set of tables for 5% interest compounded quarterly is also attached for your convenience in analyzing this case.

Present Value Table—*1.25% Per Period*

Period	(1) Present Value of $1	(2) Amount to Which $1 Will Accumulate	(3) Present Value of $ per Period Paid at End of Each Period	(4) Amount to Which $1 Paid at Beginning of Each Period Will Accumulate	(5) Amount Paid at End of Each Period Which Will Repay $1 of Initial Loan
1	98765E 00	10125E 01	98765E 00	10125E 01	10125E 01
2	97546E 00	10252E 01	19631E 01	20377E 01	50939E 00
3	96342E 00	10380E 01	29265E 01	30756E 01	34170E-00
4	95152E 00	10509E 01	38781E 01	41266E 01	25786E-00
5	93978E 00	10641E 01	48178E 01	51907E 01	20756E-00
6	92817E 00	10774E 01	57460E 01	62680E 01	17403E-00
7	91672E 00	10909E 01	66627E 01	73589E 01	15009E-00
8	90540E 00	11045E 01	75681E 01	84634E 01	13213E-00
9	89422E 00	11183E 01	84623E 01	95817E 01	11817E-00
10	88318E 00	11323E 01	93455E 01	10714E 02	10700E-00
11	87228E 00	11464E 01	10218E 02	11860E 02	97868E-01
12	86151E 00	11608E 01	11079E 02	13021E 02	90258E-01
13	85087E 00	11753E 01	11930E 02	14196E 02	83821E-01
14	84037E 00	11900E 01	12771E 02	15386E 02	78305E-01
15	82999E 00	12048E 01	13601E 02	16591E 02	73526E-01
16	81975E 00	12199E 01	14420E 02	17811E 02	69347E-01
17	80963E 00	12351E 01	15230E 02	19046E 02	65660E-01
18	79963E 00	12506E 01	16030E 02	20297E 02	62385E-01
19	78976E 00	12662E 01	16819E 02	21563E 02	59455E-01
20	78001E 00	12820E 01	17599E 02	22845E 02	56820E-01
21	77038E 00	12981E 01	18370E 02	24143E 02	54437E-01
22	76087E 00	13143E 01	19131E 02	25457E 02	52272E-01
23	75147E 00	13307E 01	19882E 02	26788E 02	50297E-01
24	74220E 00	13474E 01	20624E 02	28135E 02	48487E-01
25	73303E 00	13642E 01	21357E 02	29500E 02	46822E-01
26	72398E 00	13812E 01	22081E 02	30881E 02	45287E-01
27	71505E 00	13985E 01	22796E 02	32279E 02	43867E-01
28	70622E 00	14160E 01	23503E 02	33695E 02	42549E-01
29	69750E 00	14337E 01	24200E 02	35129E 02	41322E-01
30	68889E 00	14516E 01	24889E 02	36581E 02	40179E-01
31	68038E 00	14698E 01	25569E 02	38050E 02	39109E-01
32	67198E 00	14881E 01	26241E 02	39539E 02	38108E-01
33	66369E 00	15067E 01	26905E 02	41045E 02	37168E-01
34	65549E 00	15256E 01	27560E 02	42571E 02	36284E-01
35	64740E 00	15446E 01	28208E 02	44115E 02	35451E-01
36	63941E 00	15639E 01	28847E 02	45679E 02	34665E-01
37	63152E 00	15835E 01	29479E 02	47263E 02	33923E-01
38	62372E 00	16033E 01	30102E 02	48866E 02	33220E-01
39	61602E 00	16233E 01	30719E 02	50490E 02	32554E-01
40	60841E 00	16436E 01	31327E 02	52133E 02	31921E-01
41	60090E 00	16642E 01	31928E 02	53797E 02	31321E-01
42	59348E 00	16850E 01	32521E 02	55482E 02	30749E-01
43	58616E 00	17060E 01	33107E 02	57188E 02	30205E-01
44	57892E 00	17274E 01	33686E 02	58916E 02	29686E-01
45	57177E 00	17489E 01	34258E 02	60665E 02	29190E-01
46	56471E 00	17708E 01	34823E 02	62435E 02	28717E-01
47	55774E 00	17929E 01	35381E 02	64228E 02	28264E-01
48	55086E 00	18154E 01	35931E 02	66044E 02	27831E-01
49	54406E 00	18380E 01	36476E 02	67882E 02	27416E-01
50	53734E 00	18610E 01	37013E 02	69743E 02	27018E-01
51	53071E 00	18843E 01	37544E 02	71627E 02	26636E-01
52	52415E 00	19078E 01	38068E 02	73535E 02	26269E-01
53	51768E 00	19317E 01	38585E 02	75467E 02	25917E-01
54	51129E 00	19558E 01	39097E 02	77422E 02	25578E-01
55	50498E 00	19803E 01	39602E 02	79403E 02	25251E-01
56	49874E-00	20050E 01	40100E 02	81408E 02	24937E-01
57	49259E-00	20301E 01	40593E 02	83438E 02	24635E-01
58	48651E-00	20555E 01	41080E 02	85493E 02	24343E-01
59	48050E-00	20812E 01	41560E 02	87574E 02	24062E-01
60	47457E-00	21072E 01	42035E 02	89682E 02	23790E-01

Present Value Table—*1.25% Per Period*

Period	(1) Present Value of $1	(2) Amount to Which $1 Will Accumulate	(3) Present Value of $ per Period Paid at End of Each Period	(4) Amount to Which $1 Paid at Beginning of Each Period Will Accumulate	(5) Amount Paid at End of Each Period Which Will Repay $1 of Initial Loan	1.250% per period
61	46871E-00	21335E 01	42503E 02	91815E 02	23528E-01	
62	46292E-00	21602E 01	42966E 02	93975E 02	23274E-01	
63	45721E-00	21872E 01	43423E 02	96163E 02	23029E-01	
64	45156E-00	22145E 01	43875E 02	98377E 02	22792E-01	
65	44599E-00	22422E 01	44321E 02	10062E 03	22563E-01	
66	44048E-00	22702E 01	44761E 02	10289E 03	22341E-01	
67	43504E-00	22986E 01	45197E 02	10519E 03	22126E-01	
68	42967E-00	23274E 01	45626E 02	10752E 03	21917E-01	
69	42437E-00	23564E 01	46051E 02	10987E 03	21715E-01	
70	41913E-00	23859E 01	46470E 02	11226E 03	21519E-01	
71	41395E-00	24157E 01	46884E 02	11467E 03	21329E-01	
72	40884E-00	24459E 01	47292E 02	11712E 03	21145E-01	
73	40380E-00	24765E 01	47696E 02	11960E 03	20966E-01	
74	39881E-00	25074E 01	48095E 02	12210E 03	20792E-01	
75	39389E-00	25388E 01	48489E 02	12464E 03	20623E-01	*Annually 1 1/4%*
76	38903E-00	25705E 01	48878E 02	12721E 03	20459E-01	
77	38422E-00	26027E 01	49262E 02	12982E 03	20300E-01	
78	37948E-00	26352E 01	49642E 02	13245E 03	20144E-01	
79	37479E-00	26681E 01	50016E 02	13512E 03	19993E-01	
80	37017E-00	27015E 01	50387E 02	13782E 03	19847E-01	
81	36560E-00	27353E 01	50752E 02	14056E 03	19704E-01	*Semiannually 2 1/2%*
82	36108E-00	27694E 01	51113E 02	14332E 03	19564E-01	
83	35663E-00	28041E 01	51470E 02	14613E 03	19429E-01	
84	35222E-00	28391E 01	51822E 02	14897E 03	19297E-01	
85	34787E-00	28746E 01	52170E 02	15184E 03	19168E-01	
86	34358E-00	29105E 01	52514E 02	15475E 03	19043E-01	
87	33934E-00	29469E 01	52853E 02	15770E 03	18920E-01	
88	33515E-00	29838E 01	53188E 02	16068E 03	18801E-01	*Quarterly 5%*
89	33101E-00	30210E 01	53519E 02	16370E 03	18685E-01	
90	32692E-00	30588E 01	53846E 02	16676E 03	18571E-01	
91	32289E-00	30970E 01	54169E 02	16986E 03	18461E-01	
92	31890E-00	31358E 01	54488E 02	17300E 03	18353E-01	
93	31496E-00	31750E 01	54803E 02	17617E 03	18247E-01	
94	31108E-00	32146E 01	55114E 02	17939E 03	18144E-01	
95	30724E-00	32548E 01	55421E 02	18264E 03	18044E-01	*Monthly 15%*
96	30344E-00	32955E 01	55725E 02	18594E 03	17945E-01	
97	29970E-00	33367E 01	56024E 02	18927E 03	17849E-01	
98	29600E-00	33784E 01	56320E 02	19265E 03	17756E-01	
99	29234E-00	34206E 01	56613E 02	19607E 03	17664E-01	
100	28873E-00	34634E 01	56901E 02	19954E 03	17574E-01	

Required

1. Explain how the $6,990,000 "provision for long-term rentals on Amsterdam properties" in 1958 was determined.

2. Explain the $7,877,389 reported in 1958 for the non-current mortgage note receivable secured by properties in Amsterdam.

3. Can your explanations for (1) and (2) be reconciled with the amounts reported in Mohasco's 1967 Annual Report?

4. Consider the distinction between the current and non-current classifications in relation to such long-term receivables and obligations. What alternative apportionment between the current and non-current amounts of the mortgage note receivable might Mohasco have chosen?

5. Evaluate Mohasco's financial reporting of the 1958 transaction and the resulting receivables and obligations.

6. In what way does Mohasco's 1958 income tax situation susggest a likely motive for entering into the sale and leaseback transition? Does this motive affect your evaluation of Mohasco's financial reporting of the transaction?

Case 5-7

Associated Spring Corporation

Associated Spring Corporation is the world's largest manufacturer of custom metal parts — springs and other close tolerance engineered metal components, a producer of specialty steels, and a leading distributor of fast moving, consumable repair and replacement products for industrial, heavy equipment and automotive maintenance markets. The asset sections of Associated Spring's Consolidated Balance Sheet for December 31, 1975 and 1974 are shown.

Consolidated Balance Sheets

	1975	1974
	(in thousands)	
ASSETS		
Current Assets:		
Cash	$ 3,554	$ 4,012
Certificates of deposit	10,382	1,265
Accounts receivable, less allowances (1975—$1,604,000; 1974—$1,708,000)	29,261	29,633
Inventories:		
Finished goods	17,485	22,307
Work-in-process	6,817	9,983
Raw materials and supplies	6,296	11,699
	30,598	43,989
Prepaid expenses	3,463	755
Total Current Assets	77,258	79,654
Investments and Other Assets	1,419	1,023
Property, Plant and Equipment		
Land	2,922	2,827
Buildings	22,342	20,474
Machinery and equipment	49,451	47,529
	74,715	70,830
Less accumulated depreciation	39,779	37,098
	34,936	33,732
Investments in excess of net assets of business acquired	7,759	7,901
	$121,372	$122,310

Assume that Associated Spring uses a full accrual (estimating) method of accounting for bad debt expenses for financial accounting purposes and recognized bad debt expense of $1,213,000 in 1975. However, assume that Associated Spring recognizes bad debt expense for tax purposes only when accounts are actually written off. The Corporation's effective income tax rate was 53% for 1975 and 49% for all years prior to 1975. Written off accounts usually have been outstanding at least one year.

Required

1. What would be the balance of the deferred income taxes account at December 31, 1974? Where would this account appear in Associated Spring's December 31, 1974 Consolidated Balance Sheet?

2. What would be the amount of the net timing differences between the actual income tax payable and financial income tax expense for 1975 related to the Company's accounting for bad debts?

3. What would be the balance of the deferred income taxes account at December 31, 1975?

Case 5-8

American Savings and Loan Association

The following announcement appeared in the Friday, April 14, 1978 *Wall Street Journal:*

This announcement is neither an offer to sell nor a solicitation of an offer to buy any of these securities. The offer is made only by the Offering Circular.

April 14,

$200,000,000

AMERICAN SAVINGS AND LOAN ASSOCIATION

A Wholly-Owned Subsidiary of
FIRST CHARTER FINANCIAL CORPORATION

8½% Mortgage-Backed Bonds, Series B, Due April 15, 1984

Interest Payable April 15 and October 15

Price 99.77%
Plus accrued interest from April 15, 1978

Copies of the Offering Circular may be obtained in any State only from such of the undersigned and the other several underwriters as may lawfully offer the securities in such State.

Required

1. Assume that these bonds were issued on April 30, 1978. Give the entries American Savings and Loan made in 1978 to record the issuance of these bonds, the October 15 interest payment and the year-end accrual of interest expense. American Savings and Loan has a calendar year-end. (Use straight-line amortization.)

2. Estimate the effective interest rate paid by American assuming (for this requirement only) that the bonds were issued on April 15, 1978 at 99.77%. (Estimate to the nearest thousand, e.g., 0.049%, and use half-year periods.)

Case 5-9

Louisville Gas and Electric Company

Louisville Gas and Electric Company presented the following announcement in the Thursday, October 28, 1976 *Wall Street Journal:*

This announcement is neither an offer to sell nor a solicitation of an offer to buy any of these securities. The offer is made only by the Prospectus.

NEW ISSUE

October 28, 1976

$25,000,000

Louisville Gas and Electric Company
(a Kentucky Corporation)

8½% First Mortgage Bonds, Series due November 1, 2006

Price 101.642%
plus accrued interest from November 1, 1976

Copies of the Prospectus may be obtained in any State only from such of the undersigned as may lawfully offer the securities in such State.

Loeb Rhoades & Co.   **L.F. Rothschild & Co.**

Donaldson, Lufkin & Jenrette   **Weeden & Co.**
Securities Corporation   **Incorporated**

The *Wall Street Journal* reported that on October 28, 1976 customers bought 40% of the Company's $25 million of new 8.5% first mortgage bonds priced at 101.642 to return 8.35% in 30 years. This issue was rated triple-A by Moody's and double-A by Standard and Poor's.

Assume that the Company sold the remaining 60% of these bonds on December 1, 1976 and that the Company has a December 31, 1976 year-end.

Required   What entries would be made by the Company to account for these bonds in 1976? Assume that the bonds sold on December 1, 1976 were sold at a price of 102.338% which included accrued interest.

Case 5-10

General Host Corporation

General Host Corporation is engaged in five basic lines of business; namely, food products, convenience stores, salt and agricultural products, footwear and apparel materials, and tourism. The Consolidated Statement of Income, Consolidated Balance Sheet, and portions of Notes 6 and 11 to General Host's 1974 Consolidated Financial Statements are presented.

Consolidated Statement of Income

Fiscal Years Ended December 28, 1974 and December 29, 1973

(Dollars in thousands, except per share amounts)

	1974	1973*
Revenues:		
Sales	$ 645,506	$ 629,731
Other income	2,535	2,067
	648,041	631,798
Costs and expenses:		
Cost of sales	562,444	552,716
Selling, general and administrative	63,586	56,366
Depreciation and amortization	8,036	7,566
Interest and debt expense	9,995	9,859
	644,061	626,507
Income from continuing operations before gains on extinguishment of debt and income taxes	3,980	5,291
Gains on extinguishment of debt (Note 11)	16,863	1,176
Income from continuing operations before income taxes	20,843	6,467
Provision for income taxes (Note 8)	9,429	1,869
Income from continuing operations	11,414	4,598
Discontinued operations, net of applicable income tax benefit (Notes 8 and 10)	(575)	(758)
Income before extraordinary items	10,839	3,840
Extraordinary items, net (Note 12)	6,105	1,011
Net income	$ 16,944	$ 4,851
Per share of common stock (Note 13):		
Primary:		
Income from continuing operations	$6.18	$2.14
Discontinued operations	(.31)	(.35)
Income before extraordinary items	5.87	1.79
Extraordinary items	3.30	.47
Net income	$9.17	$2.26
Fully diluted:		
Income from continuing operations	$2.93	$1.50
Discontinued operations	(.07)	(.19)
Income before extraordinary items	2.86	1.31
Extraordinary items	1.97	.56
Net income	$4.83	$1.87
Average number of common shares outstanding	1,847,028	2,147,140

Reclassified for comparative purposes.

Consolidated Balance Sheets

December 28, 1974 and December 29, 1973

(Dollars in thousands)

	1974	1973
ASSETS		
Current assets:		
Cash	$ 4,220	$ 4,805
Short-term marketable securities, at cost which approximates market	10,022	22,123
Accounts and notes receivable, less allowance for doubtful accounts of $497 and $472	28,891	31,429
Inventories (Note 2)	46,398	42,260
Prepaid expenses	1,184	1,355
Total current assets	90,715	101,972
Investments, at cost less reserve (Note 3)	3,000	3,326
Property, plant, and equipment, at cost less accumulated depreciation and amortization of $60,829 and $55,015 (Note 4)	97,827	93,152
Other assets (Note 5)	11,522	12,295
	$203,064	$210,745
LIABILITIES AND SHAREHOLDERS' EQUITY		
Current liabilities:		
Accounts payable	$ 14,753	$ 13,159
Accrued expenses	15,446	14,457
Accrued interest payable	2,446	2,458
Current portion of long-term debt (Note 6)	2,011	1,912
Total current liabilities	34,656	31,986
Long-term debt (Note 6):		
Senior	8,960	9,920
Subordinated, less original issue discount of $20,140 and $16,598	97,790	117,038
Total long-term debt	106,750	126,958
Reserves and deferred credits (Note 7)	9,067	9,112
Commitments and contingent liabilities (Notes 14, 15 and 16)		
Shareholders' equity, per accompanying statement (Note 9):		
Common stock $1.00 par value, authorized 30,000,000 shares, issued 2,055,444 and 2,624,344 shares	2,055	2,624
Common stock purchase warrants		
Capital in excess of par value	80,802	87,119
Deficit	(23,155)	(40,099)
	59,702	49,644
Less—cost of 498,500 and 475,700 shares of common stock in treasury	7,111	6,955
Total shareholders' equity	52,591	42,689
	$203,064	$210,745

Notes to Financial Statements

6—Long-Term Debt:

	Dec. 28, 1974	Dec. 29, 1973
	(In thousands)	
Senior debt:		
Note payable to bank	$ 4,000	$ 4,000
Lease purchase obligations	3,017	3,932
Other	3,684	3,900
	10,701	11,832
Less-current portion	1,741	1,912
	8,960	9,920
Subordinated debt:		
7% subordinated debentures, due February 1, 1994, less original issue discount of $16,090—1974 and $16,598—1973	61,747	62,240
11% convertible subordinated debentures, due June 15, 1988, less original issue discount of $4,050	16,280	
5% convertible subordinated debentures, due June 15, 1988	12,621	47,204
6% cumulative income subordinated debentures, due December 1, 1990	7,412	7,594
	98,060	117,038
Less-current portion	270	
	97,790	117,038
Total long-term debt	$106,750	$126,958

The 11% convertible subordinated debentures are convertible at any time into an aggregate of 1,270,613 shares of the Company's common stock at the rate of $16 per share, subject to adjustment in certain cases. The Company may, at its option, redeem the debentures in whole or in part upon payment of a premium of 3½% prior to June 15, 1975 and at reduced amounts thereafter. The effective interest rate on the 11% debentures approximates 14% after deducting original issue discount. For financial reporting purposes, the original issue discount on the 11% debentures, in the amount of $4,050,000 at December 28, 1974, is being amortized by the "interest method" over the life of the issue. The amortization was $16,000 for the period November 1 to December 28, 1974, and will increase to approximately $580,000 in 1987.

The 5% convertible subordinated debentures are convertible at any time into an aggregate of 467,444 shares of the Company's common stock at the rate of $27 per share, subject to adjustment in certain cases. The Company may, at its option, redeem the debentures in whole or in part upon payment of a premium of 3½% prior to June 15, 1975 and at reduced amounts thereafter. During 1974 the Company repurchased $700,000 principal amount of its 5% convertible subordinated debentures for approximately $338,000 cash (See Note 11).

11—Gains on Extinguishment of Debt:

Under the terms of an exchange offer which expired on October 31, 1974, the Company issued $20,330,000 principal amount of 11% convertible subordinated debentures in exchange for $33,883,000 principal amount of its outstanding 5% convertible subordinated debentures. As a result, the Company realized a gain for financial reporting purposes of $16,112,000 after giving effect to original issue discount of $4,066,000 on the 11% debentures.

156 Cases in Financial Accounting

Required

1. Assume that unamortized debt expense on the 5% convertible debentures exchanged for 11% convertible debentures amounted to $846,000 on October 31, 1974 and that cash expenses of $661,000 were incurred in the exchange. What entry did General Host make on October 31, 1974 to record the exchange of 11% for 5% convertible subordinated debentures?

2. What entry did General Host make on December 31, 1974 to accrue interest on the 11% convertible subordinated debentures?

3. Harris J. Ashton, Chairman and President of General Host, described the exchange offer as follows in his letter to shareholders:

> On October 31, 1974 the Company successfully concluded an exchange offer for its 5% convertible debentures with 73% of the issue having been tendered. As a result, total indebtedness was reduced by $13,553,000, the Company's debt to equity ratio was substantially reduced, and book value per share significantly increased. We are quite pleased with the success of the offer as it should improve the Company's ability to obtain future financing on reasonable terms and increase the probability that the Company's convertible debentures will ultimately be converted into common stock.

Forbes (July 1, 1975: page 51) described the exchange offer as follows:

> The first few lines of General Host's 1974 income statement sing a mournful song: Pretax income from continuing operations was down 25%, to $4 million. Ah, but General Host's bottom line hums a different tune: Net income for 1974 was up — up 300%! — to a record $9.17 per share.
>
> How do you produce higher profits out of lower profits? It's one of the marvels of modern bookkeeping. In this case a nice little gimmick called "gains on extinguishment of debt.". . it's a lot easier way to make money than selling meat and tourism.

Evaluate General Host's accounting for the gain on the extinguishment of debt. Do you think that General Host should have been required to amortize this gain over the life of the debt? Why or why not?

4. Deferred Income Taxes: General Host uses the "interest method" (present value method) to amortize original issue discount for financial reporting purposes and the "straight-line method" to amortize original issue discount for federal income tax purposes (163.5 months).

Assume that none of the 11% convertible subordinated debentures were converted or repurchased in 1975. In addition, assume (a) that earnings and taxable income before interest on the 11% convertible subordinated debentures is $6,000,000 in 1975, (b) that there are no other "timing differences" between reported earnings and taxable income, (c) that there are no net operating tax loss carryforwards available and (d) that General Host's effective income tax rate was 40% in 1975.

What entry did General Host make on December 31, 1975 to record the provision for income taxes?

Case 5-11 Allegheny Airlines

The following announcement was presented in the Wednesday, November 3, 1976 *Wall Street Journal*.

Notice of Extension of Exchange Offer by

ALLEGHENY AIRLINES, INC.

To Holders of Its

6% Senior Subordinated Notes due 1986;

6% Senior Subordinated Debentures due 1983;

5½% Subordinated Debentures due 1987;

5¾% Convertible Subordinated Debentures due 1993;

and

6% Convertible Subordinated Debentures due 1993

Allegheny Airlines, Inc. ("Allegheny"), has extended until 5:00 P.M., New York time, on November 18, 1976, its offer to exchange upon the terms and conditions set forth in the Prospectus dated October 8, 1976, as supplemented as of October 29, 1976 ("Prospectus"), and related Letter of Transmittal, $750, $725, $700, $725 and $725 principal amount of its 9¼% Convertible Subordinated Debentures due 1999 ("New Debentures") for each $1,000 principal amount of its 6% Senior Subordinated Notes due 1986, 6% Senior Subordinated Debentures due 1983, 5½% Subordinated Debentures due 1987, 5¾% Convertible Subordinated Debentures due 1993 and 6% Convertible Subordinated Debentures due 1993 (collectively, "Old Debt"), respectively. Each $1,000 principal amount of New Debentures is convertible into 160 shares of Common Stock of Allegheny.

The Exchange Offer, as Extended, Will Terminate at 5:00 P.M., New York Time, on November 18, 1976, Unless Further Extended.

Allegheny will accept all Old Debt validly tendered. All tenders of Old Debt will be irrevocable.

Allegheny will pay to any securities dealer who has executed a Soliciting Dealer Agreement and who is a member in good standing of the National Association of Securities Dealers, Inc. ("NASD"), or a foreign dealer not eligible for membership in the NASD who agrees to conform to the Rules of Fair Practice of the NASD ("Soliciting Dealer"), a fee of $7.50 for each $1,000 principal amount of Old Debt validly tendered and accepted by Allegheny pursuant to the Exchange Offer, through such Soliciting Dealer's efforts and accompanied by a Letter of Transmittal in which the name of such Soliciting Dealer has been inserted with the approval of the holder of such Old Debt. There is no maximum amount of fees which may be payable to a Soliciting Dealer.

The Exchange Offer is not being made, nor will tenders be accepted from holders of Old Debt, in any jurisdiction where the making or acceptance thereof would not be in compliance with the securities or blue sky laws of such jurisdiction.

The Prospectus and Letter of Transmittal contain important information which should be read before tenders are made. Copies of the Prospectus and the Letter of Transmittal have been mailed to all holders of record of Old Debt. Additional copies may be obtained from Kuhn, Loeb & Co. or Georgeson & Co. Any questions concerning the Exchange Offer should be directed to Kuhn, Loeb & Co. (telephone collect 212-797-4256).

Excerpts from Allegheny's December 31, 1975 Balance Sheet and Notes to Financial Statements are presented.

Liabilities and Stockholders' Equity	1975	1974
	(in thousands of dollars)	
Long-Term Debt, Net of Current Maturities (note 3)	172,738	147,698
Less unamortized discount (note 1)	2,023	2,334
	170,715	145,364

(3) Long-Term Debt, Net of Current Maturities

	December 31, 1975	1974
Restated Credit Agreement:	(in thousands of dollars)	
Series A Insurance Company Notes maturing in quarterly installments of $1,000,000 each through April, 1977	$ 2,000	$ 6,000
Series D Bank Notes maturing in quarterly installments of $397,000 each through October, 1977	1,588	3,176
Series E Bank Notes maturing in quarterly installments of varying amounts through February, 1980	11,350	16,900
Series F BAC Equipment Notes maturing in quarterly installments of varying amounts through November, 1980	11,694	13,694
Series G Insurance Company Notes maturing in quarterly installments of increasing amounts from February 1976 to November, 1980	10,385	10,835
MDC Subordinated Notes maturing in quarterly installments of $1,178,000 each from Dec., 1982 to Sept., 1986	18,850	—
Revolving Credit Bank Notes maturing in quarterly installments of varying amounts from Sept., 1978 to Sept., 1982	48,000	27,500
Total Restated Credit Agreement	103,867	78,105
6% Senior Subordinated Notes maturing in equal annual installments from April, 1977 through April, 1986	13,500	13,500
5½% Subordinated Debentures due April, 1987	24,742	24,742
6% Senior Subordinated Debentures due December, 1983	2,506	2,506
5¾% Convertible Subordinated Debentures due October, 1993	14,993	14,993
6% Convertible Subordinated Debentures due January, 1993	2,525	2,525
6½% Convertible Subordinated Debentures due November, 1979	360	360
BAC 1-11 Equipment Obligations maturing in increasing monthly installments through 1981	7,945	10,967
Other Equipment Obligations maturing in various amounts through 1980	2,049	—
Other	251	—
	$172,738	$147,698

The Subordinated Notes bear interest, payable quarterly, on the unpaid amount of each installment at a rate per annum equal to 125% of the sum of the Prime Rate plus 1% until such time as they are reclassified as Senior Debt. Upon reclassification as Senior Debt, they will bear interest on the unpaid amount of each installment at a rate per annum equal to 111% of the sum of the Prime Rate plus ¾ of 1%.

The 5½% Subordinated Debentures were issued under an Indenture dated April 1, 1967. The Indenture provides that on March 31 of each of the years 1978 through 1986, the Company will provide a sinking fund sufficient to redeem 8% of the principal amount of the debentures outstanding on January 1, 1978.

With respect to the 6% Senior Subordinated Debentures due December 31, 1983, the Company will be required to provide an annual sinking fund sufficient to retire $500,000 principal amount of the debentures commencing in the year 1980.

The 5¾% Convertible Subordinated Debentures were issued under an Indenture dated October 1, 1968. Each $1,000 debenture is convertible into 43.173 shares of common stock until October 1, 1993. Prior to October 1 of each year, commencing in the year 1980, the Company will be required to provide an annual sinking fund sufficient to retire $750,000 principal amount of debentures.

The 6% Convertible Subordinated Debentures are convertible into 18.099 shares of common stock and 12.1 1979 Stock Purchase Warrants and the 6½% Convertible Subordinated Debentures are convertible into 69.493 shares of common stock for each $1,000 debenture.

Required Discuss the impact of the extension and exchange offer if it is accepted.

Case 5-12   Fairchild Industries, Inc.

Fairchild Industries, Inc. is a technologically oriented company with principal business interests in aerospace, communications and commercial/industrial products. The company was founded by Sherman Mills Fairchild, the son of one of the founders of IBM, who invented an automatic aerial camera and then developed the world's first successful enclosed-cabin monoplane—the FC-1—in which to use it. The aerial photography activity evolved into Fairchild Camera and the aviation activities evolved into Fairchild Industries which now includes the Merlin and Metro turbo-prop aircraft at Swearingen Aviation Corporation, the U.S. Airforce A-10 close support aircraft and Boeing 747 wing control surfaces at Fairchild Republic Company and airline seating at Fairchild Burns.

At December 31, 1977, Fairchild Industries included the following long-term debt in its Consolidated Balance Sheet:

Consolidated Balance Sheet

	December 31	
	1977	1976
	(in thousands)	
4⅜% Convertible Subordinated Debentures due April 1, 1992...	$25,552	$25,552
Loan Agreement dated January 10, 1972, less current maturities of $1,000,000 and $750,000.....................	3,250	4,250
Non-interest bearing notes issued by Swearingen Aviation Corporation, less unamortized imputed interest of $474,000 and $639,000 and less current maturities of $572,000 and $800,000..................................	1,294	1,649
Mortgage notes payable, less current maturities of $34,871 and $37,963..	9	44
	$30,105	$31,495

On January 12, 1978, Fairchild Industries offered to exchange $875 principal amount of 9¾% nonconvertible subordinated debentures due 1992 for each $1,000 principal amount of 4⅜% convertible subordinated debentures due 1992. The exchange offer expired on February 23, 1978, at which time $18,394,000 principal amount of 4⅜% convertible subordinated debentures had been tendered for exchange. Assume that the exchange took place on April 1, 1978 when the effective market rate of interest was 10.5%. Also, assume that Fairchild Industries has a .46 tax rate.

Required

1. What entries did Fairchild Industries make in 1978 to account for the 9¾% debentures?

2. Was the exchange economically favorable for Fairchild Industries? Support your answer with an analysis of economic effects.

Case 5-13

Pan American World Airways

Note 6 to Pan American World Airways, Inc.'s December 31, 1977 and 1976 Consolidated Financial Statements is presented.

6. Notes Payable and Long-Term Debt

	1977	1976
	(in thousands)	
Institutional loan agreements, payable in installments through 1990 at interest rates from 4.37% to 6.50%...	$293,424	$333,222
Secured Loan Agreement	21,214	
Secured Equipment Certificates	53,000	
Other notes payable		319
Convertible subordinated debentures:		
4⅞%, due 1979	4,130	4,130
4½%, due 1984	16,795	16,795
4½%, due 1986	50,236	50,236
5¼%, due 1988	27,844	30,000
5¼%, due 1989	39,910	39,910
9⅞%, due 1996 (less discount, 1977—$2,767; 1976—$2,815)	57,666	57,618
7½%, due 1998	72,633	72,633
11%, due 1999 (less discount, 1977—$969; 1976—$980)	73,328	73,317
10½%, due 2001	75,000	75,000
	785,180	753,180
Less—due within one year	29,629	25,875
Long-term debt	$755,551	$727,305

Sinking fund requirements and debt maturities for the next five years are (in thousands):

1978	$29,629
1979	35,322
1980	32,006
1981	32,182
1982	32,381

Part A: Secured Equipment Certificates

In April 1977, Pan Am issued $26,500,000 principal amount of 11½% Secured Equipment Certificates due May 15, 1994, Series A, and $26,500,000 principal amount of 11½% Secured Equipment Certificates due May 15, 1994, Series B. The net proceeds from the sale are used to finance a portion of the purchase price of two B-747SP aircraft scheduled for delivery in 1978. Pending delivery of the aircraft, scheduled for June and July of 1978, the proceeds from the sale have been deposited with and are held by the Indenture Trustee as security for the related series of Equipment Certificates.

In its Summary of Significant Accounting Policies, Pan Am states:

Capitalized Interest—Interest related to funds for major project expenditures is capitalized to reflect the appropriate cost of investment of property and equipment and the related charges to income. Interest is capitalized at the average rate currently experienced on the Company's long-term debt and is amortized over the useful lives of the related facilities and equipment.

Required

1. Do you agree with this policy? Support your position.

2. How does this situation differ from the inclusion in net income of interest charges on debt used to acquire property, plant and equipment?

Part B: Debenture Exchange

In 1976, Pan Am issued $60,558,750 principal amount of 9⅞% Convertible Subordinated Debentures, due August 1, 1996 (fair value at time of issuance of $57,725,400) and $74,299,500 principal amount of 11% Convertible Subordinated Debentures, due February 15, 1999 (fair value at time of issuance of $73,314,700) in exchange for $115,350,000 principal amount of its debentures due 1986 and $135,090,000 principal amount of its debentures due 1989, respectively. The unamortized debt issuance expense related to the principal amount of the debentures due in 1986 and 1989 was $1,885,500.

Required

1. Assume the debenture exchange occurred on July 1, 1976. What entry did Pan Am make on this date to record this exchange?

2. By what amount was interest expense increased or decreased in 1976 because of this debenture exchange?

Case 5-14 — Mobil Corporation

On July 1, 1976, Mobil Oil Corporation merged with Marcor, Inc. (the parent company of Montgomery Ward Corporation and Container Corporation of America) to form Mobil Corporation, a holding company. As part of the merger agreement, Marcor shareholders received 3,577,970 shares of Mobil Corporation Common Stock (par value, $7.50; market value, $59.19) and $673 million principal amount of Mobil Corporation's 8½% Debentures Due 2001 (market value of $642,914,000 to yield 8.95%).

Required

1. What entry did Mobil Corporation make on July 1, 1976 to record the investment in Marcor, Inc.?

2. What entry did Mobil Corporation make on December 31, 1976 (the Company's year end) to accrue interest on the 8½% Debentures? Assume that the Company used the interest method to account for these debentures.

3. Assume that Mobil Corporation's tax rate was 48% in 1976 and that the Company used the straight-line method to account for these debentures for tax purposes. What entry did Mobil Corporation make on December 31, 1976 to record the timing differences associated with these denbentures?

Section Six

Stockholders' Equity

Case 6-1   Bic Pen Corporation

The December 31, 1970 Consolidated Balance Sheet of Bic Pen Corporation included the following:

Stockholders' equity:	
Preferred Shares	$ 2,000,000
Common Shares	10,316,000
Capital Surplus	
Retained Earnings	6,035,000
	$18,351,000

The Notes to the 1970, 1971 and 1972 Consolidated Financial Statements of Bic Pen Corporation included the following selected paragraphs:

At December 31, 1970, the Preferred Shares consisted of 20,000 shares of $100 par value outstanding and the Common Shares consisted of 800,000 shares of no par value outstanding. The Preferred Share cumulative annual dividend rate was 5%. The dividend requirements unpaid on the Preferred Shares at December 31, 1970 totaled $17,000 and were paid in April 1971.

On April 29, 1971, the Corporation affected a recapitalization whereby it issued 2,910,000 Common Shares, $1 par value, in exchange for all prior Common and Preferred Shares then outstanding...

On April 30, 1971, the Corporation issued 90,000 Common Shares, $1 par value, in exchange for trademarks to be issued in Canada and Japan.

On June 16, 1971, the Corporation issued 30,000 Common Shares, $1 par value, to certain officers as restricted Share bonuses at a price of $1 per share... In connection with such Shares, $720,000, equivalent to the excess of the initial public offering price of the Shares over the aggregate sales price to the officers, was accounted for as deferred compensation with a credit to capital surplus.

The Corporation declared and paid the following cash dividends on Common Shares in 1971:

Prior to recapitalization: In April 1971 . . . an aggregate of $520,000.

Subsequent to recapitalization: In July and September 1971 . . . an aggregate of $757,000.

The Corporation also paid in April 1971, the dividend requirements on Preferred Shares through the date of recapitalization, which amounted to $42,000.

In June 1972, the Certificate of Incorporation was amended to increase the total number of Common Shares (authorized) from 4,000,000 to 10,000,000 shares.

On July 27, 1972, 210,000 Common Shares were issued in exchange for certain trademarks in Mexico and Panama, totaling $5,250,000 . . .

On July 27, 1972, the Corporation declared a 2-for-1 Share split in the form of a 100% Share Dividend of 3,240,000 Shares, $1 par value, distributable on September 7, 1972.

In 1972, the Corporation declared and paid cash dividends . . . totaling $1,603,000 . . .

Bic Pen Corporation's Consolidated Statement of Income for the years ended December 31, 1972 and 1971 is presented.

	1972	1971
	(Thousands)	
NET SALES	$47,571	$39,455
COST OF GOODS SOLD	19,892	16,376
GROSS PROFIT	27,679	23,079
SELLING, ADVERTISING AND GENERAL AND ADMINISTRATIVE EXPENSES	15,248	11,655
PROFIT FROM OPERATIONS	12,431	11,424
OTHER INCOME	269	247
Total	12,700	11,671
OTHER DEDUCTIONS	196-	504
INCOME BEFORE INCOME TAXES	12,504	11,167
PROVISION FOR INCOME TAXES	6,240	5,621
NET INCOME	$ 6,264	$ 5,546
EARNINGS PER SHARE	$1.00	$.92

Required

1. Prepare journal entries to record the above transactions and events.

2. Show how Bic Pen Corporation's stockholders' equity section would appear on December 31, 1971 and 1972.

Case 6-2   Cannon Mills

Cannon Mills manufactures and sells textile household products such as towels, sheets, pillowcases and bedspreads, knitted fabrics, sheeting fabrics, tufted and other decorative fabrics and yarn. Cannon Mills' December 31, 1972 Consolidated Balance Sheet included the following stockholders' equity section:

Consolidated Balance Sheets

Stockholders' Equity:	
Common capital stock:	
Voting, without par value (authorized, 1,100,000 shares: issued, 1,037,190 shares) — at stated value of $25 a share	$ 25,929,750
Class B, non-voting, par value $25 a share (authorized, 3,300,000 shares; issued, 1,037,009 shares)	25,925,225
Total common capital stock	$ 51,854,975
Additional capital	2,634,000
Retained earnings ($15,426,955 applied to purchase of treasury stock)	207,605,620
	$262,094,595
Less cost of treasury stock (voting — 45,600 shares; Class B — 169,846 shares)	15,426,955
	$246,667,640

Note 2 to the 1973 Consolidated Financial Statements of Cannon Mills is presented.

Recapitalization:

Effective May 25, 1973, the Company amended its Certificate of Incorporation to (1) change the value of the no par value (stated value of $25 per share) common voting stock (1,037,190 shares issued at December 31, 1972) to $5 par value common voting stock, (2) convert the previously authorized $25 par value Class B, common non-voting stock (1,037,009 shares at December 31, 1972) to $5 par value common voting stock, and (3) change the number of authorized shares from 1,100,000 shares of no par value common stock to 11,000,000 shares of $5 par value voting stock.

The Company then effected a 5-for-1 stock split for each share of the no par value common voting stock and the $25 par value Class B, common non-voting stock outstanding at the close of business on May 25, 1973.

As part of the recapitalization plan, the Company retired 45,600 shares of the no par value common voting stock and 169,846 shares of the $25 par value Class B, common non-voting stock held in its treasury at December 31, 1972, at a cost of $15,426,955. The excess ($10,041,746) of the cost of the treasury stock over its stated value or par value and the cost of fractional shares ($941), acquired in connection with the recapitalization has been deducted from Additional Capital ($1,176,765) and Retained Earnings ($8,864,981).

Required

1. What entries did Cannon Mills make on May 25, 1973 to record the recapitalization described in Note 2 above?

2. Show how Cannon Mills' stockholders' equity section would appear on December 31, 1973. During 1973 Cannon Mills reported earnings of $10,578,184 and declared a cash dividend of $8,029,769.

Case 6-3 American Consumer Industries, Inc.

American Consumer Industries is principally engaged in the operation of public refrigerated and dry warehouses and, to a lesser extent, in the production of block and cube ice for commercial and retail customers and in the processing and sale of eggs and egg products. The following stockholders' equity section was included in the Company's 1972 Consolidated Balance Sheet:

STOCKHOLDERS' EQUITY
Common stock, stated value $5 per share:
  Authorized 1,000,000 shares
   Issued 767,404 shares .... $ 3,837,020
  Additional paid-in capital 4,872,035
  Retained earnings 4,077,995
                                                      $12,787,050
Less common stock in treasury — at
  cost 87,153 shares 1,017,058
                                                      $11,769,992

Required

1. Give the journal entries necessary to record the following events:

   a.) In January 1973, the Company issued 29,139 shares of common stock in connection with a 4% stock dividend. The Company paid out cash of $8,188 in lieu of fractional shares. The fair market value of the stock was $13 per share during the first quarter of 1973.

   b.) On January 31, 1973, the Company purchased the net assets of International Freezers, Inc. (fair market value $187,000) in exchange for 17,000 shares of common stock held in treasury (cost $233,354).

   c.) On August 31, 1973, the Company purchased the capital stock of Quick Serve, Inc. in exchange for 58,320 shares of unissued common stock (fair market value $6.61 per share).

   d.) In 1973, the Company issued 1,950 shares of common stock held in the treasury (cost $26,767) in connection with the Company's (qualified) stock option plan. The exercise price was $9.00 per share. The Company's qualified stock option plan terminated on September 28, 1973 and all outstanding options expired.

   e.) In 1973, the Company purchased 3,179 shares of common stock to be held as treasury stock for $47,429.

   f.) Earnings for the year ended December 31, 1973 totaled $608,786.

2. Show how American Consumer Industries' stockholders' equity section appeared on December 31, 1973.

Case 6-4   Xonics, Inc.

Xonics, Inc.'s business generally consists of developing and selling commercially marketable technology products, applying such technology to the development of other products for which the company believes there exists a significant market, conducting research, engineering, technical and computer-oriented services for the United States government as well as others, and manufacturing and selling X-ray equipment. At March 31, 1973, Xonics' stockholders' equity section was as follows:

Common stock, $.10 par value, 10,000,000 shares authorized; shares issued: 1,143,020	$ 114,302
Additional Paid-in Capital	4,938,976
Retained Earnings	881,507
	$5,934,785
Less note receivable from stockholder and shares issued under deferred noncompete agreement	238,825
	$5,695,960

In October 1974 the Financial Accounting Standards Board issued Statement of Financial Accounting Standards No. 2 ("FAS 2") entitled "Accounting for Research and Development Costs." FAS 2 requires that "all research and development costs encompassed by (the) Statement shall be charged to expense when incurred," that such accounting "shall be applied retroactively by prior period adjustment" of the fiscal periods in which the research and development costs were incurred and that "financial statements of periods before the effective date...shall be restated to reflect the prior period adjustment."

The provisions of FAS 2 require that certain of the XERG technology and systems costs, Telepost systems costs and Acoustic sensing systems costs be charged to expense as incurred rather than deferred, as had been the previous accounting policy adopted by the Company. The effect of the FAS 2 adjustment was to reduce retained earnings by $2,186,466 at March 31, 1973 . . .

In 1973, Xonics issued 570,350 shares in connection with a three-for-two stock split. Xonics retained the $.10 par value and incurred processing costs of $6,145 in connection with the stock split.

Xonics acquired, as of October 1973, 80% of the outstanding stock of Telecommunications Industries, Inc. in exchange for 4,500 shares of the Company's common stock (valued at $47,000). The owner of the remaining 20% of Telecommunications stock has the right for an approximate five-year period ending in 1978 to exchange his 20% interest for up to 37,500 shares of Xonics' common stock contingent on an earnings formula.

As of April 1, 1973, Xonics acquired, in a transaction accounted for as a purchase, all the outstanding stock of Medical Equipment Manufacturing Company, Inc., a producer of special X-ray apparatus, in exchange for 18,000 shares of the Company's common stock. In addition, the Company may issue up to an additional 60,000 shares contingent upon cumulative earnings of Medical, as defined, during the period April 1, 1973 to March 31, 1976. Total consideration for the purchase aggregated $126,000, the value assigned to the 18,000 shares of the Company's restricted common stock issued in connection with the acquisition.

Effective March 31, 1974, the stock of two former subsidiaries, Telcom Engineering, Inc. and Telcom Construction Corporation, was sold to a group of former employees and officers of the subsidiaries for a consideration of 16,190 shares of the Company's common stock held by the purchasing group. These shares were valued at the combined net book value of the two subsidiaries ($50,826) and were retired.

In 1973, Xonics received $96,446 upon the exercise of warrants for 21,710 shares of common stock and $63,446 upon the exercise of employee stock options for 8,850 shares of common stock.

Xonics received $11,250 on account for the stockholder receivable. In addition, an employee was removed from the noncompete trust agreement. The 1,370 shares of common stock held in escrow for this employee were retired and the related cost of these shares ($23,175) was removed from the deferred noncompete agreement account.

$4,086 of the cost of the deferred noncompete agreement was amortized to profit and loss in 1973. Xonics reported a net loss of $618,507 in 1973.

In 1974, Xonics issued 192,500 shares of common stock for cash of $2,860,981. In addition, Xonics received $2,100 upon the exercise of warrants for 450 shares of common stock; $43,980 upon the exercise of employee stock options for 8,610 shares of common stock; and $12,800 for the issuance of 1,600 shares of common stock under an agreement with the employees.

Xonics received $11,250 on account for the stockholder receivable and amortized $37,481 of the cost of the deferred noncompete agreement to profit and loss in 1974. Xonics reported net income of $1,296,558 in 1974.

Required Determine the amounts that should be shown in Xonics' stockholders' equity section at March 31, 1975.

Case 6-5   Owens-Illinois, Inc. (B)

Owens-Illinois, Inc. is one of the world's leading and most diversified manufacturers of packaging products. The following shareholders' equity section was included in Owens-Illinois, Inc.'s December 31, 1975 Consolidated Balance Sheet:

Shareholders' Equity

4% preferred shares, $100 par value, 4% cumulative: 481,953 shares authorized; 141,985 shares issued and outstanding	$ 14,198,000
$4.75 convertible preference shares, $20 stated value, entitled to $100 in involuntary liquidation: 743,766 shares authorized; 663,942 shares issued and outstanding	13,279,000
Common shares, $3.125 par value: 30,000,000 authorized; 13,905,525 shares issued and outstanding	43,455,000
Capital in excess of stated value	71,599,000
Retained earnings	705,493,000
	$848,024,000

Required   Give the journal entries necessary to record the following events:

1. The Company purchased and retired 7,858 shares of the 4% preferred shares for $.649 million.

2. 6,884 shares of the $4.75 convertible preference shares were converted into 10,309 common shares.

3. $232,000 principal amount of 4½% convertible subordinated debentures and $3,000 principal amount of 5% guaranteed convertible debentures were converted into 3,964 common shares.

4. At the annual meeting of shareholders of the Company in April 1976, authorized common shares were increased from 30,000,000 to 45,000,000.

5. The Company sold 1,400,000 common shares through an offer to the general public for $77.492 million.

6. The Company acquired and cancelled 1,362,240 of its common shares in exchange for 1,226,016 shares of Owens-Corning Fiberglass Corporation common stock which the Company carried as an investment. The Owens-Corning Fiberglass stock was carried at a cost of $.712 million and had a fair market value of $72.638 million. The expenses incurred because of the exchange offer amounted to $.757 million.

7. The Company contributed 47,100 common shares having an average market value of $56.80 per share to the Owens-Illinois Stock Purchase and Savings Plan in lieu of cash.

8. The Company issued 135,315 common shares under stock option plans for an average exercise price of $45.88 per share.

9. The Board of Directors of the Company declared a two-for-one stock split of common shares to be effected by a distribution of a 100% share dividend. The $3.125 par value was retained.

Case 6-6

J.P. Stevens & Co., Inc.*

J. P. Stevens & Co., Inc. manufactures and sells cotton, synthetic, woolen and worsted fabrics, carpets, hosiery and elastic products. The Company has more than 19,000 stockholders; its capital stock is listed on the New York Stock Exchange. The price ranges per share of stock during each year 1965-68, were:

1968	67 -52
1967	57⅞-39¾
1966	80½-37¼
1965	75⅝-42¼

On March 30, 1965, J. P. Stevens & Co., Inc. made a public offering of $30,000,000 4% Convertible Subordinated 25-year Debentures due April 1, 1990. The debentures are convertible at the rate of 17.72 shares of capital stock for each $1,000 principal amount — that is, equivalent, at the principal amount, to a conversion price of $56.43 per share. The offering was made through a group of underwriters headed by Goldman, Sachs & Co. at a price of 101 or an effective interest rate of 3.96%. The issue found a ready market and trading began May 3 on the New York Stock Exchange. The proceeds were used to reduce short term indebtedness.

J. P. Stevens' Comparative Consolidated Balance Sheet as of October 30, 1965 and October 31, 1964 together with a footnote explaining the accounting procedures adopted by the Company for the 4% Convertible Subordinated Debentures, are shown.

---

*This case was prepared by Professor Robert T. Sprouse of the Graduate School of Business, Stanford University, as a basis for class discussion.

Consolidated Balance Sheets

ASSETS

	1965	1964
Current Assets:		
Cash	$ 11,340,730	$ 16,340,215
U.S. Government securities, at cost which approximates market	9,990,279	
Receivables:		
Trade	145,577,315	131,671,879
Other	11,033,708	8,013,857
	156,611,023	139,685,736
Less: Allowance for doubtful accounts	1,961,595	2,107,879
	154,649,428	137,577,857
Inventories, at the lower of cost (partly LIFO) or market—Note A	167,294,328	163,045,320
Total Current Assets	343,274,765	316,963,392
Investments, at cost or less—Note B	1,650,323	8,396,946
Miscellaneous Receivables and Other Assets	1,897,458	2,313,297
Fixed Assets, at cost:		
Land	2,195,755	2,060,386
Buildings, machinery and equipment	338,055,718	319,797,507
	340,251,473	321,857,893
Less: Accumulated depreciation	198,703,419	183,619,129
	141,548,054	138,238,764
Deferred Charges, including unamortized debt discount of $4,099,846 in 1965—Note C	7,268,030	3,212,208
	$495,638,630	$469,124,607

LIABILITIES AND SHAREOWNERS' EQUITY

	1965	1964
Current Liabilities:		
Notes payable—banks		$ 16,000,000
Current installments of long term debt	$ 4,990,632	5,264,345
Accounts payable—trade	39,437,317	36,913,446
Accrued and other liabilities	27,481,161	27,111,450
Federal income and other taxes, less U.S. Government securities of $15,806,349 in 1965	7,978,121	16,132,114
Total Current Liabilities	79,887,231	101,421,355
Long Term Debt—Note C	120,984,847	96,085,098
Other Noncurrent Liabilities	2,784,951	2,027,741
Deferred Credits—Note C	4,816,180	568,303
Shareowners' Equity—Notes C and D:		
Capital stock—par value $15 a share:		
Shares Authorized 6,500,000		
Issued 5,397,853	80,967,795	80,967,795
Capital in excess of par value	59,560,874	59,771,563
Accumulated earnings	152,513,607	132,245,920
	293,042,276	272,985,278
Less: Cost of capital stock held in treasury, 169,485 shares in 1965 and 136,091 shares in 1964	5,876,855	3,963,168
Total Shareowners' Equity	287,165,421	269,022,110
	$495,638,630	$469,124,607

Note C—Long Term Debt:

Long term debt as at October 30, 1965, exclusive of amounts due currently, consists of the following:

2¾% Promissory notes, requiring prepayments of $1,200,000 annually to 1975, and a payment of $2,400,000 in 1976	$ 13,200,000
4½% Promissory notes, requiring prepayments of $1,000,000 annually to 1977, and $2,400,000 annually from 1978 to 1981, the remaining unpaid balance becoming due in 1982	23,000,000
5¼% Promissory note, requiring prepayments of $1,000,000 annually to 1982, and $2,250,000 annually from 1983 to 1985, the remaining unpaid balance becoming due in 1986	25,000,000
4⅞% Promissory note, requiring prepayments of $1,250,000 annually from 1969 to 1987, the remaining unpaid balance becoming due in 1988	25,000,000
4% Convertible subordinated debentures due April 1, 1990, requiring sinking fund payments annually from 1976 to 1989 in amounts from 6⅔% to 13⅓% of principal amount outstanding on March 31, 1975	30,000,000
Other notes	4,784,847
	$120,984,847

In connection with the issue of the 4% convertible subordinated debentures in April, 1965, $4,200,000 was recorded as debt discount and $4,426,960, an amount deemed assignable to the convertibility feature of the debentures, was included among deferred credits. Such debt discount will be amortized by annual charges to income over the term of the outstanding debentures; however, unamortized discount applicable to debentures converted will be charged against the related deferred credit account and capital in excess of par value will be credited with a ratable portion of the remaining deferred credit balance applicable to capital stock issued upon exercise of the conversion privilege. The Company has reserved 531,600 shares of capital stock for conversion purposes.

The promissory notes and the indenture relating to the debentures include various restrictions which, among other matters, have the effect of limiting, by application of a formula, the Company's future payments of dividends (other than stock dividends) and future purchases of its capital stock. As at October 30, 1965, such payments and purchases were limited to approximately $43,000,000.

October 29, 1966 Annual Report

In its Annual Report for the 52 weeks ending October 29, 1966, J. P. Stevens' Comparative Consolidated Balance Sheet included long term debt in the amount of $113,996,472 of which $27,678,000 was represented by the 4% Convertible Subordinated Debentures due April 1, 1990. A footnote reported:

> During the year debentures amounting to $2,322,000 were converted into 41,130 shares of capital stock. These conversions resulted in additions totaling $1,704,648 to capital in excess of par value. As at October 29, 1966, 490,470 shares of capital stock were reserved for conversion purposes.

As a result of these conversions and the annual amortization, the unamortized debt discount included among the "Deferred Charges" in the October 29, 1966 Consolidated Balance Sheet was reduced to $3,628,526.

October 29, 1967 Annual Report

No further conversion took place during the 52 weeks ending October 28, 1967, but certain changes were made in accounting for the 4% Convertible Subordinated Debentures as explained in the following footnote to the Consolidated Balance Sheet:

> In compliance with an opinion of the Accounting Principles Board of the American Institute of Certified Public Accountants issued in December 1966, the amount of $4,084,303 deemed assignable to the convertibility feature of the outstanding debentures, previously carried as a deferred credit, was retroactively credited to capital in excess of par value as at October 29, 1966.

"Deferred Charges" reported in the October 28, 1967 Consolidated Balance Sheet among the "Assets" included unamortized debt discount of $3,474,121.

The above footnote referred to paragraphs 8 and 9 of Accounting Principles Board Opinion 10; these two paragraphs outlined certain accounting requirements for "convertible debt and debt issued with stock warrants." Subsequently, these accounting requirements attracted considerable attention.

Such reactions prompted the Accounting Principles Board to reconsider its position. Paragraphs 11-13 of APB Opinion 12, issued December 1967, suspended the effective date of the accounting requirement and ultimately APB Opinion 14, issued March 1969, retracted that part of the requirements of APB Opinion 10 dealing with convertible debt.

November 2, 1968 Annual Report

Meanwhile, during the 53 weeks ending November 2, 1968, J. P. Stevens & Co. "debentures amounting to $950,000 were converted into 16,826 shares of capital stock." A footnote to the November 2, 1968 financial statements reported an increase in the "Capital in Excess of Par Value" account of $570,402 resulting from "conversion of debentures (net of applicable debt discount and expense)." This transaction and the regular amortization, reduced the unamortized debt discount reported among the "Deferred Charges" to $3,205,425 at November 2, 1968.

Required

1. Recreate the journal entry giving effect to J. P. Stevens' accounting for the bond issue at time of issue and the journal entry recording the related interest expense during the fiscal period ending October 30, 1965.

2. Recreate the journal entry giving effect to the conversion of debentures amounting to $2,322,000 during 1966.

3. In what way did the apparent reasoning of the Accounting Principles Board as manifested by APB Opinion 10 differ from the apparent reasoning of J. P. Stevens at the time of bond issue?

4. Recreate the journal entry giving effect to the conversion of debentures amounting to $950,000 during 1968.

5. Consider the financial reporting of convertible debentures. Do they qualify as liabilities or should they be considered a component of stockholders' equity? How should the effects of the issuance of convertible debentures be reported—specifically, should the amount of the proceeds attributable to the convertible feature be accounted for separately?

Case 6-7

Burlington Industries, Inc.

Burlington Industries, Inc. produces finished and unfinished fabrics for apparel, yarn, hosiery, carpets and rugs, domestics, decorative fabrics, furniture, lighting and products for industrial use.

Burlington issued $40,000,000 of 5% Convertible Subordinated Debentures due 1991 on October 1, 1966 (the beginning of the Company's fiscal year). The Company determined that the debentures would have been issued at a price to yield 6.13% without the conversion feature. Consistent with APB Opinion No. 10, the Company accounted for $5,717,000 as attributable to the conversion feature.

Required

1. What entry did Burlington make on October 1, 1966 to record the proceeds from the issuance of these debentures?

2. What entries did Burlington make on September 30, 1967 and October 1, 1967?

3. The unamortized portion of debt discount was $3,678,000 on September 30, 1973. During 1974, the Company changed its accounting for the conversion feature to conform to the provisions of APB Opinion No. 14. What entry did Burlington make to record this change in accounting in 1974? What entry did Burlington make on September 30, 1974?

Case 6-8

Crane Co. vs. American Standard, Inc. et al.*

On April 17, 1968, Crane Co., brought suit against Westinghouse Air Brake Company and its ten directors to enjoin the defendants from giving effect to proxies solicited by Air Brake from its shareholders in support of a proposal to merge Air Brake into American Standard, Inc. The suit alleged misrepresentation of Standard's earnings, and false and misleading statements of other facts.

A second court action was instituted by Crane on May 6, 1968 against American Standard, Inc. and Blyth and Co., Inc. This action was based on certain transactions in Air Brake stock whereby it was alleged that Blyth, on Standard's behalf and to effect the merger manipulated and rigged the price of Air Brake stock on the New York Stock Exchange at the expense of the merged entity for the purpose of deterring tenders of Air Brake stock under a Crane exchange offer.

Both legal actions were brought to prevent the consummation of the proposed merger of Air Brake into Standard. Crane owned 1,480,623 shares, representing approximately 32% of Air Brake stock. The two actions were consolidated and tried in the U. S. District Court for the Southern District of New York on May 21, 22, 28, 29, 31 and June 3, 1968.

Included among the allegations was that in the April 8, 1968 Proxy Statement to its shareholders, Air Brake materially overstated the 1967 net income and operating performance trend of its prospective merger partner American Standard by stating the Standard's 1967 operating earnings increased by 17 cents—from $1.01 in 1966 to $1.18 in 1967. Cited specifically was American Standard's 1967 loss from devaluation of certain foreign currencies in excess of $3.3 million. This loss was not reported in American Standard's Consolidated Statement of Income; it was deducted directly from a "Reserve for foreign operations." (See Exhibit 1) Crane charged that the result was an overstatement of earnings by 33¢ per share or approximately 25% of the reported income.

History of American Standard's Reserve for Foreign Operations

In 1938, as a result of continuing foreign exchange restrictions, American Standard (then called American Radiator and Standard Sanitary Corporation) ceased its practice of consolidating foreign subsidiaries. Prior to this, the consolidated statements had included a "Foreign Exchange Valuation" reserve in the liability section of the balance sheet. (See Exhibit 2) When the foreign subsidiaries were no longer consolidated, this reserve no longer appeared.

By 1959, American Standard had decided that business conditions were

© 1969 by the Board of Trustees of the Leland Stanford Junior University

*This case was prepared by Professor Robert T. Sprouse of the Graduate School of Business, Stanford University, as a basis for class discussion.

Exhibit 1

WESTINGHOUSE AIR BRAKE COMPANY
PITTSBURGH, PENNSYLVANIA

PROXY STATEMENT

CONSOLIDATED STATEMENT OF INCOME—AMERICAN-STANDARD

The following consolidated statement of income of American Standard Inc. and subsidiaries for the five years ended December 31, 1967 has been examined by Arthur Young & Company, certified public accountants, whose report thereon appears elsewhere in this Proxy Statement. The statement should be read in conjunction with the other consolidated financial statements of American Standard Inc. and notes appearing elsewhere herein.

	\multicolumn{5}{c}{Year ended December 31}				
	1963	1964	1965	1966	1967
	\multicolumn{5}{c}{(Amounts in thousands except as indicated)}				
Income:					
Sales (a)	$527,537	$558,931	$552,646	$568,991	$599,807
Other income	1,250	1,839	1,224	904	1,903
	528,787	560,770	553,870	569,895	601,800
Costs and expense (b):					
Cost of goods sold	415,583	439,449	437,184	460,250	470,826
Selling and administrative	68,341	72,012	73,127	77,570	92,071
Research and development	7,559	8,210	9,053	10,050	11,525
Interest (c)	529	729	1,013	2,278	5,774
	492,012	520,400	520,377	550,148	580,196
Income before taxes on income	36,775	40,370	33,493	19,747	21,604
Taxes on income (including deferred income taxes) (d)	20,100	19,700	15,100	9,400	9,500
Income before extraordinary items (a)	16,675	20,670	18,393	10,347	12,104
Extraordinary items (e) (f)	–	–	–	(17,900)	1,246
Net income (loss)	16,675	20,670	18,393	(7,553)	13,350
Dividends on 7% preferred stock	307	304	302	286	252
Net income (loss) applicable to common stock	$ 16,368	$ 20,366	$ 18,091	$ (7,839)	$ 13,098
Per share of common stock:					
Income before extraordinary items (after preferred dividend requirements) (g)	$ 1.50	$ 2.03	$ 1.81	$ 1.01	$ 1.18
Extraordinary items	–	–	–	$ (1.79)	$ .12
Net income (after preferred dividend requirements) (g)	$ 1.50	$ 2.03	$ 1.81	$ (.78)	$ 1.30
Cash dividends paid	$ .80	$ 1.00	$ 1.00	$ 1.00	$ 1.00

Notes (amounts in thousands)

(a) United States and foreign operations are as follows:

	\multicolumn{5}{c}{Year ended December 31}				
	1963	1964	1965	1966	1967
Sales:					
United States	$342,962	$353,761	$351,257	$368,464	$391,910
Foreign	184,575	205,170	201,389	200,527	207,897
Consolidated	$527,537	$558,931	$552,646	$568,991	$599,807
Income before extraordinary items:					
United States	$ 4,178	$ 7,496	$ 7,949	$ 4,784	$ 5,684
Foreign	12,497	13,174	10,444	5,563	6,420
Consolidated	$ 16,675	$ 20,670	$ 18,393	$ 10,347	12,104

(b) Depreciation included above amounted to: 1963–$16,258; 1964–$17,479; 1965–$18,717; 1966–$19,628; 1967–$21,245.

Exhibit 1 (cont.)

(c) Interest expense relates principally to non-current loans payable.
(d) Taxes on income include the following:

	Year ended December 31				
	1963	1964	1965	1966	1967
Federal	$ 5,178	$ 4,266	$ 4,765	$3,606	$3,967
State	350	475	460	237	179
Foreign	14,572	14,959	9,875	5,557	5,354
	$20,100	$19,700	$15,100	$9,400	$9,500

These amounts include provisions for deferred taxes, principally from accelerated depreciation, as follows:

	1963	1964	1965	1966	1967
Federal	$ 1,350	$ 1,370	$ 227	$ (554)	$(529)
State	150	63	18	(27)	(33)
Foreign	492	468	217	656	(614)
	$ 1,992	$ 1,901	$ 462	$ 75	($1,176)

In 1967 depreciation provided in the financial statements exceeded the amount deducted for tax return purposes resulting in a reversal of taxes previously deferred.

The relationship of taxes on income to income before taxes has been affected in 1967 by foreign investment tax incentives.

(e) In accordance with Opinion No. 9 of the Accounting Principles Board of the American Institute of Certified Public Accountants which became effective in 1967, net income for the year ended December 31, 1966 has been restated to include as an extraordinary item charges which were originally reported in earned surplus. The extraordinary item represents estimated expenses and losses of $17,900 (net of related taxes of $12,570—Federal $8,321; State $399; Foreign $3,850) resulting from revaluation of certain product lines and facilities and discontinuance of the operations of Gulfstan Corporation.

(f) The extraordinary item in 1967 which is not subject to tax, represents an award determined by U.S. Foreign Claims Settlement Commission in May 1967 on a claim filed in 1965 for war damage incurred during World War II to manufacturing facilities and inventories of subsidiaries in Germany and Austria. In the annual 1967 report to shareholders this war loss recovery was identified as a separate item of income. At the recommendation of the Securities and Exchange Commission this item has been reclassified as an extraordinary item.

(g) Net income per share is based on average number of shares outstanding during each year.

(h) Reference is made to "Litigation" under the heading "Business and Properties of American-Standard" appearing elsewhere herein with respect anti-trust matters and to Note 4 to the financial statements with respect to certain dividend restrictions relating to the loans payable.

American-Standard's foreign results improved in 1967, after a two-year decline. The decline in 1965 and 1966 resulted from weakness in the economics of the principal European countries and particularly from a general decline in construction demand which, in turn, resulted in increased competitive conditions and deterioration of price levels. Contributing factors were constantly increasing costs of material and labor, and in some countries labor shortages and heavy turnover among imported workers.

In the United States, income improved from 1963 through 1965, but dropped sharply in 1966 as a result mainly of a decline in housing construction. This decline, which began in mid-1966 and continued through the first half of 1967, largely reflected unfavorable mortgage money conditions. Other factors in the 1966 decline in United States income were product problems in industrial products areas and some labor stoppages. Income improved moderately in the latter half of 1967 due to improvements in housing construction but the increase in earnings was mainly due to the inclusion of The Mosler Safe Company's operations since date of acquisition in May 1967. Mosler sales since acquisition in 1967 amounted to $51,249,000.

Exhibit 1 (Cont.)

AMERICAN STANDARD INC.
CONSOLIDATED BALANCE SHEET
December 31, 1967

ASSETS

Current assets:		
Cash		$ 42,831,000
Marketable securities, at cost which approximates market		1,325,000
Accounts receivable	$109,202,000	
Less allowance for losses	2,594,000	106,608,000
Inventories (Note 2):		
Finished goods	74,217,000	
Work in process	25,236,000	
Raw materials	42,201,000	141,654,000
Prepaid expenses		8,623,000
Total current assets		301,041,000
Investment in associated companies and unconsolidated subsidiaries (Note 1)		6,771,000
Property, plant and equipment, at cost (Note 3)		
Land	12,562,000	
Buildings	130,586,000	
Machinery and equipment	247,165,000	
Improvements in progress	14,371,000	
	404,684,000	
Less accumulated depreciation and provision for losses on disposal	252,476,000	152,208,000
Future income tax benefits		6,927,000
Excess of cost over net assets of business acquired (Note 1)		62,827,000
Other assets		8,787,000
		$538,561,000

LIABILITIES

Current liabilities:		
Loans payable		$ 30,811,000
Accounts payable		31,781,000
Accrued payrolls		22,542,000
Other accrued liabilities		27,368,000
Taxes on income		9,028,000
Total current liabilities		121,530,000
Loans payable, less current portion (Note 4)		122,852,000
Reserve for expenses resulting from revaluation of certain product lines and facilities		6,954,000
Deferred taxes on income (arising principally from accelerated depreciation)		5,639,000
Minority interests in subsidiaries:		
United States	$ 67,000	
Foreign (Note 1)	4,883,000	4,950,000
▶ Reserve for foreign operations (Note 1)		11,573,000

CAPITAL STOCK AND SURPLUS

Preferred stock—7% cumulative; $100 par value, redemption price and preference on liquidation $175 per share, $6,291,000 in the aggregate; authorized and outstanding 35,949 shares (Note 5)		3,595,000
Common stock—$5 par value; authorized 15,000,000 shares; issued 11,709,934 shares		58,550,000
Capital surplus (Notes 5 and 7)		59,314,000
Earned surplus (Note 4)		172,854,000
		294,313,000
Common stock held in treasury, 1,614,142 shares, at cost		29,250,000	265,063,000
		$538,561,000

Reference is made to accompanying notes.

Exhibit 1 (Cont.)

AMERICAN STANDARD INC.
CONSOLIDATED STATEMENT OF EARNED SURPLUS
Three Years ended December 31, 1967

	1965	1966	1967
Balance, beginning of year	$179,570,000	$187,642,000	$169,803,000
Net income (loss)	18,393,000	(7,553,000)	13,350,000
	197,963,000	180,089,000	183,153,000
Cash dividends:			
Preferred—$7.00 per share	302,000	286,000	252,000
Common—$1.00 per share	10,019,000	10,000,000	10,047,000
	10,321,000	10,286,000	10,299,000
Balance, end of year (Note 4)	$187,642,000	$169,803,000	$172,854,000

AMERICAN STANDARD INC.
Notes to Consolidated Financial Statements

1. Principles of Consolidation

All subsidiaries are consolidated except subsidiaries in the development stage or subject to exchange restrictions. The Company's investment in consolidated subsidiaries is stated at its equity in the net assets of the subsidiaries. Investment in 50% owned companies are stated at cost plus equity in undistributed earnings. All other investments are stated at cost.

In May 1967 the Company purchased substantially all the common stock of The Mosler Safe Company. The excess of cost over net assets acquired of $62,827,000 is not being amortized since there is no indication that this intangible asset has a limited term of existence. The operations of the company since the date of acquisition are included in the accompanying financial statements.

All intercompany transactions have been eliminated in the consolidated financial statement.

▶ The financial statements of the consolidated foreign subsidiaries have been converted to U. S. dollars at year-end rates of exchange except that property, plant and equipment and the related accumulated depreciation have been converted at rates of exchange quoted in the year of property additions. Unrealized exchange losses principally in England and Brazil aggregating $3,333,000 in 1967 were charged to the Reserve for Foreign Operations. The unrealized exchange gains and losses in 1965 and 1966, also transferred to the Reserve, were not material.

The net assets of the foreign subsidiaries included in the consolidated financial statements at December 31, 1967 follow:

Net working capital		$ 62,047,000
Property, plant and equipment		63,379,000
Future income tax benefits		906,000
Other assets		2,306,000
		128,638,000
Loans and other liabilities		21,091,000
Net assets		107,547,000
Applicable to minority interests in:		
Preferred stock	$ 3,751,000	
Common stock	840,000	
Capital surplus	207,000	
Earned surplus	85,000	4,883,000
Applicable to American Standard Inc.		$102,664,000

Exhibit 2

STATEMENT OF CONSOLIDATED INCOME
For the Year Ended December 31, 1937
AMERICAN RADIATOR & STANDARD SANITARY CORPORATION, SUBSIDIARY AND AFFILIATED COMPANIES

Gross Sales.		$150,854,034.59
Returns, Allowances, Discounts, Freight.		14,117,210.32
Net Sales.		136,736,824.27
Less Inter-Company Sales		17,038,669.30
		119,698,154.97
Cost of Sales.		80,285,458.00
Gross Profit		39,412,696.97
Selling and Administrative Expense.		20,864,237.88
Net Profit from Operations before Charges		18,548,459.09
Interest Received	$ 305,359.89	
Dividends from Heating and Plumbing Finance Corporation . .	165,000.000	
Rentals and Other Income.	180,230.37	650,590.26
Gross Income		19,199,049.35
Deduct:		
Expense of Idle Plants	505,910.70	
Exchange Loss on Foreign Funds Transferred.	323,378.82	
Miscellaneous	239,439.50	1,068,729.02
Net Profit before Interest, Depreciation and Government Taxes		18,130,320.33
Interest Paid.	828,680.09	
Depreciation and Depletion	4,637,925.34	
Reserve for Government Taxes	4,109,941.82	
Reserve for Surtax on Undistributed Profits.	29,398.46	9,605,945.71
		8,524,374.62
▶ Provision for Foreign Exchange Valuation.		1,000,000.00
		7,524,374.62
Minority Interests.		318,863.72
Consolidated Net Profit, transferred to Surplus.		$ 7,205,510.90

Profits of foreign affiliated companies have been converted at rates of exchange prevailing at December 31, 1937. In certain countries having exchange restrictions preventing or limiting transfer of funds at the present time, the rate of exchange used is the official rate. The net profits of affiliates operating in these countries included above total $943,379.00. During the year, $1,000,000 was charged as a provision for foreign exchange valuation in addition to the exchange loss incurred on foreign funds transferred.

Exhibit 2 (Cont.) **AMERICAN RADIATOR & STANDARD SANITARY CORPORATION, SUBSIDIARY and AFFILIATED COMPANIES**

ASSETS

Current Assets:			
Cash		$ 12,006,568.96	
Marketable Securities—German and Italian— at Foreign Quoted Values		3,238,336.71	$ 15,244,905.67
Notes and Accounts Receivable—			
Notes Receivable		1,345,233.03	
Accounts Receivable		14,036,630.36	
		15,381,863.39	
Less Reserve		1,478,692.91	13,903,170.48
Inventories at Cost or Market, Whichever is Lower— Raw Material, Work in Process, Finished Goods and Supplies			41,748,860.81
Total Current Assets			70,896,936.96
Deposits in Closed Banks (After Reserve of $236,681.13)			175,391.67
Advances to Officers and Employees (After Reserve of $400,862.54)			244,008.13
Investments:			
Investments in and Advances to Subsidiary Companies Not Consolidated—			
Heating and Plumbing Finance Companies	$ 1,059,704.33		
Spanish Company (After Reserve of $250,000.00)	571,223.65	1,630,927.98	
Stock in Treasury— 113,782 Shares Common Stock, at Cost		978,062.13	
Sundry Stocks, Bonds, Etc. (After Reserve of $1,539,874.56)		1,958,167.09	4,567,157.20
Pension Fund Investments:			
4,000 Shares Preferred Stock of the Corporation			400,000.00
Deferred Items:			
Prepaid Insurance, Rents, Taxes, Etc.		516,109.29	
Bond Discount, Product Development, Etc.		1,399,464.26	1,915,573.55
Property, Plant Goodwill, Etc. at Cost		137,221,547.61	
Less: Reserve for Depreciation and Depletion	$44,862,327.61		
Reserve for Revaluation	4,733,171.42	49,595,499.03	87,626,048.58
			$165,825,116.09

Exhibit 2 (Cont.)

LIABILITIES

Current Liabilities:		
Accrued Wages		$ 684,770.36
Notes Payable to Banks		4,947,800.00
Other Notes Payable (Includes Notes and Mortgages due after 1938−$94,898.99)		356,946.02
Accounts Payable		4,495,587.22
Reserve for Government Taxes		2,883,132.96
Total Current Liabilities		13,368,236.56
Reserves:		
Insurance	$ 233,537.75	
Pension and Benefits	569,507.76	
▶ Foreign Exchange Valuation	2,291,549.24	3,094,594.75
Long Term Obligations:		
Twenty Year 4½% Gold Debentures due May 1, 1947 (American Radiator Co.)	10,000,000.00	
Installment Notes of Subsidiary Companies		
Note Maturing 1939	300,000.00	
Notes Maturing 1939-1946	960,000.00	11,260,000.00
Minority Interests:		
Preferred Stocks		5,704,039.24
Capital Stock:		
Preferred 7% Cumulative−$100 Par Value Redeemable at $175 Per Share Authorized and Issued 47,864 Shares	4,786,400.00	
Common−no par value Authorized 15,000,000 Shares Issued 10,158,738 Shares at a stated value of	90,702,953.47	95,489,353.47
Surplus:		
Paid-in Surplus	69,064,386.85	
Less:		
Earned Surplus (Deficit) to December 31, 1936 .. $32,998,905.48		
Net Profit for Year 1937... 7,205,510.90	25,793,394.58	
	43,270,992.27	
Dividends Paid in 1937:		
Preferred 335,048.00		
Common 6,027,052.20	6,362,100.20	
Total Surplus		36,908,892.07
		$165,825,116.09
Contingent Liabilities:		
Discounted Time Payment Notes of Heating and Plumbing Finance Companies	$3,775,000.00	
All Other Drafts, Acceptances, Notes Receivable Discounted and Guarantees	573,537.10	

Current assets and liabilities of foreign affiliated companies are included in the above Balance Sheet at a valuation based on rates of exchange prevailing at the close of the year. Fixed assets and related depreciation of foreign affiliates are included on a dollar cost bases. The above current assets and liabilities include net assets of $11,862,520.35 in countries having exchange restrictions preventing or limiting transfer of funds at the present time and, in these cases, the rate of exchange used is the official rate. The changes in the reserve for foreign exchange valuation during the year, and its present status, are explained in detail in the annual report to shareholders.

such that it would again be proper to consolidate their foreign subsidiaries. Officials of the company discussed the feasibility of such action, as well as the accounting methods to be employed, with their auditors of many years, Arthur Young and Company. In so doing, the decision was made to present as part of their 1959 annual report a five-year summary of earnings in which the foreign subsidiaries were included.

In resuming the consolidation of foreign subsidiaries in 1959, American Standard again established a "Reserve for Foreign Operations," some what analagous to the reserve that appeared in their financial statements up to and including 1937. According to testimony, in establishing this reserve management took note of the fact that there had been a good many foreign exchange fluctuations, currency devaluations, or general declines in currency values in the period since the last consolidation. They also noted that other businesses had been somewhat slow to resume consolidation of foreign subsidiaries, at least partly because of the varying degrees of risk involved in foreign operations.

As a result of these and other factors, American Standard determined that a reserve of $17,500,000 was necessary to provide for the risks considered to be inherent in in their foreign operations. Note 1 to the 1959 financial statements reads as follows:

> 1. The company, effective January 1, 1959, re-established the policy followed prior to World War II of consolidating the accounts of its foreign subsidiaries. The financial statements for the year 1959 include the accounts for all foreign subsidiaries except the recently acquired Brazilian subsidiary which is still in the development stage, and the statements for the year 1958 have been restated accordingly.
>
> A reserve of $17,500,000 for foreign operations has been provided from consolidated earned surplus as at December 31, 1954. Such reserve is available to absorb all unrealized exchange gains and losses and any extraordinary gains or losses, of a material amount, that might arise from foreign operations such as the effect of major exchange fluctuations or unsettled political conditions preventing normal commercial operations. Changes in the reserve in 1959 and 1958 have been occasioned by a net unrealized exchange gain of $65,607 and a net unrealized exchange loss of $1,495,535, respectively.
>
> Capital surplus has been restated to include $11,186,201 from the consolidation of foreign subsidiaries.
>
> The asset, liability and income accounts of the consolidated foreign subsidiaries have been converted to U.S. dollars at rates of exchange quoted, generally, at the end of the respective years except that plant and equipment and related accumulated depreciation have been converted at rates of exchange quoted in the year of acquisition of the property involved.

Each year subsequent to the establishment of the reserve, it was the practice of the company to record all unrealized gains and losses on foreign exchange directly in the reserve account. The *net* aggregate charges to the reserve for the 12-year period, 1955 through 1966 inclusive were $2,594.069. (See Exhibit 3)

During 1967, due primarily to the devaluation of currency in three foreign countries, a charge of $3,332,430 was made directly to this reserve. The 1967 charge included the following amounts: British devaluation—$1,449,251; Brazilian devaluation—$1,612,152; Colombian devaluation—$264,263.

Exhibit 3

AMERICAN STANDARD INC.
RESERVE FOR FOREIGN OPERATION

A reserve for foreign operations of $17,500,000 *was provided from consolidated Earned surplus at December 31, 1954.* Such reserve is available to absorb all unrealized exchange gains or losses and any extraordinary gains or losses, of a material amount, *that might arise from foreign operations* such as the effect of major exchange fluctuations or unsettled political conditions preventing normal commercial operations.

		Change	Balance December 31
1954			$17,500,000
1955	Unrealized exchange loss, net	$(140,403)	17,359,597
1956	Unrealized exchange gain, net	161,603	17,521,200
1957	Devaluation of French franc	(1,137,812)	
	Unrealized exchange loss—other countries, net	(37,891)	
		(1,175,703)	16,345,497
1958	Devaluation of French franc	(1,511,200)	
	Unrealized exchange gain—other countries, net	15,665	
		(1,495,535)	14,849,962
1959	Unrealized exchange gain, net	65,607	14,915,569
1960	Unrealized exchange loss, net	(19,369)	14,896,200
1961	Unrealized exchange gain, net	340,599	15,236,799
1962	Unrealized exchange loss, net	(372,294)	14,864,505
1963	Unrealized exchange gain, net	10,566	14,875,071
1964	Unrealized exchange gain, net	17,311	14,892,382
1965	Unrealized exchange gain, net	5,604	14,897,986
1966	Unrealized exchange gain, net	7,945	14,905,931
1967	Devaluation of Brazilian cruzeiro (1,612,152) and English £(1,449,251)	(3,061,403)	
	Unrealized exchange loss—Colombia	(264,263)	
	Unrealized exchange loss, net	(6,814)	
		(3,332,430)	11,573,451

Witnesses for Crane Co. During the court hearings, Crane Co. called three expert witnesses to testify about American Standard's treatment of the 1967 devaluation losses. Each of these three witnesses—two partners of well-known public accounting firms and a professor of accounting from a major university—took the position that the handling of the 1967 losses was not in accordance with "generally accepted accounting principles."

The gist of the testimony was that American Standard had erred on two related counts: First, that losses of the type charged to the Reserve for Foreign Operations in 1967 were required to be included in the determination of net income; second, that the reserve was, by definition, a contingency reserve, and as such could not properly be used to absorb gains and losses that would otherwise flow through the income statement.

The authorities most often cited by these witnesses were Accounting Principles Board Opinion 9 and Chapters 6 and 12 of Accounting Research Bulletin Number 43.

Accounting Principles Board Opinion 9 requires that all items of profit and loss recognized during the period, with the sole exception of prior period adjustments, be reflected in net income. It also states that extraordinary items should be segregated from the results of ordinary operations and shown separately in the income statement, with disclosure of the nature and amounts involved. Paragraphs 21, 22, and 23 of Opinion 9 read, in part, as follows:

> 21. ... Examples of extraordinary items, ... include material gains of losses (or provision for losses) from (a) the sale or abandonment of a plant of a significant segment of the business; (b) the sale of an investment not acquired for resale; (c) the write-off of goodwill due to unusual events or developments within the period; (d) the condemnation or expropriation of properties; and (e) a major devaluation of a foreign currency.
> 22. Certain gains or losses ... regardless of size, do not constitute extraordinary items (or prior period adjustments) because they are of a character typical of the customary business activities of the entity. Examples include ... (c) gains or losses from fluctuations of foreign exchange.
> 23. Adjustments related to prior periods—and thus excluded in the determination of net income for the current period are limited to those material adjustments which (a) can be specifically identified with and directly related to the business activities of particular prior periods; and (b) are not attributable to economic events occurring subsequent to the data of the financial statements for the prior period; and (c) depend primarily on determination by persons other than management; and (d) were not susceptible of reasonable estimation prior to such determination. Such adjustments are rare in modern financial accounting.

Mr. James B. Kobak, managing partner of J. K. Lasser and Company and the first expert witness called by Crane Co., explained to the court that there are basically three kinds of reserves: liability reserves, valuation reserves, and equity reserves. As an example of a liability reserve, Mr. Kobak cited "federal income taxes that you are going to pay." "You reevaluate it every year, but it is something very specific against assets." An equity reserve on the other hand was described by Mr. Kobak as one that "came from earned surplus. It never went through the income statement."

Mr. Kobak brought out a number of points in his criticism of American Standard's handling of the devaluation losses. Excerpts from his testimony are as follows:

> They can't pin it down to what they are thinking about. In the footnote...they describe the net assets of the foreign subsidiary and they don't apply the reserve against it because the reserve is not specifically earmarked for any of those net assets.
>
> You will see in the sheet showing the history of the reserve (see Exhibit 2) that the only changes that have been in it have come from fluctuations in currency, which means that they haven't reevaluated how big this reserve should be which means it isn't a valuation reserve, it's a contingency reserve.
>
> At the time they set the $17,500,000 up, they could not have predicted 17, 18 years ago that there was going to be a devaluation of British currency in 1968, they couldn't have predicted that Brazil would have the problems that it had. This is not a real reserve; it's part of surplus, is what I am saying.
>
> This is a contingency reserve, and I have a whole bunch of reasons for it. The first one, and the basic one, is that you cannot predict in 1959 what is going to happen in 1964 or '65.
>
> The second one is that there is no movement in this reserve; nobody has pinned this to new assets. Do you realize that during the period this reserve has been in existence that the foreign assets of this company have just about doubled? If the assets have doubled, the reserve must have to get bigger, you have more to lose. If you read the very label, it says, "Items that might arise from foreign operations."
>
> You look where they put it on the balance sheets themselves right below "Minority Interest" and right above "Majority Interest."
>
> We know that it was used for devaluations in Brazil and Colombia, and these two countries were not even consolidated at the time this reserve was set up. In fact, the Colombia branch didn't even exist at that time.
>
> It is a question of fact that this cannot be a valuation reserve. It's that simple.

Mr. Kobak went on to say that, in conducting an informal poll of 301 1967 financial statements, he was only able to find 25 companies who mentioned a reserve for foreign devaluation. Of these, 22 indicated that the reserve itself was run through the income statement. Two of the remaining three had losses totalling less than three percent of their reported net income, leaving one corporation with a material loss not going through the income statement—American Standard Inc.

Mr. Kern, one of the attorneys for American Standard stressed two points in his cross-examination of Mr. Kobak: There were indeed other companies with reserves for foreign operations, and that this particular reserve was not created from American Standard's earned surplus. Excerpts from Kern's cross-examination of Kobak are shown below:

Q: You mentioned this morning the publication *Accounting Trends and Techniques*. I have the 1967 edition of that.

A: Reflecting 1966 statements.

Q: Reflecting 1966. This publication indicated that in 1966 at least 64 companies had foreign activity reserves. Did you intend by your testimony this morning to indicate that there has been a change in the number of companies reporting foreign activity reserves?

A: I intended to indicate this morning, first, that I only had 300 annual reports because the rest of them haven't been collected yet, and I believe this book covers some 600 or so. And second, I felt it was irrelevant to look at 1966 figures because this APB 9 did not become mandatory until January 1st of '67, so those figures would be relatively meaningless.

Q: So you do not know whether at this moment in time 64 companies have foreign activity reserves or not?

A: I don't know. I know what the 301 companies have, that's all. I might also say that the existence of a foreign activity reserve does not necessarily mean that the activity doesn't go through the income statement.

Q: Turning now to the American Standard reserve and the charge to it, when was that reserve created?

A: It was created in 1959, retroactive to 1954.

Q: Do you know what consideration Arthur Young & Company gave to the circumstances of the creation of that reserve in coming to their determination that a charge of these exchange losses was proper to that reserve?

· · · · · · · · · · · ·

A: I would have no idea what ideas they had at that time. I think I know, but I don't know.

Q: Are you aware of the source of this reserve?

A: Yes. It specifically has been stated on many different pieces of paper that it came from earned surplus.

Q: In making your adjustment of this situation, did you take account of the fact that the source of this reserve was unremitted earnings of the foreign subsidiaries?

A: I realize that, yes.

Q: Did you in your assessments take account of the fact that this reserve was created out of the unremitted earnings of foreign subsidiaries contemporaneously with their first consolidation with the accounts of American Standard.

A: That's correct.

Q: Are you aware that since 1959 American Standard has consistently credited and debited this reserve created for the purpose with the effects of fluctuations in foreign exchange?

A: Yes.

Q: Is it your judgment that American Standard has been wrong in this method of accounting for going on ten years?

A: It's my opinion that they have been wrong. I think until 1967 the amounts involved were not material, so I don't think it was terribly important until then.

Q: You do not believe that there is any foundation in good accounting, or in common sense, for anticipating an eventually, making provision for it, and then charging the eventuality against the provision which was made?

Mr. Castles: I object to the form of the question.
(Attorney for Crane Company)

The Court: Overruled.

On redirect examination by Mr. Castles of Lord, Day, and Lord (attorneys for Crane Co.), Mr. Kobak again discussed the difference between the three types of reserves. Some of Mr. Kobak's examples of companies alleged to be using an accounting treatment similar to American Standard were challenged.

(Mr. Kobak): ...And I will repeat. One reserve is the liability reserve like Federal income tax reserve which you know you are going to have to pay.

Another is a valuation reserve like the reserve for bad debts, or the reserve for obsolete inventory which is definable and measurable.

The third reserve is the contingency reserve, "Let's hold something for a rainy day in case something happens overseas somewhere like Mr. de Gaulle being thrown out again."

And that is what this reserve is. And any reserve set up in 1959 that could have predicted the English devaluation of the pound and how much it would be and how much it would amount to for this company—it just couldn't happen, that's all.

• • • • • • • • • • •

Mr. Gustav A. Gomprecht, managing partner of the New York office of Main Lafrentz & Co., Crane's second witness, described a contingency reserve as "... If by its very nature it does not provide for *known* losses or known or imminent losses, then it is a contingency reserve..."

Mr. Gomprecht cited Chapter 6 of Accounting Research Bulletin 43, which deals with the characteristics and handling of contingency reserves. Paragraphs 7 and 8 read as follows:

> 7. The committee is therefore of the opinion that reserves such as those created:
> a) for general undetermined contingencies, or

b) for any indefinite possible future losses, such as for example, losses on inventories not on hand or contracted for, or

c) for the purpose of reducing inventories other than to a basis which is in accordance with generally accepted accounting principles, or

d) without regard to any specific loss reasonably related to the operations of the current period, or

e) in amount not determined on the basis of any reasonable estimates of costs or losses are of such a nature that charges or credits relating to such reserves should not enter into the determination of net income.

8. Accordingly, it is the opinion of the committee that if a reserve of the type described in paragraph 7 is set up:

a) it should be created by a segregation or appropriation of earned surplus.

b) no costs or losses should be charged to it and no part of it should be transferred to income or in any way used to affect the determination of net income for any year,

c) it should be restored to earned surplus directly when such a reserve or any part thereof is no longer considered necessary, and

d) it should preferably be classified in the balance sheet as a part of shareholders' equity.

During direct examination of Mr. Gomprecht, Mr. Castles also continued with the line of questioning used earlier with Mr. Kobak:

Q: There was a reference a moment ago, Mr. Gomprecht, to a company called Abbots, I guess it is Abbots Laboratories, and I show you this document which Mr. Kern referred to, and am I correct in stating that the foreign currency devaluation loss which Abbots sustained in the period covered by that account was charged to income?

A: The income statement does not indicate in itself that there are any charges for foreign exchange losses or devaluation.

However, the statement of consolidated funds, which is the fund statement, showing the derivation of funds and what happened to the funds, indicates that they have been added back to net earnings not only depreciation but provision for deferred taxes and international operations of $1,715,000, which indicates to me that there must have been that provision from operations, although it is not separately stated on the income statement.

Mr. Castles: Thank you, sir.

A: If I may, I would like to give you an example of the treatment by Lybrand of the Cabot Corporation which I think goes right to the point.

• • • • • • • • • • • •

A: Now, to start out with, they had—they showed a comparative. In 1966, they had a reserve for extraordinary risk pertaining to foreign operations of $1,500,000.

In 1967 that reserve no longer exists. And this is what they have to say on the extraordinary items on page 22:

> ... Net income for the years 1962, 1963 and 1964, as shown in the ten-year financial summary, has been restated in accordance with the recently published opinion of the Accounting Principles Board of the American Institute of Certified Public Accountants. Except for the $1,500,000 reserve in 1962 for extraordinary risk pertaining to foreign operations, special items previously shown in those years have been reclassified as extraordinary items and included in net income. The million and a half reserve has been reflected as a deduction from retained earnings of 1962 and restored to retained earnings in 1967.

The following day, the attorneys for American Standard Inc. called as a witness Mr. William D. Conklin of Arthur Young and Company, who had been the partner-in-charge of the American Standard audit since 1958.

Mr. Conklin outlines the origin of the reserve for foreign operations, explained that they had not felt it to be necessary to restate earnings for more than five years in the 1959 financial statements, and gave his opinion that APB 9 was not applicable in this case. Excerpts from this portion of the trial are as follows:

Mr. Conklin: ... They did not go back and restate the earnings of years beyond 1954. It was not considered by them to be necessary or by us to be necessary to restate these prior years. So that at no time was the past history for a more extended period restated to show the consolidated operations.

Q: Mr. Conklin, would you please explain to his Honor the primary reason for the creation of this reserve?

A: Well, the reserve is created to provide for gains, unrealized gains and losses on foreign exchange and other major risks inherent in doing business outside the United States.

Q: When this reserve was created, was it in accordance with generally accepted accounting principles to establish such a reserve from these sources at this time?

A: Yes.

Mr. Conklin dealt with the relationship, as he saw it, between APB Opinion 9 and treatment of charges, debits and credits to this reserve. He stressed the use of the word "recognized" in APB Opinion 9.

A: ... Under Opinion 9 it states that those items are recognized in the period—and that recognition within the period does not necessarily constitute realization within the period—it only deals with those items which enter into the determination of income in that year. Any item that had been considered in the determination of income in a prior year would not fall within the recognition of the current year.

Q: In your professional judgment, does opinion 9 of the Accounting Principles Board mandate some treatment of an unrealized exchange loss different from that accorded the exchange loss in the case of American Standard in 1967.

A: Well, if the exchange loss is recognized in the determination of income for a particular year, there are provisions in the opinion as to how that would be handled in the income statement of that year.

Q: In your professional judgment, do you believe that opinion No. 9 applies to the circumstances of American Standard's reserve for unrealized exchange losses?

A: Opinion 9 does not prescribe that in the case of American Standard's accounting it would be required to include exchange gains and losses, unrealized exchange gains and losses, in the 1967 account.

During cross-examination, this witness testified that if there had not been a reserve available, the loss would have had to go through the income statement.

Crane's attorney asked Mr. Conklin where in the 1959 statement it showed that the $17.5 million had come from income and if there was any record whatsoever showing that any part of the reserve entered into the determination of income in any year.

The witness, at this stage, said that no determination was ever made as to specific years, but that the reserve did indeed come from income of these earlier years.

Other excerpts from the approximately 40 pages of recorded cross-examination are as follows:

Q: At the time this reserve was created . . . was there any Brazilian subsidiary of American Standard?

A: As of 1954, no.

Q: . . . In your opinion was the foreign operation reserve of $17.5 million a contingency reserve?

A: No.

Q: What kind of reserve was it?

A: It was a reserve for the particular purpose that it was described to cover, which is not in my opinion a contingency reserve at all.

The trial resumed at 10:00 a.m. on June 3, 1968, at which time Crane's attorney called his final witness, Professor Joel T. Wentgren.

Q: ... What type of reserve was this so-called foreign operations reserve that was created in 1959 retroactive to 1954?

A: It is a surplus reserve. It really has to be under the circumstances under which it was created. There are other reserves that we sometimes refer to as liability reserves.

Q: Was this reserve a type of reserve described in Chapter 6 as a contingency reserve?

A: Yes. If I may cite Chapter 6, it seems to me that the criteria are quite clear cut and the relevance to this particular question, I think, is quite evident.

Q: Please do.

A: First of all, referring to the reasons for really not allowing charges to be made to such reserves, it says:

> ... If a reserve so created is used to relieve the income of subsequent periods of charges that would otherwise be made against it, the income of such subsequent periods is thereby overstated. By use of the reserve in this manner profit for a given period may be significantly increased or decreased by mere whim. As a result of this practice the integrity of the financial statement is impaired and the statements tend to be misleading.

Q: Could this reserve of $17.5 million that was created out of earned surplus in 1959, retroactive to 1954 have been, under generally accepted accounting principles, properly created out of income?

A: Well, I don't think so because the nature of the losses that this reserve is presumed to have been established to cover are too nebulous. There is not enough specific reason for establishing the reserve to identify it with any prior period, that is, as a charge against income with any prior period.

The testimony included a discussion of the types of losses that could conceivably be charged against the reserve.

The Court: So that it was never intended to cover operating losses, was it?

The Witness: Well, that is not at all clear and, indeed, the description ... at the head of this schedule (see Exhibit 2) would suggest that it would, indeed, cover any kind of a gain or loss.

Q: What is that description?

A: It says: "Such reserves available to absorb all unrealized exchange gains or losses and any extraordinary gains or losses of a material amount that might arise from foreign operations such as the effect of major exchange fluctuations or unsettled political conditions preventing normal commercial operations."

The Witness: Unsettled political conditions preventing normal commercial operations, I assume would include such things as the current turmoil in France. If the strikers occupied a building and destroyed it in some way, I would assume that this language would cover that kind of a loss. It is difficult for me to believe that they had that sort of thing in mind when they set $17.5 million aside ... that in 1968 there might be such a loss in this amount.

As I say, corporations have done this—particularly historically—to a considerable extent. There is the reserve for foreign operations and the kind of reserve for domestic operations has been called reserve for contingencies. The purpose of these reserves presumably is to inform the stockholders that some day in the future some losses may occur; that we really should not be paying out all of our earnings ... so that we will be able, really, to survive such periods of diversity. But that doesn't permit the losses themselves to be charged against the reserve—Chapter 6 is very specific about that.

Professor Wentgren continued to testify, explaining what losses on foreign exchange might consist of, and citing examples of other published financial statements. At the conslusion of the cross-examination, another witness was called on behalf of American Standard.

• • • • • • • • • • • •

The second witness on behalf of American Standard was Mr. Frank T. Weston of Arthur Young and Company, a partner from the New York City home office. He testified that he was currently a member of the Accounting Principles Board and had been since 1964. Indeed, he had been a member of the subcommittee that drafted APB Opinion 9.

Excerpts from the direct examination of Mr. Weston are as follows:

A: Opinion No. 9 would not change the treatment of an item of gain or a loss for which a proper reserve had previously been established, since such a gain or loss should then be charged or credited to the reserve provided for that purpose and would not therefore be an item of income or loss in the current year to which Opinion 9 addressed itself.

Q: Is the reserve for foreign operations of American Standard a proper reserve in accordance with generally accepted accounting principles?

A: It is my understanding, based on my knowledge of the reserve and the background and all the information I have as to the reserve's establishment that it is.

The Witness: I am in our home office and do not have direct contact with clients, so I have not been in touch with the accounting records or corporation officials of American Standard nor have I studied in detail the transactions in the reserve...

The type of entry made to bring the foreign subsidiaries into consolidation in 1959 could not be handled in any other accounting way other than by bringing in the net surplus balance at that time on a retroactive basis... There is no other way to make a retroactive consolidation...

So, to summarize, I believe that this is a proper valuation type reserve, that losses or gains of the type for which it was established may properly be charged or credited to that reserve and, since there exists a reserve of that type, those items are not items of current profit and loss and Opinion No. 9, therefore, does not apply...

... The so-called valuation reserve is a reserve which is established with respect to a specific asset or a specific group of assets and it relates to the activities of the assets and in this particular case to the activities of the foreign assets of American Standard... the assets in which these earnings were reflecting were considered to require some valuation reduction, in this case, before they were introduced into the consolidation in 1959. So, they were, in effect, brought in on a net basis, net of this valuation reserve on a retroactive basis and the balance of retained earnings of the foreign subsidairies was then included in retained earnings or earned surplus of the consolidated group.

Under cross-examination, the attorney for Crane Co. returned to the issue of contingency versus valuation reserve, as exemplified by the following:

Q: ... Am I correct in stating you have to relate a valuation reserve to certain assets?

A: Yes.

Q: Now, what assets of the American Standard Company were the $17.5 million foreign operations reserve related to?

A: I understand it is the assets in Italy, France, Germany, Austria, Belgium, I believe, all foreign assets wherever located of American Standard.

Q: Now, were assets of the Brazilian subsidiary included as part of the assets with respect to which that valuation reserve was set up in 1959 effective as of 1954?

A: I am not familiar with that. My understanding is they might well have been.

Q: You don't know what ratio this $17.5 bore to the assets of these foreign subsidiaries in 1959 as of 1954, do you?

A: No.

Q: Do you know whether the Colombia subsidiary existed in 1959 or 1954?

A: No.

Q: When was the $3.3 million devaluation loss charged against income before 1967?

A: It was charged against the income of the foreign subsidiaries which were brought in consolidation in 1959.

Q: Are you saying that the $1.6 million devaluation loss in Brazil which was not consolidated as of effective date of the reserve in 1954 was charged against income in 1959 and 1954?

A: No.

Q: Or prior to 1954?

A: No.

Q: Well, when was that $1.6 million devaluation loss of the Brazilian subsidiary charged against anything, sir?

A: I might express that by expressing an analogy...

A company has an amount of accounts receivable on its books and it establishes a reserve against these receivables at December 31 based on its best idea of what is realizable.

Now, next year they had different accounts receivable on their books and they review those accounts receivable and in many cases the reserve needed at that date is exactly the same amount as the reserve needed at the prior date. So no change in the reserve is necessary.

In that sense the losses of the Brazilian subsidiary cannot be identified by year of change, but may be determined by year of determination.

Required   What type of reserve is the $17.5 million and why?

Case 6-9

Gulf & Western Industries

The following story appeared in Alan Abelson's column, "Up and Down Wall Street," in *Barron's* of February 12, 1973:

We were reminded again of the creative side of bookkeeping by the current controversy surrounding Gulf & Western. No, we don't mean the brawl with A&P. Or, whether or not the prospective acquisition of Talcott National will violate anti-trust laws. Rather, we're referring to the dispute over how G&W calculates its *fully diluted earnings per share*.

In one corner are G&W and its auditors, Ernst & Ernst. In the opposite one is a trio of analysts: Sidney J. Heller, director of the Conglomerate Service of Sterling, Grace & Co.; and Ted O'glove and Robert Olstein, who run the "Quality of Earnings Report" for Coenen & Co. By G&W's lights, in fiscal '72, on a fully diluted basis, it earned $3.30 a share. Working independently and in separate reports, Heller and O&O come up with the same total—$2.61 a share—as the true fully diluted figure.

The analysts (who, lest we be accused of impartiality, deserve high marks for a very professional job) base their argument on APB No. 15 and its subsequent "Accounting Interpretation." No. 15 laid down certain guidelines for determining fully diluted per share earnings and the interpretation elaborated on these. We blanch at even attempting to translate accountantese into English. Essentially, though, the issue turns on whether in doings its calculations, G&W properly accounted for the proceeds from the hypothetical exercise of outstanding warrants and options.

G&W chose to use those mythical proceeds to buy in convertible debentures; in doing so, moreover, it used prices at the beginning of the year rather than a yearly average price (which, as it turned out, was higher). The benefits for G&W were twofold: (a) since its converts were selling considerably below par, it was able to enrich earnings by the amount of the discount; (b) by reducing the amount of convertible debentures outstanding, it also softened the dilutive impact of those securities on the per-share figure.

What G&W should have done, the analysts say, was to use those hypothetical funds raised from warrants and options to retire straight, rather than convertible, debt and invest the rest in government securities or commercial paper (all of this, after theoretically buying in 20% of the common). Heller, in his report, points out that except for National General, all other conglomerates he is familiar with calculate their fully diluted net in this fashion. Hence, he concludes, "what G&W is doing in this instance makes their earnings non-comparable to those of most other companies." In like vein, O'glove and Olstein charge that in purchasing the convertible debt rather than the straight debt, in utilizing debt discount and beginning-of-year bond purchases in making fully diluted per share earnings calculations, G&W "violated" the accounting interpretation of APB No. 15.

What's helpful to reported earnings today, paradoxically, could prove a drag in future. O'glove and Olstein put it this way: "The unrealistic assumptions on the part of GW and its auditors regarding fully diluted earnings per share can best be exemplified by the following example. Assume GW's earnings from operations jump 15% per year for the next two fiscal years and the prices of the company's convertible bonds move substantially over par. At the end of two years, GW's earning would be approximately $93 million, up from fiscal 1972's reported $70 million. Also further assume that the warrants are exercised, the company utilizes the money to retire the 5½% convertible debentures, and the 5¼% debentures are converted by its holders.

"We believe that these assumptions, if anything, are fair to GW and do not represent unrealistic events. Under the aforementioned assumptions, the primary earnings per share would be $3.31, or the same as fiscal 1972, despite a more than 30% increment in after-tax dollar earnings. In essence, what we are saying, if GW's stock price moves upward, it would probably have a highly opposite negative effect on earnings per share computations. Thus, investors should be aware of the fact that an increasing stock price could have a negative impact on earnings per share, and hence work against the stock price moving up to the same degree as after tax earnings."

G&W and its auditors counter that the "interpretation" of APB 15 is unofficial and that their practice is both consistent (they calculated the same way last year) and fully compatible with No. 15. Our colleague, Steve Anreder, checked in with Chief Accountant Burton of the SEC to see if he had any feelings, pro or con, and discovered that the agency is actively studying the matter (as they say in official argot). "It would appear," comments Burton, "that Gulf & Western followed the letter of the opinion. But the question is whether they followed the spirit as well."

FINANCIAL HIGHLIGHTS OF FIVE YEARS OF OPERATIONS

	Dollar Amounts, Except Per Share, In Thousands				
OPERATING RESULTS—year ended July 31:	1972	1971	1970	1969	1968
Net sales and other operating revenues	$1,669,671	$1,566,327	$1,629,562	$1,563,564	$1,330,565
Net earnings from operations	69,601	55,252	49,825	50,982	67,732
Net earnings	69,411	55,576	44,771	72,050	70,366
Primary earnings per share:					
Net earnings from operations	3.31	2.61	2.26	2.15	3.00
Net earnings	3.30	2.63	2.00	3.15	3.13
Fully diluted earnings per share:					
Net earnings from operations	3.31	2.61	2.26	2.00	2.64
Net earnings	3.30	2.63	2.00	2.67	2.74
Depreciation and depletion	45,614	40,665	42,769	41,454	29,124
FINANCIAL POSITION—July 31:					
Working capital	$ 559,940	$ 478,426	$ 416,994	$ 576,510	$ 469,591
Net property, plant and equipment	607.394	584,922	552,622	525,059	518,215
Total assets	2,230,482	2,079,067	2,154,463	2,172,027	2,055,334
Shareholders' equity	673,833	621,682	580,346	590,066	537,874
Book value per common share	30.00	27.63	25.49	23.16	19.93
GENERAL STATISTICS:					
Number of shareholders:					
Common stock	45,000	51,000	54,000	51,000	43,000
Preferred stock	35,000	39,000	40,000	40,000	42,500
Capital expenditures	$ 81,767	$ 98,477	$ 86,676	$ 72,825	$ 61,587

The per share amounts have been adjusted for the stock dividends paid in fiscal years 1968 and 1969 and for the effect of the distribution to shareholders of record on July 18, 1969 of one share of stock of Transnation Development Corporation (formerly G & W Land and Development Corp.) for each 20 shares of the Company's common stock held.

Consolidated Statement of Earnings

	Year Ended July 31	
	1972	1971
Net sales and other operating revenues..........	$1,669,671,000	$1,566,327,000
Equity in earnings before income taxes of unconsolidated affiliates.....................	53,382,000	54,231,000
	$1,723,053,000	$1,620,558,000
Cost of goods sold......................	$1,263,117,000	$1,204,322,000
Selling, administrative and general expenses	267,794,000	243,163,000
Depreciation and depletion................	45,614,000	40,665,000
	$1,576,525,000	$1,488,150,000
OPERATING INCOME	$ 146,528,000	$ 132,408,000
Dividends and other income	2,610,000	3,209,000
	$ 149,138,000	$ 135,617,000
Interest expense—net.....................	58,318,000	63,360,000
Minority interest........................	3,219,000	3,255,000
Provision for income taxes—Note F...........	18,000,000	13,750,000
NET EARNINGS FROM OPERATIONS	$ 69,601,000	$ 55,252,000
Gain, no net tax effect, on exchange of securities of bank holding company subsidiary for Company debt ($.39 per share)—Note C	7,609,000	
Losses, net of income tax benefit of $5,500,000, on disposition of securities ($.40 per share)	7,799,000*	
Gain, no net tax effect, resulting from reorganization of less than wholly-owned subsidiaries, primarily from disposition of communications business interests in Canada ($.74 per share)..........		13,968,000
Estimated losses, net of income tax benefit of $21,200,000 on shutdown and disposal of unprofitable operations ($1.26 per share)		24,000,000*
Cumulative credit, net of income taxes of $5,859,000, resulting from change by insurance subsidiaries from statutory insurance reporting to generally accepted accounting principles ($.54 per share) ..		10,356,000
NET EARNINGS	$ 69,411,000	$ 55,576,000
Dividends on preferred stock other than common equivalent shares....................	$ 5,519,000	$ 5,523,000
Average common and common equivalent shares outstanding—Note G	19,373,000	19,028,000
Earnings per share—Note G:		
Net earnings from operations.............	$ 3.31	$ 2.61
Net earnings.......................	$ 3.30	$ 2.63

*Denotes deduction
See notes to consolidated financial statements

Consolidated Balance Sheets

ASSETS

	July 31 1972	July 31 1971
CURRENT ASSETS		
Cash and certificates of deposit	$ 177,042,000	$ 48,102,000
Marketable securities–at cost (estimated market value 1972–$40,371,000)	42,986,000	24,941,000
Trade receivables, less allowances (1972–$14,219,000, 1971–$14,475,000) for doubtful accounts	229,965,000	227,219,000
Inventories–Note B	400,213,000	416,834,000
Prepaid expenses, income taxes and other receivables	94,551,000	100,497,000
TOTAL CURRENT ASSETS	$ 944,757,000	$ 817,593,000
PROPERTY, PLANT AND EQUIPMENT–at cost		
Land, buildings and mines	$ 429,855,000	$ 397,684,000
Machinery, equipment and other	697,705,000	686,628,000
Construction in progress–Note H	27,177,000	21,395,000
	$1,154,737,000	$1,105,707,000
Less allowances for depreciation and depletion	547,343,000	520,785,000
	$ 607,394,000	$ 584,922,000
OTHER ASSETS		
Investment in affiliated companies and other corporate securities–Notes A and C	$ 565,206,000	$ 538,622,000
Receivables due after one year	42,294,000	58,409,000
Intangibles, deferred costs and other	70,831,000	79,521,000
	$ 678,331,000	$ 676,552,000
	$2,230,482,000	$2,079,067,000

LIABILITIES AND SHAREHOLDERS' EQUITY

	July 31 1972	July 31 1971
CURRENT LIABILITIES		
Notes payable and commercial paper	$ 85,065,000	$ 74,607,000
Current maturities of long-term debt	36,499,000	30,438,000
Trade accounts payable	93,945,000	84,552,000
Accrued expenses and other liabilities	156,208,000	134,364,000
Income taxes payable	13,100,000	15,206,000
TOTAL CURRENT LIABILITIES	$ 384,817,000	$ 339,167,000
DEFERRALS		
Liabilities due after one year	$ 71,513,000	$ 59,876,000
Income taxes	3,117,000	21,545,000
	$ 74,630,000	$ 81,421,000
LONG-TERM DEBT, less current maturities–Note D	564,680,000	486,879,000
MINORITY INTEREST–in consolidated subsidiaries	54,774,000	46,428,000
CONVERTIBLE SUBORDINATED DEBT, less current maturities–Note D	477,748,000	503,490,000
SHAREHOLDERS' EQUITY–Note E		
Convertible preferred stock (liquidation value $142,248,000)	$ 3,945,000	$ 4,410,000
$5.75 non-convertible preferred stock	40,026,000	40,726,000
Common stock	16,387,000	15,548,000
Paid-in surplus	232,467,000	228,291,000
Retained earnings–Note D	381,008,000	332,707,000
	$ 673,833,000	$ 621,682,000
	$2,230,482,000	$2,079,067,000

Consolidated Statement of Paid-In Surplus and Retained Earnings

	Year Ended July 31			
	1972		1971	
	Paid-in Surplus	Retained Earnings	Paid-in Surplus	Retained Earnings
Balance at beginning of period, excluding treasury stock	$228,291,000	$332,707,000	$226,933,000	$293,070,000
Common stock issued:				
Exercise of stock options—134,791 shares in 1972	2,914,000		520,000	
Conversion of preferred stock—757,319 shares in 1972	239,000*		138,000*	
Conversion of debentures and notes—11,427 shares in 1972	488,000			
Purchase of a business			1,118,000	
Acquisition of stock for the treasury—64,200 shares of common and 7,000 shares of $5.75 series preferred stock	484,000*	1,062,000*		
Equity transactions of subsidiaries	469,000		142,000*	
Exercise of stock purchase warrants—24,489 shares of Series A preferred stock	1,063,000			
Retirement of stock purchase warrants	35,000*			
Cash dividends:				
Paid on common stock ($.60 per share in 1972, $.50 per share in 1971)		9,630,000*		7,555,000*
Paid and accrued on preferred stock		7,955,000*		8,384,000*
Dividend paid in common stock of subsidiary		2,463,000*		
Net earnings for the year		69,411,000		55,576,000
Balance at end of period, excluding treasurey stock—Note E	$232,467,000	$381,008,000	$228,291,000	$332,707,000

*Denotes deduction
See notes to consolidated financial statements

206 Cases in Financial Accounting

	Year Ended July 31	
	1972	1971
FUNDS PROVIDED		
From operations:		
Net earnings	$ 69,411,000	$ 55,576,000
Depreciation (straight-lin method) and depletion	45,614,000	40,665,000
Deferred income taxes—non-current portion	15,081,000*	32,433,000*
Minority interest in earnings of subsidiaries	3,219,000	3,255,000
Undistributed net earnings of unconsolidated affiliates	21,097,000*	28,292,000*
Gain on exchange of securities of bank holding company subsidiary for Company debt	7,609,000*	
Estimated losses (pre-tax) on shutdown and disposal of unprofitable operations not affecting working capital		28,146,000
Other charges not affecting working capital	25,452,000	5,887,000
	$ 99,909,000	$ 72,804,000
Decrease in property, plant and equipment	23,725,000	14,771,000
Decrease in investment in affiliated companies and other securities	33,178,000	37,328,000
Issuance of long-term and convertible subordinated debt	168,614,000	106,774,000
Decrease in receivables due after one year	5,953,000	4,971,000
Exercise of stock options, conversion of debentures and notes and other issuances of stock	4,664,000	1,841,000
Decrease/Increase* in intangibles, deferred costs and other	12,119,000	6,668,000*
Increase/Decrease* in minority interest	5,127,000	3,567,000*
	$353,289,000	$228,254,000
FUNDS APPLIED		
Expenditures for property, plant and equipment	$ 81,767,000	$ 98,477,000
Net non-current assets of purchased business (primarily property, plant and equipment)	4,876,000	3,926,000
Increase in investment in affiliated companies and other corporate securities	43,298,000	11,101,000
Reduction in long-term and convertible subordinated debt (including reclassification to current maturities)	117,011,000	39,320,000
Acquisition of stock for the treasury and retirement of warrants	2,345,000	
Cash dividends	17,585,000	15,939,000
Dividend paid in common stock of subsidiary	2,463,000	
Other	2,430,000	1,941,000'
	$271,775,000	$166,822,000
INCREASE IN WORKING CAPITAL—Note I	$ 81,514,000	$ 61,432,000

*Denotes deduction
See notes to consolidated financial statements

Notes to Consolidated Financial Statements
Year ended July 31, 1972

Note A—Principles of consolidation

The consolidated financial statements include the accounts of the Company and its significant majority-owned subsidiaries other than finance and insurance subsidiaries. Investments in unconsolidated majority-owned subsidiaries. 20% or more owned companies and joint ventures are carried at cost plus equity in the increase in net assets since acquisition. Investments in other corporate stock are carried at cost.

Note B—Inventories

The amounts of inventories were determined using the following methods:

Lower of cost (primarily first-in, first-out method) or market	$322,920,000
Cost less amortization (primarily theatrical and television films)	64,318,000
Estimated net sales price (commodities, primarily sold but not shipped)	12,975,000
	$400,213,000

Note C—Investment in affiliated companies and other corporate securities

Investment in affiliated companies and other corporate securities includes $415,164,000 applicable to the Company's ownership of all of the outstanding capital stock of Associates First Capital Corporation, whose condensed consolidated financial statements (including all of its finance and insurance groups) are as follows:

	June 30	
	1972	1971
ASSETS		
Cash	$ 185,121,000	$ 151,400,000
Marketable securities, at cost—Note 1	204,409,000	242,679,000
Finance and other receivables	1,580,211,000	1,598,913,000
Other assets	78,181,000	67,160,000
	$2,047,922,000	$2,060,152,000
LIABILITIES AND SHAREHOLDER'S EQUITY		
Commercial bank deposits	$	$ 156,616,000
Insurance reserves and claims	208,190,000	184,757,000
Notes and other short-term payables	818,670,000	738,314,000
Long-term debt—Note 2	729,652,000	690,234,000
Shareholder's equity	291,410,000	290,231,000
	$2,047,922,000	$2,060,152,000

	Twelve Months Ended June 30	
	1972	1971
REVENUES—Note 3		
Financing	$ 220,447,000	$ 224,723,000
Casualty insurance	102,902,000	93,098,000
Life insurance	66,620,000	53,947,000
TOTAL REVENUES	$ 389,969,000	$ 371,768,000
Equity in earnings before income taxes of unconsolidated affiliates—Note 3	415,000	2,260,000
	$ 390,384,000	$ 374,028,000
EXPENSES		
Financing:		
Operating	$ 120,525,000	$ 109,781,000
Interest	72,941,000	87,048,000
Casualty Insurance	89,933,000	84,847,000
Life Insurance	53,586,000	42,671,000
Federal and state income taxes	24,068,000	23,527,000
	$ 361,053,000	$ 347,874,000
NET EARNINGS FROM OPERATIONS	$ 29,331,000	$ 26,154,000
Cumulative credit, net of income taxes of $5,859,000, resulting from change by insurance subsidiaries from statutory insurance reporting to generally accepted accounting principles		10,356,000
NET EARNINGS	$ 29,331,000	$ 36,510,000

Note 1—Marketable securities at June 30, 1972 consist of common and preferred stock of $96,188,000 (estimated market value of $102,091,000) and bonds (at amortized cost) of $108,221,000.

Note 2—Long-term debt at June 30, 1972 bears interest at rates from 3-3/4% to 9.31% and matures in varying amounts from 1973 to 1992.

Note 3—On November 24, 1971, securities representing 100% ownership of FBT Bancorp of Indiana, Inc. and its subsidiary, First Bank and Trust Company of South Bend, were transferred to Gulf+Western Industries, Inc. as a dividend. Gulf Western subsequently disposed of a substantial amount of these securities (including all of the common stock), principally in an exchange for Gulf+Western debt. The divestiture was made in order to comply with the recently amended Bank Holding Company Act. The disposition of FBT Bancorp of Indiana, Inc. and its subsidiary did not materially affect the financial position or results of operations of Associates First Capital Corporation. The above statement of operations does not include for either year the revenues of FBT Bancorp of Indiana, Inc. and its subsidiary, the pre-tax earnings of which are included in "equity in earnings before income taxes of unconsolidated affiliates."

Note D—Long-term debt and convertible subordinated debt

Long-term debt at July 31, 1972 includes:

Notes payable to institutional investors, interest 4% to 9¼%, primarily 5¾%, maturing 1973 to 1991	$140,643,000
Notes payable to banks, due 1975 to 1982, interest from ⅜ to ½ of 1% above the prevailing commericial loan rate of the principal lending bank	128,500,000
6½% notes due 1973 to 1985	48,635,000
6% subordinated debentures due 1975 to 1988	54,147,000
5% debentures due 1979 to 1988, convertible into common stock of the Company at $53.87 a share	49,898,000
Other notes and debentures, payable to banks and others, interest 4% to 10%, averaging approximately 6%, due in installments from 1973 to 1995	174,356,000
	$596,179,000
Less current maturities	31,499,000
	$564,680,000

Convertible subordinated debt at July 31, 1972 includes:

5½% debentures, due 1993, convertible into common stock of the Company at $56.70 a share	$385,030,000
5¼% debentures and notes, due 1973 to 1991, convertible into common stock of the Company from $43.59 to $49.02 a share	97,718,000
	$482,748,000
Less current maturities	5,000,000
	$477,748,000

Maturities of long-term debt and convertible subordinated debt during the five years ending July 31, 1977, are:

1973	$ 36,499,000
1974	29,470,000
1975	48,470,000
1976	44,120,000
1977	64,117,000

The Company has complied with restrictions and limitations required under terms of various loan agreements. Consolidated retained earnings unrestricted as to the payment of cash dividends at July 31, 1972 was $84,242,000.

Note E—Capital stock at July 31, 1972

	Shares Outstanding

Cumulative, convertible preferred stock, recorded at $2.50 par value:

$1.75 Series A—convertible into 3.367 shares of common, redeemable beginning 1974 at $65.00 a share, $25.00 liquidation value, 875,000 shares authorized, (outstanding excludes 1,500 shares held in treasury).........................207,142

$3.50 Series B—convertible into 4.208 shares of common, redeemable beginning 1974 at $100.00 a share, $100.00 liquidation value, 1,500,000 shares authorized, (outstanding excludes 35,000 shares held in treasury).......................547,252

$3.875 Series C—convertible into 1.743 shares of common, redeemable beginning 1974 at $105.00 a share, $100.00 liquidation value, 1,200,000 shares authorized, (outstanding excludes 120,500 shares held in treasury).........................823,441

Undesignated—1,425,000 shares authorized

Cumulative, non-convertible preferred stock:

$5.75 series, 5% sinking fund, redeemable at $104.50 a share, recorded at $100.00 liquidation value, 750,000 shares authorized, (outstanding excludes 18,300 shares held in treasury).......................400,257

Common stock, recorded at $1.00 par value:

150,000,000 shares authorized, (outstanding excludes 2,449,532 shares held in treasury)..........16,387,434

Each share of the preferred and common stock is entitled to one vote.

Preferred stock outstanding does not include 3,198 shares of $1.75 Series A and 6,396 shares of $5.75 series reserved for exercise of a warrant expiring in 1974 at a total exercise price of $600,000.

Common stock outstanding does not include 830,705 shares reserved for exercise of employee stock options (see below); 7,407,824 shares reserved for exercise of warrants expiring 1978 and 1986 at a total exercise price of $387,981,000; 9,904,950 shares reserved for issuance upon conversion of an aggregate of $532,646,000 principal amount of convertible debt; and 4,446,311 shares reserved for conversion of convertible preferred stock outstanding and reserved.

The Company's Stock Option Incentive Plan provides for the issuance of qualified options to key employees to purchase common stock of the Company at a price not less than fair market value on the date of grant. Transactions involving stock options were:

	Options Outstanding	
	Number of Shares	Total Option Price
Balance August 1, 1971.............	737,298	$22,084,000
Granted............	85,850	2,744,000
Exercised.........	134,791*	3,049,000*
Rescinded........	108,985*	3,774,000*
Balance July 31, 1972.............	579,372	$18,005,000
Exercisable at July 31, 1972....	194,571	

*Denotes deduction

Shares reserved for future options were 258,477 at the beginning and 251,333 at the end of the year.

Note F—Income taxes

Provision for income taxes includes United States Federal, foreign income and excess profits taxes, and state income taxes. Such provision is low in relation to earnings before taxes due to earnings of tax-exempt or low-tax-rate foreign subsidiaries, costs incurred in exploration and development of mineral reserves being capitalized for financial purposes, statutory percentage depletion allowable on earnings from mining businesses, investment tax credits (flow-through method), dividend income, tax-exempt interest income, and certain permanent differences where the tax basis of certain assets substantially exceeds their basis for financial purposes.

Provision for income taxes includes deferred tax credits of $15,980,000 for 1972 and $43,100,000 for 1971 representing future tax effects on items reported for income tax purposes in periods different than for financial purposes. Such items include theatrical film inventory amortization, provisions for depreciation, and recognition of certain expenses currently for financial purposes but in future periods for income tax purposes.

Note G—Earnings per share

Earnings per share amounts are based on the average common and common equivalent (the Company's $1.75 Series A and $3.50 Series B convertible preferred stock) shares outstanding during the respective periods.

In computing fully diluted earnings per share the following assumptions were made:
(1) exercise of all options and all warrants,
(2) use of the proceeds of such assumed exercises to purchase, at market prices, 20% of the outstanding common shares for the treasury and part of the Company's convertible debt, and
(3) conversion of the remaining convertible preferred stock and debt. Such assumed exercises and conversions did not result in dilution of the per-share amounts presented.

Note H—Commitments and contingencies

The aggregate annual rental obligations on leases in effect at July 31, 1972 approximate $17,600,000. Many of the leases also require the lessee to pay property taxes, insurance, and ordinary repairs and maintenance. Certain leases provide for additional payments based on a percentage of gross receipts. The leases have varying terms up to twenty-five years.

Pension and profit-sharing plan expense was $19,900,000 during the year ended July 31, 1972. The pension plan expense includes amortization of prior service cost over periods of thirty to forty years. The Company's policy generally is to fund an amount equal to current service cost and interest on prior service cost. As of the most recent valuation dates, the actuarially computed value of vested benefits under the pension plans exceeded the total fund assets of such plans and balance sheet accruals by approximately $50,500,000.

Estimated cost to complete construction in progress at July 31, 1972 was $29,700,000.

The Company is contingently liable for an indeterminable amount as defendant in various suits, including certain antitrust and other suits which also involve other major motion picture companies. In the opinion of counsel, these suits are without substantial merit and should not result in judgments against the Company or any of its subsidiaries which in the aggregate would have a material adverse effect on the Company's financial statements.

Note I-Working capital changes
The details of the increases/decreases* in
the elements of working capital are as follows:

	Year Ended July 31	
	1972	1971
CURRENT ASSETS		
Cash and certificates of deposit	$128,940,000	$ 16,162,000*
Marketable securities	18,045,000	3,014,000*
Trade receivables	2,746,000	32,690,000*
Inventories	16,621,000*	71,398,000*
Prepaid expenses, income taxes and other receivables	5,946,000*	16,739,000
	$127,164,000	$106,525,000*
CURRENT LIABILITIES		
Notes payable and commercial paper	$ 10,458,000	$179,819,000*
Current maturities of long-term debt	6,061,000	2,362,000
Trade accounts payable	9,393,000	18,737,000*
Accrued expenses and other liabilities	21,844,000	24,684,000
Income taxes payable	2,106,000*	3,553,000
	$ 45,650,000	$167,957,000*
INCREASE IN WORKING CAPITAL	$ 81,514,000	$ 61,432,000

REPORT TO INDEPENDENT ACCOUNTANTS

To the Shareholders and Directors
Gulf+Western Industries, Inc.

We have examined the consolidated financial statements of Gulf+Western Industries, Inc. and consolidated subsidiaries for the year ended July 31, 1972. Our examination was made in accordance with generally accepted auditing standards, and accordingly included such tests of the accounting records and such other auditing procedures as we considered necessary in the circumstances.

In our opinion, the accompanying balance sheet and statements of earnings, paid-in surplus and retained earnings, and changes in financial position present fairly the consolidated financial position of Gulf+Western Industries, Inc. and consolidated subsidiaries at July 31, 1972, and the consolidated results of their operations, changes in shareholders' equity and changes in financial position for the year then ended, in conformity with generally accepted accounting principles applied on a basis consistent with that of the preceding year.

Ernst & Ernst

New York, N.Y.
October 24, 1972

Case 6-10

National Distillers

Financial Statements of the National Distillers and Chemical Corporation (NDCC) with notes are shown.

Principles of Consolidation
The financial statements include the accounts of all majority-owned companies.

Translation of Foreign Currency Accounts
Foreign currency cash and amounts receivable or payable are translated at current exchange rates. All other balance sheet accounts are translated at rates in effect at the time acquired (i.e., historical rate).

Revenue and expense transactions, except for depreciation and amortization, are translated at the average of exchange rates in effect during the period. Provisions for depreciation and amortization are translated at the same rates as the assets to which they apply.

Resulting translation gains or losses are included in income for the year.

Inventories
Inventories are valued at the lower of cost or market. Cost is determined for the various categories of inventory using the first-in, first-out; last-in, first-out; or average cost method as deemed appropriate. Whiskey in storage for aging over a number of years is included in current assets in accordance with the general practice in the distilling industry.

Investments in Associated Companies
Investments in associated companies are accounted for under the equity method, i.e., at cost, increased or decreased by the Company's share of earnings or losses less dividends. Associated companies include significant companies in which the Company has at least a 20% but not more than a 50% interest.

Property, Plant and Equipment
Property, plant and equipment are stated at cost. Depreciation is determined for related groups of assets under the straight line method based upon their estimated useful lives; however, for income tax purposes, depreciation is based on accelerated methods and shorter useful lives where permitted.

Minor renewals or replacements and maintenance and repairs are expensed. Major replacements and improvements are capitalized. Gains or losses on disposal of assets in the normal course of business are credited or charged to accumulated depreciation. Gains or losses from abnormal dispositions are credited or charged to income.

Goodwill
The excess of the cost of acquired businesses over values assigned to net assets is classified as goodwill. In the opinion of management, goodwill (which arose from acquisitions made prior to 1970) has continuing value and it is not being amortized.

Taxes on Income
The provision for taxes on income includes the tax effects of revenue and expense transactions included in the determination of financial statement income. Where such transactions are included in the determination of taxable income in a different year, the tax effects are deferred. Investment tax credits are recognized in the year in which they are allowed for tax purposes, which is generally the year the qualified assets are placed in service.

Pensions
The Company accrues and funds pension costs annually. Costs of all principal plans are actuarially determined under projected benefit cost methods and include amounts for current service, amortization of prior service, and interest on unfunded prior service.

Research and Development
Research and development costs are charged to income as incurred.

Consolidated Statement of Income and Retained Earnings

	1975	1974 (1)
Net sales	$1,266,714,000	$1,404,679,000
Cost of goods sold	1,017,348,000	1,109,232,000
Gross profit	249,366,000	295,447,000
Selling, advertising and other divisional expenses	106,597,000	102,057,000
Operating profit of divisions	142,769,000	193,390,000
Corporate and general expenses	(9,908,000)	(9,694,000)
Interest on long-term debt	(11,497,000)	(13,085,000)
Other income (expense)—net	4,803,000	(892,000)
	126,167,000	169,719,000
Provision for taxes on income (Note 11)	(60,017,000)	(84,738,000)
Minority interests in earnings of subsidiaries	(3,458,000)	(3,204,000)
Share of earnings of associated companies—net (Note 5)	10,256,000	12,616,000
Income from continuing operations	72,948,000	94,393,000
Loss on discontinued operation net of tax recovery (Note 2)	(7,971,000)	(4,716,000)
Income before extraordinary charge	64,977,000	89,677,000
Extraordinary charge—proposed settlement of litigation (Note 3)	(2,568,000)	
Net income for the year	62,409,000	89,677,000
Retained earnings at beginning of year	416,507,000	352,923,000
Dividends paid		
$100 Preferred—$4.25 per share	566,000	625,000
$ 50 Preferred—$2.25 per share	248,000	270,000
Common—$1.20 per share in 1975; $1.025 per share in 1974	29,516,000	25,198,000
Retained earnings at end of year (Note 10)	$ 448,586,000	$ 416,507,000
Primary earnings per common share (Note 1)		
Continuing operations	$2.94	$3.80
Discontinued operation	(.33)	(.19)
Extraordinary charge	(.10)	
Net income	$2.51	$3.61
Fully diluted earnings per common share (Note 1)		
Continuing operations		
Discontinued operation		
Extraordinary charge		
Net income		

(1) Reclassified—See Note 2

Consolidated Balance Sheets
December 31

	1975	1974
Assets		
Current Assets		
Cash	$ 49,202,000	$ 56,551,000
Short-term investments—at lower of cost or market	56,435,000	49,850,000
Accounts and notes receivable—less allowance for doubtful accounts: $1,734,000—1975; $1,600,000—1974	209,188,000	203,951,000
Inventories (Note 4)	301,391,000	325,948,000
Prepaid expenses and other assets (Note 2)	13,148,000	5,014,000
Total current assets	629,364,000	641,314,000
Investments in Associated Companies (Note 5)	40,820,000	35,042,000
Miscellaneous Investments and Other Receivables—at cost	11,154,000	6,756,000
Deferred Charges and Other Assets	5,233,000	3,965,000
Property, Plant and Equipment (Note 7)	322,427,000	316,328,000
Goodwill—at cost	15,199,000	15,199,000
	$1,024,197,000	$1,018,604,000
Liabilities and Stockholders' Equity		
Current Liabilities		
Accounts payable and accrued liabilities	$ 94,735,000	$ 81,524,000
Federal excise taxes payable	30,831,000	26,402,000
Taxes on income	19,715,000	49,831,000
Loans payable to banks and others	5,159,000	12,715,000
Long-term debt payable within one year (Note 8)	13,327,000	10,313,000
Total current liabilities	163,767,000	180,785,000
Long-Term Debt Payable After One Year (Note 8)	185,403,000	197,030,000
Deferred Taxes on Income and Other Deferred Credits (Note 11)	57,402,000	51,620,000
Minority Interests in Subsidiary Companies	22,281,000	24,320,000
Preferred Stock (Note 9)	17,310,000	19,590,000
Common Stockholders' Equity (Note 10)	578,034,000	545,259,000
Contingencies (Note 13)		
	$1,024,197,000	$1,018,604,000

Notes to Financial Statements

Note 1 Earnings per Common Share

Primary earnings per common share were computed by dividing net income applicable to common stock by the weighted average number of shares of common stock outstanding during the year. For purposes of this computation certain unissued shares subject to stock options have been included in the weighted average. Fully diluted earnings per common share were determined by dividing net income as above, adjusted for interest on convertible debentures after related income tax effect, by the weighted average as above plus the number of shares which would have been issued at the beginning of each year on conversion of convertible debentures.

Note 2 Loss on Discontinued Operation

In November 1975, the Company discontinued the manufacture and sale of double-knit apparel fabrics and wrote down the inventories, plant, equipment and other assets of the operation to estimated realizable value.

The loss on discontinued operation comprises the following:

	Year Ended December 31,	
	1975	1974
Net sales	$14,250,000	$25,424,000
Costs and expenses	19,570,000	34,529,000
Loss before income taxes	5,320,000	9,105,000
Less income tax recovery	(2,560,000)	(4,389,000)
Net loss from operations	2,760,000	4,716,000
Estimated loss on disposal of knitting operation (less income tax recovery of $3,926,000)	5,211,000	
Loss on discontinued operation	$ 7,971,000	$ 4,716,000

The estimated loss on disposal of the knitting operation includes the writedown of assets, provision for severance costs and continuing costs during the period required to dispose of the properties. The income tax recovery applicable to such loss has been reduced by $457,000 representing the loss of investment tax credits taken in prior years.

The estimated realizable value of the knitting assets at December 31, 1975 was $5,050,000, which amount is included in Prepaid Expenses and Other Assets. Sale of these assets is expected to be completed in 1976.

The 1974 consolidated statement of income has been reclassified to conform to the 1975 presentation.

Note 3 Extraordinary Charge

In December 1975, a settlement agreement was submitted for approval to the Federal District Court in New York which provides for termination of a class action against the Company and others alleging violations of the Federal Securities Laws in connection with the 1973 exchange offer under which National shares owned by the class plaintiffs were exchanged for shares, owned by the Company, of the Company's subsidiary Almadén Vineyards, Inc. Under the settlement agreement National has paid $3,000,000 into a fund which, after deduction of fees and expenses approved by the Court, will be disbursed to eligible members of the class who submit and substantiate claims. No tax recoveries are anticipated with respect to the settlement.

If the settlement agreement is

approved by the Court the cost to the Company, including legal expenses and after giving effect to recovery on insurance, would be $2,568,000, which has been provided in 1975 as an extraordinary charge. In December 1973, the Company credited to income an extraordinary gain of $25,868,000 as a result of the exchange offer.

Note 4 Inventories

	December 31,	
	1975	1974
Finished goods	$ 91,880,000	$ 99,334,000
Work in process	24,112,000	25,220,000
Raw materials and supplies	54,117,000	59,588,000
	170,109,000	184,142,000
Bulk whiskey, other spirits and wines in bond	131,282,000	141,806,000
	$301,391,000	$325,948,000

Inventory costs of $99,707,000 at December 31, 1975 and $112,233,000 at December 31, 1974 were determined under the last-in, first-out method. The remaining inventory costs were determined under either the first-in, first-out or average cost method. If inventories valued under the last-in, first-out method had been determined under first-in, first-out or average cost methods, inventory value would have been increased by approximately $73,000,000 at December 31, 1975 and $79,000,000 at December 31, 1974.

Note 5 Investments in Associated Companies

National's investments in associated companies amounted to $40,820,000 and $35,042,000 at December 31, 1975 and 1974, respectively.

The Company's principal investments in associated companies consist of 50% interests in two U.S. corporations, National Helium Corporation and National Petro Chemicals Corporation, a 50% interest in RMI Company, a domestic partnership, and a 28% interest in Poliolefinas S.A., a Brazilian corporation. Summary financial information for associated companies as a group is as follows:

The Company's share of the undistributed earnings of associated companies was $18,672,000 at December 31, 1975.

The Company includes its share of the income or loss of RMI Company in computing its taxable income. The resulting tax expense or benefit is included in share of earnings of associated companies.

National Helium Corporation's net income for 1975 was substantially below that of 1974 because of a curtailed supply of natural gas feedstock with a lower hydrocarbon content, and lower selling prices for the natural gas liquids it produces.

	1975	1974
Total assets	$204,694,000	$212,418,000
Combined equity	87,616,000	77,558,000
National's share of equity	40,820,000	35,042,000
Revenues	207,607,000	191,057,000
National's share of earnings	10,256,000	12,616,000
National's share of dividends	5,443,000	9,948,000

Prior to 1974, National Helium's major source of revenue was from the sale of helium to the U.S. Government under a long-term contract. The Government served notice to terminate the contract as of April 4, 1973 and refused to accept deliveries of helium on and after November 12, 1973. In May 1975, National Helium filed an action against the Government in the U.S. Court of Claims for breach of contract seeking recovery of $21,700,000 (plus interest) for helium delivered and substantial damages for loss of future profits. The outcome of this action cannot be predicted at this time.

If the Government's right to terminate the contract is upheld, National Helium is entitled under the contract to either convey its helium plant to the Government at a formula price or to retain the plant and receive any excess of depreciated cost over market value of the plant.

The Company is contingently liable in respect of indebtedness of certain of the associated companies for moneys borrowed. At December 31, 1975, the maximum amount of such contingent liability is estimated at $18,500,000, assuming the other investor in one of the associated companies involved makes its required contribution should the liability arise.

Note 6 Foreign Currency Translation

1975 foreign currency translation adjustments increased income by $528,000, compared with a $3,513,000 charge in 1974. The 1974 charge included a write-off of the unamortized balance of $2,965,000 applicable to foreign currency long-term debt as of the beginning of that year.

Note 7 Property, Plant and Equipment

	December 31, 1975	December 31, 1974
Land and land improvements	$ 32,804,000	$ 33,843,000
Buildings	118,629,000	119,059,000
Machinery and equipment	453,169,000	444,058,000
Other	22,270,000	22,530,000
Construction in progress	32,447,000	18,854,000
	659,319,000	638,344,000
Less—Accumulated depreciation	336,892,000	322,016,000
	$322,427,000	$316,328,000

Annual rates used in computing depreciation are as follows: Buildings 2½% to 5%; Machinery and equipment 5% to 10%.

Note 8 Long-Term Debt

The December 31, 1975 amounts in the following summary have been reduced by $9,137,000 principal amount of certain issues reacquired by the Company which will be used to satisfy future sinking fund requirements. The payments to be made on long-term debt during each of the years 1977-1980 are $12,247,000, $11,839,000, $17,454,000 and $17,164,000, respectively.

At December 31, 1975, the 4½% debentures were convertible into 2,311,551 shares of common stock at a conversion price of $25.02 per share.

	December 31,	
	1975	1974
Convertible subordinated debentures 4½% due 1978-1992	$ 57,835,000	$ 57,845,000
Sinking fund debentures 5% due 1976-1983	19,352,000	22,336,000
Promissory notes 5⅜% due 1976-1986	45,000,000	45,750,000
Promissory notes 4⅜% due 1976-1977	1,500,000	2,800,000
Promissory note 5% due 1976-1985	24,450,000	26,750,000
Foreign subsidiary loans due 1976-1982, average rate 7.85%	30,069,000	34,978,000
Foreign subsidiary loan from customer due 1976-1984 net of discount ($9,274,000—1975; $7,050,000—1974) imputed at 9½%	16,626,000	11,500,000
Other	3,898,000	5,384,000
	198,730,000	207,343,000
Long-term debt payable within one year	13,327,000	10,313,000
Long-term debt payable after one year	$185,403,000	$197,030,000

Note 9
Preferred Stock

	1975		1974	
	Shares	Amount	Shares	Amount
$100 cumulative preferred 4¼% Authorized—500,000 shares Outstanding				
Beginning of year	138,330	$13,833,000	166,650	$16,665,000
Reacquired	(16,500)	(1,650,000)	(28,320)	(2,832,000)
End of year	121,830	12,183,000	138,330	13,833,000
$50 cumulative preferred 4½% Authorized and outstanding				
Beginning of year	115,140	5,757,000	129,940	6,497,000
Reacquired	(12,600)	(630,000)	(14,800)	(740,000)
End of year	102,540	5,127,000	115,140	5,757,000
		$17,310,000		$19,590,000

At December 31, 1975 the Company held 65,048 shares of $100 preferred stock and 39,350 shares of $50 preferred stock which can be used to satisfy sinking fund provisions that require the annual redemption of 13,702 shares of $100 preferred and 6,061 shares of $50 preferred. The required redemptions have been made through 1975. The preferred shares are callable at par.

Note 10
Common Stockholders' Equity

	1975		1974	
	Shares	Amount	Shares	Amount
Common Stock—$2.50 Par Authorized—40,000,000 shares Issued				
Beginning of year	26,790,258	$164,734,000	26,790,220	$163,960,000
Stock options exercised	3,450	45,000		
Issued on conversion of debentures	386	10,000	38	1,000
Excess of par over cost of preferred stock reacquired		629,000		773,000
End of year	26,794,094	165,418,000	26,790,258	164,734,000
Less				
Common stock in treasury, at cost				
Beginning of year	2,201,751	35,982,000	2,139,463	35,074,000
Acquired by purchase	150,680	2,388,000	2,100	30,000
Conversion of contingent shares under Incentive Compensation Plan			60,188	878,000
Exchanged for minority interest in subsidiary	(151,616)	(2,400,000)		
End of year	2,200,815	35,970,000	2,201,751	35,982,000
Common stock outstanding at end of year	24,593,279	129,448,000	24,588,507	128,752,000
Retained Earnings—end of year		448,586,000		416,507,000
Common Stockholders' Equity		$578,034,000		$545,259,000

Prior to 1974 the Company's Incentive Compensation Plan provided for the awarding of shares contingently to certain employees. On December 27, 1973, the plan was amended to provide that contingent awards for 1973 and subsequent years be made in the form of Common Stock Equivalency Units. Each unit has a value equivalent to the market value of a share of the Company's common stock. During 1974, 60,188 contingent shares awarded prior to the amendment were converted at the option of the participants into such units. The accrued liability applicable to such units is included in accounts payable and accrued liabilities.

The Company has granted, upon various terms and conditions, options to key employees to purchase shares of the Company's common stock at prices equal to the market value of the stock at date of grant. One term which is unique to the options granted in June 1975 is that a holder may surrender an exercisable option, in whole or in part, in exchange for a payment equal to the excess of the market value of the stock on the day of surrender over the option price. Such payment is to be made approximately one-half in whole shares of the Company's stock (based on the stock's market value on the day of surrender) and the balance in cash. At December 31, 1975, there were outstanding options for 383,000 shares which may be surrendered under such provision and $242,000 has been accrued in anticipation of settlement of such right to surrender.

Changes in shares under option during 1975 and 1974 were as follows:

	Option Shares	
	1975	1974
Outstanding—beginning of year	302,425	314,325
Granted ($15.625 per share)	388,000	
Exercised	(3,450)	
Cancelled	(122,375)	(11,900)
Outstanding—end of year ($13.00-$17.00 per share)	564,600	302,425
Exercisable—end of year	108,300	168,975

At December 31, 1975, 27,775 shares were available for future grant.

The terms of indentures and note agreements relating to certain of the long-term debt and terms of the preferred stock impose certain restrictions on the payment of cash dividends on the common stock or acquisition of preferred and common stock by the Company. Retained earnings available for these purposes under the most restrictive agreement amounted to approximately $217,000,000 at December 31, 1975.

Note 11
Provision for Taxes on Income

	December 31,	
	1975	1974
Current		
United States (net of investment tax credits of $2,222,000 in 1975 and $819,000 in 1974)	$34,359,000	$55,134,000
Foreign	9,027,000	15,634,000
State and local	6,582,000	6,957,000
	49,968,000	77,725,000
Tax effect of timing differences		
United States	4,139,000	2,331,000
Foreign	(576,000)	293,000
	3,563,000	2,624,000
Provision for taxes on income	$53,531,000	$80,349,000
Applicable to:		
Tax on continuing operations	$60,017,000	$84,738,000
Tax recovery on discontinued operation	(6,486,000)	(4,389,000)
	$53,531,000	$80,349,000

The tax effects of timing differences arise from the recognition of certain items of revenue and expense for tax purposes in years different from those in which they are recognized in the financial statements. The tax effects of these items which are added to (deducted from) the amount currently payable in determining the provision for taxes on income are as follows:

	1975	1974
Depreciation expense	$ 4,860,000	$ 1,055,000
Facilities disposal costs	(1,937,000)	(1,166,000)
Other items	640,000	2,735,000
Total tax effect of timing differences	$ 3,563,000	$ 2,624,000

Required   Given the data on Primary EPS *but not* for Fully diluted EPS, derive each of the letters in the table below. Do not use plug figures. (See Note 1 to the financial statements).

Income from continuing operations	$72,948,000
Additions and/or subtractions	(a)
Income from continuing operations after allowing for dilution	(b)
Weighted Average number of shares used to compute primary EPS	(c)
Additions and/or subtractions	(d)
Total shares (fully diluted)	(e)
Fully diluted EPS Continuing Operations	(f)

Case 6-11

Bunker-Ramo Corporation

The Annual Report for Bunker-Ramo for the year ended December 31, 1971 indicated the following:

Consolidated Balance Sheets

	Year Ended December 31, 1971	1970
NET REVENUES	$224,669,407	$231,797,142
COST AND EXPENSES:		
Cost of sales and services	172,824,898	173,310,599
Selling, general, and administrative expenses	41,407,501	41,235,431
Total	214,232,399	214,546,030
INCOME FROM OPERATIONS	10,437,008	17,251,112
OTHER EXPENSE (INCOME):		
Interest expense	5,840,832	4,504,830
Equity in income of affiliates — net of tax	(270,000)	(635,615)
Other income — net	(960,397)	(1,799,116)
Total	4,610,435	2,070,099
INCOME BEFORE INCOME TAXES	5,826,573	15,181,013
PROVISION FOR INCOME TAXES		
Current	855,800	3,535,000
Deferred	714,200	2,505,000
Total	1,570,000	6,040,000
NET INCOME	$ 4,256,573	$ 9,141,013
NET INCOME PER SHARE OF COMMON STOCK (including dilutive common stock equivalents)	$0.085	$0.36

Bunker-Ramo reported the same income figure of $9,141,013 in their annual report issued for the year ending December 31, 1970. However they reported net income per share of $0.39. On page 19 in their Financial Review section of the 1970 report they state:

"Earnings per common share are based upon 23,575,685 weighted average shares of common stock, including common stock equivalents [amounting to

5,435,449 shares] outstanding during 1970 as compared with 23,567,480 during 1969. The preferred stock, stock options and warrants are considered common stock equivalents and the computation of the weighted average common shares outstanding has been increased to give effect to the assumed conversion of preferred stock and the applicable exercise of stock options and warrants. Earnings per common share, assuming full dilution, do not differ from earnings per common share, including common stock equivalents."

The Financial Review continues:

Dividends

"During 1970, four quarterly dividends of 37½ cents per share were paid on the cumulative convertible preferred stock. No dividend payments were made on the common stock.

Total dividends paid in 1970 were $2,697,075 compared with $2,733,347 in 1969."

Required

1. Why did Bunker-Ramo restate their earnings per share figures in their 1971 Annual Report?

2. Derive the 36 cents-per-share figure reported in the 1971 Annual Report for 1970 earnings.

3. Bunker-Ramo reported 53 cents per share for 1969. What impact did the convertible preferred stock have on the EPS calculation in that year? Why? (Assume the same number of preferred shares are convertible in 1969.)

4. Suppose reported earnings per share had been 50 cents in 1969 rather than $.53. What impact should the convertible preferred have had on the computation of the EPS figure?

5. Is the mistake the firm's or is it the auditor's?

Case 6-12

Computer Sciences Corporation (CSC)

Computer Sciences Corporation provides a broad range of technical and management services required to apply computer and communications equipment to the tasks of collecting, communicating, processing, storing and presenting information. The Company also provides a number of proprietary data services of which the most significant is operation of a remote data processing service called INFONET. The Company manufactures no equipment.

Consolidated Statement of Earnings

	YEAR ENDED	
	March 31, 1978	April 1, 1977
REVENUES:		
Contract Services operations	$199,068,000	$176,976,000
Data Services operations	77,844,000	57,769,000
	276,912,000	234,745,000
EXPENSES:		
Contract Services operations:		
Costs of services, excluding depreciation	163,176,000	144,778,000
Operating overhead	12,941,000	10,267,000
Depreciation and amortization	3,246,000	5,129,000
	179,363,000	160,174,000
Data Services operations:		
Costs of services, excluding depreciation	48,912,000	35,627,000
Operating overhead	6,154,000	3,927,000
Depreciation and amortization	6,533,000	4,508,000
	61,599,000	44,062,000
OPERATING INCOME, BEFORE CORPORATE CHARGES:		
Contract Services operations	19,705,000	16,802,000
Data Services operations	16,245,000	13,707,000
	35,950,000	30,509,000
CORPORATE CHARGES:		
Interest expense	3,547,000	3,609,000
General and administrative	6,316,000	5,680,000
	9,863,000	9,289,000
Income before taxes and extraordinary item	26,087,000	21,220,000
TAXES ON INCOME (Note 3)	12,207,000	9,585,000
EARNINGS BEFORE EXTRAORDINARY ITEM	13,880,000	11,635,000
Extraordinary item—reduction of income tax expense resulting from use of a prior year's net operating loss	—	3,000,000
NET EARNINGS	$ 13,880,000	$ 14,635,000

Liabilities and Stockholders' Equity

	March 31, 1978	April 1, 1977
CURRENT LIABILITIES:		
Current maturities of long-term liabilities (Note 5)	$ 2,173,000	$ 1,832,000
Accounts payable	7,085,000	4,998,000
Accrued payroll and related costs	19,344,000	14,526,000
Other accrued expenses	9,248,000	7,010,000
Federal, state and foreign income taxes (Note 3)	18,120,000	10,068,000
Total current liabilities	55,970,000	38,434,000
LONG-TERM LIABILITIES, excluding current maturities (Note 5)	7,345,000	6,166,000
COMMITMENTS AND CONTINGENT LIABILITIES (Note 6)	—	—
6% SUBORDINATED CONVERTIBLE DEBENTURES, due September 15, 1994, net of $461,000 (1978) and $489,000 (1977) unamortized discount (Note 7)	49,530,000	49,502,000
STOCKHOLDERS' EQUITY (Notes 7 and 8):		
Preferred stock, par value $1 per share; authorized 1,000,000 shares; none issued	—	—
Common stock, par value $1 per share; authorized 25,000,000 shares; issued 14,412,817 shares (1978) and 14,342,917 (1977)	14,413,000	14,343,000
Additional paid-in capital	9,786,000	9,794,000
Earnings retained for use in business	26,539,000	12,903,000
	50,738,000	37,040,000
Less common stock in treasury, at cost, 1,500,000 shares in 1978 and no shares in 1977	11,575,000	—
(See Notes to Consolidated Financial Statements)	39,163,000	37,040,000
	$152,008,000	$131,142,000

Consolidated Statement of Stockholders' Equity

	Common stock Shares	Common stock Amount	Additional paid-in capital	Earnings retained for use in business (deficit)	Treasury stock
Balance at April 2, 1976	14,301,717	$14,302,000	$9,723,000	$ (1,732,000)	$ —
Exercise of stock options	41,200	41,000	71,000	—	—
Net earnings	—	—	—	14,635,000	—
Balance at April 1, 1977	14,342,917	14,343,000	9,794,000	12,903,000	—
Exercise of stock options	69,900	70,000	148,000	—	—
Net earnings	—	—	—	13,880,000	—
Purchase of outstanding warrants	—	—	(156,000)	(244,000)	—
Purchase of 1,500,000 shares of treasury stock	—	—	—	—	(11,575,000)
Balance at March 31, 1978	14,412,817	$14,413,000	$9,786,000	$26,539,000	$(11,575,000)

CSC's 1978 Consolidated Statement of Earnings, Consolidated Balance Sheets (Liabilities and Stockholders' Equity Sections Only), Consolidated Statement of Stockholders' Equity and selected Notes to Consolidated Financial Statements are presented.

The 6% Subordinated Convertible Debentures are not considered to be common stock equivalents. Assume that during fiscal 1978 (which ends on March 31, 1978) the average option price was $4.66 per share, the average market price was $8.50 per share and the average number of options outstanding was for 543,584 shares. The market price was $9.25 per share on March 31, 1978.

Notes to Consolidated Financial Statements

Note 7 – 6% Subordinated Convertible Debentures

The 6% subordinated convertible debentures, due 1994, are convertible into common stock at $27.00 per share. At March 31, 1978, 1,851,518 shares of common stock were reserved for conversion of the debentures. Beginning in September 1980, annual sinking fund payments are required of not less than 5% nor more than 10% of the aggregate principal amount of debentures outstanding. Upon 30 days' written notice, the Company may redeem all outstanding debentures or any portion thereof at an annually declining rate of 103.3% in 1978 to par in 1989 and thereafter.

The indenture covering the issuance of the debentures contains restrictions relating to the payment of dividends or payment for the acquisition of the Company's outstanding capital stock. At March 31, 1978, such payments could not exceed $9,576,000 in the aggregate.

Note 8 – Common Stock

In October 1977, the Company repurchased 1,500,000 shares of its common stock from the Jones Foundation, a non-profit California corporation, for $11,575,000.

In accordance with a prior agreement with certain banks, the Company had issued to the banks warrants to purchase 250,000 shares of the Company's common stock at an exercise price of $6.00 per share, expiring March 31, 1978. The Company repurchased the warrants from the banks for $400,000, effective July 1, 1977.

The Company has two plans under which options to purchase shares of common stock may be granted to officers and key managerial and technical employees of the Company and its subsidiaries at prices equal to fair market value at date of grant. Options are exercisable in cumulative annual installments commencing at various times from date of grant until expiration either five years or 10 years from date of grant.

At March 31, 1978, options for the purchase of 589,950 shares of the Company's common stock were outstanding, of which 163,100 shares were exercisable; 109,800 shares of common stock were available for the granting of future options.

Status of all optioned shares is as follows:

	1978	1977
Outstanding—beginning of year	497,575	484,850
Granted during year, at prices ranging from $7.13 to $9.75 (1978) and $5.63 to $8.63 (1977)	203,000	135,500
Exercised during year, at prices ranging from $2.06 to $6.44 (1978) and $2.06 to $4.50 (1977)	(69,900)	(41,200)
Expired during year, at prices ranging from $2.06 to $8.63 (1978) and $2.56 to $16.31 (1977)	(40,725)	(81,575)
Outstanding—end of year, at prices ranging from $1.88 to $9.75 (1978) and $1.88 to $8.63 (1977)	589,950	497,575

Other Information

CSC Stock

Common stock of Computer Sciences Corporation is listed and traded on the New York Stock Exchange and Pacific Stock Exchange. The ticker symbol is "CSC."

The table shows the high and low prices of the Company's common stock on the New York Stock Exchange for each quarter during the last two calendar years, and to date in 1978. No dividends have been paid during this period.

Calendar Quarter	1978 High	1978 Low	1977 High	1977 Low	1976 High	1976 Low
1st	10½	8⅛	8⅞	7	7⅞	4
2nd	12*	9⅞*	8¼	6¾	7⅜	5⅞
3rd	—	—	9⅜	7⅝	7⅜	6
4th	—	—	9⅝	7⅜	7¼	5¼

*Through May 31, 1978

Required Assume that the options exercised were evenly distributed throughout the year and that the treasury shares were purchased on October 1, 1977.

1. Calculate the numerator for the primary earnings per share calculation for 1978.

2. Calculate the numerator for the fully diluted earnings per share calculation for 1978.

3. Calculate the weighted average number of shares of common stock outstanding during 1978.

4. Calculate the number of shares under outstanding options that should be considered common stock equivalents and included in the denominator of the primary earnings per share calculation for 1978.

5. Calculate the incremental number of shares under outstanding options that should be included in the denominator of the fully diluted earnings per share calculation for 1978.

Case 6-13

McDonnell Douglas Corporation

McDonnell Douglas Corporation's Consolidated Statement of Earnings and Consolidated Statement of Shareholders' Equity for the year ended December 31, 1976 and excerpts from Note G from the Notes to Consolidated Financial Statements are presented.

Consolidated Statement of Earnings

Years Ended 31 December	1976	1975
Income		
Sales	$3,543,713,215	$3,255,668,229
Other income	40,061,955	55,191,490
	3,583,775,170	3,310,859,719
Costs and Expenses		
Cost of products and services	2,965,305,884	2,720,515,784
Research and development	105,566,398	132,207,082
Administrative and general	309,322,988	292,064,862
Interest and debt expense	23,933,255	40,294,125
Income taxes, *Note F*	70,791,403	40,128,150
	3,474,919,928	3,225,210,003
Net Earnings	$ 108,855,242	$ 85,649,716

Earnings Per Share, *Note O*

Consolidated Statement of Shareholders' Equity

Years Ended 31 December 1976 and 1975

	Common Stock	Capital In Excess Of Par Value	Earnings Retained For Growth	Treasury Shares
Shareholders' Equity at 1 January 1975	$38,215,178	$307,703,110	$452,631,660	($26,199,595)
Cash dividends declared—$.40 a share			(14,505,965)	
Treasury shares (225,845) issued under the Incentive Compensation Plan		498,818		2,989,445
Net earnings			85,649,716	
Shareholders' Equity at 31 December 1975	38,215,178	308,201,928	523,775,411	(23,210,150)
Cash dividends declared—$.44 a share			(16,062,644)	
Treasury shares (212,928) issued under the Incentive Compensation Plan		1,821,935		2,818,466
Stock options exercised	70,877	863,351		
Net earnings			108,855,242	
Shareholders' Equity at 31 December 1976	$38,286,055	$310,887,214	$616,568,009	($20,391,684)

G. Long-Term Debt
The long-term debt outstanding is detailed below:

31 DECEMBER	1976	1975
Unsecured notes	$ 50,000,000	$150,000,000
4¾% Convertible Subordinated Debentures	61,894,000	61,894,000
5% Sinking Fund Debentures	4,912,000	6,936,000
Space Center Secured Notes	17,210,233	18,988,081
Other	9,811,161	12,525,537
	143,827,394	250,343,618
Less current maturities	5,811,871	4,684,469
	$138,015,523	$245,659,149

The Indenture for the 4¾% Convertible Subordinated Debentures, due 1 July 1991, provides for retirement of a minimum (on a cumulative basis) of $4,285,000 of these Debentures annually, beginning in 1977, through conversion, purchase and cancellation, or operation of a sinking fund. At 31 December 1976 sinking fund requirements through 1979 and $251,000 of the 1980 requirement had been fulfilled, principally through purchase of Debentures in the open market. The Debentures are callable at any time (but at a premium to 30 June 1985) and are convertible at $30.61 per share into MDC Common Stock. The conversion price and shares reserved for conversion are subject to adjustment in accordance with antidilution provisions of the indenture. At 31 December 1976, 2,022,020 shares of unissued Common Stock were reserved for conversion of Debentures.

The 4¾% Convertible Subordinated Debentures are considered to be common stock equivalents. Since 1959 McDonnell Douglas has granted stock options to officers and key employees. Assume that during 1976 the average option price was $16.92 per share and the average number of options outstanding was for 988,500 shares. The average market prices of McDonnell Douglas Common Stock during 1976 were:

Quarter	High	Low	Average
1	18 7/8	14 3/4	16.81
2	24 7/8	17 1/2	20.30
3	26	20 5/8	24.275
4	24 3/8	21 1/4	23.18

Required Calculate McDonnell Douglas Corporation's earnings per common and common equivalent share for the year ended December 31, 1976.

Case 6-14

Georgia-Pacific Corporation (B)

Selected portions of Georgia-Pacific's 1977 Annual Report are presented.

Consolidated Balance Sheets

Amounts and shares in thousands

	1977	1976
Assets		
Current assets		
Cash	$ 11,000	$ 25,000
Receivables (less reserves of $7,000 in 1977 and $6,000 in 1976)	356,000	295,000
Inventories, at the lower of cost or market (Note 3)	449,000	423,000
Prepaid expenses	9,000	10,000
Total current assets	825,000	753,000
Natural resources, at cost less depletion (Note 4)		
Timber and timberlands	385,000	331,000
Coal, minerals, natural gas and oil	36,000	30,000
	421,000	361,000
Property, plant and equipment (Note 4)		
Land, buildings, machinery and equipment, at cost	2,657,000	2,285,000
Less—Reserves for depreciation	995,000	836,000
	1,662,000	1,449,000
Noncurrent receivables and other assets	21,000	21,000
	$2,929,000	$2,584,000

	As of December 31	
	1977	1976
Liabilities		
Current liabilities		
Current portion of long-term debt	$ 46,000	$ 37,000
Accounts payable and accrued liabilities	254,000	207,000
Current income taxes	65,000	67,000
	365,000	311,000
Commercial paper and other short-term notes supported by confirmed seasonal bank lines of credit (Note 9)	13,000	222,000
Total current liabilities (Note 9)	378,000	533,000
Long-term debt, excluding current portion (Note 9)	607,000	318,000
Convertible subordinated debentures 5¼% due 1996 (Note 10)	125,000	125,000
Deferred income taxes (Note 6)	280,000	250,000
Employee stock purchase plan (Note 11)	10,000	6,000
Capital stock and surplus (Notes 7, 11 and 12)		
Common stock, par value $.80 (authorized 150,000 shares; issued 102,806 shares in 1977)	82,000	79,000
Paid-in surplus	1,021,000	906,000
Earned surplus	428,000	369,000
Less—Common stock held in treasury, at cost (58 shares in 1977)	(2,000)	(2,000)
	1,529,000	1,352,000
	$2,929,000	$2,584,000

Statements of Consolidated Income

Amounts in thousands (except per share amounts)

	Year ended December 31	
	1977	1976
Net sales	**$3,675,000**	$3,038,000
Costs and expenses		
Cost of sales	**2,820,000**	2,332,000
Selling, general and administrative expenses	**194,000**	161,000
Depreciation and depletion (Notes 4 and 6)	**175,000**	151,000
Interest expense (less interest capitalized on construction projects of $18,000 in 1977 and $13,000 in 1976) (Note 4)	**33,000**	38,000
Provision for income taxes (Note 6)	**191,000**	141,000
	3,413,000	2,823,000
Net income	**$ 262,000**	$ 215,000
Income per share of common stock (Notes 2 and 10)		
Primary	**$ 2.54**	$ 2.12
Fully diluted	**$**	$

Notes to Financial Statements

Accounting Practices

1. Principles of Presentation

The consolidated financial statements include the accounts of Georgia-Pacific Corporation and all subsidiaries (the corporation) after elimination of intercompany balances and transactions.

2. Income per Share of Common Stock

Primary income per share of common stock has been computed based on the weighted average number of shares outstanding, assuming issuance of shares under stock option and stock purchase plans, adjusted retroactively for shares issued in stock dividends and for the 3-for-2 stock split in 1976. Fully diluted income per share of common stock, in addition, assumes conversion of the convertible subordinated debentures.

3. Inventory Valuation

The last-in, first-out (LIFO) method of inventory valuation is utilized for the majority of inventories at manufacturing facilities, while the average cost method is used for all other inventories. Inventory costs are determined on the basis of the average cost of materials, labor and plant overhead. All inventories are valued at the lower of cost or market as summarized below:

Method of valuation	**1977**	1976
Average cost	**$294,000**	$269,000
LIFO	**155,000**	154,000
	$449,000	$423,000

If LIFO inventories were valued at the lower of average cost or market, such inventories would have been $40,000, $34,000 and $30,000 higher than those reported at December 31, 1977, 1976 and 1975, respectively. The corporation uses the dollar value pool method for computing LIFO inventories; therefore it is not possible to present a breakdown of inventories between finished goods, raw materials and supplies.

4. Depletion, Depreciation and Capitalization Policies

The corporation amortizes its timber costs over the total fiber that will be available during the estimated growth cycle. Timber carrying costs are expensed as incurred.

All costs of exploring for and developing domestic oil and gas reserves are capitalized using the full-cost method of accounting and charged to operations on the basis of units-of-production over the estimated life of future production. The Financial Accounting Standards Board has adopted rules that prohibit the use of the full-cost method of accounting. If the new rules, which will apply to the corporation in 1979, had been in effect for the years ended December 31, 1977 and 1976, net income would have been reduced by $2,000 and $1,000, respectively.

Provisions for depreciation of buildings, machinery and equipment are computed on the straight-line or units-of-production method using composite rates based upon the estimated service lives of the various units of property. The ranges of composite rates for the principal classes of property and equipment are as follows:

Land improvements	5 to 7%
Buildings	2 to 5%
Machinery and equipment	5 to 20%

Maintenance and repairs and replacements of minor units of property are charged to expense as incurred. Replacements of major units of property are capitalized and the replaced properties retired.

All dollar amounts, except per share amounts, are in thousands

No gain or loss is recognized on normal property dispositions; property cost is credited to the asset accounts and charged to the depreciation reserve accounts and any proceeds are credited to the depreciation reserve accounts. When there are abnormal dispositions of property, the cost and related depreciation reserves are removed from the accounts and any gain or loss is reflected in income.

The corporation capitalizes interest during construction periods based upon the interest cost on debt incurred to finance construction projects. Such interest is charged to the property and equipment accounts and amortized over the approximate life of the related assets in order to properly match expenses with revenues resulting from the facilities. Capitalized interest, less related amortization and income taxes, amounted to $5,000 and $3,000 for the years ended December 31, 1977 and 1976, respectively.

The corporation defers net operating costs on new construction projects during the start-up phase and amortizes the deferral over approximately seven years. The amounts deferred for new project start-up costs were not significant in 1977 and 1976.

5. Pension and Stock Bonus Plans

Substantially all of the corporation's hourly employees participate in a number of noncontributory pension plans. Contribution to most of these plans is based upon hourly rates set forth in various contracts. The corporation also has a noncontributory stock bonus plan for salaried employees wherein an amount up to 10% of the eligible employee's annual salary, if certain conditions are met, is contributed to the plan. Total contributions accrued for all plans were $24,000 in 1977 and $21,000 in 1976, including charges for normal cost and amortization of prior service costs over periods ranging from ten to thirty years. At December 31, 1977, the unfunded prior service cost of plans administered solely or jointly by the corporation was approximately $45,000 and the actuarially computed value of vested benefits of these plans was approximately $14,000 in excess of the market value of plan assets. The increase in costs in 1977 compared to 1976 is attributable primarily to increases in benefits under the hourly plans. The corporation follows the policy of funding substantially all pension costs.

6. Income Taxes and Investment Credit

The provision for income taxes includes deferred taxes of $30,000 in 1977 and $35,000 in 1976. Deferred income taxes result from timing differences in the recognition of revenue and expense for financial and tax reporting purposes. The sources of these differences and the tax effect of each are summarized as follows:

	1977	1976
Excess of tax depreciation over financial depreciation	**$25,000**	$28,000
Capitalized interest, net of amortization	**4,000**	2,000
Others, including start-up costs and depletion timing differences	**1,000**	5,000
	$30,000	$35,000

The corporation realized investment tax credits of $29,000 in 1977 and $18,000 in 1976. The credits realized since 1962, less amortization credited to depreciation expense to date ($12,000 in 1977 and $11,000 in 1976), totaled $63,000 at December 31, 1977, and are included in the reserves for depreciation.

The difference between the ordinary Federal income tax rate and the corporation's effective income tax rate is summarized as follows:

	1977	1976
Federal income tax rate	**48%**	48%
Increase (decrease) as a result of		
Value of timber appreciation taxed at capital gains rate	**(6)**	(7)
State income taxes, net of Federal tax benefit	**2**	2
Others, including amortization of investment credit	**(2)**	(3)
Effective income tax rate	**42%**	40%

7. Stock Options

The corporation has granted key employees options to purchase common stock pursuant to the 1963 Employee Stock Option Plan and the 1974 Employee Stock Option Plan. No further options may be granted under the 1963 Plan. The 1974 Plan provides for issuance of options covering up to 1,723,000 shares at a price which shall not be less than 85% of the fair market value at the date of the grant. The excess, if any, of the fair market value at the date of grant over the option price is amortized to expense over the life of the option with a corresponding credit to paid-in surplus. When the stock options are exercised, the proceeds (including tax benefits to the corporation arising as a result of the exercise) are credited to the appropriate capital stock and surplus accounts. In addition, the corporation pays the optionees a cash bonus upon exercise of options granted under the 1974 Plan. The bonus, which represents the amount of individual tax liability estimated to be created as a result of the option exercise, is accrued based on the exercisable shares and charged to expense over the term of the option.

Under the 1974 Plan, as amended, officers of the corporation, excluding the Chairman, may surrender options in exchange for shares of common stock having an aggregate market value on the date of surrender equal to the difference between the market value and option price of the shares covered by the surrendered options. The excess of the fair market value over the option price or, for amended options, over the fair market value on the date of amendment, is amortized to expense over the life of such options with a corresponding credit to paid-in surplus.

Other

8. Addition (Reduction) to Working Capital

	1977	1976
Cash	$ (14,000)	$ (23,000)
Receivables	61,000	45,000
Inventories	26,000	46,000
Prepaid expenses	(1,000)	3,000
Current portion of long-term debt	(9,000)	62,000
Accounts payable and accrued liabilities	(47,000)	(77,000)
Current income taxes	2,000	(42,000)
Commercial paper and other short-term notes	209,000	(222,000)
	$ 227,000	$(208,000)

9. Long-Term Debt

	1977	1976
Insurance companies	$ 96,000	$ 114,000
Revenue bonds	158,000	158,000
Notes	200,000	—
Commercial paper and other short-term notes supported by revolving line of credit	100,000	—
Others, including banks and purchase contracts	53,000	46,000
	$ 607,000	$ 318,000

The average interest rate for debt at year-end was approximately 6.4%.

At December 31, 1977, $207,000 of long-term debt was secured by property and timber at a net book value of $282,000, including $194,000 (original cost $321,000) relating to certain manufacturing and pollution control facilities which were financed with the proceeds from revenue bonds issued by governmental units and guaranteed by the corporation. The corporation leases such facilities from the governmental units and pays all costs incidental to ownership of the properties. Upon repayment of the bonds, the corporation may at its option acquire the properties for a nominal amount. Accordingly, the leased facilities are included in property, plant and equipment and the related amortization charges are included in depreciation expense.

Repayment of principal through 1982 on long-term debt outstanding is as follows:

1979	$ 47,000
1980	138,000
1981	21,000
1982	119,000

In May 1977, the corporation replaced a $300,000 confirmed seasonal line of credit with a $250,000 unsecured revolving line of credit ("evergreen line") and a $100,000 unsecured seasonal line of credit ("seasonal line"). The evergreen line, which expires on June 30, 1980, consists of separate agreements with a number of banks. Each agreement may be terminated upon ten days' notice by the corporation or upon fifteen months' written notice by a participating bank. The seasonal line also consists of separate agreements which have varying provisions relating to review and renewal of each bank's participation in the line. Neither of the lines carry commitment fees or long-term conversion features. Under the evergreen line, the corporation has agreed to maintain bank deposits on an annual average basis amounting to 10% of the evergreen line plus 10% of all loans outstanding thereunder. The Board of Directors of the corporation has authorized the use of these lines up to a maximum of $300,000.

The corporation uses the evergreen line of credit to support short-term borrowings. The maximum amount of short-term borrowings outstanding at any time during 1977 was $256,000. The daily average amount of such borrowings outstanding during 1977 was $110,000 and the average interest rate for such borrowings was 5.7% during the period. As of December 31, 1977, current liabilities exclude and long-term debt includes $100,000 of commercial paper and short-term notes. The corporation currently intends to maintain borrowings of at least $100,000 supported by the evergreen line.

10. Convertible Subordinated Debentures

The 5¼% (due 1996) debentures were convertible into common stock at $30.87 per share at December 31, 1977. The conversion price is subject to adjustment for certain changes in the capital structure including common stock splits.

In January and November 1976, the corporation called for the redemption of its 5¾% and 6¼% debentures, respectively. As a result, substantially all of the debentures were converted into shares of common stock. Pro forma income per share, assuming conversion of the debentures on January 1, 1976, was $2.10 for the year ended December 31, 1976

11. Capital Stock

A summary of the common stock transactions for the year ended December 31, 1977, is as follows:

	Issued Shares	Issued Amount	Treasury Shares	Treasury Amount
Beginning balance	98,723,000	$79,000	52,000	$2,000
Add (deduct):				
Stock dividends on common stock (4%)	3,901,000	3,000	—	—
Stock sold	77,000	—	—	—
Stock issued for acquisitions	105,000	—	—	—
Purchases, at cost	—	—	6,000	—
Ending balance	102,806,000	$82,000	58,000	$2,000

At December 31, 1977, the following authorized shares of common stock of the corporation, adjusted for declaration of stock dividends, were reserved for issue as follows:

Exercise of stock options	803,000
Conversion of the 5¼% Convertible Subordinated Debentures	4,047,000
Employee Stock Purchase Plan	440,000
	5,290,000

The shares reserved for stock options cover shares which may be issued to key employees under the 1963 Employee Stock Option Plan and the 1974 Employee Stock Option Plan.

Options for 803,000 shares were outstanding as of December 31, 1977, including options for 3,000 shares granted under the 1963 Plan, at prices ranging from $18.25 to $30.09 per share. Of these, 504,000 shares were exercisable. During 1977, options for 34,000 shares were granted and options for 38,000 shares were canceled. Options for 3,000 shares under the 1963 Plan and options for 53,000 shares under the 1974 Plan were exercised during the year at prices ranging from $18.71 to $29.05.

As of December 31, 1977, 440,000 shares of common stock were subscribed at $26.54 per share under the 1976 Employee Stock Purchase Plan. Subscribers have the option to receive their payments plus interest at the rate of 6% per annum in lieu of stock. The Plan expires on March 31, 1978.

The shares and prices relating to the Stock Option Plans and the Employee Stock Purchase Plan are subject to adjustment for certain changes in the capital structure, including common stock splits.

Required

Using the footnotes and primary earnings per share information to derive each of the letters in the following table and calculate fully diluted earnings per share.

Net income	$262,000
Additions and/or subtractions	a
Income after allowing for dilution	b
Weighted average number of shares to compute primary EPS	c
Additions and/or subtractions	d
Total shares (fully diluted)	e
Fully diluted EPS	f

Section Seven

Intercorporate Investments

Case 7-1

W.R. Grace and Co. (B)

The following note is from the 1975 financial statements of W. R. Grace and Company.

Notes to Financial Statements
(dollar amounts in thousands except per share)

Note 6—Marketable Securities:

Current marketable securities are carried at cost which approximates market except that equity securities at a cost of $17,532 (1974–$23,767) have been reduced by a valuation reserve of $3,037 (1974–$6,900) to adjust their carrying value to approximate market. The noncurrent portfolio of marketable equity securities is included in noncurrent assets at a cost of $9,579 which is lower than aggregate market (1974–at cost $7,458).

Net gains realized on the sale of marketable equity securities were $604 (1974–None). Aggregate unrealized gains and losses related to marketable equity securities in the portfolios at December 31, 1975, are as follows:

	Gains	Losses
Current	$ —	$ 3,037
Noncurrent	$11,253	$ 3,422

The Current Assets of W. R. Grace show (among other items)

	1975	1974
Marketable Securities	$46,498,000	$87,233,000

Required

1. Give summary entries relative to current marketable securities for 1975. Assume the gains realized in 1975 through sale are attributable to the marketable securities classified as current. (Note: no valuation reserve is shown on the balance sheet.)

2. What entry (or entries) are necessary for 1975 for marketable securities classified as noncurrent?

Case 7-2 Cooper Laboratories, Inc.

Consolidated Balance Sheets

Assets	1976	1975
Current assets:		
Cash (Note 8)	$ 4,311	$ 3,095
Receivables:		
Trade, less allowance for doubtful accounts of $889 in 1976 and $780 in 1975	12,354	14,106
Other	1,836	3,372
	14,190	17,478
Inventories (Note 1):		
Raw materials	5,090	5,665
Work-in-process	3,952	3,546
Finished goods	5,828	6,550
	14,870	15,761
Prepaid expenses	900	686
Total current assets	34,271	37,020
Property, plant and equipment, at cost (including land not used in operations of $12,083 in 1976 and 1975) (Note 7)	43,090	44,141
Less accumulated depreciation (Note 1)	10,466	10,109
	32,624	34,032
Investment in non-consolidated subsidiaries (Notes 2 and 3)	5,046	3,508
Intangible assets, net of amortization (Note 1):		
Trademarks, patents and agreements	6,856	8,273
Excess cost over net assets acquired	1,213	1,369
	8,069	9,642
Long-term investment in equity security carried at cost in 1976 and at market in 1975 (Note 1)	12,275	1,628
Other assets	1,809	2,289
	$94,094	$88,119

Liabilities and Stockholders' Equity		
Current liabilities:		
Notes payable (Note 8)	$ 1,435	$ 1,550
Current installments of long-term debt (Note 8)	792	1,136
Accounts payable and accrued expenses	11,799	11,154
Income taxes payable (Notes 1, 4 and 5)	2,483	1,978
Total current liabilities	16,509	15,818
Long-term debt (Notes 5 and 8):		
Bank credit agreements	5,000	5,000
4½% Convertible Subordinated Debentures due 1992	7,172	17,837
7½% Convertible Subordinated Debentures due 1991	10,284	10,282
10½% Subordinated Debentures due 1992	6,134	–
Other, less current installments	1,380	2,387
	29,970	35,506
Deferred income taxes (Notes 1, 4 and 5)	1,188	–
Reserve for discontinued operations (Note 2)	131	1,065
Minority interest in subsidiaries	100	100
Commitments and contingent liabilities (Notes 11 and 12)		
Stockholders' equity (Notes 1, 8, 9 and 10):		
Common stock, $.10 par value. Authorized 10,000,000 shares; issued 6,594,640 in 1976 and 6,591,765 in 1975	659	659
Additional paid-in capital	29,530	29,515
Retained earnings (net of unrealized loss on long-term investment in equity security in 1975)	16,007	5,456
Total stockholders' equity	46,196	35,630
	$94,094	$88,119

Cooper Laboratories, Inc. is principally engaged in the development, manufacture and sale of medical and dental products, sold either by prescription or over-the-counter without a prescription, and primarily promoted to physicians, dentists and pharmacists.

Cooper's Consolidated Balance Sheets as of October 31, 1976 and 1975 are presented. (Amounts in thousands.)

Long-term investment in equity security at October 31, 1976 represents the Company's investment in 288,000 shares (70,000 at October 31, 1975) of common stock of Barnes-Hind Pharmaceuticals, Inc. This temporary investment is carried at lower of cost or market and represents approximately 38% (9% at October 31, 1975) of the outstanding common stock of Barnes-Hind. The market value of the long-term investment was $17,352,000 at October 31, 1976. A valuation allowance in the amount of $1,149,000 was established at October 31, 1975 because market was lower than cost.

Required

1. What was the cost of Cooper's long-term investment in equity security at October 31, 1975?

2. How much did Cooper pay for the additional 218,000 shares of common stock of Barnes-Hind it acquired during 1976?

Case 7-3   The Charter Company

The Charter Company is a diversified multi-industry corporation with a primary revenue and asset base in the petroleum industry. The Company also conducts operations in communications and insurance.

Consolidated Balance Sheets

(in thousands)

Assets	1977	1976
Current assets:		
Cash	$ 27,078	15,977
Receivables	152,509	91,558
Refundable Federal income taxes	–	12,900
Inventories	109,609	50,246
Assets held for sale, net	–	10,931
Prepaid expenses	6,342	9,518
Total current assets	295,538	191,128
Investments in real estate, net	43,517	55,684
Investments	64,604	76,200
Property, plant and equipment		
Cost	246,462	216,205
Less accumulated depreciation and amortization	55,879	43,689
	190,583	172,516
Long-term receivables, excluding current installments	13,034	3,257
Intangibles resulting from acquisitions, net	47,705	17,749
Other assets	14,759	6,320
	$669,740	522,854

Liabilities and Stockholders' Equity	1977	1976
Current liabilities:		
Notes payable	$ 16,889	21,419
Current installments of long-term debt, excluding real estate debt	19,951	18,481
Accounts payable and accrued expenses	191,143	116,054
Income taxes	12,635	7,405
Total current liabilities	243,619	163,359
Real estate debt	16,101	33,077
Long-term debt, excluding current installments	174,840	145,235
Deferred credits and minority interest	37,538	18,316
Deferred income taxes	34,474	16,453
Stockholders' equity (notes 7, 10, 11 and 12):		
Preferred stock	426	432
Common stock	17,566	17,566
Additional paid-in capital	59,072	58,252
Retained earnings	89,813	74,438
Net unrealized loss on investment securities	(3,709)	(4,279)
Total stockholders' equity	163,168	146,409
Commitments and contingencies		
	$669,740	522,854

Charter's investments included marketable equity securities of $5,705,000 and $3,787,000 at December 31, 1977 and 1976, respectively. These securities were stated net of any allowance for unrealized losses.

Required

1. What was the cost of Charter's acquisition of marketable equity securities in 1977? (No equity securities were sold in 1977.)

2. What entry did Charter make in 1977 to adjust the allowance for unrealized losses account?

3. How much of the adjustment to the allowance for unrealized losses account was included in Charter's 1977 Consolidated Statement of Earnings.

Case 7-4

Corning Glass Works (B)

Corning Glass Works is an international producer of glass and glass-ceramic products, and related products involving corollary technologies, for use in the home, science and industry. It traces its origin to a glass business established in 1851.

Corning's 1976 and 1975 Consolidated Balance Sheets (Asset Section Only) and its Consolidated Statements of Income and Retained Earnings are presented.

Consolidated Balance Sheets

January 2, 1977, and December 23, 1975 (in thousands)	1976	1975
Assets		
Current Assets		
Cash	$ 20,425	$ 19,723
Short-term investments, at cost which approximates market value	165,216	91,876
Receivables, net of doubtful accounts and allowances $6,724/1976; $6,691/1975	135,696	142,833
Inventories	154,647	142,471
Prepaid expenses including deferred taxes on income	38,802	17,454
Total current assets	$514,786	$414,357
Investments		
Associated companies, at equity	$142,715	$121,027
Other at cost	3,488	3,490
	$146,203	$124,517

Consolidated Statements of Income and Retained Earnings

Years Ending January 2, 1977, and December 23, 1975 (In thousands)	1976	1975
Net sales	$1,025,905	$938,959
Cost of sales	701,647	708,455
	324,258	230,504
Selling general and administrative expenses	166,773	151,819
Research and development expenses	48,857	42,285
	215,630	194,104
Income from Operations	103,628	36,400
Royalty, interest and dividend income	18,038	11,317
Interest expense	(19,704)	(21,302)
Other income (deductions), net	3,745	(5,211)
Taxes on income	(51,374)	(7,723)
Income before minority interest and equity earnings	58,833	12,981
Minority interest in (earnings) loss of subsidiaries	(595)	2,617
Equity in earnings of associated companies	25,475	15,539
Net Income (per share, $4.74/1976; $1.76/1975)	83,713	31,137
Retained Earnings at beginning of year	446,031	439,649
Dividends		
Preferred stock—$3.50 per share	(11)	(14)
Common stock—per share, $1.50/1976; $1.40/1975	(26,431)	(24,691)
Retained Earnings at end of year	$503,302	$446,081

Corning Glass Works and Subsidiary Companies

Required

1. Note that Corning's Consolidated Balance Sheets include investments in associated companies accounted for at equity in net assets. Assume that Corning made no additional investments in these companies in 1976. Dividends received from these companies were how much in 1976?

2. Also note that Corning's Consolidated Balance Sheets include an investment accounted for at cost. This investment is in Owens-Corning Fiberglass Corporation. Corning received dividends from this investment of $3,715,000 in 1976. The market value of this investment was about $263,012,000 on January 2, 1977 and $173,162,000 at December 28, 1975. How much additional income (loss) before taxes would have been reported in Corning's Consolidated Income Statement in 1976 if it had used the market method to account for this investment?

Case 7-5

Harte-Hanks Newspapers, Inc.

Harte-Hanks Newspapers, Inc. and its subsidiaries are primarily engaged in publishing daily, Sunday and weekly newspapers in 21 communities. In September 1972, the company acquired the Republic Publishing Company, which published the Yakima Herald-Republic, a morning and Sunday newspaper in Yakima, Washington, from W. H. Robertson and related persons for 485,200 shares of the company's common stock.

The company's common stock was traded in the over-the-counter market. Set forth below for the periods indicated is the range of bid prices as reported by National Quotation Bureau Incorporated.

1972:	High Bid	Low Bid
First Quarter (from March 7)	29 1/8	21 1/2
Second Quarter	33 1/4	25
Third Quarter (through Sept. 21)	31 3/4	26

The foregoing prices represent quotations between dealers, do not include retail markup, markdown or commission and do not necessarily represent actual transactions.

The Consolidated Income Statements for the period ended June 30, 1972 and the Consolidated Balance Sheets as of June 30, 1972 of both Harte-Hanks Newspapers, Inc. and Subsidiaries and Republic Publishing Company are presented. Assume that Harte-Hanks Newspapers, Inc.'s June 30, 1972 financial statements are to be retroactively restated to reflect the acquisition or merger in September 1972 of Republic Publishing Company.

Statement of Operations

	Year Ended December 31					Year Ended
	1967	1968	1969	1970	1971	June 30, 1972
	(unaudited)	(unaudited)				
Revenues:						
Newspaper advertising	$2,265,996	$2,419,732	$2,593,342	$2,693,969	$3,089,159	$3,339,339
Newspaper circulation	699,307	739,219	800,785	875,124	914,515	918,241
Other	62,921	48,978	69,946	81,983	54,123	62,378
	3,028,224	3,207,929	3,459,073	3,651,076	4,057,797	4,319,958
Costs and expenses:						
Editorial, production and distribution	1,757,396	1,770,653	1,856,732	2,054,863	2,284,120	2,392,124
Advertising, selling, general and administrative	700,146	793,239	871,034	890,496	987,008	1,067,819
Depreciaton and amortization	221,933	224,913	195,601	194,537	165,434	156,386
	2,679,475	2,788,805	2,923,367	3,139,896	3,436,562	3,616,329
Income Before Federal Income Taxes and Extraordinary Items	348,749	419,124	535,706	511,180	621,235	703,629
Federal income taxes—						
Current	151,455	191,724	281,967	267,993	291,954	361,636
Deferred (credit)	323	22,144	(11,839)	(27,154)	(13,779)	(41,084)
	151,778	213,868	270,128	240,839	278,175	320,552
Income Before Extraordinary Items	196,971	205,256	265,578	270,341	343,060	383,077
Extraordinary items	305,122	—	—	(42,097)	(1,130,000)	—
Net Income (Loss)	$ 502,093	$ 205,256	$ 265,578	$ 228,244	($ 786,940)	$ 383,077

STATEMENT OF CONSOLIDATED INCOME

The following statement of consolidated income of Harte-Hanks Newspapers, Inc. (Company) and subsidiaries includes, for the period from January 29, 1971 (date Company's operations began) to June 30, 1972, the results of operations of the Company; for the five years ended June 30, 1972, the results of operations of the Company's affiliates and subsidiaries acquired in poolings of interests in fiscal years 1971 and 1972; and, from the respective dates of acquisition, the results of operations of companies purchased in fiscal years 1971 and 1972 (see Note A). The statement for the four years ended June 30, 1972, has been examined by Ernst & Ernst, independent accountants, whose report thereon appears elsewhere in this Prospectus. The statement for the year ended June 30, 1968, is unaudited, but the Company believes that all adjustments (consisting only of normal recurring accruals) necessary for a fair presentation have been made. The statement should be read in conjunction with the other financial statements and notes thereto included elsewhere in this Prospectus.

	Year Ended June 30,				
	1968	1969	1970	1971	1972
	(unaudited)				
	(In Thousands, Except Share Amounts)				
Revenues:					
Newspaper advertising	$22,487	$25,006	$26,250	$28,585	$39,963
Newspaper circulation	6,133	6,755	7,003	7,523	10,655
Television revenues	2,572	2,958	3,018	2,904	3,244
Other newspaper revenues	431	706	587	644	723
Miscellaneous income	245	246	344	332	280
	31,868	35,671	37,202	39,988	54,865
Costs and expenses:					
Editorial, production and distribution	19,529	21,937	23,340	25,110	30,819
Advertising, selling, general and administrative	6,629	7,480	7,947	8,781	14,680
Depreciation and amortization (excluding goodwill)	962	995	948	962	1,374
Interest—principally on long-term debt	204	152	150	186	773
Miscellaneous expense	–	17	22	5	36
	27,324	30,581	32,407	35,044	47,682
Income Before Income Taxes, Goodwill Amortization and Extraordinary Items	4,544	5,090	4,795	4,944	7,183
Income taxes—Note 3:					
Current	2,003	2,635	2,122	2,012	3,169
Deferred (credit)	–	(163)	(21)	78	32
	2,003	2,472	2,101	2,090	3,201
Income Before Goodwill Amortization and Extraordinary Items	2,541	2,618	2,694	2,584	3,982
Goodwill amortization (deduction)—Note A	–	–	–	(15)	(367)
Income Before Extraordinary Items	2,541	2,618	2,694	2,839	3,615
Extraordinary items (net of applicable income tax)—Note 4	98	(1)	12	1,063	–
Net Income	$ 2,639	$ 2,617	$ 2,706	$ 3,092	$ 3,615
Average number of shares of Common Stock outstanding after giving retroactive effect to the shares issued in the reorganization and poolings of interests—Note A	3,119,247	3,119,247	3,119,247	3,119,247	3,268,989
Earnings per average share of Common Stock:					
Income before goodwill amortization and extraordinary items	$.81	$.84	$.87	$ .91	$1.22
Goodwill amortization	–	–	–	–	(.11)
Income before extraordinary items	.81	.84	.84	.91	1.11
Extraordinary items	.03	–	–	.34	–
Net income	$.84	$.84	$.87	$1.25	$1.11
Dividends paid per share—Note 5				$ .15	$ .20

See notes to statement of consolidated income and notes to financial statements of Harte-Hanks Newspapers, Inc. and subsidiaries.

Harte-Hanks Consolidated Balance Sheets
June 30, 1972

ASSETS

Current Assets
Cash	$ 5,027,447
Trade receivables, less allowance for doubtful accounts of $278,672	6,007,985
Inventories of newsprint and operating supplies—at lower of cost (first-in, first-out method) or market—	1,488,639
Prepaid expenses	583,321
Total Current Assets	13,107,392

Investments and Other Assets
Investment in affiliate—at cost plus equity in undistributed earnings—	708,848
Marketable securities—at cost (approximate market of $566,167)	210,045
Other assets	952,242
	1,871,135

Property, Plan and Equipment—on the basis of cost—
Land	2,248,600
Buildings and improvements	11,132,497
Equipment and furniture	15,067,610
	28,488,707
Less allowances for depreciation	10,565,700
	17,883,007
Construction and equipment installations in progress (estimated additional cost to complete of $2,000,000)	389,817
	18,272,824

Intangible Assets and Deferred Charges—At Cost
Goodwill, net of amortization of $383,184—	25,635,072
Agreements not to compete, deferred compensation and other deferred charges, net of amortization of $265,279—	508,195
	26,143,267
	$59,394,618

LIABILITIES AND STOCKHOLDERS' EQUITY

Current Liabilities
Notes payable	$ 147,707
Accounts payable	2,039,158
Accrued expenses and other liabilities	2,001,664
Prepaid subscriptions	524,255
Federal income taxes, including deferred	861,753
Current portion of long-term debt	5,205,063
Total Current Liabilities	10,779,600
Long-Term Debt—less current portion	11,845,276
Other Liabilities	186,558

Stockholders' Equity
Preferred Stock, issuable in series, par value $1 a share: authorized—$2,500,000 shares; outstanding—none	—
Common Stock, par value $1 a share: authorized—7,500,000 shares; issued and outstanding—3,480,347 shares, including 2,000 shares held in treasury	3,480,347
Additional paid-in capital	6,955,330
Retained earnings	26,149,507
Cost of treasury (deduction)	(2,000)
	36,583,184
Commitments and Contingent Liabilities	$59,394,618

Republic Consolidated Balance Sheets
June 30, 1972

ASSETS

Current Assets

Cash	$ 541,839
Trade receivables, less allowance for doubtful accounts of $15,000	301,398
Current maturities of municipal bonds including accrued interest	34,635
Inventory of newsprint—at lower of cost (first-in, first-out method) or market	60,112
Prepaid expenses	9,876
Total Current Assets	947,860

Investments and Other Assets

Long-term portion of municipal bonds	86,754
Other investments less allowance for losses of $1,080,000	170,000
Other	44,713
	301,467

Property, Plant and Equipment—on the basis of cost

Land	198,337
Building and improvements	1,595,036
Equipment and furniture	1,420,114
	3,213,487
Less allowances for depreciation	1,806,433
	1,407,054
Construction and equipment installations in progress (estimated additional cost to complete of $240,000)	221,869
	1,628,923
	$2,878,250

LIABILITIES AND STOCKHOLDERS' EQUITY

Current Liabilities

Accounts payable	$ 317,358
Accrued expenses and other liabilities	302,880
Prepaid subscriptions	68,954
Federal income taxes, including deferred	40,436
Total Current Liabilities	729,628

Stockholders' Equity

Preferred Stock, 5% cumulative, par value $100 a share: authorized—20,000 shares; issued and outstanding—16,319 shares	1,631,900
Common Stock:	
Class A—(voting) par value $10 a share; authorized—3,500 shares; issued and outstanding—2,600 shares	26,000
Class B—(nonvoting) par value $10 a share; authorized—31,500 shares; issued and outstanding—23,400 shares	234,000
Additional paid-in capital	5,543
Retained earnings	251,179
	2,148,622
	$2,878,250

Required

1. Assume that the market price of Harte-Hanks Newspapers, Inc.'s common stock was $30.00 per share on June 30, 1972.

   a) What entry would Harte-Hanks Newspapers, Inc. have made on June 30, 1972 to record the issuance of its common shares if the acquisition were treated as a "purchase?" Describe the effects of this entry on Harte-Hanks Newspapers, Inc.'s consolidated income statement and balance sheet at June 30, 1972.

   b) What entry would Harte-Hanks Newspapers, Inc. have made on June 30, 1972 to record the issuance of its common shares if the acquisition were treated as a "pooling of interests?" Describe the effects of this entry on Harte-Hanks Newspapers, Inc.'s consolidated income statement and balance sheet at June 30, 1972.

2. Why might the management of Harte-Hanks Newspapers, Inc. prefer to treat the acquisition as a pooling of interests?

3. A preliminary prospectus dated September 22, 1972 disclosed the offering of 800,000 shares of Harte-Hanks Newspapers, Inc. The prospectus revealed that 274,400 shares were being sold by the company and 525,600 shares by certain "selling stockholders." Prominent among the selling stockholders were former Republic stockholders who were offering some 455,040 shares for sale. The preliminary prospectus suggested that Harte-Hanks Newspapers, Inc. may have effected a pooling of interests with a "bailout."

   a) What is a "bailout?"

   b) Under what conditions is a pooling of interests with a bailout acceptable under generally accepted accounting principles?

   c) Do you believe that the acquisition of Republic Publishing Company was, in substance, a pooling of interests? Why or why not?

Case 7-6

Time, Incorporated

In May, 1973, Time, Incorporated (Time) filed a Form S-14 Registration Statement with the Securities and Exchange Commission. This statement described a proposed issuance of stock for the purpose of effecting a merger with Temple Industries, Inc. (Temple).

Time is primarily engaged in publishing magazines, books, records, and related products, producing pulp, paperboard, paper, and other paper products and timber, and is also engaged in the sale of products and services to the graphic arts industry, newspaper publishing, the marketing of information relating to the movement of grocery products, radio and television broadcasting, cable television, and film production and distribution. Temple is primarily engaged in the manufacture and sale of building materials and other consumer and industrial products and is also engaged in mortgage banking, real estate, and construction operations.

The principal offices and timberlands of Temple are located in East Texas near the offices and timberlands of Time's pulp and paper operation. Time's pulp and paper operation is a significant supplier of timber to Temple and Temple supplies a substantial amount of sawmill residue utilized in Time's pulp and paper operation.

In 1971, Time sold to Temple approximately 25,000 acres of timber and development lands in exchange for cash and notes, and granted Temple options to purchase approximately 1,500 additional acres. As of March 31, 1973, approximately $7,428,000 of such notes remained outstanding: $357,000 is reflected in current receivables and payables and $7,071,000 is reflected in other assets and long-term debt. Also, as of March 31, 1973, there is about $3,909,000 in intercompany profits related to intercompany sales and purchases of timber and timberland included in the financial statements of Time and Temple.

The proposed merger was designed to be a "tax-free" reorganization under Section 368 of the Internal Revenue Code, and as a pooling of interests for financial reporting purposes. On May 23, 1973, the closing price of Temple was $16 5/8; the maximum proposed offering price for each share of Time was $33.25. Time proposed to issue about 3,089,413 shares of its common stock in exchange for 6,178,826 shares of Temple's common stock.

TIME, INC. CONSOLIDATED BALANCE SHEET

(in thousands of dollars)

ASSETS

	December 31, 1972	March 31, 1973 (unaudited)
Current Assets:		
Cash	$ 25,067	$ 23,420
Marketable securities—at cost U.S. Government and other short-term securities (approximately market)	32,846	35,524
Preferred and common stock (quoted market prices $32,003,000 and $31,020,000)	26,887	27,831
Receivables, less allowances of $14,704,000 and $13,509,000	85,017	73,479
Notes receivable—current portion	4,875	4,875
Inventories—at the lower of cost or market		
Work in process and finished goods	37,251	35,489
Paper and other materials	12,716	12,293
Prepaid expenses	24,615	25,175
Total Current Assets	249,274	238,086
Other Investments		
Companies 20% or more owned—at equity	38,998	41,102
Other—at cost less allowances of $10,497,000 in 1972 and 1973	11,008	11,254
	50,006	52,356
Property and Equipment—on the basis of cost		
Buildings	60,843	60,911
Machinery and equipment	169,221	171,103
Leasehold improvements	17,040	17,191
	247,104	249,205
Less allowances for depreciation and amortization	114,722	117,760
	132,382	131,445
Timber and timberland, less depletion	22,237	22,091
Land	6,818	6,818
	161,437	160,354
Excess of Purchase Prices Over Net Tangible Assets of Acquired Properties	20,489	20,434
Notes Receivable	34,125	34,125
Other Assets	26,645	27,353
	$541,976	$532,708

LIABILITIES AND STOCKHOLDERS' EQUITY

	December 31, 1972	March 31, 1973 (unaudited)
Current Liabilities:		
Accounts payable and accrued expenses	$ 61,093	$ 60,379
Liabilities in connection with suspension of LIFE magazine	16,375	4,401
Employee compensation and profit-sharing contributions	7,775	2,961
Federal and foreign income taxes	966	5,516
Loans and current portion of long-term debt	3,580	24,333
Total Current Liabilities	89,789	97,590
Unearned Portion of Paid Subscriptions	67,053	69,177
Long-Term Debt	92,097	70,871
Deferred Federal Income Taxes	30,624	30,007
Other Liabilities	7,214	7,454
Stockholders' Equity		
Common Stock—$1 par value; authorized 10,000,000 shares; issued and outstanding 7,286,000 shares in 1972 and 7,298,000 shares in 1973	7,286	7,298
Additional paid-in capital	23,836	24,406
Retained income	224,077	225,905
	255,199	257,609
	$541,976	$532,708

TEMPLE INDUSTRIES CONSOLIDATED BALANCE SHEETS

	December 31, 1972	March 31, 1973 (unaudited)
ASSETS	(in thousands of dollars)	
Current Assets:		
Cash	$ 2,454	$ 2,823
Reveivables—		
Trade	8,837	13,132
Current portion of long-term notes receivable	520	541
Other	307	991
Allowance for doubtful accounts	(199)	(351)
Inventories, principally at the lower of average cost or market	10,391	10,062
Developed real estate, held for resale	900	900
Prepaid expenses and other	555	746
Total current assets	$ 23,765	$ 28,844
Real Estate, held for development and resale	8,038	8,079
Timber and Timberlands, at cost less depletion	14,961	13,936
Investments:		
Investments in and advances to unconsolidated subsidiaries and related companies—		
Lumbermen's Investment Corporation—		
Investment	4,846	5,229
Notes receivable	225	225
Federal income taxes receivable	55	310
Other—		
Investment	1,400	1,410
Notes receivable	1,428	1,469
Long-term notes receivable, less current maturities—		
Employees	250	250
Other	1,922	1,965
Other	964	958
	11,090	11,816
Property, Plant and Equipment, at cost		
Buildings, machinery, and equipment	77,575	80,613
Less—Accumulated depreciation	27,029	27,332
	50,546	53,281
Deferred Charges and Other Assets:		
Deferred Federal income tax charges	1,089	1,094
Other assets	1,825	1,798
	2,914	2,892
	$111,314	$118,848

	December 31, 1972	March 31, 1973 (unaudited)
LIABILITIES AND SHAREHOLDERS' INVESTMENT	(in thousands of dollars)	
Current Liabilities:		
Short-term notes payable	$ 404	$ 492
Current maturities of long-term liabilities	3,661	3,666
Accounts payable	4,106	4,185
Dividends payable	416	493
Accrued liabilities—		
Salaries and wages	666	866
Taxes, other than income	911	721
Retirement plan	418	117
Other	823	1,355
Federal income taxes payable	2,890	3,589
Total current liabilities	$ 14,295	$ 15,484
Long-Term Liabilities, excluding current maturities		
Notes payable	14,899	17,593
Lease obligations	4,090	4,970
	18,989	22,563
Deferred Federal Income Taxes	3,356	3,504
Shareholders' Investment:		
Common stock, $1.66 2/3 par, 20,000,000 shares authorized, 6,178,826 shares issued in 1972 and 1973	10,298	10,298
Capital in excess of par value	16,673	16,520
Retained earnings	47,703	50,480
	74,674	77,298
Less—Treasury stock, at cost, 500 shares	—	1
	74,674	77,297
	$111,314	$118,848

Required

1. Using the financial statements of Time and Temple, show how the stockholders' equity section of Time's Balance sheet would have appeared if the proposed merger had taken place on March 31, 1973.

2. Now, assume that the proposed combination of Time and Temple was to be accounted for as a purchase rather than as a pooling of interests. Using the financial statements, show how the stockholders' equity section of Time's Balance Sheet would have appeared if the acquisition of Temple had taken place on March 31, 1973.

3. Describe how the asset and liability sections of Time's March 31, 1973 Balance Sheet would *differ* if the combination of Time and Temple had been accounted for as a purchase instead of as a pooling of interests.

Case 7-7
Rockwell International

Rockwell International is a diversified corporation engaged in the manufacture, sale, research and development of many products for commercial and aerospace markets. On April 9, 1974, Rockwell exchanged 2,932,000 shares of its common stock having a fair value of $27 per share for all the outstanding common stock of Admiral, a corporation engaged in the manufacture, distribution and sale of consumer products in the home entertainment and household appliance fields. The merger of Admiral and Rockwell was accounted for as a *purchase*.

The December 31, 1973 stockholders' equity sections of Admiral and Rockwell's consolidated balance sheets are presented.

Stockholders' Equity: Admiral Corporation	1973
Preferred stock, no par value—300,000 shares authorized; none issued.	
Common stock, $1 par value: Authorized—9,000,000 shares Issued—5,903,191	$ 5,903,000
Capital in excess of par value	19,991,000
Retained earnings	78,980,000
	$104,874,000
Less cost of 40,000 shares of common stock in the treasury	320,000
	$104,554,000

Stockholders' Equity: Rockwell Corporation	1973
Capital stock:	
Preferred stock, without par value:	
Series A	$ 3,700,000
Series B	2,500,000
Common Stock, $1 par value	27,300,000
Additional capital	159,000,000
Retained earnings	759,200,000
	$951,700,000

Required

1. Assume that the merger of Admiral with Rockwell took place on December 31, 1973.

    a) What entry would have been made by Rockwell on December 31, 1973 to record its acquisition of Admiral?

b) At December 31, 1973, the fair value of Admiral's property and equipment exceeded its book value by $3,421,000. What entry would have been made by Rockwell on December 31, 1973 to include Admiral's assets and liabilities in its 1973 consolidated financial statements?

2. Assume that the merger of Admiral and Rockwell took place on December 31, 1973. What entry would have been made by Rockwell on December 31, 1973 if this merger had been accounted for as a pooling of interests?

Case 7-8

Giddings and Lewis Machine Tool Company

A. The 1965 and 1964 Stockholders' equity sections of Giddings and Lewis' consolidated balance sheet are presented.

Giddings and Lewis

	1965	1964
Stockholders' equity:		
Common stock, $2.00 par value		
Authorized–750,000 shares (106,667 shares reserved for debenture conversion and 9,606 shares for stock options)		
Issued and outstanding–1965, 510,998 shares; 1964, 489,212 shares	$ 1,021,996	$ 978,424
Capital in excess of par value	6,073,857	5,685,924
Retained earnings, exclusive of earnings capitalized	9,634,062	8,270,702
Total shareholders' equity	16,729,915	14,935,050
	$29,750,706	$24,088,974

The following events occurred during the first six months of 1966:

a) Giddings' income for the first six months was $906,040.
b) Cash dividends of $129,188 were declared and paid.
c) Options for 4,555 shares were exercised for a total consideration of $96,612.
d) $45,000 of the convertible debentures were converted into 1,200 shares of common stock.

B. The 1965 and 1964 Stockholders' equity sections of Gisholt's consolidated balance sheets are presented.

Gisholt

	1965	1964
Stockholders' equity:		
Common stock, $10 par value; 750,000 shares authorized, 411,180 shares issued.	$ 4,111,800	$ 3,738,000
Capital in excess of par value	1,223,623	999,343
Retained earnings	6,390,682	5,485,273
	$11,726,105	$10,222,616

The following events occurred during the first six months of 1966:

a) Gisholt's income for the first six months was $844,260.
b) A 10% stock dividend was issued on the stock outstanding at December 31, 1965. The total market value of these shares was $796,661.
c) Options for 39,787 shares were exercised for a total consideration of $506,380.
d) A cash dividend of $147,172 was declared and paid during the six month period.

e) On June 30, 1966, Giddings and Lewis merged with Gisholt. To accomplish this merger, Giddings and Lewis first split its stock on a 3 for 2 basis (the $2 par value was retained). Next, Giddings and Lewis exchanged (issued) one share of its stock for each outstanding share of Gisholt. Thus, Gisholt was no longer a separate legal entity, but merely became a division of Giddings and Lewis. The merger was accounted for as a pooling of interests. At June 30, 1966, the market value of a share of Giddings and Lewis stock was $27.00 (after adjusting for the stock split) and the market value of a share of Gisholt was $25.00.

Required

1. Show how the stockholders' equity section of Giddings would appear at June 30, 1966.

2. Show how the stockholders' equity section of Gisholt would appear at June 30, 1966.

3. Show how the stockholders' equity section of Giddings and Lewis' balance sheet would appear immediately after the merger.

4. Show how the stockholders' equity section of Giddings and Lewis' balance sheet would have appeared immediately after the merger if the merger had been accounted for as a *purchase* instead of a pooling of interests.

Case 7-9

Borg-Warner Corporation

The following article appeared in *The Wall Street Journal* on Thursday, November 30, 1978:

Borg-Warner Could Acquire Firestone Cheaply, but Its Strategy May Backfire

By Bernard Wysocki Jr.
and Ralph E. Winter
Staff Reporters of The Wall Street Journal

Borg-Warner Corp. is getting a chance to acquire Firestone Tire & Rubber Co. at what is deemed a very cheap price, but its strategy is a risky one that may backfire if Firestone's much-publicized problems are bigger than Borg-Warner management believes.

That's the consensus of several securities analysts and other close observers of the merger plan announded by the two companies late Tuesday. Under the plan to bring about one of the largest corporate mergers ever, Borg-Warner and Firestone are planning to combine the two companies into a new holding company that would have annual sales of more than $6 billion and assets of about $5 billion.

"The big question is, how badly has Firestone been hurt by all this governmental stuff?" asks one Wall Street analyst, referring to an expensive government-imposed recall of about 7.5 million Firestone, "500" steel-belted radial tires alleged to have a safety defect. "And how much trouble is Borg-Warner going to have turning (Firestone) around?" the analyst asks.

Merger Could Pay Off

Observers believe that if Firestone's problems are temporary—as Borg-Warner officials insist— the merger could pay off in a huge way. And Borg-Warner officials say that the new holding company will be able to use accounting procedures to shelter from taxes up to $630 million of future earnings. Those accounting procedures stem from the proposed purchase price of Firestone's common shares, Borg-Warner says.

Borg-Warner is a Chicago-based concern with interests in automotive, air-conditioning, industrial, chemicals and plastics and other products. In 1977, the company earned $104 million, or $4.93 a share, on sales of $2.03 billion.

Firestone is the nation's second-largest tiremaker, based in Akron, Ohio. In the fiscal year ended Oct. 31, 1977, the company earned $110.2 million, or $1.92 a share, on sales of $4.43 billion.

Terms of Transaction

Under terms of the transaction, the new holding company would have three classes of securities: common stock, convertible preferred stock and debentures.

Borg-Warner shareholders would get one share of the new holding company's common stock for each share of Borg-Warner stock. Firestone holders would have the option of receiving holding company convertible preferred stock or debentures, with a minimum of 30% and a maximum of 40% of Firestone's approximately 57.6 million common being exchangeable for debentures. And therein lies a key reason for the proposed transaction, say sources close to Borg-Warner.

Borg-Warner says the new holding company will pay Firestone holders about $870 million in convertible preferred and debentures for their Firestone common shares. That's about 15% above the depressed market value of Firestone's common, but well below the estimated $1.5 billion book value of Firestone.

The difference between the "purchase price" and the book value is about $630 million. Borg-Warner says it will use that difference "to provide for asset write-downs to realistic values where appropriate," and to provide liability reserves for measureable future losses."

Protect Future Earnings

The reserve then could be used to protect the future earnings of the holding company from being torpedoed by losses that the Firestone or other holding-company unit might suffer from plant closings, unfunded pension liabilities, product-liability suits or other events that ordinarily might prompt the company to establish a loss reserve that automatically would hurt earnings. The effect of the plan would be to establish a reserve and a "valuation adjustment," whereby such losses would be absorbed in the balance sheet and wouldn't be in the profit and loss statement, sources said.

Some analysts figure that this write-down would result in a loss that could be used to shield future profit of the company from federal income taxes.

Some analysts can't see the logic of the merger as it affects Borg-Warner, however, in the past few years, Borg-Warner has made several attempts to diversify into businesses that aren't closely tied to the automotive business or other sectors of the economy that are highly subceptible to cyclical downturns. But the tire business is very closely tied to the automotive business, and Firestone has more of its overall business in tires than any of the other major tire companies.

Some Wall Streeters fault Borg-Warner for an inability to devise a local long-term strategy. "I don't follow the company any more" as a result, says an analyst who regards Firestone as an albatross for Borg-Warner.

Loss for Year

Back in 1977, before the Firestone radial "500" fiasco broke, Mr. Riley said it was the company's goal to return to a 5% after-tax margin on sales, which the company last achieved in 1973, when profit was 5.2% of sales. Mr. Riley said last year that it might take a couple of years to regain that target profit margin.

The combined costs of plant closings and the big recall campaign will result in a loss for the year ended Oct. 31, 1978, which the company will report in a couple of weeks. Earnings for fiscal 1979 will be distorted by the recall.

But if, as Firestone and Borg-Warner officials say, the damage done by the recall is only temporary, and in a couple of years the company does start earnings a 5% return on sales, profit for Borg-Warner shareholders could be substantial. Assuming sales in fiscal 1980 or 1981 are in excess of $5 billion. (A fairly safe assumption), a 5% return would produce earnings of $250 million, and even a

4% margin would result in more than $200 million profit.

If 35% of Firestone's 57.6 million shares outstanding are exchanged for debentures, interest on the resulting $320 million of debentures would be $32 million pretax, or around $17 million after taxes. The dividend on preferred stock to be issued in exchange for the other 37.5 million shares would be about $49 million. Thus, the annual cost of servicing the securities to be issued to Firestone holders would be about $66 million after taxes.

Should Firestone's businesses rebound to that 4% or 5% after-tax profit margin area, the holding company would have $134 million to $184 million a year earnings applicable to common stock. Even a 2.5% return equaling the fiscal 1977 performance, would provide $59 million for common holders. Initially, of course, the common will be held by present Borg-Warner holders.

From the Firestone holder's viewpoint, the transaction offers either an opportunity to sell out of an unhappy situation or protection of the dividend in exchange for a reduced equity participation, depending on whether the holder accepts debentures or preferred stock.

While $16 of debentures isn't a high price for Firestone stock in historical perspective, it is about a 30% premium over the recent market price of around $12.50 a share. The price ranged from $15 to $23.75 during 1977, before the controversy over the radial 500 erupted.

Some analysts have said that only the dividend of $1.10 a share annualy prevented Firestone stock from sinking lower during the recall battle. While Mr. Riley said at the time of the recall announcement that there wasn't any "present plan to change" the 27½ cent quarterly dividend, some analysts have speculated that a cut might become necessary next year.

The dividend costs Firestone about $63 million a year, and that drain could be painful while the company is handing out five million free tires and paying dealers $7.50 apiece to mount them on the customer's car. In addition, the company expects to give four million new tires at half price to buyers of radial 500 and related tires who bought their suspect tires before the offical recall period.

Major Factors

The trend of foreign earnings, profits from nontire operations and from sales of tires outside the recall agreement would be major factors in determining whether Firestone could maintain its dividend without depleting its operating capital.

The $1.30-a-share dividend on the holding company preferred should be safe, as it would be backed by earnings of Borg-Warner as well as Firestone.

The Firestone holder who accepts the holding company preferred eventually could convert those securities into common, and benefit from any earnings progress of the combined company. But Firestone holders would hold a lesser equity than they have currently.

Assuming that holders of 65% of Firestone stock accept the preferred, those 37.5 million shares of preferred of the combined company could be converted into 11.3 million common shares of the combined company, compared with 21.5 million common shares that the Borg-Warner holders would get. As Firestone is a substantially larger company than Borg-Warner, that could have to be considered to be a dilution of the equity position of Firestone holders. After five years, those preferred shares may convert into as many as 15 million common shares of the combined company, depending on market price of the common during the period.

However, Borg-Warner would be taking a considerable risk in exchange for the earnings opportunity. Bringing Firestone's profit back to a respectable margin on sales may be a lengthy and difficult job.

Tires are relatively interchangeable. A motorist who has any lingering doubt about Firestone tires as a result of the publicity about the radial "500s" can readily buy any one of a dozen other company brands, or countless private labels sold by major retailers and filling stations.

As Firestone does a good chunk of private-label business itself, the company could pick up a few of the sales from customers trying to dodge the Firestone brand, but there's a potential for a significant loss in volume by Firestone and its company-owned stores. With excess capacity in the industry anyway, the company could find it hard to keep its plants running at profitable levels, once it has supplied the tires needed for the recall program.

Assume that Borg-Warner created a holding company called BWC on December 1, 1978. The market price of Borg-Warner's common stock was $28 1/8 and the market price of Firestone's common stock was $13 1/4 on December 1, 1978. The net worth sections of Borg-Warner and Firestone each reflect about 15% of invested capital and the remainder is reinvested earnings.

Required

1. Assume that BWC acquired 35% of the outstanding shares of Firestone for debentures and the remainder for preferred stock on December 1, 1978.

   a) What entry would have been made by BWC on December 1, 1978 to record this acquisition?

   b) What entry would have been made by BWC on December 1, 1978 to include Firestone's assets and liabilities in its consolidated financial statement?

2. Assume that BWC and Firestone decided to merge and that one share of BWC $1.00 par value stock was exchanged for each two shares of Firestone common stock on December 1, 1978. What entry would have been made by BWC on December 1, 1978 if this merger had been accounted for as a pooling of interests?

3. Describe how the asset and liability sections of BWC's Consolidated Balance Sheet would have differed if the acquisition of Firestone had been accounted for as a pooling of interests instead of as a purchase.

Case 7-10

Crestek, Inc.

Crestek, Inc. was founded in 1961, initially to manufacture and sell relatively simple ultrasonic cleaning devices. As a result of a 1973 reorganization and restructuring and subsequent development, Crestek has evolved into a specialist in designing, engineering and manufacturing custom automated industrial cleaning systems, some of which employ high frequency sound waves (ultrasonics). At June 30, 1980, Crestek had assets of about $2,020,315, liabilities and redeemable preferred stock of about $1,303,183, and the following Shareholders' Equity section:

Shareholders' Equity

Common stock without par value. Authorized 2,000,000 shares; issued 614,675 at $.083 stated value...........................	$ 51,018
Additional paid-in capital........................	277,473
Less redemption price in excess of fair value of preferred stock at date of issue...............	(131,069)
Retained Earnings (since July 1, 1972)............	519,710
Total common Shareholders' Equity...............	$717,132

A proxy statement dated December 2, 1980 described a proposed merger between Crestek, Inc. and UTI, a California holding company. UTI's operating subsidiaries, both of which were wholly-owned, were UTI-Spectrotherm which was primarily engaged in the development, manufacture and sale of analytic instruments and Uthe Technology, Inc. which was primarily engaged in the development, manufacture and sale of semiconductor assembly and test equipment. Crestek proposed to acquire the operations of Uthe Technology, Inc. At June 30, 1980, Uthe had assets of about $1,243,050, liabilities of $973,300, and retained earnings of $189,844. At June 30, 1980, the market value of Crestek common stock was $10.25 per share.

Two merger plans were described in the proxy statement. Under the "merger plan," UTI will be dissolved. Shareholders of UTI will receive one share of UTI-Spectrotherm for each of the 207,148 shares of UTI common stock held at June 30, 1980. After this distribution, each shareholder of UTI will hold equal amounts of UTI stock and UTI-Spectrotherm stock. The merger of Uthe Technology, Inc. and Crestek will be accomplished by having shareholders of UTI receive 115,000 shares of Crestek common stock in exchange for their UTI common stock. These shareholders would receive up to an aggregate of 50,000 additional shares of Crestek common stock if Uthe Technology, Inc. achieves certain profit objectives during the four year period ended June 30, 1984. The "merger plan" will not be effected unless a ruling is received from the Internal Revenue Service that the "merger plan" will result in no gain or loss for tax purposes for UTI shareholders.

If no such ruling is received by June 1, 1981, an "alternative merger plan" will be effected in which Crestek will issue to UTI 11,500 shares of Series I Preferred Stock which is convertible into an aggregate of 115,000 shares of Crestek common stock in exchange for the operations of Uthe Technology, Inc. UTI would receive up to an additional 50,000 shares of Crestek common stock if the business being acquired by Crestek achieves certain profit objectives during the four year period ended June 30, 1984. UTI will not distribute any Crestek stock to its shareholders under the "alternative merger plan." The "alternative merger plan" will result in no gain or loss for UTI shareholders for tax purposes.

Required

1. Should Crestek have accounted for this merger with Uthe Technology, Inc. as a "purchase" or as a "pooling of interests" for financial accounting purposes? Why?

2. Assume that the merger plan was effected on June 30, 1980.

    a. What entry would have been made by Crestek to record the merger?

    b. What entry would have been made by Crestek to include Uthe's assets and liabilities in its consolidated financial statements? (Hint: This is the elimination entry.)

3. Assume that 40,000 shares of Crestek common stock will be issued on June 30, 1984 based on Uthe's performance to that date. Also assume that Crestek's common stock has a fair market value of $20.00 per share on June 30, 1984. What entry (or entries) will be made by Crestek to record the issuance of these shares?

Case 7-11   Emhart Corporation

A. The December 31, 1975 and 1974 Consolidated Balance Sheets of Emhart Corporation are presented. Note that amounts for Emhart's Investment in USM (United Shoe Machinery) Corporation and Stockholders' Equity are missing.

B. Investment in USM: In July 1974, Emhart acquired 1,241,500 shares of common stock of USM Corporation, which constituted approximately 30% of USM's outstanding common stock and 23.5% of its outstanding voting stock, for cash of $31,197,000. Emhart's share of USM's 1974 earnings and dividends was $1,190,000 and $310,000, respectively.

In November 1975, Emhart acquired an additional 1,242,247 shares of common stock of USM, increasing its ownership to approximately 60% of USM's outstanding common stock and 47% of its outstanding voting stock, for cash of $30,105,000. Emhart's share of USM's 1975 earnings and dividends amounted to $5,263,000 and $1,428,000, respectively.

C. Business Combination: On December 18, 1975, Emhart and USM jointly announced an agreement in principle to merge. USM (United Shoe Machinery) is engaged in the production of a broad line of products serving such major industries as footwear, automotive, rubber and plastic, construction, and appliances.

The management of Emhart and USM believed that the merger would allow the stockholders of both Emhart and USM to more fully and directly participate in the combined operating results of the two companies, that the combined diversity of economic resources would present the potential of realizing opportunities not available to either company alone and that the consolidation of management strengths should result in operating efficiencies, as well as in more effective world-wide cost controls and profit maximization.

The USM Consolidated Balance Sheets at December 31, 1975 and February 28, 1975 are presented. At the effective time of the merger (assumed to be January 1, 1976), the stockholders of Emhart and USM will receive "New Emhart" Preference or Common Stock as follows:

Each outstanding share of Emhart Common Stock will be converted into one share of New Emhart Common Stock, par value of $1.00 per share.

Each outstanding share of USM Common Stock will be exchanged for 1.125 shares of New Emhart Common Stock, par value of $1.00 per share.

EMHART CONSOLIDATED BALANCE SHEET
December 31, 1975 and 1974
(In thousands except share amounts)

ASSETS	1975	1974
CURRENT ASSETS:		
Cash	$ 6,898	$ 6,853
Time deposits and short-term investments—at cost which approximates market	3,196	1,797
Notes and accounts receivable:		
Trade (less allowance of $4,098 in 1975 and $4,062 in 1974)	52,613	59,872
Other	2,664	2,684
Inventories (Notes 1 and 3)	89,395	97,823
Prepaid expenses, etc.	1,967	1,041
Current assets of discontinued operations (Note 4)		13,347
Total current assets	156,733	183,417
INVESTMENTS (Notes 1 and 5):		
USM Corporation common stock	12,361	
Other investments		535
Total investments		
PROPERTY, PLANT AND EQUIPMENT (Note 1):		
Land	3,210	2,746
Buildings	41,179	40,755
Machinery and equipment	81,634	75,658
Total	126,023	119,159
Less accumulated depreciation and amortization	67,250	61,586
Property, plant and equipment—net	58,773	57,573
NONCURRENT ASSETS OF DISCONTINUED OPERATIONS (Note 4)		4,111
DEFERRED CHARGES, ETC.	579	246
TOTAL	$294,463	$277,959

LIABILITIES AND STOCKHOLDERS' EQUITY	1975	1974
CURRENT LIABILITIES:		
Notes payable to banks (Note 6)	$ 21,249	$ 17,136
Current instalments of long-term debt	1,292	1,770
Accounts payable—trade	13,842	23,526
Customers deposits	2,877	4,907
Taxes, etc. withheld	2,506	2,125
Income taxes (Note 1)	3,814	6,347
Accrued liabilities:		
Other taxes	2,092	2,045
Salaries and wages	6,991	7,135
Other	11,547	10,975
Current liabilities of discontinued operations (Note 4)		2,437
Total current liabilities	66,210	78,403
NONCURRENT LIABILITIES:		
Long-term debt (Note 7)	24,365	11,495
Pension liabilities (Note 10)	5,560	4,427
Total noncurrent liabilities	29,925	15,922
DEFERRED INCOME TAXES (Note 1)	7,986	7,856
COMMITMENTS AND CONTINGENT LIABILITIES (Notes 9 and 10)		
Total liabilities	104,121	102,181
STOCKHOLDERS' EQUITY (Notes 1, 7 and 8):		
Capital stock:		
Preferred stock—authorized, 1,000,000 shares without par value; none issued		
Common stock—authorized, 8,000,000 shares of $6.25 par value each; outstanding, 1975—6,204,073 shares, 1974—6,204,052 shares	38,940	38,940
Capital surplus	52,743	52,743
Retained earnings	99,173	84,609
Total	190,856	176,292
Less treasury stock—at cost	514	514
Stockholders' equity	190,342	175,778
TOTAL	$294,463	$277,959

USM CORPORATION AND SUBSIDIARIES

CONSOLIDATED BALANCE SHEET

(In Thousands of Dollars)

ASSETS	December 31, 1975		February 28, 1975	
Current assets:				
Cash (including time deposits of $2,543,000 and $394,000)		$ 13,930		$ 7,670
Short-term investments at cost, which approximates market		229		479
Accounts and notes receivable:				
Trade, less allowances for doubtful accounts of $7,405,000 and $7,707,000	$102,170		$119,337	
Other	4,201	106,371	3,581	122,918
Inventories (note H):				
Raw materials	41,212		52,614	
Work in progress	59,973		66,264	
Finished goods	83,872	185,057	98,533	217,411
Deferred income taxes (note M)		14,227		14,127
Prepaid expenses		6,344		5,552
Total current assets		326,158		368,157
Machinery for leasing:				
Machines leased to customers at cost, less accumulated depreciation (note I) of $46,180,000 and $47,655,000, and machines returned from lease, net of accumulated depreciation and machines and parts, finished and in progress, on hand at cost, $8,995,000 and $13,426,000		42,754		49,022
Property, plant and equipment at cost:				
Land and buildings	92,143		91,309	
Manufacturing machinery, tools and equipment	160,657		158,101	
Vehicles, furniture and other	21,975		21,834	
Unfinished construction	5,099		3,894	
	279,874		275,138	
Less accumulated depreciation (note I)	151,317	128,557	144,041	131,097
Investments in affiliated companies (note D)		4,627		4,927
Goodwill, patent rights and other intangibles at cost, less amortization of $3,184,000 and $3,156,000 (note J)		28,014		28,705
Deferred charges and other assets		8,880		11,036
		$538,990		$592,944

LIABILITIES	December 31, 1975	February 28, 1975
Current liabilities:		
Short-term loans including current portion of long-term debt (note P)	$ 24,850	$ 40,189
Accounts and notes payable, trade	38,807	58,692
Income taxes (note M)	9,631	17,997
Dividends payable	1,772	8,068
Accrued pension expense (Note K)	7,924	3,425
Accrued payrolls	3,893	5,684
Customer deposits	7,457	
Accrued expenses and other liabilities	32,302	34,303
Total current liabilities	126,636	168,358
Long-term debt (note P)	99,919	121,862
Provision for unfunded international pensions (note K)	15,955	16,052
Deferred income taxes (note M)	22,116	15,908
Excess of net assets over cost of acquired companies (note J)	1,162	1,636
Other noncurrent liabilities	6,206	7,142
Minority interest consisting of capital stock of $625,000 and $631,000 and retained earnings of $132,000 and $165,000 (note E)	757	796
Litigation and contingent liabilities (note R)		

SHAREHOLDERS' EQUITY

	December 31, 1975	February 28, 1975
Capital Stock (notes S, T and U):		
Preferred, 6% Cumulative, par value $25 per share, authorized 600,000 shares; issued 423,908 shares (Outstanding 200,000 shares with par value of $5,000,000 after deducting treasury shares as shown below)	$ 10,598	$ 10,598
Convertible Preference, $2.10 Series, cumulative, without par value, authorized 778,800 shares, outstanding 692,832 and 722,780 shares	34,642	36,139
Preference, without par value, authorized 600,000 shares		
Common, par value $12.50 per share, authorized 10,000,000 shares; issued 4,216,817 and 4,181,480 shares (Outstanding 4,179,238 shares with par value of $52,240,000 and 4,143,546 shares with par value of $51,794,000 after deducting treasury shares as shown below)	52,709	52,268
Additional paid-in capital (note U)	16,581	15,529
Retained earnings per accompanying statement (notes A(1), B, C, D, M and P)	160,195	155,158
	274,725	269,692
Less cost of shares in treasury (Preferred: 223,908 shares ($7,582,000); Common: 37,579 ($904,000) and 37,934 shares ($920,000))	8,486	8,502
	266,239	261,190
	$538,990	$592,944

264 Cases in Financial Accounting

Each outstanding share of USM 6% Preferred Stock will be exchanged for 1.15 shares of New Emhart Common Stock, par value of $1.00 per share.

Each outstanding share of USM Convertible Preference Stock will be exchanged for one share of New Emhart $2.10 Convertible Preference Stock, without par value.

Schedule of Changes in Consolidated Stockholders' Equity

	Common Stock	Capital Surplus	Retained Earnings	Treasury Stock
Balance, December 31, 1972– 5,196,390 shares issued; 88,588 shares in the treasury	$32,477	$45,637	$74,903	$(3,048)
Net Income in 1973 of $17,437				
Cash Dividends in 1973 of $6,297				
Purchases of 127,410 shares for treasury for $2,717				
Balance, December 31, 1973– _____ shares issued; _____ shares in treasury				
Net Income for 1974 of $20,406				
Cash Dividends in 1974 of $6,598				
Stock Dividend of 1,034,009 shares–Fair Market Value of $15,242				
Issuance of 189,651 treasury shares costing $5,251 for acquisition of Fellows Corporation having a fair value of $3,578				
Balance, December 31, 1974– _____ shares issued; _____ shares in the treasury				
Net Income for 1975 of $22,630				
Cash Dividends in 1975 of $8,066				
Balance, December 31, 1975– _____ shares issued; _____ shares in the treasury				

Required

1. Stockholders' Equity: Complete the schedule of changes in Emhart's Consolidated Stockholders' Equity presented and enter the balances for December 31, 1975 and 1974 on the financial statements.

2. What entries would have been made by Emhart in 1974 and 1975 to account for its Investment in USM if it had used the cost method?

3. What entries would have been made by Emhart in 1974 and 1975 to account for its Investment in USM if it had used the equity method?

4. Emhart actually used the equity method to account for its Investment in USM in 1974 and 1975. What was the balance of the Investment in USM account at December 31, 1974 and 1975? Enter the amounts on the balance sheet.

5. What entry would have been made by Emhart on January 1, 1976 to record the conversion of Emhart Common Stock into New Emhart Common Stock?

6. What entry would have been made by Emhart on January 1, 1976 to record the acquisition of all of the USM Preference and Common Stock not held by Emhart at December 31, 1975 in exchange for New Emhart Preference and Common Stock? The market value of New Emhart Common Stock was $22 per share and the market value of New Emhart Preference Stock was $27 per share on January 1, 1976. The purchase method was used to account for this acquisition.

7. What was the carrying value of Emhart's Investment in USM on January 1, 1976 after the acquisition of USM was complete?

8. Show how Emhart's stockholders' equity section would have appeared on January 1, 1976 after the acquisition of USM.

9. Now assume that Emhart held no interest in USM at December 31, 1975. What entry would have been made by Emhart to record the merger with USM on January 1, 1976 assuming that the pooling of interests method was used? (Assume that the assigned value of New Emhart Preference Stock was $27 per share and that USM treasury stock was cancelled.)

10. Show how Emhart's stockholders' equity section would have appeared on January 1, 1976 after the merger with USM.

11. How would any difference between the carrying value of Emhart's Investment in USM using the purchase method (requirement 7 above) and the carrying value of this investment using the pooling of interests method (as in requirement 9 above) be accounted for under generally accepted accounting principles?

Section Eight

Changes in Financial Position

Case 8-1

Richard D. Brew and Company

Richard D. Brew and Company's 1972 and 1971 Statements of Operations and Deficit and Balance Sheets are presented.

STATEMENT OF OPERATIONS AND DEFICIT
Years ended December 31, 1972 and 1971

	1972	1971
Net sales	$1,011,989	$1,533,364
Operating costs and expenses:		
Cost of sales	879,636	1,326,189
Administrative and selling	385,288	311,799
	1,264,924	1,637,988
	(252,935)	(104,624)
Other income (deductions):		
Interest, net	(26,755)	(17,177)
Rental income, net	5,348	5,706
Gain on sale of land	8,602	—
	(12,805)	(11,471)
Net loss (Notes 1 and 6)	(265,740)	(116,095)
Deficit at beginning of year	(320,768)	(204,673)
Deficit at end of year	$(586,508)	$(320,768)
Net loss per share of common stock	$(.70)	$(.31)

See accompanying notes.

Consolidated Balance Sheets

ASSETS

Current assets:	1972	1971
Cash	$ 27,109	$ 22,354
Accounts receivable (Note 5)	227,640	209,853
Inventories (Note 5):		
Raw materials and supplies	91,885	103,276
Work in process	89,457	96,611
Finished goods	4,914	9,488
	186,256	209,375
Prepaid expenses	3,633	3,152
Total current assets	444,638	444,734
Property, plant and equipment, at cost (Note 5):		
Land	3,600	21,572
Buildings and improvements	341,414	327,037
Machinery and equipment	310,611	246,731
Furniture and fixtures	58,157	56,108
Motor vehicles	1,972	1,972
	715,754	653,420
Less accumulated depreciation	409,170	379,581
Net property, plant and equipment	306,584	273,839
Other assets:		
Amount due from licensee (Note 3)	–	10,000
Other	17,988	20,020
	17,988	30,020
	$769,210	$748,593

LIABILITIES AND STOCKHOLDERS' EQUITY

Current liabilities:	1972	1971
Demand notes payable to bank (Note 5)	$487,000	$175,000
Other notes payable	8,000	–
Accounts payable	89,667	124,592
Accrued liabilities	29,828	24,480
Long-term debt due within one year (Note 5)	36,418	24,990
Total current liabilities	650,913	349,062
Long-term debt due after one year:		
4-½% first mortgage note, payable monthly to December 1974	8,715	17,060
6% second mortgage note, payable monthly to September 1975	15,023	23,828
9% second mortgage note, payable monthly to June 1977	16,916	–
Chattel mortgage note, payable quarterly to September 1974, interest at 1% over prime rate (Note 5)	–	15,260
Total long-term debt	40,654	56,148
Stockholders' equity:		
Common stock, $1.00 par value; 500,000 shares authorized, 380,100 shares issued and outstanding (Note 4)	380,100	380,100
Capital in excess of par value	284,051	284,051
Deficit	(586,508)	(320,768)
Total stockholders' equity	77,643	343,383
	$769,210	$748,593

See accompanying notes.

Notes to Financial Statements

December 31, 1972 and 1971

1. Presentation of financial statements

Operating losses in recent years have placed a strain on the Company's ability to meet current operating needs. It is management's opinion that certain actions being taken will improve the Company's operating results. However, there can be no assurance that such improvement will be attained.

2. Accounting policies

The following is a summary of the principal accounting policies:

Inventories:
Inventories are valued at the lower of cost (first-in, first-out basis) or market, net of advance payments received for work in process.

Cost of the work in process inventories represents accumulated costs of material, labor and overhead. Market is realizable value after allowances for disposal costs.

Depreciation:
Substantially all of the machinery and equipment is being depreciated on the straight-line method. The buildings are being depreciated on the sum-of-the-years'-digits method.

3. License agreement

In December 1970 the Company entered into an agreement with General Engineering Company (Radcliffe) Limited of Manchester, England, whereby General was granted an exclusive license to manufacture, advertise and sell vacuum furnaces and related products in the "Licensed Territory", as defined (primarily Europe). Originally for a term of six years, the agreement was amended in November 1972 to cover seven years and renews automatically from year to year after December 1977.

The agreement provides for the payment of royalties to the Company at 7-½% of licensed sales with minimum royalties of $100,000 during the seven-year term unless the Company and General mutually agree to an earlier termination.

4. Stock options

At December 31, 1971 options granted to a key employee were outstanding and exercisable at $2.1375 per share as to 4,800 and 4,300 shares, respectively. During 1972, these options terminated.

5. Demand notes payable to bank

On January 12, 1973 notes payable to bank ($487,000) and chattel mortgage due September 1974 ($15,260) were replaced by a 7-½% demand note payable secured by a lien on accounts receivable, inventories, machinery and equipment and by an additional mortgage on other real and personal property.

6. Federal income tax

At December 31, 1972 the Company had a net operating loss carryforward for federal income tax purposes of approximately $468,000 which is available to reduce future taxable income. Of this amount, approximately $83,000 expires in 1973, $5,000 in 1975, $113,000 in 1976 and the balance of $267,000 in 1977. Investment tax credit carryforwards of approximately $5,300 are available to reduce future federal income tax liability and expire in various years through 1979.

Assume that:

a) The sale of land was the only disposition of property and plant and equipment in 1972

b) Patents were sold for cash on October 15, 1972.

c) Proceeds from the issuance of long-term debt were $20,925 in 1972.

Required Prepare a schedule of changes in net working capital and a statement of sources and uses of funds, defined as net working capital, for 1972.

Case 8-2

Oxford Pendaflex Corporation

Oxford Pendaflex Corporation's 1974 and 1973 Consolidated Balance Sheets, Statement of Consolidated Earnings, Statement of Consolidated Retained Earnings, and Notes to Consolidated Financial Statements are presented.

Statement of Consolidated Earnings

	Mar. 31, 1974	Mar. 31, 1973
Net sales	$45,614,404	$37,532,351
Cost of sales	28,639,359	23,713,507
Gross profit	16,975,045	13,818,844
Selling, warehousing and administrative expenses	12,009,279	9,926,878
	4,965,766	3,891,968
Other deductions, net	279,684	231,704
Earnings before provision for Federal and foreign taxes on income and minority interests	4,686,082	3,660,264
Provision for Federal and foreign taxes on income (notes 1(e) and 4)	2,039,900	1,833,600
Earnings before minority interests	2,646,182	1,826,664
Minority interests in earnings of foreign subsidiaries	151,684	21,274
Net earnings	$ 2,494,498	$ 1,805,390
Average shares of common stock outstanding	1,244,500	1,244,500
Net earnings per share	$2.00	$1.45

See accompanying notes to consolidated financial statements.

Statement of Consolidated Retained Earnings

	Mar. 31, 1974	Mar. 31, 1974
Balance at beginning of year	$12,267,958	$11,084,819
Net earnings	2,494,498	1,805,390
	14,762,456	12,890,209
Cash dividends on common stock ($.50 per share in 1974 and 1973)	(622,251)	(622,251)
Balance at end of year	$14,140,205	$12,287,958

See accompanying notes to consolidated financial statements.

Consolidated Balance Sheets

ASSETS	1974	1973
Current Assets:		
Cash	$ 500,055	$ 1,041,462
Accounts receivable, less allowances— 1974, $82,386; 1973, $64,779 (note 3)	10,038,530	6,979,435
Inventories (at lower of average cost or market):		
Raw materials	4,187,401	2,585,214
Work in process	1,046,751	823,483
Finished goods	3,297,733	3,118,201
	8,531,885	6,506,878
Prepaid expenses	273,849	183,548
Total current assets	19,344,319	14,711,323
Property, plant and equipment, at cost (notes 1(c) and 3):		
Land and improvements	1,312,608	784,448
Buildings	5,859,875	5,841,621
Machinery and equipment	8,682,149	7,404,905
	15,854,632	14,030,974
Less accumulated depreciation	6,554,206	5,929,300
	9,300,426	8,101,674
Construction in progress	1,900,065	555,710
	11,200,491	8,657,384
Other assets:		
Intangible assets, at amortized cost (note 1(d))	619,569	693,889
Miscellaneous	49,938	71,701
	669,507	765,590
	$31,214,317	$24,134,297

LIABILITIES AND STOCKHOLDERS' EQUITY	1974	1973
Current liabilities:		
Bank loans (note 2)	$ 2,757,821	$ 1,955,050
Current portion of long-term debt (note 3)	724,684	639,791
Accounts payable and accrued expenses	5,117,314	2,731,922
Federal income taxes (notes 1(e) and 4)	—	161,362
Dividends payable	155,562	155,562
Total current liabilities	8,755,381	5,643,687
Deferred Federal income taxes (notes 1(c) and 4)	806,922	540,700
Long-term debt, less current portion (note 3)	3,887,617	2,264,492
Minority interests in foreign subsidiaries (note 1(a))	394,582	187,850
Stockholders' equity (note 5):		
Capital stock:		
Preferred stock, $1 par value, 1,000,000 shares authorized and unissued	—	—
Common stock, $2.50 par value. 2,500,000 shares authorized; 1,244,500 shares issued in 1974 and 1973	3,111,250	3,111,250
Additional paid-in capital	118,360	118,360
Retained earnings	14,140,205	12,267,958
Total stockholders' equity	17,369,815	15,497,568
Commitments (note 6)		
	$31,214,317	$24,134,297

Notes to Consolidated Financial Statements

(1) SUMMARY OF SIGNIFICANT ACCOUNTING POLICIES

(a) Principles of Consolidation

The accompanying financial statements include the accounts of all subsidiaries. All significant intercompany accounts and transactions have been eliminated in consolidation.

Subsidiaries operating outside of the United States represent 21% of consolidated total assets (19% in 1973); 23% of consolidated net sales (21% in 1973); and 38% of consolidated net earnings (13% in 1973).

Current asset and current liability accounts of foreign subsidiaries have been translated at rates of exchange in effect at year-end, noncurrent accounts and depreciation expense at historical rates, and income and other expense accounts at the average rates of exchange in effect during the years. Exchange adjustments resulting in net gains are deferred and in net losses charged to operations. Such exchange adjustments have not been material in 1974 or 1973.

The Company has not provided for any taxes on unremitted earnings of its foreign subsidiaries, since all of such earnings have been or are expected to be reinvested in the operations. Unremitted earnings amount to approximately $1,298,200 and $340,500 at March 31, 1974 and 1973, respectively.

(b) Acquisition

During 1974, Oxford Pendaflex Canada Limited, a Canadian subsidiary, purchased in assets and undertakings of two companies in the office products business for a total consideration of approximately $498,000 ($203,000 paid in cash, $165,000 of liabilities assumed, and $130,000 in a note payable due in 1976). The purchase price exceeded the net assets acquired by $105,000 which is being amortized over a twenty-year period.

(c) Property, Plant and Equipment

In 1974, Oxford sold property that originally cost $345,000 for $174,000. Accumulated Depreciation to date of sale was $171,000 on this property.

It is the policy of the Company to provide for depreciation on plant and equipment by charges against earnings over their estimated useful lives principally on a straight-line method for financial reporting and on an accelerated method for tax purposes. (See note 4 for the amount of deferred taxes included in the statement of consolidated earnings). Depreciation in the amount of $795,859 and $722,214 was charged to operations in fiscal 1974 and 1973, respectively.

(d) Intangible Assets

In 1974, Oxford's amortization of Goodwill amounted to $143,000 and its amortization of other intangible assets amounted to $36,000.

Intangible assets represent the excess cost over net book value of assets acquired and patents and trademarks of acquired subsidiaries, and are being amortized on a straight-line method over periods ranging from fifteen to twenty years.

(e) Investment Tax Credits

The Company follows the policy of reducing Federal income taxes currently for the amounts of computed allowable investment credit. The provision for Federal income taxes in the accompanying statement of consolidated earnings has been reduced by investment tax credits amounting to $57,000 and $37,000, in fiscal 1974 and 1973, respectively.

(f) Pension Plans

The Company has several pension and supplemental retirement plans which cover substantially all employees. The Company's policy is to fund pension costs accrued. Pension costs accrued include amortization of prior service costs over a period of thirty years. At January 1, 1974, the latest date for which calculations have been made, pension fund assets exceeded the vested benefit liabilities under the plans while unfunded past service costs amounted to approximately $456,000. The cost of contributions to the plans for the years ended March 31, 1974 and 1973, amounted to $296,203 and $279,323, respectively.

(2) SHORT-TERM BORROWINGS

Bank loans represent principally short-term unsecured notes payable with interest based on the prime commercial rate. The aggregate maximum amount of these short-term borrowings at any month-end during fiscal 1974 was $3,951,000. The average aggregate short-term borrowings outstanding during the year based on month-end balances, amounted to approximately $2,152,000, with a related average interest rate of approximately 9%.

(3) LONG-TERM DEBT

In 1974, Oxford reduced its long-term debt by $1,432,000 in one set of transactions. At March 31, 1974, long-term debt consisted of the following:

	Interest rate	Security	Date due	Amount
Mortgages (a)	6-6¼%	Land and buildings	1974-1992	$ 571,605
Term bank loans (b)	½% above prime rate	None	1974-1979	2,000,000
Revolving credit agreement (b)	1% above prime rate	None	1979	1,000,000
Other bank loan (c)	1½% above prime rate	Accounts receivable	1974-1977	432,086
Notes payable (d)	None—4%	None	1974-1977	310,423
Long-term obligation relating to capitalized lease (less unamortized discount in the amount of $123,511 based on imputed interest rate of 7% (e)]	7%	Land and buildings	1974-1985	298,187
				4,612,301
Less current portion				724,684
				$3,887,617

(a) Land and buildings with a book value of approximately $2,074,626 are pledged as security under the above mortgages.

(b) During fiscal 1974, the Company entered into a revolving credit and term loan agreement with two banks. The revolving credit agreements, which expires January 1, 1979, permits borrowings up to a maximum of $3,000,000. The term loan arrangement provides for borrowings up to a maximum of $2,000,000, repayable in semiannual installments, to January 1, 1979.

The terms of the aforementioned agreement require, among other things, the maintenance of minimum working capital and tangible net worth, limitations on additional borrowings and capital expenditures, and restrictions as to the payment of cash dividends. At March 31, 1974, retained earnings available for the payment of dividends amounted to approximately $4,285,000.

(c) The bank loan in the amount of $432,086 relates to the acquisition of certain Canadian companies and is a demand note that has been included in long-term debt inasmuch as the bank, while reserving the option to call the loan, has agreed to a semiannual principal repayment of $73,000 through 1977. This loan is secured by accounts receivabe of the Canadian companies $2,182,000.

(d) Principally, notes issued in conjunction with the acquisitions of the Canadian companies in 1972 and 1974.

(e) During fiscal 1973, the Company entered into a sale and lease-back arrangement with respect to its Augusta, Georgia facilities. Such arrangement provided for the sale of the existing facilities to a development authority in Georgia and the construction of additional facilities by that authority. Simultaneously the Company entered a twelve-year lease agreement with the authority regarding these facilities. Under the terms of the lease, the Company pays aggregate annual rentals amounting to approximately $38,000, including interest. The lease agreement also provides the Company with an option to purchase the facilities at the end of the lease period for a nominal amount. The transaction has been accounted for as an installment purchase of the facilities and, accordingly, the cost of the facilities has been reflected in property, plant and equipment in the accompanying consolidated balance sheet at the present value of the total lease obligation, discounted at a 7% interest rate. Concurrently, the same amount has been reflected in long-term debt above.

(4) TAXES ON INCOME

The provision for Federal and foreign taxes on income includes the following:

	1974 United States Federal	1974 Canadian and other foreign	1974 Total	1973 total
Current	$1,177,500	627,700	1,805,200	1,765,000
Deferred	121,100	113,600	234,700	68,600
	$1,298,600	741,300	2,039,900	1,833,600

The deferred portion of taxes for both 1974 and 1973 results from computing depreciation under different methods for financial reporting and tax purposes as explained in note 1(c).

The Company's effective tax rate of 43.5% for fiscal 1974 is less than the Federal statutory rate of 48% primarily because of investment tax credits offset against the provision and income of foreign subsidiaries which is not expected to be subject to United States Federal income taxes.

(5) STOCK OPTIONS AND STOCK PURCHASE PLAN

On July 21, 1970, the Board of Directors and stockholders adopted a qualified stock option plan which permits the granting of options to key employees to purchase not more than an aggregate of 60,000 shares of the Company's authorized but unissued or reacquired common stock and a qualified employee stock purchase plan reserving 40,000 shares of common stock for subscription by eligible employees. Under the qualified stock option plan, options may be granted for a period of five years from the date of plan adoption and are exercisable for a period of five years from the date of grant. Under the qualified employee stock purchase plan, subscriptions may be offered once during each fiscal year through 1975 to eligible employees, based upon a subscription formula. The combined total of options granted and subscriptions offered may not exceed an aggregate of 25,000 shares in each year.

Options to purchase 25,000 shares of stock at a price of $9.125 per share were granted under the qualified stock option plan for key employees during 1974, and 14,000 shares of stock at a price of $11.875 per share were granted during 1973. To date, no options have been exercised under this plan.

Subscriptions to purchase 10,000 shares of stock at a price of $12.50 per share were offered under the qualified employee stock purchase plan during fiscal 1973. Such shares are not issuable until two years from the date of subscription. At March 31, 1974, 6,482 shares were under subscription.

(6) COMMITMENTS

At March 31, 1974 the Company and its subsidiaries were obligated under building leases expiring between 1977 and 1994. Minimum annual rentals under these obligations are as follows: 1975–$484,000; 1976–$484,000; 1977–$382,000; 1978–$329,000; 1979–$322,000; 1980 to 1984–$1,564,000; 1985 to 1989–$1,506,000; 1990 to 1994–$284,360.

Required Using the information provided in Oxford Pendaflex's Consolidated Financial Statements, prepare a schedule of changes in net working capital and a statement of sources and uses of funds, defined as net working capital, for 1974.

Case 8-3

Evans Products Company

Evans Products Company manufactures and markets a wide range of building products through its manufacturing facilities and retail building materials stores (Grossman's Stores).

Assumptions

1. Proceeds from the issuance of long-term debt during 1975 amounted to $2,647,000.

2. During 1975, Evans acquired property, plant and equipment costing $13,325,000 and sold property, plant and equipment for its book value of $34,139,000.

3. All amortized expenses in the Statement of Results of Operations relate to the excess of cost over net assets of businesses purchased and deferred charges, etc. included in "Other Assets" in the Balance Sheet presented.

CONSOLIDATED BALANCE SHEET

December 31 (In thousands)	1975	1974
ASSETS		
CURRENT ASSETS		
Cash	$ 12,476	$ 21,760
Refundable taxes on earnings	1,204	12,333
Receivables	88,204	107,913
Inventories	133,802	181,397
Prepaid expenses	4,974	5,784
Total Current Assets	240,660	329,187
DISCONTINUED FACILITIES HELD FOR SALE	9,071	17,422
PROPERTY, PLANT AND EQUIPMENT	139,037	172,894
INVESTMENTS IN UNCONSOLIDATED SUBSIDIARIES	143,237	136,758
DEFERRED TAX BENEFITS	10,618	21,771
OTHER ASSETS	22,668	31,073
	$565,291	$709,105
LIABILITIES AND SHAREHOLDERS' INVESTMENT		
CURRENT LIABILITIES		
Notes payable	$ —	$ 5,871
Accounts payable and accruals	65,351	98,915
Accrued losses on discontinued facilities	2,639	11,995
Current portion of long-term debt	2,249	3,723
Total Current Liabilities	70,239	120,504
SENIOR LONG-TERM DEBT	227,162	332,697
CONVERTIBLE SUBORDINATED DEBENTURES	49,942	49,942
SHAREHOLDERS' INVESTMENT	217,948	205,962
	$565,291	$709,105

The accompanying notes are an integral part of this statement.

STATEMENT OF RESULTS OF OPERATIONS

	1975	1974
REVENUES		
Sales	$774,297	$1,109,982
Other income	7,322	5,611
Gain on sale of assets	13,506	1,883
Earnings before taxes of unconsolidated subsidiaries	15,889	15,416
	811,014	1,132,892
COSTS AND EXPENSES		
Costs of operations	687,963	1,040,156
Selling and administrative	53,305	79,403
Depreciation and amortization	14,773	16,798
Interest	29,867	41,411
Estimated losses of discontinued facilities	2,950	35,038
	788,858	1,212,806
EARNINGS (LOSS) BEFORE TAXES	22,156	(79,914)
TAXES ON EARNINGS		
Current	725	(10,700)
Deferred	8,775	(24,800)
	9,500	(35,500)
NET EARNINGS (LOSS)	$ 12,656	$ (44,414)
PER COMMON SHARE		
Primary	$ .74	$ (2.69)
Assuming full dilution	$ .73	$ (2.69)

STATEMENT OF SHAREHOLDERS' INVESTMENT

	Shares Outstanding		Amount	
	1975	1974	1975	1974
PREFERRED				
5¼% series	53	56	$ 5,250	$ 5,625
COMMON				
Common stock	16,986	16,986	16,986	16,986
Paid-in capital			151,238	151,238
Retained earnings			48,427	36,066
			221,901	209,915
Less treasury stock at cost	369	369	3,953	3,953
	16,617	16,617	$217,948	$205,962

DETAILS OF COMMON SHAREHOLDERS' INVESTMENT

	Common Stock	Paid-in Capital	Retained Earnings
Balance at January 1, 1974	$16,986	$151,130	$ 88,268
Net loss			(44,414)
Cash dividends			(7,788)
Miscellaneous		108	
Balance at December 31, 1974	16,986	151,238	36,066
Net earnings			12,656
Cash dividends			(295)
Balance at December 31, 1975	$16,986	$151,238	$ 48,427

There are 4,900,500 shares of no par preferred stock authorized. The 5¼% cumulative preferred stock has a stated value of $100 a share, and required redemption of 3,750 shares annually at a price of $100 a share.

The common stock has a par value of $1 a share, and 30,000,000 shares are authorized.

Required Using the financial statements presented and the stated assumptions, prepare a statement of sources and uses of funds, defined as net working capital, for 1975.

Case 8-4

General DataComm Industries, Inc.

General DataComm Industries, Inc. is the largest independent manufacturer of data transmission equipment. General DataComm's 1977 Consolidated Financial Statements are presented.

Consolidated Balance Sheets

September 30, 1977 and 1976

	1977	1976
Assets:		
Current assets:		
Cash	$ 592,000	$ 470,000
Accounts receivable, trade (Note 6)	3,580,000	3,600,000
Due from leasing subsidiaries	180,000	43,000
Inventories (Notes 3 and 6)	7,492,000	5,488,000
Prepaid expenses and other	264,000	173,000
Total current assets	12,108,000	9,774,000
Investment in and advances to leasing subsidiaries (Note 5)	547,000	422,000
Property, plant and equipment, net (Notes 4, 6 and 8)	4,281,000	2,378,000
Deferred international market development costs, net (Note 1)	268,000	412,000
Other assets	93,000	154,000
	$17,297,000	$13,140,000
Liabilities and Stockholders' Equity:		
Current liabilities:		
Accounts payable, trade	$ 1,664,000	$ 1,777,000
Accrued expenses	892,000	584,000
Income taxes payable	468,000	146,000
Capital lease obligations	184,000	139,000
Mortgages payable	89,000	—
Total current liabilities	3,297,000	2,646,000
Revolving credit notes (Note 6)	4,700,000	5,000,000
Mortgages payable (Note 7)	2,068,000	—
Capital lease obligations (Note 8)	304,000	270,000
Deferred income taxes	293,000	—
Deferred income (Note 1)	229,000	161,000
Stockholders' equity (Notes 6 and 10):		
Common stock	147,000	145,000
Capital in excess of par value	5,458,000	5,424,000
Retained earnings (deficit)	816,000	(491,000)
Less, treasury stock, at cost	(15,000)	(15,000)
Total stockholders' equity	6,406,000	5,063,000
	$17,297,000	$13,140,000

Consolidated Statements of Stockholders' Equity

Years ended September 30, 1977 and 1976

	Common Stock				Capital In Excess of Par	Retained Earnings (Deficit)	Total Stockholders' Equity
	Shares Issued	Amount	Treasury Stock Shares	Amount			
Balance September 30, 1975	1,448,640	$145,000	30,600	($15,000)	$5,442,000	($1,306,000)	$4,266,000
Exercise of stock options	400				1,000		1,000
Repurchase of common stock for treasury			1,000				
Repurchase of 75,000 stock purchase warrants					(19,000)	(38,000)	(57,000)
Net income						853,000	853,000
Balance September 30, 1976	1,449,040	145,000	31,600	(15,000)	5,424,000	(491,000)	5,063,000
Exercise of stock options	18,440	2,000			34,000		36,000
Net income						1,307,000	1,307,000
Balance September 30, 1977	**1,467,480**	**$147,000**	**31,600**	**($15,000)**	**$5,458,000**	**$816,000**	**$6,406,000**

Consolidated Statements of Income

Years ended September 30, 1977 and 1976

	1977	1976
Net revenues:		
Sales (Note 2)	$20,032,000	$15,956,000
Equity in net income of leasing subsidiaries (Note 5)	90,000	102,000
	20,122,000	16,058,000
Costs and expenses:		
Cost of sales	12,112,000	9,911,000
Selling, general and administrative	3,954,000	3,427,000
Research and product development	1,429,000	1,196,000
	17,495,000	14,534,000
Operating income	2,627,000	1,524,000
Other income (expense):		
Interest	(603,000)	(647,000)
Other, net	(16,000)	41,000
	(619,000)	(606,000)
Income before income taxes and extraordinary credit	2,008,000	918,000
Provision for income taxes (Note 11)	701,000	439,000
Income before extraordinary credit	1,307,000	479,000
Extraordinary credit, tax benefit from carryforward of net operating losses	—	374,000
Net income	**$ 1,307,000**	**$ 853,000**
Earnings per common share:		
Primary:		
Before extraordinary credit	$.88	$.34
Extraordinary credit	—	.26
Net income	$.88	$.60
Fully diluted	**$.86**	**—**

Notes to Financial Statements

September 30, 1977 and 1976

1. Summary of Significant Accounting Policies

*Principles of Consolidation—*The consolidated financial statements include the accounts of all domestic and foreign subsidiaries except leasing subsidiaries, which are accounted for under the equity method (see Note 5). Certain amounts for 1976 have been reclassified to conform with the current year's presentation.

*Inventories—*Inventories are stated at the lower of cost (computed on average methods which approximate the first-in, first-out method) or market. Market represents replacement cost for raw material and net realizable value for work-in-process and finished goods.

*Property, Plant and Equipment—*Property, plant and equipment is stated at cost, and depreciated on the straight-line method over the following estimated lives:

Building and Improvements	20 years
Test Equipment and Fixtures	5 to 10 years
Machinery and Equipment	3 to 10 years
Leasehold Improvements	Lease Term

Certain test equipment and fixtures and certain other equipment consist of material, internal manufacturing and engineering labor and overhead costs incurred in their construction.

Maintenance and repairs are charged to expense as incurred, and betterments and improvements are capitalized. Cost and accumulated depreciation of assets retired or otherwise disposed of are eliminated and any resulting gain or loss is reflected in operations.

*Deferred Costs—*International market development costs, consisting primarily of direct salaries and administrative costs and travel expense, are accumulated by country and deferred. Following commencement of profitable operations in a country these costs are amortized over five years. If no significant profitable operations appear likely, related deferred costs are charged to operations. Accumulated amortization of international market development costs amounted to $323,000 and $210,000 in 1977 and 1976, respectively.

*Revenue Recognition—*The leasing subsidiaries use the finance method of accounting for all leases which are equivalent to sales. Under this method, the unearned finance income represents the excess of aggregate future rentals and unguaranteed residual value over the cost of the equipment. Such income is recognized using the "sum-of-the-months digits" method over the life of the lease. All other leases are accounted for using the operating method. Under this method, rental income from leases is recorded in equal monthly amounts over the life of the lease and equipment is depreciated using the straight-line method over a five year life. Manufacturing profit is recognized by General DataComm at the time of sale of equipment to the leasing subsidiaries when such equipment is subject to sales type leases and in equal monthly amounts over the depreciable life of the equipment when subject to operating leases.

*Income Taxes—*General DataComm files a consolidated federal income tax return. For financial reporting purposes the leasing subsidiaries are not consolidated and provide federal income taxes under a sharing arrangement whereby the leasing subsidiaries provide taxes at a 48% rate less the surtax exemption.

Deferred income taxes are provided to reflect timing differences between financial and tax reporting.

Investment tax credits are included as a reduction of the provision for income taxes on the "flow-through" method.

*Earnings Per Share—*Primary earnings per share are based on the weighted average number of common and common equivalent shares outstanding. Common equivalent shares include dilutive stock options and warrants. Fully diluted earnings per share have been determined as stated previously, adjusted as to options and warrants for market prices at the end of the period.

2. Sales in Foreign Countries

General DataComm markets its products worldwide. Sales in 1977 and 1976 to customers outside the U.S., principally in Canada, Europe and the Far East, aggregated $6,070,000 and $6,493,000, respectively.

3. Inventories

Inventories consist of the following:

	1977	1976
Raw Materials	$2,586,000	$1,983,000
Work-In-Process	2,400,000	762,000
Finished Goods	2,506,000	2,743,000
	$7,492,000	$5,488,000

4. Property, Plant and Equipment

Property, plant and equipment consists of the following:

	1977	1976
Land	$ 337,000	—
Building & improvements	1,659,000	—
Test equipment & fixtures (Note 8)	2,739,000	$2,680,000
Machinery and equipment	1,048,000	1,121,000
Leasehold improvements	288,000	199,000
	6,071,000	4,000,000
Less, accumulated depreciation and amortization	1,790,000	1,622,000
	$4,281,000	$2,378,000

Depreciation and amortization expense in 1977 and 1976 amounted to $829,000 and $604,000, respectively.

5. Leasing Subsidiaries

The following condensed financial information combines DataComm Leasing Corporation and two other leasing subsidiaries, which are 100% owned by General DataComm:

	1977	1976
Cash	$ 23,000	$ 31,000
Receivables (net of unearned finance income) and residual values	645,000	1,219,000
Operating lease rental equipment, net of accumulated depreciation	450,000	213,000
Total assets	1,118,000	1,463,000
Accrued expenses and amounts currently payable to General DataComm and affiliates	189,000	54,000
Notes and other payables	382,000	987,000
Total liabilities	571,000	1,041,000
Net equity	$547,000	$422,000
Net revenue	$507,000	$428,000
Income before income taxes	$163,000	$186,000
Net income	$ 90,000	$102,000

Notes:

(a) *Basis of financial data—*General DataComm's leasing subsidiaries purchase equipment, for lease to others, from General DataComm, their present sole supplier. The aggregate cost of such purchases amounted to $439,000 in 1977 and $857,000 in 1976, at prices comparable to those contained in General DataComm's price list. In addition, General DataComm charged the leasing subsidiaries $20,000 and $19,000 in 1977 and 1976, respectively, for administrative services. The terms of the aforementioned transactions were established by negotiation between the parties.

(b) *Notes and other payables—*In 1976 the leasing subsidiaries obtained a significant portion of the financing necessary to purchase equipment from General DataComm by utilizing the individual lease contracts and related equipment as collateral for borrowings. The interest rates on these borrowings range between 12% and 15% with principal generally payable as the related contracts receivable become due. In 1977 all financing was provided by General DataComm with no interest charge.

(c) *Net equity—*General DataComm's net equity in the leasing subsidiaries is represented by:

	1977	1976
Accounts receivable— due after one year	$115,000	$ 80,000
Subordinated non-interest bearing note, due July 20, 2073	100,000	100,000
Equity	332,000	242,000
	$547,000	$422,000

(d) *Operating Leases—*The following is a schedule by years of minimum future rental revenues on non-cancellable operating leases as of September 30, 1977:

1978	$174,000	
1979	114,000	
1980	14,000	
	$302,000	

6. Revolving Credit Notes

Revolving credit notes were outstanding in fiscal year 1977 under a bank revolving credit loan agreement which was superceded by a new revolving credit agreement in November 1977. Under the terms of the original agreement, General DataComm could borrow up to $6,000,000 based on a lending formula related to accounts receivable, inventory and net fixed assets. The notes were collateralized by substantially all the assets of General DataComm except land, buildings, and the common stock of the leasing subsidiaries. The agreement provided, among other things, for maintenance of specified working capital, net worth, and debt to net worth requirements. It also limited investments and capital expenditures, and prohibited payments of cash dividends. The original revolving credit notes had interest at 2½% over the bank's prime rate plus a ½% commitment fee on the average daily unused amount. In addition, General DataComm was required to maintain compensating balances based on the level of borrowing. During 1977 the maximum revolving credit notes payable at any month end were $5,400,000 and the average borrowings were $5,131,000. The daily weighted average interest rate during fiscal 1977 was 9.1%.

The new revolving credit agreement provides for a maximum borrowing line of $9,000,000, has similar collateral, lending formula and restrictive covenants as the original agreement, bears interest at 2¼% over the bank's prime rate, plus a ½% commitment fee on the average daily unused amount and requires no compensating balances. The balance of such revolving credit loan on October 31, 1980 will convert to a four year term loan with interest at 2¾% over the bank's prime rate, payable in sixteen equal quarterly payments.

7. Mortgages Payable

In connection with the purchase of the Danbury facilities, General DataComm assumed existing first and second mortgages on the property and arranged for a third mortgage to finance closing costs and renovations. Under the terms of the third mortgage General DataComm may borrow up to $1,079,000 with payments beginning the third quarter of fiscal 1978. The following schedule shows the principal terms of each mortgage:

8. Capital Leases

General DataComm leases certain test equipment and fixtures (with a cost of $854,000) which are classified as property, plant and equipment. The following is a schedule, by years, of future minimum lease payments together with the present value of the net minimum lease payments as of September 30, 1977:

1978	$219,000
1979	163,000
1980	134,000
1981	56,000
1982	10,000
	582,000
Less, amounts representing interest	94,000
Present value of net minimum lease payments	$488,000

9. Operating Leases

Operating leases are principally comprised of two non-cancellable leases for plant and office space. As a result of the relocation to Danbury, General DataComm has no immediate need for this space. Accordingly, General DataComm has entered into a sublease for one facility which provides for sublease rentals in excess of its rental expense. General DataComm has retained the right to return to this facility on the first renewal option date. General DataComm expects to sublease the other facility for an amount at least equal to its rental expense. Rental expense in 1977 and 1976 amounted to $226,000 and $198,000, respectively.

10. Capital Stock

At September 30, 1977 there were 5,000,000 common shares, par value $.10, authorized and 1,000,000 shares of $1.00 par value preferred stock authorized but not issued.

Under General DataComm's qualified stock option plans, 129,210 shares of common stock have been reserved for grants to officers and key employees at a price of not less than 100% of the fair market value on the date of grant. Options expire five years from the date of grant and become exercisable in installments after the first year. No charges are made to income for qualified options granted under these plans. When shares are issued on exercise of options, the excess of amounts paid over par value is credited to capital in excess of par value.

At September 30, 1977 options were outstanding under these plans for 121,400 common shares (of which 13,800 were exercisable) having an aggregate option price of $374,219 at prices ranging from $.6875 to $9.125 per share (equal to market prices at the date of grant) and 7,810 shares were available for grant. In 1977, 18,440 options were exercised at prices ranging from $.6875 to $5.25 per share, options were granted for 52,400 shares and options or 25,760 shares were cancelled or terminated.

In connection with the original revolving credit loan agreement (see Note 6), General DataComm has 20,000 detachable stock purchase warrants outstanding at a value of $.25 per warrant. The warrants are exercisable at $5.00 per share, subject to adjustment for anti-dilution provisions, until October 31, 1979.

11. Income Taxes

The provision for income taxes is comprised of the following:

	1977	1976
Current:		
Federal	$274,000	$306,000
State	153,000	29,000
Foreign	(19,000)	104,000
	408,000	439,000
Deferred	293,000	—
	$701,000	$439,000

	Interest Rate	Principal Outstanding 9/30/77	Monthly Installments (Principal and Interest)	Maturity Date	Principal Balance Payable at Maturity
First mortgage	6½%	$1,568,000	$15,000	10/1/87	$464,000
Second mortgage	7½%	149,000	1,000	3/1/88	62,000
Third mortgage	9¼%	440,000	4,000	3/1/88	370,000

The provision for income taxes in 1977 includes the utilization of $300,000 of investment tax credit carryforwards.

Deferred taxes consist of accelerated depreciation ($126,000), income deferral from the conversion of financing leases to operating leases ($52,000), DISC income ($48,000) and miscellaneous other ($67,000).

The following reconciles income taxes computed at the United States federal statutory rate to the provision for income taxes:

	1977	1976
U.S. tax on income at statutory rate	48.0%	48.0%
Investment credits	(18.8)	—
Equity in net income of leasing subsidiaries, net of income tax	(2.1)	(5.3)
Excess foreign provision over U.S. statutory rate	—	2.6
State and local income taxes	6.8	1.6
Other, net	1.0	.9
	34.9%	47.8%

Required Assuming that during 1977 General DataComm sold property, plant and equipment costing $793,000 for their book value, prepare a statement of sources and uses of funds, defined as net working capital, for 1977.

Case 8-5

FlightSafety International

FlightSafety International operates 16 Learning Centers in the United States and abroad. The Company is the leading high technology training organization for professional aircraft pilots and technicians.

FlightSafety's 1976 and 1975 Consolidated Statements of Income and Retained Earnings and Consolidated Balance Sheets are presented.

Purchases of equipment and facilities totaled $8,412,897 in 1976.

Note 5 to FlightSafety's Consolidated Financial Statements is shown.

Note 5—Common Stock and Capital in Excess of Par Value:

Changes in issued common stock and capital in excess of par value were as follows:

	Common Stock Shares	Common Stock Amount	Capital in excess of par value
Balance December 31, 1974	1,496,393	$149,639	$1,801,930
Exercise of stock options	7,425	743	56,182
Balance December 31, 1975	1,503,818	150,382	1,858,112
Two-for-one stock split	1,509,153	150,915	(150,915)
Exercise of stock options	14,335	1,434	67,478
Balance December 31, 1976	3,027,306	$302,731	$1,774,675

Consolidated Statements of Income and Retained Earnings

	Year ended December 31, 1976	1975
Pilot training and other revenue (Note 1)	$15,727,148	$13,432,527
Expenses:		
Salaries and wages	4,334,092	3,719,518
Other operating	1,120,983	752,579
Depreciation and amortization	1,672,080	1,467,862
Rent and occupancy	390,868	330,561
General and administrative	1,465,238	1,360,485
	8,983,261	7,631,005
Income before income taxes	6,743,887	5,801,522
Taxes on income (Notes 1 and 3)	2,707,000	2,696,000
Net income for the year	4,036,887	3,105,522
Retained earnings, beginning of year	12,711,258	9,605,736
Dividends declared	(272,008)	
Retained earnings, end of year	$16,476,137	$12,711,258
Net income per share (Note 1)	$1.34	$1.04

Consolidated Balance Sheets

Assets	December 31, 1976	December 31, 1975
Current assets:		
Cash and short-term investments	$ 1,146,550	$ 2,879,765
Notes and accounts receivable, less allowance for doubtful accounts of $415,700 ($388,000 in 1975)	3,625,122	2,480,842
Inventories, principally spare parts, at lower of current cost or market	368,723	199,419
Unbilled training fees and expenses	158,937	422,084
Prepaid expenses, deposits and other current assets	217,376	149,915
Accumulated income tax prepayments (Note 1)	1,053,000	534,000
Total current assets	6,569,708	6,666,025
Equipment and facilities, at cost (Notes 1 and 2)	29,838,898	21,480,570
Less—accumulated depreciation and amortization	(9,905,674)	(8,266,888)
	19,933,224	13,213,682
Notes receivable due after one year	145,895	198,639
	$26,648,827	$20,078,346

Liabilities and stockholders' equity		
Current liabilities:		
Accounts payable and accrued expenses	$ 1,371,246	$ 1,259,281
Equipment purchases	1,146,278	1,121,505
Dividends payable	90,819	
Income taxes payable	770,312	1,018,449
Unearned income for contract training to be earned in one year (Note 1)	2,080,629	1,212,371
Total current liabilities	5,459,284	4,611,606
Note payable to bank (Note 4)	1,500,000	
Unearned income for contract training to be earned after one year		22,215
Accumulated income tax reductions (Note 1)	1,136,000	724,773
Total liabilities	8,095,284	5,358,594
Stockholders' equity (Notes 5 and 6):		
Common stock, par value $.10 Authorized-4,000,000 shares Issued and outstanding 3,027,306 shares (3,007,636 in 1975)	302,731	150,382
Capital in excess of par value	1,774,675	1,858,112
Retained earnings	16,476,137	12,711,258
Total stockholders' equity	18,553,543	14,719,752
Commitments (Notes 2 and 7)		
	$26,648,827	$20,078,346

Required Using these financial statements and the additional information, prepare a statement of sources and uses of funds, defined as net working capital, for 1976.

Case 8-6

Gardner-Denver

The financial statements for Gardner-Denver for the year ended December 31, 1975 are presented. Gardner-Denver was founded 117 years ago and is a leading producer of quality rock-drilling machinery. Its output is used by those industries involved in developing the earth's resources.

Consolidated Balance Sheets

Assets December 31:	1975	1974
	(in thousands)	*(in thousands)*
Current Assets		
Cash	$ 7,818	$ 9,374
Short-term investments, at cost which approximates market	11,309	—
Accounts and notes receivable, less allowances of $3,231,000 in 1975 and $3,050,000 in 1974	86,911	88,047
Inventories (Note 1)	159,983	140,948
Total current assets	$266,021	$238,369
Other Assets	$ 17,107	$ 15,256
Plant and Equipment		
Land and improvements	$ 5,579	$ 4,512
Buildings	37,527	34,329
Machinery and equipment	117,875	108,309
Construction in progress	1,150	1,343
	$162,131	$148,493
Less—Accumulated depreciation	73,779	64,032
	$ 88,352	$ 84,461
	$371,480	$338,086

Liabilities and Stockholders' Equity		
Current Liabilities		
Loans payable (Note 5)	$ 3,390	$ 7,053
Accounts payable and accrued liabilities	32,826	39,896
Accrued income taxes	15,142	7,806
Total current liabilities	$ 51,358	$ 54,755
Long-term Debt (Note 5)	$ 58,707	$ 68,383
Deferred Income Taxes (Note 4)	$ 12,978	$ 8,576
Minority Interest in Foreign Subsidiary	$ 3,738	$ 1,337
Stockholders' Equity (Notes 2, 6 and 8)		
Common stock	$ 95,318	$ 90,906
Paid-in capital	17,800	1,138
Retained earnings	131,581	112,991
	$244,699	$205,035
	$371,480	$338,086

Statements of Consolidated Income

Year ended December 31:	1975	1974
	(in thousands)	*(in thousands)*
Net Sales	$423,140	$355,437
Costs and Expenses		
Manufacturing cost of products sold	$279,008	$234,525
Selling and administrative	78,906	66,368
Interest	6,573	6,984
Other income, net	(2,691)	(2,260)
	$361,796	$305,617
Income Before Income Taxes	$ 61,344	$ 49,820
Income taxes (Note 4)		
Current	$ 25,171	$ 17,887
Deferred	3,631	5,487
	$ 28,802	$ 23,374
Net Income	$ 32,542	$ 26,446
Net Income Per Share	$ 1.74	$ 1.46

Consolidated Statement of Stockholders' Equity

	Common Stock Shares	Par Value	Paid-In Capital	Retained Earnings
		(in thousands)		
Balance December 31, 1973, as previously reported	16,522	$82,609	$ 735	$ 96,726
Common stock issued in connection with poolings	1,627	8,138	–	2,554
Balance December 31, 1973, as restated	18,149	$90,747	$ 735	$ 99,280
Net income	–	–	–	26,446
Cash dividends (per share $.76)	–	–	–	(12,735)
Common stock issued under option plans	32	159	403	–
Balance December 31, 1974	18,181	$90,906	$1,138	$112,991
Net income	–	–	–	32,542
Cash dividends (per share $.76)	–	–	–	(13,952)
Common stock issued:				
Under option plans	29	141	336	–
Public offering	850	4,250	16,266	–
By pooled company prior to acquisition	4	21	60	–
Balance December 31, 1975	19,064	$95,318	$17,800	$131,581

The only notes you will need are:

Note 2: Plant and Equipment Sales

During 1975, the Company sold equipment with an original cost of $1,770,000 for $10,000. There was a loss of $500,000 recognized on this transaction which was included in other income (net).

288 Cases in Financial Accounting

Note 4: Income tax expense for 1975 is composed of the following:

Current		
U.S. Federal	$18,372	
Foreign	5,270	
State and Local	1,529	
	$25,171	
Deferred		
Tax on DISC Companies		
Deferred for Tax	$ 3,871	
Deferred Investment Tax Credit	70	
Other, net	461	
	$ 4,402	
Tax on Income from		
Installment Sales	(771)	
Deferred Taxes Per Income		
Statement	$ 3,631	

Note 5: On December 15, 1975, bonds with a face value of $9,676,000 were retired for $9,676,000. Bond discount had been recognized on these bonds (and other Company Debt) to the amount of $10,000 in 1975 and is reflected in interest expense.

Required Using the following schedule, complete the Consolidated Statement of Changes in Financial Position. (Hint: Derive the net change in working capital from the Consolidated Balance Sheet and enter this item first.)

Gardner-Denver Company and Subsidiaries
Consolidated Statement of Changes in Financial Position
Year Ended December 31, 1975

Sources of Working Capital		(in thousands)
Net Income		$_____
Expenditures Not Requiring Funds		
Depreciation	_____	
Deferred Income Taxes	_____	
Bond Discount Amortized	_____	
Loss on Sale of Assets	_____	_____
Sale of Common Stock		_____
Total Sources		$_____
Applications		
Plant and Equipment Additions		$_____
Increase in Other Assets		1,851
Retirement of Long-Term Debt		_____
Dividends		_____
Less Increase in Minority Interest		(2,401)
Total Applications		$_____
Increase (Decrease) in Working Capital		$_____

Case 8-7

Georgia-Pacific Corporation (C)

Georgia-Pacific's Consolidated Financial Statements for 1975 and 1976 are presented.

Consolidated Balance Sheets

Amounts in thousands

	1976	1975
Assets		
Current assets:		
Cash	$ 25,600	$ 31,800
Marketable securities, at quoted market (cost $20,100 in 1975)	—	16,600
Receivables (less reserves of $6,100 in 1976 and $5,900 in 1975)	294,700	250,000
Inventories, at the lower of cost or market (Note 3)	423,000	376,700
Prepaid expenses	9,700	6,600
Total current assets	753,000	681,700
Natural resources, at cost less depletion (Note 4):		
Timber and timberlands	330,500	319,900
Coal, minerals, natural gas and oil	30,300	26,800
	360,800	346,700
Property, plant and equipment (Note 4):		
Land, buildings, machinery and equipment, at cost	2,284,900	2,049,900
Less—Reserves for depreciation	835,800	721,900
	1,449,100	1,328,000
Noncurrent receivables and other assets	21,100	47,500
	$2,584,000	$2,403,900
Liabilities		
Current liabilities:		
Current portion of long-term debt	$ 36,900	$ 98,600
Accounts payable and accrued liabilities	206,700	130,100
Current income taxes	67,200	25,600
	310,800	254,300
Commercial paper and other short-term notes supported by confirmed seasonal bank lines of credit	222,600	—
Total current liabilities	533,400	254,300
Long-term debt, excluding current portion (Note 8)	317,700	606,900
Convertible subordinated debentures (Note 9):		
5¾% due 1994	—	75,000
5¼% due 1996	125,000	125,000
6¼% due 2000	—	100,000
Deferred income taxes (Notes 1 and 6)	250,000	215,000
Employee stock purchase plan (Note 10)	5,800	—
Capital stock and surplus (Notes 7, 10 and 11):		
Common stock	79,000	48,300
Paid-in surplus	905,700	701,300
Earned surplus	368,800	279,900
Less—Common stock held in treasury, at cost	(1,400)	(1,800)
	1,352,100	1,027,700
	$2,584,000	$2,403,900

Statements of Consolidated Income

	1976	1975
Net sales	$3,038,000	$2,358,600
Costs and expenses:		
Cost of sales	2,331,900	1,798,900
Selling, general and administrative expenses	160,700	144,600
Depreciation and depletion (Notes 4 and 6)	151,400	133,800
Interest expense (less interest capitalized on construction projects of $12,800 in 1976 and $18,800 in 1975) (Note 4)	37,700	49,800
Provision for income taxes (Note 6)	141,000	83,500
	2,822,700	2,210,600
Net income	$ 215,300	$ 148,000
Income per share of common stock (Notes 2 and 9):		
Primary	$ 2.21	$ 1.60
Fully diluted	$ 2.13	$ 1.53

Notes to Financial Statements

Accounting Practices

1. Principles of Presentation:

The consolidated financial statements include the accounts of Georgia-Pacific Corporation and all subsidiaries (the corporation) after elimination of inter-company balances and transactions.

In 1975, the corporation acquired all the outstanding shares of Exchange Oil & Gas Corporation (Exchange) in a pooling-of-interests transaction. In connection with this acquisition Exchange adopted the full-cost method of accounting for oil and gas properties and elected to retroactively provide deferred income taxes of $10,000 with respect to intangible drilling and development costs.

2. Income per Share of Common Stock:

Primary income per share of common stock has been computed based on the weighted average number of shares outstanding, assuming issuance of shares under stock option and stock purchase plans, adjusted retroactively for shares issued in stock dividends through December 31, 1976, and for the 3-for-2 stock split of June 25, 1976. Fully diluted income per share of common stock, in addition, assumes conversion of the convertible subordinated debentures. The 2% stock dividend declared January 31, 1977, has not been reflected in the income per share computations.

3. Inventory Valuation:

The last-in, first-out (LIFO) method of inventory valuation is utilized for the majority of inventories at manufacturing facilities, while the average cost method is used for all other inventories. Inventory costs are determined on the basis of the average cost of materials, labor and plant overhead. All inventories are valued at the lower of cost or market as summarized below:

Method of valuation	1976	1975
Average cost	$269,100	$230,400
LIFO	153,900	146,300
	$423,000	$376,700

If LIFO inventories were valued at the lower of average cost or market, such inventories would have been $33,500 and $29,700 higher than those reported at December 31, 1976 and 1975, respectively. The corporation uses the dollar value pool method for computing LIFO inventories; therefore it is not possible to present a breakdown of inventories between finished goods, raw materials and supplies.

4. Depletion, Depreciation and Capitalization Policies:

The corporation amortizes its timber costs over the total fiber that will be available during the estimated growth cycle. Timber carrying costs are expensed as incurred.

All costs of exploring for and developing domestic oil and gas reserves are capitalized using the full-cost method of accounting and charged to operations on the basis of units-of-production over the estimated life of future production.

Provisions for depreciation of buildings, machinery and equipment are computed on the straight-line or units-of-production method using composite rates based upon the estimated service lives of the various units of property. The ranges of composite rates for the principal classes of property and equipment are as follows:

Land improvements	5 to 7%
Buildings	2 to 5%
Machinery and equipment	5 to 20%

Maintenance and repairs and replacements of minor units of property are charged to expense as incurred. Replacement of major units of property are capitalized and the replaced properties retired. No gain or loss is recognized on normal property dispositions; property cost is credited to the asset accounts and charged to the depreciation reserve accounts and any proceeds are credited to the depreciation reserve accounts. When there are abnormal dispositions of property, the cost and related depreciation reserves are removed from the accounts and any gain or loss is reflected in income.

The corporation capitalizes interest during construction periods based upon the interest cost on debt incurred to finance construction projects. Such interest is charged to the property and equipment account and amortized over the life of the related assets in order to properly match expenses with revenues resulting from the facilities. Capitalized interest, less related amortization and income taxes, amounted to $3,100 and $6,700 for the years ended December 31, 1976 and 1975, respectively.

The corporation defers net operating costs on new construction projects during the start-up phase and amortizes the deferral over approximately seven years. The amount deferred was $4,800 in 1975. New project start-up costs were not significant in 1976.

5. Pension and Stock Bonus Plans:

The corporation has a number of noncontributory pension plans covering substantially all its hourly employees. Contribution to most of these plans is based upon hourly rates set forth in various contracts. The corporation also has a noncontributory stock bonus plan for salaried employees wherein an amount up to 10% of the eligible employee's annual salary, if certain conditions are met, is contributed to the plan. Total contributions accrued for all plans were $20,700 in 1976 and $17,100 in 1975, including charges for normal cost and amortization of prior service costs over periods ranging from ten to thirty years. The increase in costs in 1976 compared to 1975 is attributable primarily to increases in benefits under the hourly plans. The corporation funds substantially all pension costs accrued.

At December 31, 1976, the unfunded prior service costs of all plans was approximately $20,000 and the actuarially computed value of vested benefits was approximately $3,400 in excess of the market value of plan assets.

The Pension Reform Act of 1974 required the corporation to amend its pension plans to conform with certain provisions of the Act. All such plan amendments have been finalized, and the effect of these amendments has no significant impact on the corporation's annual pension cost.

6. Income Taxes and Investment Credit:

The provision for income taxes includes deferred taxes of $35,000 in 1976 and $40,000 in 1975. Deferred income taxes result from timing differences in the recognition of revenue and expense for financial and tax reporting purposes. The sources of these differences and the tax effect of each are summarized as follows:

	1976	1975
Excess of tax depreciation over financial depreciation	$28,000	$28,900
Capitalized interest, net of amortization	2,400	6,500
Others, including start-up costs and depletion timing differences	4,600	4,600
	$35,000	$40,000

The corporation realized investment tax credits of $17,600 in 1976 and $15,800 in 1975. The credits realized since 1962, less amortization credited to depreciation expense to date ($10,700 in 1976 and $8,400 in 1975), totaled $45,800 at December 31, 1976, and are included in the reserves for depreciation.

The difference between the ordinary Federal income tax rate and the corporation's effective income tax rate is summarized as follows:

	1976	1975
Federal income tax rate	48%	48%
Increase (decrease) as a result of—		
Value of timber appreciation taxed at capital gains rates	(7)	(11)
State income taxes, net of Federal tax benefit	2	2
Others, including amortization of investment credit	(3)	(3)
Effective income tax rate	40%	36%

Independent Auditor's Report

To the Stockholders and Board of Directors of Georgia-Pacific Corporation:

We have examined the consolidated balance sheets of Georgia-Pacific Corporation (a Georgia corporation) and subsidiaries as of December 31, 1976 and 1975, and the related statements of consolidated income, surplus and changes in financial position for the years then ended. Our examination was made in accordance with generally accepted auditing standards, and accordingly included such tests of the accounting records and such other auditing procedures as we considered necessary in the circumstances.

In our opinion, the accompanying financial statements present fairly the financial position of Georgia-Pacific Corporation and subsidiaries as of December 31, 1976 and 1975, and the results of their operations and the changes in their financial position for the years then ended, in conformity with generally accepted accounting principles consistently applied during the periods.

Arthur Andersen + Co.

Portland, Oregon,
February 11, 1977.

Additional Information

a) During 1976 the firm raised $31,900 from banks on a long-term basis.

b) Transactions in Capital stock and surplus account resulted in cash of $174,200.

c) Non-current receivables and other assets represents deferred charges, such as prepaid insurance, which increased by $10,000 during 1976, and long-term receivables converted to cash.

Required

Using these statements and the additional information, complete the Statement of Changes in Consolidated Financial Position for 1976.

Georgia Pacific Corporation
Statement of Changes in Consolidated Financial Position
Year Ended 12/31/76

Sources of Funds $
   Net Income
   Noncash charges to income (identify each item)

   Proceeds from Stock issued
   Bank Financing
   Conversion of Long-term Receivables
   Other (Employee stock purchase plans)

Total Sources $_____

Uses of Funds
   Prepayments $
   Cash Dividends
   Debt Reduction
   Purchase of Timber and Natural Resources
   Additions to plant and equipment

Total Uses

Net Change in Working Capital $_____

Change in Current Assets less Current Liabilities per
   Balance Sheet $_____

Case 8-8

Allegheny Ludlum Industries, Inc. (B)

The following announcements appeared in the May 1, 1978 issue of *Business Week*. Wilkinson Match Limited's Ordinary shares were selling at $6 per share on April 10 and April 12, 1978. Allegheny's common shares were selling at $20 per share on both dates. True Temper's shares were not actively traded.

This announcement appears as a matter of record only.

April 10, 1978

ALLEGHENY LUDLUM INDUSTRIES, INC.

has purchased 6,500,000 Ordinary shares of

WILKINSON MATCH LIMITED

from

Svenska Tändsticks AB

The undersigned assisted Allegheny Ludlum Industries, Inc. in the negotiation of this transaction.

SMITH BARNEY, HARRIS UPHAM & CO.
Incorporated

> *This announcement appears as a matter of record only.*
>
> April 12, 1978
>
> **ALLEGHENY LUDLUM INDUSTRIES, INC.**
>
> has sold
>
> **True Temper Corporation**
>
> to
>
> **WILKINSON MATCH LIMITED**
>
> for 6,200,000 Ordinary shares of Wilkinson Match Limited
> and other considerations
>
> ---
>
> *The undersigned assisted Allegheny Ludlum Industries, Inc.
> in the negotiation of this transaction.*
>
> **SMITH BARNEY, HARRIS UPHAM & CO.**
> Incorporated

Required

1. How would Allegheny report the April 10, 1978 item in its Statement of Sources and Uses of Funds? What amount would it report?

2. How would Wilkinson report the April 10, 1978 item in its Statement of Sources and Uses of Funds, assuming it was reporting this item in accordance with generally accepted accounting principles? What amount would it report?

3. True Temper was included in Allegheny's records as a long-term investment at a cost of $36,000,000. Wilkinson Match Limited was quoted at $6 per share. Allegheny's Statement of Sources and Uses of Funds began with Net Income After Taxes of $832,671,000. What was the impact of this transaction on total sources and on total uses of funds for Allegheny?

Section Nine

Price-Level and Fair Value Accounting

Case 9-1

Westwood Manufacturing*

Mary Barton, president of Westwood Manufacturing was meeting with her chief financial officer Frank Linn. It was early March and the firm's financial statements had just reached her desk. It was clear from her expression that she was concerned about something.

"Frank," she began, "I am pleased with the continual rise in our earnings and in general with the appearance of financial health that our financial reports reflect. However, I wonder if we are in as good financial condition as our reports seem to indicate. What concerns me is the impact of inflation on our ability to compete successfully. In particular, we have been paying out most of our earnings as dividends. Further, we have not made any major capital investments in some time although several substantial renovations are in the planning stage for late this year. I wonder if you could review our statements with an eye to the impact of inflation on our financial condition. When do you think you could get me the necessary revised statements?"

Frank Linn, who had been taking notes from time to time looked up with a degree of concern. "What we will need to do is adjust the reports to reflect the impact of price changes. One way this can be done is to adjust the nonmonetary items, such as plant and equipment, for the average change in prices. If I recall correctly, the recommended index is the Consumer Price Index for All Urban Consumers. This index is relatively easy to obtain and is a measure of the impact of inflation on general purchasing power." Since our investment in plant and equipment is not excessive, this should both give us an idea of the impact of inflation while simultaneously being acceptable under existing FASB guidelines as a means of reporting this information to shareholders.

"The first problem as I see it," he continued, "is to obtain realistic data concerning the acquisition dates for our fixed assets. We will need to put several people on this for a week or two and then it will take another week at least to do the calculations. Even then, I suspect, there will be a good deal of guess work. Are you sure the figures will be worth the effort?"

President Barton had listened closely to the remarks of her senior financial aide. She now looked out her 54th floor window over the Manhatten skyline for several minutes as she considered Frank's concerns. A decisive person, it did not take her long and she quickly turned to address Mr. Linn.

"Frank," she began, "our stockholder meeting is in three weeks and I want to meet with the Board of Directors a week before that to discuss ex-

---

*The idea for this case was suggested by the case Forever Stores written by David Clark under the supervision of Professor John K. Shank.

pansion, dividend policy and several other issues. I want this data from you in no more than one week. Put what ever internal resources on it you need and can spare from routine duties. One issue, however, still bothers me. I am concerned with the impact of inflation on this firm. We don't buy a general economy-wide market basket of goods. Our purchases are more limited in scope. Shouldn't we use a measure of the price change that is more indicative of what we buy?"

"I had not considered that point," Frank said. "Let me give the idea some thought as to both the concept and its implementation and get back to you. We can't begin any comprehensive adjustment calculations until we have gathered some data on acquisition dates anyway."

"Ok Frank," said President Barton with some evident disappointment apparently because Frank could not respond immediately to her concern," but I will be gone for the next few days. Perhaps you had better go ahead, but be prepared to defend your selection of a price index to the Board as well as to me. As you know there are several finance experts on the board as well as those, like myself, with a marketing orientation."

Frank indicated he would get right on the problem and hoped the President would have a successful trip.

Westwood Manufacturing
Statement of Financial Position
December 31, 1975 and 1976

		Figures in Thousands	
		1976	1975
Assets			
(1)	Cash	$ 3,700	$ 2,800
(2)	Accounts Receivable–Net	47,200	46,500
(3)	Inventories	27,600	23,200
		$78,500	$72,500
(4)	Land	5,000	5,000
(5)	Plant and Equipment–Net	5,304	5,680
(6)	Investment in Hays Timber Co.	4,000	4,000
	Total Assets	$92,804	$87,180
Equities			
(7)	Accounts Payable	$22,300	$18,700
(8)	Accrued Wages	4,400	4,600
(9)	Income Taxes	1,200	1,000
		$27,900	$24,300
(10)	Deferred Taxes	8,485	7,815
(11)	Bonds Outstanding Less Discount	14,820	14,805
		$51,205	$46,920
(12)	Common Stock No Par	28,000	28,000
(13)	Contributed Capital	5,000	5,000
(14)	Retained Earnings	8,599	7,260
	Total Equities	$92,804	$87,180

Notes to the Statement of Financial Position

1. Inventories are accounted for on a FIFO basis.

2. The company moved to its present site in 1962 when it acquired the land and productive facilities of the Appalachian Furniture Company.

3. Plant and Equipment (data gathered by Mr. Linn from plant records, 000 omitted)

Year Acquired	Cost	Depreciation 12/31/75	Plant and Equipment Net 12/31/76	12/31/75
1974	$1,200	$ 96 48	$1,056	$1,104
1971	1,800	360	1,368	1,440
1966	2,000	800	1,120	1,200
1962	4,400	2,464	1,760	1,936
	$9,400	$3,720	$5,304	$5,680

Depreciation is calculated using the straight-line method based on a 25 year life with no salvage. A full year's depreciation is taken in the year of acquisition.

4. The investment in Hays Timber was acquired in 1969.

5. Assume the deferred taxes were generated evenly over the past 10 years.

6. Assume sales and cash expenses are incurred evenly over the year.

7. Bonds maturing January 1, 1989 in the amount of $15,000,000 were issued January 1, 1969 at 98.

8. Common Stock and Contributed Capital were issued as follows:

1963	Common Stock	$15,000,000
1963	Contributed Capital	5,000,000
1968	Common Stock	13,000,000

(1967 = 100)

Year	CPI	Relative Index 12/31/76	12/31/75
1962	90.6	1.918	1.823
1963	91.7	1.895	1.806
1964	92.9	1.871	1.783
1965	94.5	1.839	1.752
1966	97.2	1.788	1.704
1967	100.0	1.738	1.656
1968	104.2	1.668	1.589
1969	109.8	1.583	1.508
1970	116.3	1.494	1.424
1971	121.3	1.433	1.365
1972	125.3	1.387	1.322
1973	133.1	1.306	1.244
1974	147.7	1.177	1.121
1975	161.2	1.078	1.027
1976	170.5	1.019	—

			Relative Index	
Quarter		Deflator	12/31/76	12/31/75
1975–	I	157.2	1.106	1.053
	II	159.3	1.091	1.040
	III	162.8	1.068	1.017
	IV	165.6	1.050	1.000
1976–	I	167.1	1.040	—
	II	169.2	1.027	—
	III	171.9	1.011	—
	IV	173.8	1.000	—

Westwood Manufacturing
Statement of Income
Year Ended 12/31/76
(Thousands)

(15)	Sales..................................		$94,135
(16)	Cost of Goods Sold	$73,040	
(17)	Depreciation Expense.......................	377	
(18)	Administrative and Selling Expenses	14,985	
(19)	Interest Paid.............................	1,215	89,617
	Income Before Taxes		$ 4,518
(20)	Income Taxes............................		2,103
	Income After Taxes........................		$ 2,415

Westwood Manufacturing
Statement of Retained Earnings
December 31, 1976
(Thousands)

(21)	Retained Earnings 12/31/75		$ 7,246
	Additional Income After Taxes	$ 2,415	
(22)	Subtract Dividends Paid	(1,077)	1,338
	Retained Earnings 12/31/76		$ 8,584

Notes to Statement of Income and Retained Earnings

1. The Cost of Sales is determined on a FIFO basis: (000 omitted)

Inventory 1/1/76	$23,200
Purchases	77,440
Inventory 12/31/76	27,600

2. Interest was paid 6/30/76. Dividends were declared on December 1, 1976 and paid December 31, 1976.

3. Closing Inventories for 1976 and 1975 were purchased in the fourth quarter of 1976 and 1975 respectively.

Required

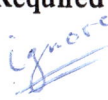

1. Consider the issue of the appropriate adjustment process to use in obtaining the inflation adjusted financial statements of Westwood. Take a position and defend it.

2. Assume, regardless of your response to part (1), that you have elected to use the CPI. Provide supplementary statements consistent with FAS 33 for Westwood for 1976 using the data supplied. Additional information is given below:

    a. The weighted average current cost of items sold per dealer price lists is $4 per unit. The company sold 19,196,000 items in 1976.

    b. The current value of depreciable assets was as follows: (000 omitted)

	Total	1974	1971	1966	1962
12/31/74	$15,000:				
12/31/75	25,000:	$3,191	$4,787	$5,319	$11,702
12/31/76	28,000:	3,574	5,362	5,957	13,107

    c. The current value of inventories based on dealer price lists was as follows: (000 omitted)

12/31/74	$22,000
12/31/75	24,000
12/31/76	27,000

3. Comment on any policy issues you detect based on this exercise. Relate these issues to Westwood.

Case 9-2

Ayrshire Collieries Corporation

The last annual report of Ayrshire Collieries Corporation is presented below. From 1948 to 1968 Ayrshire included a provision for "price-level depreciation" in its Statements of Consolidated Income. The following excerpt is from Ayrshire's "The Year in Review" section of its 1968 annual report:

> Our net income is stated after deducting the expense entitled Price-Level Depreciation. In deducting this expense from income we are reporting our income in a manner that reflects the additional depreciation expense on property, plant and equipment consumed during the year when measured in current purchasing power of the dollar over that consumed when merely measured by historical cost. Depreciation customerily reported does not properly reflect the decline in the purchasing power of the original or historical dollar. Such historical reporting expresses depreciation expense in terms of the number of dollars spent in the year of acquisition.
>
> The number of these historical dollars never changes—but their purchasing power does change. The practice of amortizing historic cost over the physical life of property and equipment results in the recovery of diminishing purchasing power each year as inflation continues. For example, investments in property and plant last year were made when the Bureau of Labor Statistics Consumer Price Index registered 116.0. Today that index figure is 120.9, representing a decrease in the purchasing power of the dollar of 4.2% in only 12 months. In recognizing price-level depreciation accounting, our expense for the year was $366,917 more than if it had been calculated on the basis of historical cost alone.

Statements of Consolidated Income

	Year Ended June 30	
	1968	**1967**
Revenues:		
Sales of coal and coke	$59,684,111	$62,008,842
Income from other product, royalties, interest, rentals, etc.	1,474,863	1,180,785
Equity in net income of nonconsolidated companies (Note 5)	884,560	647,780
	62,043,534	63,837,407
Expenses:		
Cost of products sold and other operating charges, exclusive of items listed below	47,711,790	49,919,638
Depreciation and depletion (Notes 4 and 5)	3,112,837	3,545,058
Selling, administrative and general expenses	4,043,491	3,940,821
Interest expense	1,098,118	1,213,163
	55,966,236	58,618,680
Income Before Federal Income Taxes And Extraordinary Items	6,077,298	5,218,727
Provision for Federal Income Taxes (Note 4):		
Current	411,402	842,300
Deferred	895,000	248,630
Investment tax credit (net)	188,598	106,070
	1,495,000	1,197,000
Income Before Extraordinary Items	4,582,298	4,021,727
Extraordinary Items, net of income taxes (Note 3)(per share: 1968-$11)	87,710	–
Net Income (conventional net income before deducting provision for price-level depreciation expense)	4,670,008	4,021,727
Provision for price-level depreciation (Notes 1 and 5)	366,917	352,274
Net Income, after deducting provision for price-level depreciation (per share: 1968–$5.45; 1967–$4.64)	$ 4,303,091	$ 3,669,453

Consolidated Balance Sheets

Assets

	June 30 1968	June 30 1967
Current Assets:		
Cash	$ 4,902,284	$ 3,827,307
Marketable securities (including U.S. Government securities of $3,000,000 and $5,857,615, respectively), at cost	3,481,634	9,970,553
Accounts receivable (less reserved of $100,799 and $95,799, respectively)	8,194,234	7,801,148
Coal and other products, at market or less	916,378	417,344
Federal income tax effect from production payment (Note 4)	1,512,000	960,000
	19,006,530	22,976,352
Property, Plant and Equipment, at cost (Note 5):		
Plant and equipment (including leased equipment of $5,083,242 in 1968)	71,184,018	60,990,853
Less—Accumulated depreciation	34,390,973	31,310,602
	36,793,045	29,680,251
Coal lands and rights (less accumulated depletion of $5,027,228 and $4,594,944, respectively) (Note 4)	34,539,181	30,850,753
Construction in progress	6,224,206	4,900,889
	77,556,432	65,431,893
Investments:		
Investments in nonconsolidated companies, at cost plus equity in undistributed income	4,994,209	4,099,517
Cash surrender value of life insurance	90,723	176,291
Other	186,178	158,379
	5,271,110	4,434,187
Prepaid Expenses and Deferred Charges:		
Repair parts and supplies	3,602,407	3,337,736
Other	1,150,918	876,168
	4,753,325	4,213,904
	$106,587,397	$97,056,336

Liabilities and Shareholders' Equity

	June 30 1968	June 30 1967
Current Liabilities:		
Accounts payable and accrued expenses	$ 5,314,402	$ 4,815,782
Federal income taxes	1,398,351	1,126,564
Current requirements on long-term obligations	5,263,515	2,917,197
Proceeds from production payment	3,000,000	2,000,000
	14,976,268	10,859,543
Long-Term Obligations:		
5% unsecured note, due serially to 1975	15,000,000	16,875,000
5% equipment note, due serially to 1974	2,500,000	2,875,000
Royalty and land purchase contracts, due serially to 2012	7,276,661	7,395,172
Equipment purchase contracts	155,425	2,199,629
6% lease obligation, due quarterly to 1980	4,694,950	—
Other	—	31,420
	26,627,036	29,376,221
Reserves and Deferred Items:		
Work stoppage expense	—	300,000
Reclamation expense	498,000	—
Deferred Federal income taxes (Note 4)	4,901,831	4,006,831
Unamortized investment tax credit (Note 4)	607,897	419,299
	6,007,728	4,726,130
Contingent Liability (Note 7)		
Shareholders' Equity:		
Common stock, par value $3 per share, authorized 800,000 shares; issued and outstanding 790,145 shares	2,370,435	2,370,435
Paid-in surplus (no change during the year)	8,687,816	8,687,816
Capital maintained by recognition of price-level depreciation (Note 1)	4,609,546	4,242,629
Earned surplus	40,308,568	36,793,562
	55,976,365	52,094,442
	$106,587,397	$97,056,336

The accompanying notes to consolidated financial statements are an integral part of these statements.

Statements of Consolidated Earned Surplus

	Year Ended June 30	
	1968	1967
Balance, at beginning of year	$36,793,562	$33,912,194
Net income, after deducting provision for price-level depreciation	4,303,091	3,669,453
	41,096,653	37,581,647
Cash dividends, $1.00 per share	788,085	788,085
Balance, at end of year	$40,308,568	$36,793,562

The accompanying notes to consolidated financial statements are an integral part of these statements.

Notes to Consolidated Financial Statements

(1) PRICE-LEVEL DEPRECIATION

The provision for price-level depreciation represents the excess of depreciation expense measured by the current purchasing power of the dollar over depreciation expense measured by the purchasing power of the dollar at the dates of acquisition or construction of the Companies' depreciable property, as measured by general price-level indices. The Companies believe the provision for price-level depreciation should be deducted before arriving at net income, but are informed that such treatment would not be in conformity with "generally accepted accounting principles." Reference is made to the opinion of Arthur Andersen & Co.

(2) PENSION PROGRAM

The Company and its subsidiaries have pension plans covering substantially all of their employees. The total pension expense for the year was $271,946, which includes current service costs and provisions to amortize past service costs over ten years. As of June 30, 1968, the total of the pension fund was sufficient to cover the actuarily computed value of vested benefits.

The Companies also made payments of $3,507,687 to employee retirement and welfare funds not administered by the Companies, as required under the terms of collective bargaining agreements.

(3) EXTRAORDINARY ITEMS

Extraordinary items included in the Statement of Consolidated Income for the year ended June 30, 1968, net of Federal income taxes, consists of the following:

Income:	
Interest received on settlement of prior year's Federal income taxes	$ 91,760
Reserves provided in prior years which, in the Company's opinion, are no longer needed	338,343
	430,103
Expenses:	
Estimated cost of required reclamation of disturbed coal lands	247,000
Write off of abandoned equipment	53,721
Expenses incurred in connection with a proposed sale or merger of the Companies	41,672
	342,393
	$ 87,710

(4) FEDERAL INCOME TAXES AND INVESTMENT TAX CREDIT

The Companies elected, with respect to certain fixed assets acquired since June 30, 1954, to compute depreciation for Federal income tax purposes on an accelerated basis, but for all other accounting purposes to compute depreciation on the straightline or unit of production basis as used in prior years. The Companies have also elected to deduct in the year of expenditure certain development costs and advance royalty payments for Federal income tax purposes which were capitalized for accounting purposes. The tax reductions resulting from these additional deductions have been credited to a reserve for deferred Federal income taxes to provide for the additional taxes payable in future years when the book depreciation and amortization with respect to particular assets will exceed the amount deductible for tax purposes. As additional taxes become payable, this reserve will be charged.

As a result of a recent pronouncement of the American Institute of Certified Public Accountants, deferred Federal income taxes applicable to advance royalty payments and certain development expenses and the Federal income tax effect on the proceeds from production payments have been reclassified in the June 30, 1967, balance sheet.

The Federal investment tax credit earned is deferred and amortized over the estimated service lives of the related property. In addition to the investment tax credits allowed to date, a carry forward of approximately $840,000 is available which expires in 1972 and 1973.

(5) CHANGE IN SERVICE LIVES OF PROPERTY

In 1968, the estimated service lives of certain property of Aryshire Collieries Corporation and two of its nonconsolidated subsidiaries were extended. These changes result from extending the term of existing coal contracts or entering into new coal contracts.

Accordingly, these changes do not represent changes in the consistent application of accounting principles, but do affect the comparability of the financial statements. The approximate effect of these changes for the year ended June 30, 1968, was as follows:

	Amount Net of Tax Effect
Decrease in depreciation expense	$ 61,000
Decrease in provision for price-level depreciation	31,000
Increase in equity in net income of nonconsolidated companies	154,000
Increase in net income, after deducting provision for price-level depreciation	$246,000

(6) PROPOSED SALE OR MERGER OF COMPANY

The Company has retained an agent to assist in current negotiations for a proposed sale of the Company's assets or merger with another corporation. The effective data of any such transaction and the effect, if any, upon the June 30, 1968, financial statements are not presently determinable.

(7) CONTINGENT LIABILITY

The Company has made certain advance royalty payments in 1968 in connection with a matter for which no liability is presently recorded. Legal counsel believes that the Company has a liability, the amount of which is uncertain. It is the Company's opinion that any such liability would not have a material effect on the June 30, 1968, financial statements.

The following paragraph was included in the auditor's opinion:

> Generally accepted principles of accounting for cost of property consumed in operations are based on historical costs and do not recognize the effect of changes in the purchasing power of the dollar since dates of acquisition or construction of the Companies' depreciable property. In our opinion, therefore, the consolidated net income for the year is more fairly presented after deducting the provision for price-level depreciation because such provision does recognize the effect of changes in the purchasing power of the dollar.

Required

1. Ayrshire reported a conventional net income before deducting the provision for price-level depreciation and a net income after deducting this provision.

    a) Which of these net income figures did Ayrshire use in reporting earnings per share?

    b) Which of these net income figures do you consider to be more meaningful in evaluating the potential earning power of Ayrshire or in comparing the performance of Ayrshire with other companies in the same industry?

2. What is the nature of depreciation as it is typically measured in accounting? How would you exlain the "provision for price-level depreciation" reported by Ayrshire?

3. **In what way(s) is the "provision for price-level depreciation" consistent and/or inconsistent with the related accounts reported in Ayrshire's balance sheet?**

4. What entry did Ayrshire make to record the price-level depreciation for 1968? Explain the effects of this entry on assets, stockholders' equity and net income.

5. Why was the treatment preferred by Ayrshire not in conformity with generally accepted accounting principles?

6. Do you agree with the auditors that net income for the year was more fairly presented after deducting the provision for price-level depreciation?

Case 9-3   Crane Company

Crane Company serves industrial, building, and construction markets with fluid and pollution control products, steel products, building products and aerospace and aircraft products. Crane Company's 1977 and 1976 Consolidated Statements of Income are presented.

Consolidated Statement of Income
CRANE CO. AND SUBSIDIARIES
FOR YEARS ENDED DECEMBER 31

	1977	1976
Net Sales	$1,133,822,269	$1,087,605,797
Operating Costs and Expenses:		
Cost of sales	916,846,784	866,531,695
Selling, general and administrative	105,665,342	104,098,743
Depreciation	44,191,500†	36,380,436
	1,066,703,626	1,007,010,874
Operating Profit	67,118,643	80,594,923
Other Income (Deductions):		
Interest—net	(18,698,083)	(18,764,292)
Dividend income on investments	3,932,461	2,609,300
Miscellaneous—net*	26,441,871	12,338,181
	11,676,249	(3,816,811)
Income Before Income Taxes	78,794,892	76,778,112
Provision for Income Taxes	12,623,727	28,819,335
Net Income	$ 66,171,165	$ 47,958,777
Net income per common share:		
Average shares outstanding*	$6.52	$4.61
Assuming conversion of debentures	6.17	4.31

†Changed from straight-line to accelerated depreciation, which increased depreciation by $5,538,000 in 1977.

In 1977, Crane Company changed from the straight-line method to the accelerated method of computing depreciation for buildings, plant and equipment. The new method eliminated a substantial reporting difference between financial and income tax basis. Crane Company's composite income tax rate was 50% in 1977 and 1976. The provision for income taxes was composed of the following:

	1977	1976
	(in thousands)	
Tax effect of timing differences:		
Depreciation	$ 0	$ 2,370
Other	2,503	2,719
Deferred income taxes	2,503	5,089
Current income taxes	12,571	18,658
	$15,074	$23,747

Income taxes on non-recurring transactions were a credit of $2,450,000 for 1977 and a charge of $5,072,000 for 1976.

Required

1. In their letter to shareholders, D.C. Fabiani (President) and T.M. Evans (Chairman) stated that the accelerated method "gives a closer assessment of the earnings level necessary to allow replacement of plant, property and equipment in today's inflationary economic environment." Do you agree with this statement? Why or why not?

2. Calculate the net income for 1976 if accelerated methods had been used for financial reporting.

3. Would your answer to question 2 be the same if Crane Company's tax rate was 80 percent? If not, would it be higher or lower and by how much?

4. What type of accounting change is involved here? Did Crane Company properly account for the change?

Case 9-4

Indiana Telephone Corporation

Since 1954 Indiana Telephone Corporation has presented two sets of financial statements. One set has shown the results under conventional historical cost accounting and the other has shown results under historical cost restated for changes in the purchasing power of the dollar. The following excerpts are from Indiana Telephone's Summary of Significant Accounting Policies:

a) Explanation of Financial Statements

> In the accompanying financial statements, costs measured by the dollars disbursed at the time of the expenditure are shown in "Column A—Historical Cost." In "Column B—Historical Cost Restated for Changes in Purchasing Power of Dollar" (where the amounts in A and B differ), these dollars of cost have been restated in terms of the price level at December 31, 1972, as measured by the Gross National Product Implicit Price Deflator. Since 1954, the Corporation has presented supplemental financial information recognizing the effect of the change in the purchasing power of the dollar relating to telephone plant and depreciation expense in the annual report to shareholders.
>
> In computing the amounts set forth in Column B of the accompanying financial statements, the Corporation has followed the methods set forth in Statement No. 3 released in June, 1969, by the Accounting Principles Board of the American Institute of Certified Public Accountants, except that, contrary to Statement No. 3, the effects of price-level changes on long-term debt and preferred stock have been reflected as income in the year in which the debt and preferred stock are retired (as required by the specific instruments under which they were issued) and not refinanced. The Accounting Principles Board has tentatively taken the position that all such amounts should be taken into income in the year of price-level change. In the opinion of the Corporation's management and of its independent public accountants, such tentative viewpoint of the Accounting Principles Board does not result in a proper determination of income for the period. "Unrealized Effects of Price-Level Changes" recognizes the excess of adjustments on the Statement of Assets over the adjustments of Common Shareholders' Interest.
>
> Dollars are a means of expressing purchasing power at the time of their use. Conversion or restatement of dollars of differing purchasing power to the purchasing power of the dollar at the date of conversion results in all the dollars being treated as mathematical likes for the purpose of significant data. The resulting financial statements recognize the change in price levels between the periods of expenditure of funds and the periods of use of property. Accordingly, the earnings, results of operations, assets and other data available for use by management and other readers of financial statements provide important information and comparisons not otherwise available.

310 Cases in Financial Accounting

No one would attempt to add, subtract, multiply, or divide marks, dollars and pounds. The failure to change the tittle of the monetary unit may be partially responsible for this violation of mathematical principle. This conceals the fact that mathematical unlikes are being used and therefore unfortunate results have been produced by generally accepted accounting methods.

b) Recovery of Capital & Return of Capital

Under the law of Indiana, the Corporation is entitled to recover the fair value of its property used and useful in public service by accruing depreciation based on the "fair value" thereof and is entitled to earn a fair return on such "fair value." The amount shown in Column B for telephone plant approximates the fair value of the property as determined based on the principles followed by the Public Service Commission of Indiana in an order dated September 1, 1967, authorizing the Corporation to increase its subscriber rates.

In the accompanying financial statements, Column A includes depreciation expense based on historical cost and Column B includes depreciation expense, as well as other expenses, on the basis of historical cost repriced in current dollars to reflect the changes in the purchasing power of the dollar. Also, the annual reports to the Indiana Commission are in the same basic form shown herein.

It must be kept in mind that this determination of depreciation expense is a year-to-year estimate and there are involved the questions of obsolescense, foresight, and judgment giving due consideration to maintenance, but the regulatory process does not adjust even to this accurately.

In 1971 the Corporation petitioned the Indiana Commission for approval to increase its depreciation rates to a level to reflect properly these factors, but certain of these rates were not approved. If all of the requested rates were applied to the average cost of depreciable property accounts in 1972 and 1971, depreciation expense, operating income, and net income (net of applicable income tax effects), as shown in the accompanying financial statements, would have been as follows:

	Column A Historical Cost	
	1972	*1971*
Depreciation provision	$2,109,258	$1,997,871
Operating income	2,666,421	2,278,248
Net income	2,097,384	1,770,351

	Column B Historical Cost Restated for Changes in Purchasing Power of Dollar	
	1972	*1971*
Depreciation provision	$2,690,932	$2,644,049
Operating income	2,134,276	1,788,662
Net income	1,514,636	1,244,263

If use of property, obsolescence and current denominators (in the case of monetary inflation) are used accurately by way of keeping the allowable expense of depreciation current and rates sufficient to return it along with a fair return, and the proceeds are immediately invested in property used and useful in the public service, there more likely will be a real return of capital and a fair return thereon. However, if monetary inflation continues, as it usually does, purchasing power of capital is unlikely ever to be truly returned. It must be observed there is a substantial lag in the regulatory process. In rate making there is no guarantee of recovery of capital or of an adequate rate of return to the Corporation. This is an added risk which should be considered in estimating a fair return.

Since the present Internal Revenue Code does not recognize the costs measured in current dollars, they are not deductible for computing Federal income tax payments, and the Corporation in fact pays taxes on alleged earnings which do not exist in true purchasing power. If they were deductible, as they should be, reductions in Federal income taxes as shown in Column B of $312,000 in 1972 and $274,000 in 1971 would result. By requiring the use of the Uniform System of Accounts for utility accounting and by virtue of the Internal Revenue Code, the Government has condemned and confiscated during the last 8 years over $1.3 million (in terms of the dollars of the years in which they were paid) of the assets of this Corporation through taxation of overstated earnings. This is true to a greater or lesser extent in each case where we have been able to ascertain the facts. We do not understand why this is currently concealed by management and accountants—to their detriment.

Indiana Telephone's 1972 and 1971 Statements of Income and Statements of Assets and Statements of Capital are presented. The auditor's report included the following paragraphs:

AUDITORS' REPORT

To the Shareholders of Indiana Telephone Corporation:

We have examined the statements of assets and capital of INDIANA TELEPHONE CORPORATION (an Indiana corporation) as of December 31, 1972, and the related statements of income, retained earnings, and changes in financial position for the year then ended. Our examination was made in accordance with generally accepted auditing standards and accordingly included such tests of the accounting records and such other auditing procedures as we considered necessary in the circumstances. We have previously examined and reported on the financial statements for the preceding year.

In our opinion, the accompanying financial statements shown under Column A present fairly the financial position of the Corporation as of December 31, 1972, and the results of its operations and the changes in its financial position for the year then ended, in conformity with generally accepted accounting principles applied on a basis consistent with that of the preceding year.

In our opinion, however, the accompanying financial statements shown under Column B more fairly present the financial position of the Corporation as of December 31, 1972, and the results of its operations for the year then ended, as recognition has been given to changes in the purchasing power of the dollar, as explained in Note 1(a).

ARTHUR ANDERSEN & CO.

Indianapolis, Indiana,
March 2, 1973.

Statement of Income

	Column A Historical Cost 1972	1971	Column B Historical Cost Restated for Changes in Purchasing Power of Dollar 1972	1971
OPERATING REVENUES:				
Local service	$ 6,187,012	$ 5,744,356	$ 6,242,998	$ 5,964,020
Toll service	5,208,814	4,852,156	5,255,949	5,037,703
Miscellaneous	337,136	304,522	340,187	316,167
Total operating revenues	11,732,962	10,901,034	11,839,134	11,317,890
OPERATING EXPENSES:				
Depreciation provision, Note 1 (b)	2,053,700	1,943,551	2,620,440	2,572,577
Maintenance	1,548,758	1,486,495	1,562,773	1,550,974
Total depreciation and maintenance	3,602,458	3,430,046	4,183,213	4,123,551
Traffic	1,101,833	1,226,906	1,111,803	1,274,544
Commercial	581,311	511,661	586,571	531,227
General and administrative	1,003,875	1,055,318	1,015,121	1,100,994
State, local and miscellaneous Federal taxes	967,974	912,601	976,733	947,499
Federal income taxes, Note 1 (b)				
Currently payable	1,363,382	1,132,500	1,375,719	1,175,807
Deferred until future years	264,200	315,800	266,591	327,876
Deferred investment tax credit (net)	152,618	9,708	145,524	3,361
Total operating expenses	9,037,651	8,594,540	9,661,275	9,484,859
OPERATING INCOME	2,695,311	2,306,494	2,177,859	1,833,031
INCOME DEDUCTIONS:				
Interest on funded debt	789,579	651,195	796,724	676,097
Other deductions	41,540	36,828	53,285	41,445
Allowance for funds used during construction (credit), Note 1 (d)	(141,241)	(63,905)	(142,519)	(66,349)
Other income (credit)	(196,647)	(177,974)	(198,426)	(184,780)
Nonoperating Federal income taxes	92,500	82,000	93,337	85,136
Gain from retirement of long-term debt through operation of sinking fund (credit)	(11,985)	(15,192)	(12,093)	(15,773)
Price-level gain from retirement of long-term debt (credit), Note 1 (a)	—	—	(36,528)	(62,985)
Gain from retirement of preferred stock through operation of sinking fund (credit)	(4,709)	(5,055)	(4,752)	(5,248)
Price-level gain from retirement of preferred stock (credit), Note 1 (a)	—	—	(14,034)	(13,298)
Price-level loss from other monetary items	—	—	84,646	90,154
Total income deductions	569,037	507,897	619,640	544,399
NET INCOME, Note 1 (a)	2,126,274	1,798,597	1,558,219	1,288,632
Preferred stock dividends applicable to the period	94,890	96,209	95,749	99,888
EARNINGS APPLICABLE TO COMMON STOCK	$ 2,031,384	$ 1,702,388	$ 1,462,470	$ 1,188,744
EARNINGS PER COMMON SHARE	$ 4.16	$ 3.49	$ 3.00	$ 2.44
BOOK VALUE PER SHARE	$ 24.82	$ 21.45	$ 23.01	$ 20.81
Stations in service at end of year	80,439	75,016	80,439	75,016

Statement of Assets

	Column A Historical Cost	Column B Historical Cost Restated for Changes in Purchasing Power of Dollar
TELEPHONE PLANT, at original cost, Note 1 (a):		
In service	$37,084,382	$47,050,796
Less—Accumulated depreciation	11,842,883	16,041,306
	25,241,499	31,009,490
Plant under construction	968,792	977,559
	26,210,291	31,987,049
WORKING CAPITAL:		
Current assets—		
Cash	795,971	795,971
Temporary cash investments accumulated for construction—at cost, which approximates market	4,482,550	4,482,550
Accounts receivable, less reserve	1,498,689	1,498,689
Materials and supplies	602,669	612,751
Prepayments	144,090	145,394
	7,523,969	7,535,355
Current liabilities—		
Sinking fund obligations, Note 2	121,000	121,000
Accounts payable	819,978	819,978
Advance billings	338,760	338,760
Dividends payable	168,904	168,904
Federal income taxes, Note 1 (b)	494,297	494,297
Other accrued taxes	677,736	677,736
Other current liabilities	986,941	986,941
	3,607,616	3,607,616
Net working capital	3,916,353	3,927,739
OTHER:		
Debt expense being amortized, Note 1 (c)	208,617	264,648
Other deferred charges	18,553	19,070
Other deferred credits	(40,818)	(41,187)
Deferred Federal income taxes, Note 1 (b)	(1,599,454)	(1,765,204)
Unamortized investment tax credit, Note 1 (e)	(544,396)	(632,744)
	(1,957,498)	(2,155,417)
TOTAL INVESTMENT IN TELEPHONE BUSINESS	$28,169,146	$33,759,371

Statement of Capital

	Column A Historical Cost Amount	Ratio	Column B Historical Cost Restated for Changes in Purchasing Power of Dollar Amount	Ratio
FIRST MORTGAGE SINKING FUND BONDS:				
Series 6, 5⅜% due September 1, 1991	$ 1,820,000		$ 1,820,000	
Series 7, 4¾% due May 1, 1994	1,974,000		1,974,000	
Series 8, 4¾% due July 1, 2005	2,869,000		2,869,000	
Series 9, 6½% due October 1, 2007	2,910,000		2,910,000	
Series 10, 7¾% due June 1, 2008	4,875,000		4,875,000	
Less—Current sinking funds, Note 2	(101,000)		(101,000)	
Total first mortgage sinking fund bonds	14,347,000	51%	14,347,000	43%
PREFERRED STOCK (no maturity):				
Cumulative, sinking fund, par value $100 per share, 30,000 shares authorized of which 10,000 are unissued—				
1950 Series 4.80%	235,000		235,000	
1951 Series 4.80%	239,800		239,800	
1954 Series 5¼%	327,800		327,800	
1956 Series 5%	252,900		252,900	
1967 Series 6⅛%	679,000		679,000	
Less—Current sinking funds, Note 2	(20,000)		(20,000)	
Total preferred stock	1,714,500	6	1,714,500	5
COMMON SHAREHOLDERS' INTEREST:				
Common stock, no par value, authorized 500,000 shares, issued 492,086 shares	4,251,785		6,678,779	
Retained earnings ($3,147,223 restricted as to the payment of cash dividends on common stock, Note 4)	7,937,320		4,675,412	
	12,189,105		11,354,191	
Less—Treasury stock, 4,336 shares, at cost	(5,192)		(8,130)	
Stock discount and expense	(76,267)		(123,194)	
Total common shareholders' interest	12,107,646	43	11,222,867	33
UNREALIZED EFFECTS OF PRICE-LEVEL CHANGES, Note 1 (a)	—	—	6,475,004	19
TOTAL INVESTMENT IN TELEPHONE BUSINESS	$28,169,146	100%	$33,759,371	100%

Required

1. Do you agree with Indiana Telephone's method of accounting for the effects of price-level changes on long-term debt and preferred stock? Was the net income in Column B higher or lower in 1972 because of this method? Explain.

2. Explain the meaning and derivation of the "Unrealized Effects of Price-Level Changes" account in the Statement of Capital.

3. Where would the $6,475,004 of unrealized effects of price-level changes in 1972 have been reported if Indiana Telephone had used the methods described in Statement No. 3 to restate historical cost for changes in the purchasing power of the dollar?

4. Have the cumulative effects of changes in the purchasing power of the dollar to December 31, 1972 been positive or negative? Explain.

5. Do you agree with the auditors that the numbers in Column B "more fairly present" Indiana Telephone's financial situation? **Why or why not?**

Case 9-5   Iowa Beef Processors

Iowa Beef Processors (IBP) was incorporated in 1960 under the name Iowa Beef Packers Inc. with headquarters in Denison, Iowa. The Company was reincorporated in Delaware in 1969 and its name changed in 1970. IBP was first listed on the NYSE in 1968.

The Company markets fresh beef and beef carcasses nationwide to food retailers and food service outlets. The Company also markets by-products and pork, accounting for about ten percent of its sales.

The following excerpt from the description of the Company's Operating Descriptions reflects their concern with the impact of inflation on their business.

Inflation Accounting

This is the third year that IBP has included in its Annual Report to stockholders accounting data which aims to shed light on the impact of inflation on its operations. This was a pioneering disclosure by IBP in an effort to be candid with its investors. Even now, according to December 26, 1977 *Business Week*, "relatively few companies" publish such data to stockholders in their annual reports, although the Securities and Exchange Commission now requires certain data in its Form 10-K report partially revealing the effect of inflation.

The essence of this new accounting approach is the replacement of historical costs with current values. Thus, the figures on most fixed assets and inventories would be calculated to show current replacement costs. According to a study reported in the same *Business Week* article, it would cost the average big corporation (in the 175 company survey) twice as much to replace its productive capacity today, and 25 percent more to replace its inventories, than when these assets were purchased. However, different industries are affected differently. IBP's exhibits using current-value accounting appear in this report following the traditional statements.

IBP's financial statements, shown, are based first on a historical-cost basis and then on a current-value basis. Only the notes to the current-value statements are supplied.

Liabilities & Stockholders' Equity

	October 29, 1977	October 30, 1976
CURRENT LIABILITIES:		
Notes payable (Note D)	$ 4,000,000	$ —
Accounts payable and accrued expenses (Note H)	22,646,000	23,242,000
Salaries, wages, bonuses and amounts withheld from employees	11,053,000	9,889,000
Federal and state income taxes	1,805,000	16,514,000
Current maturities on long-term obligations	2,019,000	2,325,000
TOTAL CURRENT LIABILITIES	41,523,000	51,970,000
DEFERRED INCOME TAXES	14,066,000	11,460,000
LONG-TERM OBLIGATIONS (Notes D and E)	59,307,000	55,715,000
CONTINGENCIES (Note I)		
STOCKHOLDERS' EQUITY (Notes E and F):		
Common stock, par value $1.50 a share: Authorized—12,000,000 shares Issued—4,420,978 and 4,382,659	6,631,000	6,574,000
Additional paid-in capital	19,445,000	18,981,000
Retained earnings	137,289,000	109,508,000
	163,365,000	135,063,000
Less common stock in treasury, at cost—37,208 and 40,200 shares	734,000	771,000
Stockholders' Equity, net shares outstanding— 4,383,770 and 4,342,459	162,631,000	134,292,000
	$277,527,000	$253,437,000

Consolidated Statements of Earnings

	October 29, 1977	October 30, 1976
Sales	$2,023,765,000	$2,077,158,000
Cost of products sold	1,937,823,000	1,990,176,000
	85,942,000	86,982,000
Expenses:		
Selling, general and administrative	27,787,000	24,374,000
Interest costs incurred	3,541,000	3,666,000
Less interest capitalized on construction	(260,000)	—
	31,068,000	28,040,000
Earnings before income taxes	54,874,000	58,942,000
Income taxes (Note G)	24,909,000	30,164,000
Net earnings	$ 29,965,000	$ 28,778,000
Net earnings per common and common equivalent share	$6.29	$6.17

Consolidated Statements of Stockholders' Equity

	Common Stock Shares	Common Stock Amount	Additional paid-in capital	Retained earnings	Treasury stock
Balance, November 1, 1975	2,891,646	$4,337,000	$20,741,000	$ 82,479,000	$ —
Common stock options exercised:					
Qualified stock options	24,127	37,000	363,000	—	—
Non-qualified stock options	6,000	9,000	68,000	—	—
Shares acquired for treasury (40,200)	—	—	—	—	(771,000)
Cash dividends paid, $.40 per share	—	—	—	(1,749,000)	—
Three-for-two stock split (Note A)	1,460,886	2,191,000	(2,191,000)	—	—
Net earnings	—	—	—	28,778,000	—
Balance, October 30, 1976	4,382,659	6,574,000	18,981,000	109,508,000	(771,000)
Common stock options exercised	38,319	57,000	445,000	—	—
Shares acquired for treasury (8,726)	—	—	—	—	(194,000)
Treasury shares issued (11,718) (Note B)	—	—	19,000	—	231,000
Cash dividends paid, $.50 per share	—	—	—	(2,184,000)	—
Net earnings	—	—	—	29,965,000	—
Balance, October 29, 1977	4,420,978	$6,631,000	$19,445,000	$137,289,000	$(734,000)

Current-Value Consolidated Balance Sheets

	Current Value October 29, 1977	Current Value October 30, 1976	Historical Cost October 29, 1977
Assets			
CURRENT ASSETS:			
Cash	$ 15,549	$ 11,582	$ 15,549
Accounts receivable, less allowance for doubtful accounts	98,513	89,019	98,513
Inventories	32,239	38,199	32,239
Deferred tax benefit	—	—	1,578
Prepaid expenses	1,182	533	1,182
Total Current Assets	147,483	139,333	149,061
PROPERTY, PLANT AND EQUIPMENT:			
Land and land improvements	19,136	16,284	13,224
Buildings and stockyards	73,875	77,390	43,675
Equipment	158,236	127,053	98,541
Construction in progress	11,101	4,251	10,830
	262,348	224,978	166,270
Less—accumulated depreciation	83,111	69,397	42,292
—imputed income taxes	41,696	35,925	—
	137,541	119,656	123,978
OTHER ASSETS	1,090	1,966	4,488
	$286,114	$260,955	$277,527
Liabilities and Stockholders' Equity			
CURRENT LIABILITIES:			
Notes payable	$ 4,000	$ —	$ 4,000
Accounts payable and accrued liabilities	32,121	30,992	33,699
Federal and state income taxes	1,805	16,514	1,805
Current maturities on long-term obligations	2,019	2,325	2,019
Total Current Liabilities	39,945	49,831	41,523
DEFERRED INCOME TAXES	—	—	14,066
LONG-TERM OBLIGATIONS	58,079	54,284	59,307
STOCKHOLDERS' EQUITY	188,090	156,840	162,631
	$286,114	$260,955	$277,527

Consolidated Statements of Net Results of Operations & Changes in Value

	Current Value October 29, 1977	Current Value October 30, 1976	Historical Cost October 29, 1977
RESULTS OF OPERATIONS:			
Sales	$2,023,765	$2,077,158	$2,023,765
Less—cost of products sold	1,947,130	1,991,188	1,937,823
—inventory value change	(3,700)	4,000	—
	1,943,430	1,995,188	1,937,823
	80,335	81,970	85,942
Expenses:			
Selling, general and administrative	27,926	24,746	27,787
Interest expense	3,258	3,703	3,281
Income taxes	21,742	30,302	24,909
	52,926	58,751	55,977
Net results of operations and inventory value change	27,409	23,219	29,965
CHANGES IN VALUE:			
Change in current costs of depreciable assets during the year	6,383	5,709	—
Change in current value of debt and interest	173	(1,265)	—
Change in other imputed taxes	(1,072)	1,628	—
Amount required to recognize impact on stockholders' equity of increase in the general price level during the year	(9,003)	(6,402)	—
TOTAL OF NET RESULTS OF OPERATIONS AND CHANGES IN VALUE	$ 23,890	$ 22,889	$ 29,965

Current-Value Consolidated Statements of Stockholders' Equity

	Current Value October 29, 1977	Current Value October 30, 1976	Historical Cost October 29, 1977
Balance at beginning of year	$156,840	$ 129,602	$ 134,292
Amount required to recognize impact on stockholders' equity of increase in general price level during the year	9,003	6,402	—
Restated balance at beginning of year	165,843	136,004	134,292
Common stock options exercised	512	488	502
Shares acquired for treasury	(204)	(771)	(194)
Treasury shares issued	259	—	250
Cash dividends paid	(2,210)	(1,770)	(2,184)
Net results of operations and changes in value during the year	23,890	22,889	29,965
Balance at end of year	$188,090	$ 156,840	$ 162,631

Notes to Current-Value Statements

1. General:

In the inflationary environment of the past several years, financial information reported on the conventional basis of historical costs fails to fully reflect economic reality of the financial condition and results of operations of business enterprises. As a result, the Company is presenting financial statements reflecting the current values of its assets, liabilities, operating results and changes in value by estimating:

a. The current replacement cost for assets and resources expected to be retained and net realizable value for assets expected to be disposed of.

b. The present value of estimated future cash outflows for liabilities.

c. The imputed income taxes relative to the difference in current-value and income tax bases of assets and liabilities.

d. The effects of changes in general purchasing power on the net resources of the Company.

2. Current Assets and Liabilities:

Current assets and liabilities are stated on the same basis as the historical cost basis financial statements except for imputed taxes which have been deducted from accounts payable and accrued liabilities.

3. Inventories and Cost of Product Sold:

Inventories reported at the year ends are unchanged from the historical cost basis statements since the inventories are stated at amounts that approximate current replacement cost due to the short time span between purchases and sales of inventories. However, the prices for live cattle, dressed carcasses, processed cuts and by-products all fluctuated during the years. The prices of these products generally increased during fiscal 1977 and generally declined during fiscal 1976. The inventory value changes (gain of $3,700,000 in 1977 and loss of $4,000,000 in 1976) as reported in the Consolidated Statements of Net Results of Operations and Changes in Value represent the net changes in the value of inventories held throughout the respective years. The inventory value changes are measured from the date the product is received until the product is shipped.

4. Property, Plant and Equipment:

Property, plant and equipment is stated at current replacement cost less accumulated depreciation and imputed income taxes. Current replacement cost was developed principally by using engineering estimates for the cost of replacing existing productive capacity after giving recognition to technological changes and methods by which replacement would be expected to be made. The costs so determined have not been adjusted for anticipated reductions in operating expenses as such reductions are not estimated to be significant. Accumulated depreciation has been restated to reflect depreciation which would have been incurred in 1977, 1976 and prior years based on the current replacement costs. Current-value depreciation expense for 1977 and 1976 was $5,746,000 and $5,384,000 greater than the respective historical cost amounts. Such depreciation was calculated on average replacement costs using the straight-line method and the historical rates for existing facilities. Costs of products sold and selling, general and administrative expenses have been charged for the increased current-value depreciation during the years. The increase in replacement cost (net of imputed income taxes) of property, plant and equipment during the years is reported as a value change in the Consolidated Statements of Net Results of Operations and Changes in Value.

5. Long-term Obligations:

Long-term obligations are stated at the present value of future cash flows (net of imputed income taxes) based on the current applicable interest rates at the statement dates. The rates include an element for estimated financing costs. Current-value interest expense is calculated at average current rates for the years.

6. Income Taxes:

Income taxes at rates approximating 50% have been imputed on the differences between current-value and income tax bases of assets and liabilities. The amounts of imputed taxes that have been deducted from the related assets and liabilities (added in the case of other assets) in the current-value balance sheets are shown below:

	October 29, 1977	October 30, 1976
Property, plant and equipment	$41,696,000	$35,925,000
Accounts payable and accrued liabilities	1,578,000	2,139,000
Long-term obligations	1,228,000	1,406,000
Other assets	—	511,000

All changes in imputed taxes are reported as changes in value in the Consolidated Statements of Net Results of Operations and Changes in Value.

Income tax expense shown in the current-value results of operations is the amount currently payable.

7. Stockholders' Equity:

The amounts of aggregate earnings required during the years to maintain the general purchasing power of stockholders' equity are shown as decreases in changes in value. Such amounts are measured by the GNP Implicit Price Deflator and are comprised of the following:

	Year (52 Weeks) Ended	
	October 29, 1977	October 30, 1976
Net non-monetary assets	$9,216,000	$7,306,000
Net monetary assets-liabilities	574,000	(330,000)
Operations	(787,000)	(574,000)
	$9,003,000	$6,402,000

Stockholders' equity at the beginning of the years and the amounts shown for sales and purchases of stock and dividends paid during the years have been restated as appropriate to give effect to the increase in general price level during the years.

8. Restatement of Prior Year's Current-Value Statements:

The current-value financial statements for 1976 have been restated for the imputation of income taxes on the differences between current-value and income tax bases of property, plant and equipment, other assets and long-term obligations.

9. Notes to Historical Cost Basis Financial Statements:

The current-value financial statements and the historical cost basis information contained therein should be read in conjunction with the notes to the historical cost basis financial statements.

Current-Value Accountants' Report

Board of Directors and Stockholders
Iowa Beef Processors, Inc.
Dakota City, Nebraska

The accompanying consolidated current-value balance sheets of Iowa Beef Processors, Inc. and subsidiaries as of October 29, 1977, and October 30, 1976 and the related current-value statements of net results of operations and changes in value and statements of stockholders' equity for the years then ended have been prepared on a current-value basis of accounting as more fully discussed in Note 1. The current-value basis differs significantly from, and is not in accordance with, generally accepted accounting principles. Further, the current-value financial statements are not intended to measure the net realizable value or market value of the Company taken as a whole.

Because current-value accounting is presently in an experimental stage, uniform criteria for the preparation and presentation of current-value financial information have not yet been established and acceptable alternatives exist as to the nature and content; accordingly, as experimentation proceeds, the principles followed in the accompanying current-value financial statements may be modified.

Our examination of the current-value financial statements was made in accordance with generally accepted auditing standards and, accordingly, included a review of selected data used to obtain current values and such other auditing procedures we considered necessary in the circumstances. In our opinion, the current-value financial statements referred to above are a reasonable and appropriate presentation of the information set forth therein on the basis indicated in Note 1, which basis has been applied in a manner consistent with that of the preceding year after restatement (Note 8).

Touche Ross & Co. December 23, 1977
Certified Public Accountants
Omaha, Nebraska

Required

1. Comment on the auditor's position with respect to the current value statements.

2. Can you explain why the historical amount for accounts payable and accrued liabilities exceeds the current value amount?

3. Does the firm attempt to allow for general changes in purchasing power as well as for specific changes caused by movements in replacement prices?

4. What was the net change in the current value of the depreciable assets during the year?

5. What were the primary causes of the change in reported values as reported in the Consolidated Statement of Net Results of Operations and Changes in Value for 1977?

6. Were the effects of the changes due to the use of current values significant to the Company?

Case 9-6   The Rouse Company

In early August 1975, James W. Rouse, Chairman of the Board of the Rouse Company called in his Chief Executive Officer, Mathias J. DeVito and the Senior Vice-President, R. Harwood Beville, to discuss the failure of the company's reports to reflect the economic realities of its business.

Rouse, a Maryland-based real estate developer, develops and operates shopping centers that it builds rather than developing them for resale to outsiders. By 1976 they had developed 24 such centers. They were also the developers of the "new town" of Columbia, Maryland.

The issue that occasioned the meeting was the results from the sale over the last 2 years of 50 percent interests in 7 of its shopping centers to outsiders to raise working capital. Rouse obtained $24 million in cash. But J. W. noted that the firm's equity in those interests had shown up negatively on the books. He was concerned about the effects of such values on the company's share values and on its ability to raise funds in the capital market. He asked DeVito and Beville to study the situation and see what could be done. J. W. ended the meeting by saying "we are worth $10 a share, yet we are selling at less than $5. It is not fair that there is no way to communicate our firm's value to the market."

Beville pointed out that for the last 3 years the company carried a special "value added" table in the "letter to shareholders" section. The Chairman noted that such a table, while of some value, does not obtain the auditors blessing. "A bank loan officer can't take that table to his committee," he said.

Later that month, the SEC's then Chief Accountant, John C. Burton, suggested that companies experiment with new financial measures "to enable investors to obtain more relevant information about the current economics of a business enterprise in an inflationary economy." [On March 23, 1976 the SEC published Accounting Series Release No. 190. ASR 190 by way of Rule 3-17 amending Regulation S-X requires all SEC registrants with inventories and gross property, plant, and equipment which aggregate more than $100 million and which comprise more than 10% of total assets, to disclose certain specified replacement cost data in financial statements filed with the SEC.]

R. Harwood Beville, Senior Vice-President, upon hearing the 1975 statement by Burton commented to President Mathias J. DeVito, "By God, that's what we've been trying to do all along."

The company and its outside auditor immediately sat down to hammer out some common objectives. To justify the cost ("substantially less than $100,000," Beville says), Rouse insisted that the result had to be significantly more informative than what the company already was doing. And for added credibility, it insisted on auditor certification.

Initially, Peat Marwick was reluctant to go so far. Current value was unexplored territory, alive with possible pitfalls including vulnerability to stockholder suits if something went awry. But the big CPA firm finally agreed to provide some form of certification if it were convinced of the over-all fairness of the current-value numbers and if the results were also certified by an independent real estate appraiser. It also was essential to persuade the SEC to go along.

Throughout the fall of 1975, Rouse and the auditors developed a working financial model to collect the new current-value data, and late last winter they took it to the SEC. After meetings with Burton and his staff, Rouse was given the gree light in March. For the next three months the company compiled its valuations, and the final audit was made during the summer. The results are provided in the company's statements and selected notes for the fiscal year ending May 31, 1976.

Financial Review

Fiscal 1976 has been a year of great improvement in the company's operating results and financial position—and in the way in which the financial position is reported. As reviewed in preceding sections of this report, the company has developed a current value accounting and financial reporting model which presents the financial position of the company in terms of current values. This current value presentation, which supplements the cost basis (historical cost) financial statements, has been audited by Peat, Marwick, Mitchell & Co. Our current value presentation, including the related notes, is intended to respond to the recent Accounting Series Release issued by the Securities and Exchange Commission which calls for disclosure of the replacement cost of our "productive capacity." Because of the significant differences between the cost basis and current value basis presentations, it is especially important that the notes to these presentations be read as an integral part of these financial statements.

In addition to the current value presentation contained in this financial review section, note 11 to the consolidated financial statements describes the accounting for the sales of interests in certain of our retail centers during 1976 and 1975. These sales have had a significantly favorable impact on the company's operating results and financial position.

The contents of this financial review section have been arranged as follows:

- Consolidated Cost Basis and Current Value Basis Financial Statements—pages 20 to 24;
- The Report of the Company's Independent Certified Public Accountants and the Report of Independent Real Estate Consultants—pages 25 and 26;
- Notes to Consolidated Financial Statements—pages 27 to 41; and
- Five-Year Supplemental Financial Information, including certain operating results and management's analysis, for each of the company's operating divisions—pages 42 to 47.

The Five-Year Summary of Earnings Before Non-Cash Charges reports the operating results of each operating division before deductions for:

- Depreciation of real estate and related personal property;
- Amortization of deferred costs related to properties; and
- Deferred income taxes.

Management has consistently stated that, in its opinion, "earnings before non-cash charges" is the best measurement of the company's operating performance. Our current value presentation, which indicates that the current value of our operating properties exceeds the original cost, supports the use of this measurement as a valid indicator of the company's performance.

In last year's Annual Report to Shareholders, the company indicated that the International Council of Shopping Centers (ICSC) was considering the adoption of "earnings before non-cash charges" as the primary performance measurement to be reported by investment builders. The ICSC's Board of Trustees, at their recent annual meeting, approved the basic report of a special committee recommending that this measure become the primary performance measurement of investment builders.

Those readers who wish to receive a copy of the company's annual Form 10-K filed with the Securities and Exchange Commission may do so by contacting Mr. David L. Tripp, Director of Investor Relations, The Rouse Company, Columbia, Maryland 21044.

Consolidated Cost Basis and Current Value Basis Balance Sheets

Assets	— 1976 —		1975
	Current Value Basis (note 1)	Cost Basis	Cost Basis
Property and deferred costs of projects (notes 3 and 9):			
Operating properties:			
Current value	$372,105		
Cost		$314,205	$297,766
Less accumulated depreciation and amortization		54,230	50,542
		259,975	247,224
Construction and development in progress	60,075	60,075	60,226
Pre-construction costs, net	7,761	7,761	7,723
Other furniture, fixtures and equipment, net	4,459	3,734	4,105
Net property and deferred costs of projects	444,400	331,545	319,278
Mortgage banking (notes 4 and 9):			
Notes receivable	15,760	15,742	8,730
Accounts receivable	674	674	855
	16,434	16,416	9,585
Investment operations (notes 5 and 9):			
Notes receivable	15,190	15,190	20,827
Real estate owned	9,755	9,755	12,219
Accounts receivable	203	203	708
	25,148	25,148	33,754
Less reserve for possible loan losses	3,950	3,950	2,405
	21,198	21,198	31,349
Net investment in Rouse-Wates (note 6)	3,364	3,364	1,650
Due from HRD (note 7)	692	692	755
Other assets and deferred charges, primarily prepaid expenses and deposits	7,364	7,364	7,078
Accounts and notes receivable (note 8)	10,058	10,058	9,163
Cash and temporary investments	3,805	3,805	6,007
Total assets	$507,315	$394,442	$384,865

Liabilities, Deferred Credits and Shareholders' Equity

Debt (note 9):			
Debt not carrying a parent company guarantee of repayment:			
Debt of operating properties	$208,962	$208,962	$236,627
Debt of properties under development	17,484	17,484	4,229
Debt of parent company and debt carrying a parent company guarantee of repayment:			
Debt of operating properties	44,265	44,265	18,984
Debt of properties under development	23,888	23,888	23,827
Term loan credit notes payable:			
Parent company	18,250	18,250	25,400
Investment operations	13,800	13,800	19,481
Senior subordinated notes payable	12,096	12,096	13,432
Other debt	4,097	4,097	4,798
Notes payable—Mortgage banking	15,522	15,522	8,640
Accounts payable and accrued expenses	15,877	15,877	17,486
Commitments and contingencies (notes 4, 6, 13, 14 and 16)			
Deferred credits:			
Deferred gains on sale-leasebacks of property (note 2)	2,243	2,243	2,275
Deferral associated with sales of interests in retail centers (note 11)	1,936	1,936	1,939
Shareholders' equity:			
Capital stock (note 12):			
$6 Cumulative Preferred stock of $100 par value per share. Authorized 25,000 shares; issued 24,991 shares	2,499	2,499	2,499
Common stock of 1¢ par value per share. Authorized 20,000,000 shares; issued 14,077,524 shares in 1976 and 13,991,524 shares in 1975	141	141	140
Total capital stock	2,640	2,640	2,639
Additional paid-in capital	20,171	20,171	20,103
Deficit	(6,491)	(6,491)	(14,697)
Revaluation equity (note 1 (c))	112,873		
	129,193	16,320	8,045
Less common stock held in treasury, 1,164,940 shares at cost	298	298	298
Total shareholders' equity	128,895	16,022	7,747
Total liabilities, deferred credits and shareholders' equity	$507,315	$394,442	$384,865

Statement of Operations

	1976	1975
Continuing operations		
Revenues	$73,712	$73,087
Expenses exclusive of depreciation and amortization	70,280	73,904
	3,432	(817)
Depreciation and amortization (note 3)	8,208	8,308
	(4,776)	(9,125)
Gain on sales of interests in retail centers (note 11)	13,229	10,208
Earnings from continuing operations before income taxes and extraordinary credit	8,453	1,083
Federal and state income taxes (notes 2 and 10):		
Current, state	97	57
Tax effect of accounting loss carryovers in 1976 and charge equivalent to tax benefit recognized under discontinued operations in 1975	4,000	500
	4,097	557
Earnings from continuing operations before extraordinary credit	4,356	526
Discontinued operations		
Additions to reserve for loss on disposal of assets of Rouse-Wates (note 6)	—	(1,200)
Tax benefit equivalent to tax charged to continuing operations in 1975 (note 2)	—	500
Loss from discontinued operations	—	(700)
Earnings (loss) before extraordinary credit	4,356	(174)
Extraordinary credit		
Tax credit caused by the availability of accounting loss carryovers (note 2):		
Continuing operations	1,200	—
Discontinued operations	2,800	—
	4,000	—
Net earnings (loss)	$ 8,356	$ (174)
Earnings (loss) per common share after provision for dividends on Preferred stock (note 15):		
Continuing operations	$ .33	$ .03
Discontinued operations	—	(.06)
Extraordinary credit	.31	—
Net earnings (loss)	$ .64	$ (.03)

Statement of Shareholders' Equity

	$6 Cumulative Preferred stock	Common stock	Additional paid-in capital	Deficit
Balance at May 31, 1974	$2,499	$140	$20,077	$(14,373)
Net loss	—	—	—	(174)
Dividends on $6 Cumulative Preferred stock	—	—	—	(150)
Other	—	—	26	—
Balance at May 31, 1975	2,499	140	20,103	(14,697)
Net earnings	—	—	—	8,356
Dividends on $6 Cumulative Preferred stock	—	—	—	(150)
Other	—	1	68	—
Balance at May 31, 1976	$2,499	$141	$20,171	$ (6,491)

Statement of Changes in Financial Position

	1976	1975
Earnings from continuing operations before extraordinary credit	$ 4,356	$ 526
Depreciation and amortization	8,208	8,308
	12,564	8,834
Tax credits caused by availability of accounting loss carryovers in 1976 and deferred income tax in 1975:		
Continuing operations	1,200	—
Discontinued operations	2,800	500
Funds provided by continuing operations after extraordinary credit	16,564	9,334
Dividends on Preferred stock	150	150
	16,414	9,184
Mortgage principal payments—operating properties	3,641	3,724
Funds provided by continuing operations after extraordinary credit, Preferred stock dividends and mortgage principal payments	12,773	5,460
Additions to reserves charged to operations, net of write-offs:		
Additions to reserve for potentially unsuccessful pre-construction efforts, net	950	2,374
Additions to reserve for possible loan losses, net	1,545	2,200
Total additions to reserves charged to operations, net	2,495	4,574
Other funds generated:		
Project related debt, including term loan credit notes payable of $25,400 in 1975	45,568	57,395
Borrowings other than project related debt	6,992	2,422
Disposition of properties:		
Net book value of interests in retail centers sold	21,512	15,902
Net book value of other dispositions	2,744	923
Transfers to joint ventures, net	3,982	1,376
Decrease in amounts due from HRD	63	4,104
Increase in accounts payable and accrued expenses	—	2,370
Decrease in receivables	880	17,480
Other, net	—	1,976
Total other funds generated	81,741	103,948
Other funds disbursed:		
Construction and development of projects	47,867	41,347
Improvements to existing operating properties	1,589	1,418
Other property additions	207	1,699
Repayment of borrowings other than project related debt	8,810	19,917
Repayment of project debt other than mortgage principal payments, including demand bank loans payable of $25,400 in 1975	13,331	26,751
Mortgages assumed by purchasers of interests in retail centers	23,832	16,542
Increase in advances to Rouse-Wates	1,714	3,487
Decrease in accounts payable and accrued expenses	1,609	—
Other, net	252	—
Total other funds disbursed	99,211	111,161
Increase (decrease) in cash and temporary investments	(2,202)	2,821
Cash and temporary investments at beginning of year	6,007	3,186
Cash and temporary investments at end of year	$ 3,805	$ 6,007

The Board of Directors
The Rouse Company:

We have examined the consolidated balance sheets of The Rouse Company and subsidiaries as of May 31, 1976 and 1975 and the related consolidated statements of operations, shareholders' equity and changes in financial position for the years then ended. Our examination was made in accordance with generally accepted auditing standards, and accordingly included such tests of the accounting records and such other auditing procedures as we considered necessary in the circumstances. We did not examine the consolidated financial statements of Rouse-Wates, Incorporated and subsidiaries (Rouse-Wates) for the years ended May 31, 1976 and 1975. The financial statements of Rouse-Wates were examined by other auditors whose qualified report thereon has been furnished to us, and our opinion expressed herein, insofar as it relates to the amounts included for Rouse-Wates, is based solely upon the report of the other auditors. See note 6 to the consolidated financial statements for information relative to The Rouse Company's investment in and advances to Rouse-Wates and its impact on the results of operations of The Rouse Company.

As explained in note 6, Rouse-Wates' financial statements have been prepared on a liquidation basis as of and for the years ended May 31, 1976 and 1975 and reserves have been provided for estimated losses on the disposition of assets. As described in the report of the other auditors, the determination of such reserves "involves subjective judgment which is not susceptible to substantiation by auditing procedures." The opinion of the other auditors is "subject to the effect on the financial statements of any adjustments, which in our judgment could be material, arising because of differences between the estimates referred to (above) and the actual amounts ultimately realized or incurred and subject to The Rouse Company making additional advances as needed to enable the company (Rouse-Wates) to meet the obligations to its creditors."

As described in note 1, the financial statements include a consolidated balance sheet as of May 31, 1976 prepared on a current value basis to supplement the financial statements prepared on the cost basis. The current value basis of presentation provides relevant information about the current financial position of the company which is not provided by financial statements prepared on the historical cost basis. The current value basis of presentation differs significantly from the historical cost basis required by generally accepted accounting principles.

In our opinion, based upon our examination and the report of the other auditors and subject to the effect on the financial statements of the company of the matters underlying the qualification taken by the other auditors, the aforementioned consolidated financial statements stated on a cost basis present fairly the financial position of The Rouse Company and its subsidiaries at May 31, 1976 and 1975 and the results of their operations and the changes in their financial position for the years then ended, in conformity with generally accepted accounting principles applied on a consistent basis; and the consolidated current value basis balance sheet as of May 31, 1976 is presented fairly on the basis indicated in the preceding paragraph and the note referred to therein.

August 12, 1976

Peat, Marwick, Mitchell & Co.

Peat, Marwick, Mitchell & Co.
and
The Board of Directors
The Rouse Company:

You have asked us to review and comment upon estimates of the fair market value of the equity in certain real property interests owned by The Rouse Company (TRC) and its subsidiaries as of May 31, 1976. The specific properties and interests are identified as "In Operation" on the "Projects of The Rouse Company" table on pages 50 and 51 of the Annual Report for the year ended May 31, 1976. The properties have been appraised and the equity values estimated by the staff of TRC. All properties were appraised subject to existing leases and financing.

We have completed our review and analysis of the data, value estimates, and summary reports submitted to us by TRC. The total equity value estimated by TRC as of May 31, 1976 as indicated in Note 1 of Notes to Consolidated Financial Statements is:

One Hundred and Thirteen Million, Eight Hundred and Twenty Thousand Dollars
$113,820,000.

As a result of our review and analysis of the data and the appraisal reports, we concur with this estimate of the total value of the property interests appraised.

Concurrence is defined as an aggregate valuation of the equity interests as prepared by TRC with a variation of less than 10%, in our opinion, from the probable value we would estimate in a full and complete appraisal of the same equity interests. A 10% variation between appraisers is generally considered a reasonable range of value and implies substantial agreement as to the most probable fair market value of the property.

The above value is the sum total of the individual values of the individual property interests. No assumptions have been made with respect to a bulk sale of the entire holdings or groups of property interests.

Throughout this review assignment we have relied entirely upon TRC's interpretation and summaries of leases, operating agreements, mortgages, partnership agreements, etc. While we have had complete and unrestricted access to all underlying documents and have on occasion examined the applicable legal instruments, the vast majority of the data has been provided in summary form by TRC. We have found no discrepancies in this data and have assumed all such information to be accurate and complete. The basic assumptions used by TRC are fair and reasonable.

We have also been supplied with historical revenue and expense data for the fiscal years 1974 through 1976 which we understand Peat, Marwick, Mitchell & Co. has reviewed and found to be accurate in all material respects. The individual value estimates prepared by TRC meet all prudent tests of documentation, credibility, technique, and rationale.

Although our assignment was to review and analyze appraisals prepared by TRC, we have physically inspected a selected sampling of the properties including 9 retail centers, 3 office buildings, and the Village of Cross Keys.

Our review of these appraisals has been made in conformity with and subject to the requirements of the Code of Professional Ethics and Standards of Professional Conduct of the American Institute of Real Estate Appraisers of the National Association of Realtors.

We hereby certify that James D. Landauer Associates, Inc. was employed to review the estimates of fair market value of the equity interests in the subject properties prepared by TRC.

Neither James D. Landauer Associates, Inc. nor the undersigned have any present or contemplated future interest in the real estate or in The Rouse Company. We have no personal interest or bias with respect to the subject matter of the appraisals reviewed or the parties involved.

To the best of our knowledge and belief the facts upon which the analyses and conclusions are based are true and correct. No one other than the undersigned, assisted by members of our staff, performed the analyses and reached the conclusions resulting in the opinion concerning the appraisals of the properties expressed in this letter.

We hereby authorize the publication of this letter of opinion in its entirety along with the current value financial statements in TRC's annual report to its shareholders and to the Securities and Exchange Commission for the fiscal year ended May 31, 1976.

Sincerely,

James D. Landauer Associates, Inc.

John B. Bailey, M.A.I., C.R.E.
Senior Vice President

Peter F. Korpacz, M.A.I.
Vice President & Chief Appraiser

August 11, 1976

Notes to Consolidated Financial Statements

(1) Current value presentation

(a) Development of current value reporting

The management of The Rouse Company has consistently stated that the current value of its operating properties, its major asset, far exceeds the net book value of these assets as reflected in the financial statements prepared in accordance with generally accepted accounting principles. In a special report contained in the 1975 Annual Report to Shareholders, we described the process of creating a high quality operating property and the process by which its value is increased over time through professional merchandising and management. In the company's last several annual reports, management has supported its position by reporting an estimate of the value of the company's operating properties. Again, because generally accepted accounting principles do not allow us to report these values in the cost basis (historical cost) financial statements, we reported such values in the letter to shareholders. This was done because we believe that reporting the current value of assets is an integral and important part of reporting the actual economics of the company's financial position—the economics which, in fact, are the basis for developing, financing, operating and selling the operating property assets of investment builders.

Over the past year the company has developed a current value financial reporting format which places the current value of all of our resources in the context of a full statement of financial position. Our presentation takes a step beyond the Securities and Exchange Commission's recent requirement for certain companies to disclose replacement cost information in notes to the cost basis financial statements. It is our intention to make this current value reporting a continuing part of our formal financial statements on an annual basis.

In addition to their normal involvement, our auditors, Peat, Marwick, Mitchell & Co., engaged the services of James D. Landauer Associates, Inc. (Landauer), real estate consultants, who reviewed and analyzed our estimates of the value of our operating properties. Our estimates of value were based on an evaluation of the history and future of each operating property and included for each retail center:
- a complete five-year market study covering basic demographic and market volume projections plus competitive alignment and market share expectations;
- tenant-by-tenant analyses of lease terms, sales performance and rent projections for the next five years; and
- analyses of projections of operating expenses over the next five years (including those portions passed on to tenants under lease agreements) plus financing costs—principal, interest and lender participations.

Landauer rendered an opinion to our auditors stating their concurrence with our estimates of these values. Landauer's opinion is contained on page 26. Our auditors' opinion respecting the consolidated current value basis balance sheet is contained in their report on page 25.

The company's financial position on a current value basis is reported on pages 20 and 21 as a supplementary column alongside our cost basis balance sheet. The current value and net book value is shown for each asset category, and the $112,873,000 aggregate increment of current value over net book value has been reflected in shareholders' equity as "revaluation equity." We believe this consolidated current value balance sheet more realistically reflects the economics of the company's cumulative operations and financial position.

The consolidated current value basis balance sheet recognizes the value of the company's assets based on the presumption that such assets will be retained and utilized by the company for a significant period of time. This current value basis balance sheet does not necessarily represent the liquidation value of assets or of the company. The most significant difference in value (comparing the current value of assets against the cost basis net book values) is in our operating properties. The values of these particular properties approximate the current investment which investors would make to purchase 100% of the company's interest in their present and future cash flow streams. We believe that the investment value of a property's cash flow stream is the most appropriate measurement of the current value of the asset and, therefore, of its net replacement cost. These values also represent the economic value of the company's income-producing resources—value which is utilized by the company as a source of capital. In the context of a two-year program to improve the company's liquidity and general financial condition, approximately $29,000,000 of equity value in operating properties has been received in cash through sales of partial interests in seven operating properties and the refinancing of three others.

(b) Bases of valuation

The bases of management's estimates of current values are as follows:

- The current value of the company's operating property assets has been defined as each property's equity value, (i.e., the value of its future net cash flow after paying both interest and principal on the debt specifically related to the property) plus the outstanding balance of related debt. Net cash flow represents the operating revenues less all operating expenses, current taxes and ground rents, debt principal, interest and participations to lessors, lenders and equity partners. The estimate of each property's equity value was based on criteria currently utilized by investors in income-producing real estate. The valuations recognized the considerable differences between properties in terms of quality, age, outlook and risk. Landauer, independent real estate consultants, reviewed, analyzed and concurred with our $113,820,000 appraised value of the company's equity interest in operating properties. Concurrence, as used by Landauer, is defined as a variation of less than 10% from the probable value that might be estimated by Landauer in a full and complete appraisal. Landauer did not review our valuation of fringe land contiguous to operating properties—land not being utilized in the operations of such properties or as security for project mortgages. The company's estimate of the gross value of this fringe land (approximately 150 acres) is $7,073,000.
- Construction and development in progress and pre-construction costs are carried at the same values as in the cost basis financial statements—values which represent the lower of cost or net realizable value. While the company believes that the properties under construction (some of which will open in the next several months) have value in excess of stated cost, management has taken the more conservative position in not adjusting the cost basis by any value increment.
- Other furniture, fixtures and equipment is valued at its current replacement cost which was determined by reference to recent prices of similar assets and estimates of the current cost to duplicate similar assets. The gross replacement cost of furniture, fixtures and equipment is $5,856,000, which reflects an increase of $941,000 over the cost basis. The related accumulated depreciation and amortization was $1,397,000 after an increase of $216,000 to reflect that portion of the increase in current replacement cost of the assets which would have been charged to operations through May 31, 1976.
- Mortgage banking notes receivable represent mortgage notes held for sale to long-term investors usually under pre-arranged take-out commitments from such investors. The mortgages are purchased from developers at a price which may be different from the price at which the company will ultimately resell such mortgages. Those notes for which sale commitments have been pre-arranged are carried at the commitment price. The remainder of the notes are carried at their market value. This value exceeds the cost basis by $18,000 at May 31, 1976.
- The following resources are carried on the current value balance sheet at the lower of cost or net realizable value—the same stated value as on the cost basis balance sheet:
  —Mortgage banking accounts receivable (net of doubtful receivable reserves);
  —accounts of the Investment operations, including notes and accounts receivable and real estate owned (net of loan loss reserves);
  —the company's net investment in Rouse-Wates (net of liquidation reserves);
  —amounts due from HRD;
  —other assets and deferred charges;
  —accounts and notes receivable (net of doubtful receivable reserves); and
  —cash and temporary investments.
  The stated values of these accounts represent their current value as the underlying assets will be realized in the relatively near-term.
- All liability accounts are carried at the same stated value as in the cost basis balance sheet. Long-term debt relating to our operating properties is carried at the same amount as in the cost basis statement because the difference between the current value and cost basis of such debt, if any, is an integral part of the revaluation equity attributable to operating properties. A significant portion of the debt which is not specifically related to our operating properties carries interest rates which fluctuate with the prime interest rate. Therefore, the outstanding balance of this debt represents its current value. This is also the case with the notes payable—Mortgage banking.

The application of the foregoing methods for estimating current value represents the best judgment of management based upon its current evaluation of the economy and money markets today and in the future. These kinds of judgments regarding the economy and money markets are not subject to precise quantification or verification, and may change from time to time as economic and market factors, and management's evaluation of them, change.

(c) Revaluation equity

The aggregate difference between the current value basis and cost basis net book value of the company's assets is carried as revaluation equity in the shareholders' equity section of the consolidated current value basis balance sheet. The components of this revaluation equity at May 31, 1976 are as follows:

Operating properties:	
Value of equity interests.	$113,820,000
Outstanding balance of debt related to equity interests, excluding $2,015,000 of debt related to fringe land.	251,212,000
	365,032,000
Value of fringe land.	7,073,000
Total asset value.	372,105,000
Depreciated cost of operating properties.	259,975,000
Revaluation equity in operating properties.	112,130,000
Mortgage banking notes receivable.	18,000
Other furniture, fixtures and equipment, net of accumulated depreciation and amortization.	725,000
Total revaluation equity.	$112,873,000

No income tax charge has been imputed against the revaluation equity as the differences between the current value and cost basis net book value of our properties and the changes in these increments over the lives of such properties will not enter into the determination of taxable income until such differences are realized over the long-term through future operations or sales. Although realization of current values through future operations or sales will ultimately enter into the determination of taxable income, management has no current intention to sell additional operating properties and, therefore, such realization is expected to occur over an extended period of time. Consequently, the payment of Federal income taxes, based on the company's anticipated business activities and existing Federal income tax laws, will be made over an extended, indefinite future time period. Accordingly, the current value of the future obligation for Federal income taxes is indeterminable at this time.

Presently, our current value reporting model does not include a statement of operating results and/or annual changes in value. One reason for this is that comparable values as of the beginning of fiscal year 1976 are not available. While the company, in previous years, had provided a conservative estimate of the values of its operating properties, these estimates did not undergo the rigorous process, including external professional review and analysis, which the May 31, 1976 valuations have undergone. In addition, we have not defined what we believe to be the most appropriate information or format for reporting periodic operating results and value changes. This reporting will be developed as we, along with others in our industry, define the appropriate information and presentations.

(d) Replacement cost of assets

On March 23, 1976, the Securities and Exchange Commission (SEC) issued Accounting Series Release No. 190 requiring disclosure of certain replacement cost data. The SEC's requirements, as described in Accounting Series Release No. 190, "were designed to enable investors to obtain more relevant information about the current economics of a business enterprise in an inflationary economy than that provided solely by financial statements prepared on the basis of historical cost." Assets of the company subject to the SEC's disclosure requirements include operating properties and furniture, fixtures and equipment. The current value of furniture, fixtures and equipment in the consolidated current value balance sheet represents the replacement cost of such assets. While management's valuation of operating properties is based on the current value of cash flow rather than the cost to reconstruct such properties, management believes that this current value is the most appropriate measure of the cost of replacing the cash flow stream generated by income-producing properties held as long-term assets. If the current values of these resources were ratably charged to operations in the same manner as is used in the company's cost basis financial statements, the depreciation and amortization charged to 1976 operating results would total approximately $10,100,000, the majority of which relates to operating properties. Because the value of these properties, as reflected in the current value balance sheet, represents the current value of such properties at May 31, 1976, depreciation and amortization related to operating properties would have no effect on the net asset values of properties or on shareholders' equity as reflected in the consolidated current value balance sheet.

(2) Summary of significant accounting policies

(a) Principles of statement presentation

The consolidated financial statements include the accounts of The Rouse Company, all subsidiaries and partnerships in which it has majority interest and control, and the company's proportionate share of the assets, liabilities, revenues and expenses of unincorporated retail center joint ventures in which it has joint interest and control with other venturers. Significant intercompany transactions have been eliminated in consolidation.

The company's investment in Rouse-Wates, Incorporated (Rouse-Wates) is accounted for as a discontinued operation. The reserve for loss on disposal of the assets of Rouse-Wates was established in 1974 and increased in 1975. Tax credits resulting from the availability of accounting loss carryovers from Rouse-Wates have been recorded in 1976 and 1975 as explained in note 2(h).

Certain amounts in 1975 have been reclassified to conform with the presentation for 1976.

(b) Property

The company capitalizes construction and development costs associated with the development of projects and land held for development or sale. Among these costs are real estate taxes, interest and other carrying charges, applicable salary and related costs and pre-construction costs as described in note 2(d). These costs are classified as construction and development in progress until the project becomes operational or is sold at which time the accumulated project costs are transferred to operating property categories or charged to cost of sales, respectively.

In 1976, the company reviewed the proposed uses of all parcels of land contiguous to its operating properties which were classified as construction and development in progress. This review was to ascertain the effects, if any, that local and national conditions in the real estate market were having on the prospective uses of the parcels and the time frame of such uses. As a result of this evaluation, the company reclassified the costs of all land parcels where specific development programs were not currently authorized by management to operating property categories and commenced charging the related carrying costs to operations. The costs associated with land parcels where development programs are authorized remain in the construction and development in progress classification and carrying costs continue to be capitalized. The effect of this change in classification, made as of March 1, 1976, reduced net earnings for 1976 by $191,000.

Depreciation of property for financial reporting purposes is computed primarily by the use of the straight-line method using a composite life of 40 years. Maintenance and repair costs are expensed against operations as incurred, while significant improvements and replacements are charged to the appropriate property accounts. Minor retirements or dispositions of property are accounted for by charging the cost of the property to accumulated depreciation thereby reflecting the related gains or losses in future depreciation charges. Major retirements or dispositions of depreciable property are accounted for by removing the cost of the property and related accumulated depreciation from the respective accounts and recognizing the related gain or loss in current operations.

(c) Deferred costs of projects

In addition to the construction and development costs of projects, certain other costs related to projects are capitalized and amortized over the periods benefited by the expenditures. The costs of acquiring leasehold interests are amortized over the terms of the respective leases. Costs associated with securing long-term debt are amortized over the terms of the related debt. Pre-operating expenses incurred prior to placing a project in operation are amortized over a period of five years from the date the project is opened. Expenditures associated with negotiating leases with tenants and prospective tenants prior to the opening of the project are amortized over the weighted average term of the project's initial leases (usually 10 to 15 years). Costs of re-leasing are expensed as incurred.

(d) Pre-construction costs

The pre-construction stage of project development includes efforts and related costs to achieve land control, to obtain requisite zoning, to secure department store tenants, to obtain financing commitments and to accomplish other initial tasks which are essential to the development of a project. Pre-construction costs include salaries and related manpower costs, land option payments, legal and architectural fees, feasibility study costs, other direct expenditures and interest charges. These costs are transferred to construction and development in progress when the pre-construction tasks are achieved.

The company provides for the costs of potentially unsuccessful pre-construction efforts by charges to operations. The amount of the reserve and, therefore, additions to the reserve are based upon an evaluation of the probability of the company's discontinuing its efforts on projects in their pre-construction stage of development.

Other development costs charged directly to operations include the costs associated with the initial evaluations of new projects, carrying costs associated with certain pre-construction projects which have a high probability of being discontinued and, in 1975, a reserve for loss of $600,000 on a project developed for sale. This reserve represents the estimated total project costs in excess of the estimated total project proceeds. Project costs include land, building costs, applicable salary and related costs, selling costs, real estate taxes, interest and other carrying costs through the estimated construction and sales period of the project.

(e) Accounting for costs during lease-up periods

When properties are initially opened, certain carrying costs such as interest, ground rents, real estate taxes and insurance are capitalized or expensed during the lease-up period. For retail centers, these costs are expensed as operating costs monthly based on the ratio of actual occupancy to total leasable space until occupancy reaches 90%, but no longer than twelve months after opening in 1976 and six months after opening in 1975. The 1976 change in the maximum lease-up period from six to twelve months for retail centers opening after 1975 is based on the actual leasing experience of the company and others. The change in the maximum lease-up period had no effect in 1976. Under this policy, the costs charged to capital accounts were $841,000 in 1976 and $46,000 in 1975; the amounts expensed were $1,071,000 in 1976 and $184,000 in 1975. The company has a similar lease-up policy for office buildings; however, no office buildings were in the lease-up period during 1976 and 1975.

(f) Deferred gains on sale-leasebacks of properties

Gains from sale-leaseback transactions are deferred for financial reporting purposes and amortized over the terms of the respective leases as reductions of rental costs. Amortization of such deferred gains amounted to $32,000 in 1976 and 1975.

(g) Property sales and costs of sales
The company accounts for sales of real estate in accordance with the guidelines set forth in the American Institute of Certified Public Accountants' accounting guide, *Accounting for Profit Recognition on Sales of Real Estate.* Proceeds from the sale of fringe land classified in operating properties categories, as explained in note 2(b), are credited to the cost of operating properties.

(h) Income taxes
Deferred income taxes are provided for the timing differences between accounting earnings and taxable income (loss) as described in note 10. For accounting purposes, the tax effect of accounting loss carryovers, aggregating $4,000,000 in 1976 and included in the results of continuing operations, has been offset by an extraordinary credit which has been identified as relating to continuing operations and to discontinued operations based on the amount of accounting loss carryovers attributable to each.

Investment tax credits, which are not material, will be carried forward to reduce the Federal income tax provision in the years the credits are utilized. No provision has been made for taxes on the undistributed earnings of foreign subsidiaries as the company does not intend to make such distributions.

Required

1. Rouse is in the business of developing and operating properties, primarily large shopping centers. The current values of these properties are figured on the basis of what investors would have to pay for similar income properties on today's market. How much do these values exceed their cost basis?

2. What amount of accumulated depreciation does Rouse show in its current-value-basis statements? How was the amount determined?

3. What approach was used to value Rouse's other property?

4. Why are mortgage notes receivable valued differently under the current value basis while other receivables are not?

5. What changes do you note in the firm's liabilities reported under the current-value and cost basis?

6. What does the revaluation equity account reflect?

7. To reduce its corporate debt during 1975 and 1976, Rouse sold a 50% interest in 7 of its 24 shopping centers to outsiders, netting $24 million in cash. Rouse's equity in these interests showed up negatively on its books to the tune of $3 million. How could this be so and why would Rouse cite this fact as a reason for favoring current values?

8. In what major ways does the reporting approach for current values used by Rouse differ from the replacement-cost disclosures that are required by the SEC?

9. What methods were used by Rouse to make its current-value estimates? Is the method consistent with the approach used by most purchasers of major real estate parcels? What value did Rouse obtain?

10. What did the Chairman mean by "the auditor's blessing?" Do you believe the new current value statements will make it easier for the firm to raise capital? Do you believe the new disclosure would result in an increase in the price of the firm's stock?

11. Do you see any potential problems with the approach by Rouse?

Case 9-7

Bethlehem Steel Corporation (B)

Bethlehem Steel Corporation's Consolidated Income Statement and Balance Sheets for 1976 and 1975 are presented. The Information on Replacement Costs required by Rule 3–17 of Regulation S-X of the SEC as filed on Bethlehem Steel's Form 10-K is also presented.

	1976	1975
	(dollars in millions)	
Revenues:		
Net sales	$5,248.0	$4,977.2
Interest, dividends and other income	56.7	51.1
	$5,304.7	$5,028.3
Costs and Expenses:		
Cost of sales	$4,082.1	$3,854.3
Depreciation	275.6	234.2
Pensions (Note J)	261.2	198.4
Selling, administrative and general expense	234.7	220.0
Interest and other debt charges	77.7	63.4
Taxes (including income taxes of $26,000,000 and $41,000,000) (Note K)	205.4	216.0
	$5,136.7	$4,786.3
Net Income ($3.85 and $5.54 per share)	$ 168.0	$ 242.0
Income Invested in the Business, January 1	2,105.3	1,983.4
	$2,273.3	$2,225.4
Deduct: Dividends ($2.00 and $2.75 per share)	87.4	120.1
Income Invested in the Business, December 31	$2,185.9	$2,105.3

Consolidated Balance Sheets

December 31
(dollars in millions)

	1976	1975
Assets		
Current Assets:		
Cash	$ 45.6	$ 59.7
Marketable securities, at cost (approximately market)	355.6	306.9
Receivables, less allowances of $6,100,000 and $5,800,000	421.5	401.7
Inventories (Note B)	834.1	619.9
Total Current Assets	$1,656.8	$1,388.2
Investments and Long-term Receivables:		
Investments in associated companies accounted for by equity method (Note D)	116.9	114.3
Investments in other associated enterprises	97.4	94.1
Long-term receivables	24.8	23.9
Pollution control funds held in trust	35.6	58.3
Property, Plant and Equipment (Note C)	2,963.4	2,854.3
Miscellaneous Assets (Note E)	44.2	58.4
Total	$4,939.1	$4,591.5
Liabilities and Stockholders' Equity		
Current Liabilities:		
Accounts payable	$ 274.8	$ 239.7
Accrued employment costs	241.5	234.6
Accrued taxes (Note K)	127.5	94.7
Debt due within one year	12.9	24.2
Other current liabilities	127.3	125.8
Total Current Liabilities	$ 784.0	$ 719.0
Liabilities Payable After One Year	140.8	140.0
Deferred Income Taxes (Note K)	298.6	263.6
Long-term Debt (Note F)	1,023.1	856.9
Commitments (Note G)		
Stockholders' Equity (Note H):		
Common Stock—$8 par value—Authorized 80,000,000 shares; issued 45,987,118 shares	$ 576.0	$ 576.0
Income invested in the business	2,185.9	2,105.3
	$2,761.9	$2,681.3
Less—2,321,540 and 2,321,925 shares of Common Stock held in treasury, at cost	69.3	69.3
Total Stockholders' Equity	$2,692.6	$2,612.0
Total	$4,939.1	$4,591.5

Bethlehem Steel Corporation Form 10-K Information Based on Estimates of Replacement Cost (unaudited)

The statements below are made to comply with Rule 3-17 of Regulation S-X of the Securities and Exchange Commission, which requires disclosure of information (based on estimates) on the current replacement cost of inventories; the cost of sales on the basis of the replacement cost of the goods or services at the time of sale; gross (new) and depreciated replacement cost of productive capacity; and depreciation expense on a replacement cost basis; accompanied by a description of the methods employed in determining replacement costs and other information which the management believes is necessary to prevent the data from being misleading. The table below should be read in conjunction with the subsequent explanations and is expressly made subject to the entire narrative portion hereof, including such explanations.

	On Basis of	
	Estimated Replacement Cost (unaudited)	Historical Cost
	(dollars in millions)	
At December 31, 1976		
Inventories	$ 1,555	$ 834
Property, plant and equipment, excluding depletable mineral properties, land and construction in progress		
Gross...........................	$16,010	$5,839
Net of accumulated depreciation.......	$ 4,947	$2,352
For the year 1976		
Cost of sales (excluding estimated cost savings—see explanation below)	$ 4,132	$4,082
Depreciation, excluding depletion..........	$ 594	$ 274

Inventories valued on a LIFO basis, which account for approximately 85% of the consolidated book value of inventories, have been adjusted to estimated replacement cost by using the most recent purchase price or production cost. Other inventories have not been adjusted because it is estimated that book value approximates replacement cost.

The estimates of current replacement cost of present property, plant and equipment, excluding depletable mineral properties, land and construction in progress, were determined as follows:

> Approximately 85% of such property, plant and equipment was valued by the use of estimated current facility replacement costs per ton of capacity. These estimates are based on a number of factors, such as actual construction costs of recent installations, estimated costs of authorized but incomplete projects and quotations from vendors and reflect the latest feasible technology and environmental controls as well as economic and commercial considerations.

> The estimates of current replacement cost of the remainder of such property, plant and equipment were determined by indexing historical costs.

The cost of sales has not been adjusted to reflect $535 million of estimated cost savings which could reasonably be expected from the facilities utilized to calculate the estimated replacement cost of such property, plant and equipment. The estimate of cost savings is based on efficiencies of new

332 Cases in Financial Accounting

equipment actually installed or new equipment presently available from vendors and is consistent with the concepts and assumptions utilized in estimating such replacement cost. The estimate of cost savings does not take into account, among other things, the cost of the capital required to replace such property, plant and equipment. Such estimate is based on present conditions and should not be considered indicative of any actual future cost savings or the possible effect thereof on financial results.

Bethlehem Steel Corporation Annual Report

M. Replacement Cost Information (Unaudited)

As required by Rule 3-17 of Regulation S-X of the Securities and Exchange Commission, Bethlehem's Annual Report on Form 10-K (a copy of which is available upon request) contains information (based on estimates) on the current replacement cost of inventories; the cost of sales on the basis of the replacement cost of the goods or services at the time of sale; gross (new) and depreciated replacement cost of productive capacity; and depreciation expense on a replacement cost basis. Such information (which must be read in conjunction with the explanations thereof contained in such Annual Report on Form 10-K and is expressly made subject to such explanations and the other qualifications set forth therein) shows that, on the basis of estimated replacement cost, inventories, property, plant and equipment and depreciation expense would be significantly greater and cost of sales, as adjusted to reflect estimated cost savings, would be less than on the basis of historical cost.

Required

1. Calculate the total effect on Net Income Per Share of using replacement costs using all disclosures made to the SEC for 1976.

2. Determine the change in Return on Assets for 1976 from using replacement costs.

3. What is the primary cause for the increased replacement cost value over historical cost in determining cost of sales?

4. Do the replacement cost estimates represent the current value of existing property, plant and equipment? Why or why not?

5. Does the information set forth in the Form 10-K show the overall effect of inflation on Net Income and the Balance Sheet of Bethlehem Steel?

Case 9-8

Barber-Ellis of Canada, Ltd. (A)

Barber-Ellis presented a Balance Sheet and a Statement of Earnings on a current replacement cost basis as a supplementary part of its 1974 annual report. The Company's Current Replacement Cost Balance Sheet (Asset Section Only) and Statement of Earnings and Retained Earnings are presented.

Current Replacement Cost Balance Sheet

ASSETS	Current Replacement Cost (Note 1)	Historical Cost (Note 3)
CURRENT		
Cash	$ 29,783	$ 29,783
Accounts receivable	12,074,945	12,074,945
Inventories	10,366,804	10,117,804
Prepaid expenses	249,545	249,545
	$22,721,077	$22,472,077
Property, plant and equipment	$15,164,198	$11,261,927
Accumulated depreciation	(8,074,486)	(5,817,772)
Unamortized excess of purchase price of subsidiaries over fair value of net assets acquired	–	816,067
	$29,810,789	$28,732,299

Current Replacement Cost Statement of Earnings and Retained Earnings

	Current Replacement Cost (Note 2)	Historical Cost (Note 3)
NET SALES	$69,058,300	$69,058,300
COSTS AND EXPENSES		
Cost of products sold	$51,373,580	$50,389,580
Selling, general and administration	10,705,281	10,705,281
Depreciation and amortization	1,095,567	786,969
Interest—long-term debt	381,884	381,884
Interest—current	590,284	590,284
	$64,146,596	$62,853,998
Earnings before income taxes	$ 4,911,704	$ 6,204,302
Provision for income taxes	2,927,442	2,927,442
NET EARNINGS	$ 1,984,262	$ 3,276,860
Retained earnings, beginning of year	7,939,344	7,939,344
	$ 9,923,606	$11,216,204
Adjustment of prior years' depreciation on current replacement cost of plant and equipment	$ 1,948,116	–
Dividends	973,837	$ 973,837
RETAINED EARNINGS, END OF YEAR	$ 7,001,653	$10,242,367
Earnings Per Share		
Basic	$ 4.30	$ 7.09
Fully diluted	4.22	6.96

Required

1. What entries did Barber-Ellis make in 1974 to adjust property, plant and equipment to replacement cost?

2. In its annual report, Barber-Ellis stated that "if our economy is to function effectively, it is essential that management, investors and governments clearly understand the changed financial conditions that inflation creates." Using the information presented, list some of the changes in financial conditions that inflation creates. Why are these changes important?

Case 9-9

The Barber-Ellis Group (B)

The Barber-Ellis Group included a complete set of supplementary consolidated financial statements on a current replacement cost basis in its 1977 annual report. Excerpts from these statements are presented.

Consolidated Current Replacement Cost Balance Sheet

as at December 31, 1977 (With comparative figures for 1976)

Assets	1977	1976
Current		
Accounts receivable	$13,383,659	$12,626,534
Inventories	12,628,865	11,883,053
Prepaid expenses	295,811	240,661
	26,308,335	24,750,248
Property, plant and equipment (Note 2)	9,232,510	8,693,930
	$35,540,845	$33,444,178

Consolidated Current Replacement Cost Statement of Earnings

for the year ended December 31, 1977 (With comparative figures for 1976)

	1977	1976
Net sales	$92,173,649	$79,839,547
Costs and expenses		
Cost of products sold	70,099,460	60,179,363
Selling, general and administrative	16,390,467	14,604,213
Depreciation and amortization	1,309,207	1,260,522
Interest		
Long-term debt	348,962	360,573
Current debt, net of dividend income of $78,904 (1977)	714,042	765,372
	88,862,138	77,170,043
Earnings before income taxes	3,311,511	2,669,504
Provision for income taxes	1,776,484	1,386,758
Net earnings	$ 1,535,027	$ 1,282,746
Earnings per share	$3.28	$2.73

Consolidated Statement of Revaluation Account

for the year ended December 31, 1977 (With comparative figures for 1976)

	1977	1976
Balance at beginning of year	$ 8,172,631	$ 6,725,502
Add		
Revaluation of property, plant and equipment at end of year.	2,282,942	1,447,129
Revaluation of cost of products sold during year	450,000	—
Balance at end of year	$10,905,573	$ 8,172,631

Property, plant and equipment

	1977 Current replacement cost	1977 Accumulated depreciation	1976 Current replacement cost	1976 Accumulated depreciation
Land	$ 1,151,924	$ —	$ 915,383	$ —
Plant and equipment	22,567,873	14,487,287	19,690,841	11,912,294
	$23,719,797	$14,487,287	$20,606,224	$11,912,294

The current replacement of costs of property and plant are based upon independent appraisals by quantity surveyors of the Canadian Institute of Quantity Surveyors or by accredited appraisers of the Appraisal Institute of Canada. Where appraisals for buildings were completed at dates other than at December 31, 1977, the appraised values were adjusted by the Non-Residential Construction Price Index developed by Statistics Canada. Land is stated at its most recent appraised value determined during the previous four years.

The current replacement cost of equipment is determined from recent suppliers' prices and estimates made by those suppliers.

Provision for depreciation is computed generally on the diminishing-balance method at the following rates:

Buildings	5%
Machinery and equipment	20%

As a result of the revaluation of fixed assets in the current year, accumulated depreciation representing the expired portion of the useful lives of those assets has been increased by $1,446,165 and this amount has been charged to retained earnings.

Required

Expenditures for property, plant and equipment totaled $1,057,243 in 1977 and proceeds from the disposal of equipment amounted to $54,699. Reconstruct the entries Barber-Ellis made in 1977 to account for its property, plant and equipment on a current replacement cost basis.